Educational Leadership and Planning for Technology

SECOND EDITION

Anthony G. Picciano
Hunter College
City University of New York

Merrill,
an imprint of Prentice Hall
Upper Saddle River, New Jersey   Columbus, Ohio

To E.B.

Library of Congress Cataloging-in-Publication Data

Picciano, Anthony G.
    Educational leadership and planning for technology / Anthony G. Picciano.—2nd ed.
      p. cm.
    Rev. ed. of: Computers in the schools. ©1994.
    Includes bibliographical references and index.
    ISBN 0-13-262122-3 (alk. paper)
      1. Education—Data processing—Planning. 2. Computer managed instruction—Planning. 3. Computer-assisted instruction—Planning. 4. School management and organization—Data processing—Planning.   I. Picciano, Anthony G. Computers in the schools. II. Title.
    LB1028.43.P536   1998
    370'.285—dc21

                              96-52859
                              CIP

Cover art: © Diana Ong/Super Stock
Editor: Debra A. Stollenwerk
Production Editor: Alexandrina Benedicto Wolf
Photo Editor: Linda Gray
Design Coordinator: Karrie M. Converse
Text Designer: STELLARViSIONs
Cover Designer: Brian Deep
Production Manager: Deidra M. Schwartz
Electronic Text Management: Marilyn Wilson Phelps, Matthew Williams, Karen L. Bretz, Tracey B. Ward
Director of Marketing: Kevin Flanagan
Marketing Manager: Suzanne Stanton
Advertising/Marketing Coordinator: Julie Shough

This book was set in Garamond by Prentice Hall and was printed and bound by R.R. Donnelley & Sons Company. The cover was printed by Phoenix Color Corp.

Earlier edition, entitled *Computers in the schools: a guide to planning and administration,* © 1994 by Macmillan Publishing.

Photo credits: pp. 1, 39, 77, and 206 Courtesy of International Business Machines Corporation. Unauthorized use not permitted; p. 2 by Jean-Claude Lejeune; pp. 15, 57, and 171 by Barbara Schwartz/Merrill; pp. 58, 153, 154, 228, and 252 by Scott Cunningham/Merrill; p. 105 by Maria Stenzel/Courtesy of Jason Foundation for Education; p. 126 Courtesy of Space Telescope Science Institute; p. 190 by Anne Vega/Merrill; and p. 251 Courtesy of National Aeronautics and Space Administration.

Printed in the United States of America
10 9 8 7 6 5 4 3 2 1

ISBN: 0-13-262122-3

Prentice-Hall International (UK) Limited, *London*
Prentice-Hall of Australia Pty. Limited, *Sydney*
Prentice-Hall of Canada, Inc., *Toronto*
Prentice-Hall Hispanoamericana, S. A., *Mexico*
Prentice-Hall of India Private Limited, *New Delhi*
Prentice-Hall of Japan, Inc., *Tokyo*
Simon & Schuster Asia Pte. Ltd., *Singapore*
Editora Prentice-Hall do Brasil, Ltda., *Rio de Janeiro*

Preface

The purpose of this book is to provide educators with both the theoretical and the practical considerations for planning and implementing technology, particularly computer applications, in schools. Basic concepts of technology and planning that use systems theory are presented. Emphasis is placed on the importance of the total application of technology as opposed to any individual component, be it hardware, software, facilities, personnel, or finances. The book is meant to form a foundation from which educators will provide leadership and become agents for realizing the powerful potential of technology in their schools.

The material is designed for practicing administrators and other educators such as teachers, computer coordinators, and media specialists who are involved in initiating and supporting computer technology in their schools. This book is most appropriate as a text in a preservice or in-service course on computer applications designed primarily for school administrators.

ORGANIZATION

This book is divided into four sections: I, Basic Concepts and Foundations; II, Applications; III, Planning and Implementation; and IV, A Look to the Future. Although each chapter can be read independently, the material is meant to be read sequentially chapter by chapter. Following the text, several supplemental sections are presented for reference: Appendix A is a review of basic computer concepts and terminology; Appendix B is a workshop activity designed to provide an introductory hands-on experience with administrative software being used in many schools; Appendix C may serve as a checklist to help educators evaluate instructional software; and the glossary provides a quick reference for technical terms used in the text.

Section I: Basic Concepts and Foundations

This section provides the basic concepts and foundation material for an overall understanding of the themes and major issues related to planning for technology in schools and school systems. It is directed specifically to those who are or will be leading their schools in planning for technology. This section concludes with a chapter on pedagogical and social issues related to technology that should be considered as part of the planning process. Readers who are not familiar with basic computer concepts or terminology should review Appendix A before preceding beyond this section.

Section II: Applications

This section provides four chapters on the nature of computer applications used for both administration and instruction. Although similar in some respects, enough differences exist in the nature, design, and policies associated with administrative and instructional applications that they require separate treatments. This section devotes two chapters to discussions of newer technologies such as multimedia and data communications.

Section III: Planning and Implementation

This section presents specific material on the primary components of planning for and administering computer technology in schools. Entire chapters are devoted to the five components of every computer application: hardware, software, staff development, facilities, and finances. Section III is also designed to provide practical information on evaluating and implementing these components.

Section IV: A Look to the Future

This concluding section is meant to make the reader aware of major trends that have and will continue to affect the evolution of technology. Although it reviews some of the material already covered in previous chapters, this section is not a summary of the book. This section also takes a realistic glimpse at the future and the significant role that technology will be playing in education.

End-of-Chapter Activities

Each chapter concludes with key concepts and questions, suggested activities, and/or case studies. These are provided to stimulate thought and discussion on the material presented. They also attempt to relate the material to situations that exist in schools. The case studies, though having some basis in fact, are fictitious and designed to put the reader in the position of leaders having to make decisions about computer technology and related issues. Reference lists are also provided at the end of each chapter.

WHAT IS NEW IN THIS EDITION

The second edition of this book differs from the first edition in several ways.

- All chapters have been revised to keep up with current thinking and advances in technology as applied to education.
- Two substantive chapters have been added on newer technologies such as multimedia and data communications, including the Internet.
- The organization has changed slightly in response to suggestions provided by reviewers and users of the first edition. The number of sections has increased from three to four as described earlier, because of the additional chapters and material provided in the new edition. A new section focuses on applications. Because students and practitioners are more computer literate than several years ago, Basic Concepts of Computer Technology (formerly Chapter 2) is now provided as Appendix A for reference or review. Technology, Learning, and Equity Issues (Chapter 3) is presented earlier in the text, following the chapter on basic concepts of planning. Finally, although two former appendices (Introduction to Operating Systems, and Introduction to Logo) are no longer included, this material can easily be made up by using on-line tutorials that are now provided as part of these basic software packages.

DEFINITION OF TERMS

Technology is a general term that can be applied to a variety of administrative and instructional applications involving calculators, overhead projectors, telephones, television, and so forth. In this book, *technology* refers primarily to computer and computer-related technologies such as data communications, interactive video, and digital television.

School districts sometimes are referred to as small, medium, or large, depending on their enrollment:

Small: less than 600 students
Medium: 600 or more and less than 25,000 students
Large: more than 25,000 students

School districts in the United States generally are governed by independently elected or appointed boards of education with the power to raise taxes and issue bonds. Some districts, particularly those in urban areas, are governed by other governmental entities such as a municipality, from which they receive an operating budget. Unless otherwise noted, references to school districts include *all* school districts. In some cases, the term *municipally governed* is used to refer specifically to those school districts described earlier.

ACKNOWLEDGMENTS

I gratefully acknowledge the guidance and assistance provided by the staff at Merrill/Prentice Hall, especially Debbie Stollenwerk, Penny Burleson, Alex Wolf, Laura Larson, and Linda Gray.

I would also like to thank the following reviewers for their valuable feedback: Dale L. Brubaker, University of North Carolina–Greensboro; Leticia Ekhaml, West Georgia College; Larry W. Hughes, University of Houston; Lawrence O. Picus, University of Southern California; and Nancy H. Vick, Longwood College.

In addition, I have benefitted significantly from my professional associations with a number of colleagues, specifically: the faculty in the Department of Curriculum and Teaching at Hunter College; the administration, staff, and faculty fellows at the Open Systems Laboratory at the City University of New York; and all of the school administrators who provided source material and who are truly leading their schools in creative uses of technology.

Especially important to my efforts were the students in the Administration and Supervision Program at Hunter College. They are an industrious group of future leaders who provided me with insight in presenting this topic and continually help me to learn about our schools.

Lastly, Michael and Dawn Marie have always helped me to be a better person.

Anthony G. Picciano

Contents

3 Technology, Learning, and Equity Issues   39

Section II

Applications   57

4 Computer Applications in Educational Administration   58

5 Computer Applications in Instruction   77

6 Multimedia in Education   105

7 Data Communications, the Internet, and Educational Applications   126

Section III

Planning and Implementation 153

8 Hardware Planning and Evaluation 154

9 Software Selection and Evaluation 171

10 Staff Development 190

11 Computer Facilities   206

12 Financial Planning   228

Section IV
A Look to the Future   251

13 Trends and the Future   252

A   Basic Concepts of Computer Technology   269

B   An Introduction to Administrative Software   291

C   Instructional Software Evaluation Factors   304

Glossary   309

Index   319

Section I

Basic Concepts and Foundations

1

Introduction to Technology and Planning

A t a national computing conference held in June 1992, Dr. Robert D. Ballard, a senior scientist at the Woods Hole Oceanographic Institute, delivered a paper entitled "Living a Dream" in which he described the development of a new project that he termed "telepresence." Using computers, satellite telecommunications, fiber optics, and robotics, this project allows scientists on land to experience deep-sea explorations by manipulating a robotic system, named the ARGO/JASON, by remote control. Using deep-sea image technology, scientists in their offices and laboratories see everything that they could see if they were actually on the ocean floor.

In sharing his experience of seeing the development and success of this system, Ballard compared it to other events in his life, which included substantiating theories involving plate tectonics and continental drift, discovering mountains higher than Everest, seeing canyons deeper than the Grand Canyon, and locating the *RMS Titanic* 12,460 feet deep in the North Atlantic Ocean. However, one of his major goals now is to share these experiences with children. Through an initial series of "downlink" sites across the United States, in the most ambitious ARGO/JASON undertaking ever, 600,000 students were able to watch a deep-sea exploration of active volcanoes just off the Galápagos Islands. Ballard indicated that the highlight of this event was when young children at the remote sites actually took turns steering and manipulating the arms of the deep-sea robots. Ballard said that seeing the expressions of wonder and excitement on the faces of these children was a joy incomparable to any other.

Ballard's description is used here to illustrate the potential of technology in adding to children's educational experiences. While not every school can be a downlink site for the ARGO/JASON system, by using technology educators can add significantly to children's experiences. ARGO/JASON stands as the culmination of many hours of planning and the investment of millions of dollars. However, what was critical to success was the fact that an individual had a vision of something he wanted to do and was able to lead others in accomplishing it. Thousands of educators in schools around the country are in positions similar to that of Ballard. They can lead others in developing and implementing projects and programs that will surely touch children's lives. They need vision and resources, but, most important, they need the will to share and accomplish their goals with others.

PURPOSE

To describe the purpose of this book requires a discussion of the purposes of schools and schooling. Educational technology, to be successful, must be integrated into the main functions of schools and not just as something separate and apart. Technology for technology's sake is an expensive and generally futile endeavor in education. However, when integrated into an educator's vision of what children and young adults need to learn about the world and themselves, then technology can be an effective tool in achieving that vision.

Views differ among educators and communities regarding the purposes of schools and schooling. For some, education should focus on the intellectual and emotional needs of children. For others, the focus may be a society's social and economic needs. Fundamental to most of these views is a sense that children, as a result of an education, will come away with a desire to learn more about themselves, others, and the world about them. Drawing from experiential theories, a basic assumption is that children are born with a natural curiosity about the world, and the main function of schooling should be to stimulate that curiosity. Once the desire to learn has been instilled, children will learn a great deal on their own. Schooling succeeds when children begin to learn through experiences and by learning are motivated to experience more, so that a cycle of life-long learning and experiencing evolves. Seymour Sarason (1995) describes this concept most succinctly:

> If when a child is motivated to learn more about self and the world, then I would say that schooling has achieved its overarching purpose. . . . [T]he student knows that the more you know the more you need to know. . . . To want to continue to explore, to find answers to personally meaningful questions, issues, and possibilities is the most important purpose of schooling. (p. 135)

The role of technology in achieving this purpose can be made evident by briefly describing its relationship to education. For most of the 20th century, technology in education centered on print media. Paper, pens, books, and chalk were critical for communicating ideas, accessing information, and learning about the world. As we enter the 21st century, electronic media has begun to replace the print media. Word processing, E-mail, fax-modems, video, CD-ROMs, multimedia, and the Internet have become the common tools for communicating ideas and accessing information. The morning newspaper is now read to provide additional insight to what was already seen and heard on the nightly news broadcast. The linearity of the sentence, paragraph, and page is used in conjunction with hypertext branching and searching. The one-dimensionality of the lecture achieves depth and perspective as it is integrated into multiple-interactive dialogues and small-group discussions on local and international data communications networks. In sum, technology is becoming the tool of choice for communicating in, accessing, and learning about our world. As such, it should be integrated with any educational vision or plan that attempts to help individuals, including children, understand this world.

The purpose of this book is to provide educators with both the theoretical framework and the practical considerations for planning and implementing technology, particularly computer applications, in schools. Basic concepts of technology and planning that use systems theory are presented. Emphasis is placed throughout this book on the importance of the total application of technology in the educational enterprise—more so than on any individual component, be it hardware, software, facilities, or staff. Lastly, this book is meant to form the foundation from which educators will look ahead and become the agents for realizing the powerful potential of technology in their schools.

THE POTENTIAL IN PRIMARY AND SECONDARY SCHOOLS

"For many firms using computers . . . is an absolute necessity." So says James O'Brien (1989, p. 33), in the third edition of a standard textbook on the use of computers in business organizations. His readers would accept this statement with little reservation. Computer technology has become such an integral part of most business operations, both large and small, that it is a given, as fundamental as accounting, finance, marketing, and management. Architects, engineers, bankers, and salespersons routinely use computers for various aspects of their jobs, whether to draw designs, look up customers' accounts, or record purchases.

The same is true for many organizations in the public sector. High-technology agencies such as the Department of Defense, NASA, and the Federal Aviation Administration are totally dependent on computers for all aspects of their operations and literally could not function without them. Weapons systems, the space shuttle missions, and air traffic are controlled almost exclusively by computer technology. Most other public agencies, such as the Internal Revenue Service and the Social Security Administration, also rely on sophisticated information retrieval systems to conduct their operations. Take a walk through a hospital, a library, or a college, and you likely will see technology routinely used to monitor a patient's heartbeat, borrow a book, or conduct research.

Those who have studied and observed the use of computers in primary and secondary education see a substantially different picture. Instead of treating computing as a foregone conclusion, educators appear interested in the potential of the technology but also express reservations. For example:

It is important . . . that we not present microcomputers with unbridled enthusiasm. (Geisert & Futrell, 1995, p. 4)

Others have even lamented that education is the worse because of this infusion of technology. (Simonson & Thompson, 1994, p. 5)

Bringing about [technological] changes will not be easy. Schools are complex organizations. (Knapp & Glenn, 1996, p. 13)

[Although some have realized the potential of technology,] there are also many teachers who have not seen this potential, teachers whose use of technology is marginal, limited and unenthusiastic. (U.S. Congress, Office of Technology Assessment, 1995, p. 8)

Although schools have started to use technology, these quotes reflect the fact that educators are still cautious and concerned about the impact. To a degree, American schools have fallen behind other industries and organizations, both private and public, in benefiting from technology. We can make airline reservations, buy lottery tickets, withdraw money, or tally a cart of groceries electronically at the push of a button or the wave of a wand. Yet, the vast majority of primary and secondary schools rely on intensive manual efforts to conduct one of our most important "businesses," that is, the education of children. Why this has occurred is an important starting point for the study of planning and administering technology in primary and secondary schools.

THE BEGINNING YEARS

Primary and secondary schools were effectively excluded in the early years of the computer revolution (1960s and 1970s) for a variety of reasons. Much of the earliest software provided for computers was designed for data-processing applications rather than for educational purposes. The exceptions were several scientific software languages and packages that were useful in organized research activities and major military-industrial and space exploration projects. International Business Machines (IBM), which dominated the entire computer industry and provided much of the leadership, developed products for organizations that were already part of an office machine customer base, such as users of typewriters and punch-card equipment. Although extremely active in higher-education markets (to familiarize future business leaders and engineers with its products), IBM was not as active in marketing to primary and secondary schools. In a 1988 article in *Think,* an IBM publication, Jim Dezell, the general manager of IBM's Educational Systems, said, "We were way behind, way behind. . . . As recently as three years ago, the only IBM software in education . . . the company was offering was *Writing to Read.* . . . We had no installed base or customer references" (Grimm, 1988, p. 5).

From the educational perspective, schools have a long tradition of being people oriented rather than machine oriented. In addition to teaching, schools provide nourishment, health, recreation, and other social services to their students. A fundamental concept of teacher education is to "nurture" children and to take care of the "whole" child. As a result, in their earliest courses teachers are trained to be child oriented. Many of them considered most of the earlier computer technology as an impersonal approach to teaching, particularly in the primary grades, and have not embraced it. Furthermore, many of today's teachers, especially those over the age of 40, likely did not receive formal training in computer technology in their undergraduate programs. As a result, this technology did not become a routine part of their repertoire of teaching tools.

When major advances in computer technology were being made in the 1960s and 1970s, schools themselves were going through significant changes. No other organizations in this country were affected as much by the major social issues of the times as were the primary and secondary schools. Racial integration, bilingual education, and the rights of persons with disabling conditions have affected all aspects of society. However, it was the schools that were called on to spearhead changes in the way the United States would resolve these issues. While private businesses and many governmental agencies were gradually changing, major and sudden changes were occurring in the nation's schools. These changes rightfully dominated much of the planning that school administrators and education policy makers did and became the major priorities for improving the schools and their instructional programs.

Finally, while some larger school districts could afford it, most of the 15,000-plus school districts in the nation did not have adequate financial resources to invest in the new computer technology. Although businesses were willing to invest resources in designing and developing computer applications, schools used their available resources for other priorities. Smaller school districts could afford neither the hardware nor expensive support staff that the large mainframe computer systems of the 1960s and early 1970s required. While some districts made pioneering attempts to use time-sharing systems provided by universities, state and local agencies, and educational consortia, these efforts did not affect the vast majority of teachers and students in the schools. As late as 1980, after reviewing the results of several national surveys, H. J. Becker (1991) estimated that no more than 50,000 microcomputers or computer terminals were available in the nation's primary and secondary schools. With more than 40 million students and a student-computer ratio of 800:1, this technology was surely not a part of their educational experiences.

Without hardware, software, or training and with other more important and pressing priorities, primary and secondary schools on the whole did not enter the technology revolution that occurred in the 1960s and 1970s. However, the situation changed in the late 1970s and early 1980s with the introduction of microcomputers. Major new computer manufacturers such as Apple, Commodore, Tandy, and Atari were genuinely interested in marketing their products to schools. They were also interested in the children's market in general and provided hardware and software that could be used in the home for playing electronic games. Teachers and school administrators began to observe that more and more children were becoming computer literate at home. Parents also were becoming more familiar with computer technology as their workplaces began to require them to use it for a variety of tasks. New software companies such as Sunburst, Broderbund, Tom Snyder Productions, Davidson, and Scholastic appeared almost overnight with educational software that was more appealing and pedagogically more interesting than any developed in the previous 20 years. As a result, schools finally began to make meaningful investments in computer technology in the 1980s.

Although unquestionably behind other American enterprises and still in the initial stages of fitting computer technology into their overall education program, schools are beginning to make significant strides. The time has come for administrators and teachers to take control and harness the power of the technology at their disposal. This task involves engaging in thoughtful evaluation, discarding or improving what does not work, accepting and building on what does, and carefully planning for new applications.

STEADY PROGRESS IN ADMINISTRATIVE SYSTEMS

Computer applications in education can be divided into two major categories: **administrative** and **instructional**. Administrative applications support the administrative functions of a district or school. Examples include database management and transaction-processing systems such as student demographics, grading, budgeting, payroll, personnel, scheduling, and inventory control, all of which are designed for and used primarily by administrative staff. Instructional applications support teaching and learning activities that are designed for and used mainly by teachers, school library media specialists, and students. The background, implementation, and planning for these two major categories of applications are different and need to be distinguished.

Administrative systems have progressed more steadily than instructional applications because they are very similar to the data-processing applications in private industry and public agencies. Customer and product database management systems in private businesses resemble student and course systems in schools; furthermore, personnel, payroll, and financial database systems designed for public agencies are identical to those used in schools. As a result, schools were able to draw on the expertise and software products developed for general data-processing applications for their own administrative operations. Computer manufacturers, software developers, and data-processing service bureaus could market many of the same products to schools, private industry, and government agencies. Many of the larger school districts were able to afford and use the benefits of these data-processing applications. For example, school districts governed by local municipalities generally were required to follow the same administrative procedures established for all the other agencies under the municipality's jurisdiction. This was especially true for financial applications such as budgeting, payroll, and purchasing. As municipalities began to computerize these applications, so did the school districts.

In the late 1960s and 1970s, state education departments became much more active in data collection and evaluation activities, partly because of the reporting requirements of the federal government regarding entitlement programs, and partly because of a desire and need to understand better what the schools were doing. Schools increasingly were required to provide data on student demographics, performance, and expenditures. To streamline these data collection activities, some states (e.g., Florida, Minnesota, Texas) established statewide computer networks to assist the school districts. Administrators soon were able to use these networks not only to fulfill the reporting requirements but also to meet their own informational and other administrative needs.

By the 1970s and 1980s, as microcomputers became available, many school districts were converting existing applications or developing new ones to meet their administrative needs. Even districts with very little access to computing before this period were able to draw on the experiences of other districts and utilize established software products.

INSTRUCTIONAL SYSTEMS SHOW PROMISE

The quotes at the beginning of this chapter that refer to the potential of computer technology reflect the thinking of educators regarding the instructional rather than the administrative uses of computers in the schools. Educational and survey research findings (Quality Education Data, 1996; Robyler, Castine, & King, 1988; Sheingold & Hadley, 1990; U.S. Congress, Office of Technology Assessment, 1995) regarding the benefits of computing technology remain inconclusive, but the general opinions are that

- more schools are acquiring technology and establishing instructional applications than ever before,
- the software has improved,

- administrators and teachers are not convinced of the benefits, and
- they are not sure of the future.

In summary, while most schools have begun to invest in technology, others are struggling with it for various reasons in terms of a teaching philosophy, the benefits, and problems in implementation.

As mentioned previously, most of the early research and development that went into software development was directed to improving data-processing applications that were prevalent in businesses and many public agencies. Such research concentrated on data and information flow and was primarily concerned with improving speed and other transaction-processing features. Although critical to high-volume, service-oriented organizations such as banks, insurance companies, stock brokerage houses, and many governmental agencies, these features were of minimal value to teaching and learning. Several of the early attempts at developing packages for schools consisted of copies and conversions of software developed primarily for businesses and other organizations. For example, the Bank Street College of Education, which enjoys an excellent reputation for having developed a variety of very interesting educational software packages, started by converting standard word-processing (Bank Street Writer) and database management (Bank Street Filer) software for use in primary and secondary schools.

Many of the earliest instructional software applications developed in primary and secondary schools in the 1960s and 1970s were the drill-and-practice variety and concentrated on providing repetitive exercises for learning basic skills. Although drill and practice is widely used by teachers using flash cards and other manual techniques, when delivered electronically on computers it became the topic of much debate (Gagné, 1977; Trumbull, 1986; Yates, 1983). Although drill and practice has proponents, many teachers were not receptive to the early software developed in the 1960s and 1970s. Some, in fact, were turned off to computing technology in general and viewed it as an impersonal, "Big Brother is watching" approach.

Even if schools wanted to use software, they still had to overcome financial and other technical hurdles to do so effectively before 1980. To deliver computing power to the classroom using a large mainframe or even a minicomputer system required a significant organizational commitment. Hardware costs alone made it prohibitive for many school districts to even consider. Other problems (e.g., establishing data communications networks to allow student access, attracting and training highly paid technicians, building environmentally controlled facilities) made it impossible for all but some of the larger districts.

In the early 1980s, with the proliferation of microcomputers, some of these problems were overcome. Hardware costs decreased dramatically. Software began to be designed for children. Although intended more for entertainment than education, video games were effective in breaking down the first barriers that prevented children from using computer technology. In addition, video games such as Pac-Man and Space Invaders relied heavily on motion and graphics that added significantly to their appeal to children. As a result, a good deal of software research and development in the 1980s was devoted to improving graphics, not just for children but for adult and business applications also. Thousands of titles of software packages now exist that were designed for children and are very appropriate for use in primary and secondary schools. According to data collected in a national survey by Quality Education Data (1996), 98% of all public schools had acquired some form of computer technology by 1990. By 1995, significant investments continued to be made by schools in acquiring newer technologies such as CD-ROMs (51% of all public schools), modems (45%), videodisc players (34%), local area networks (35%), and satellite dishes (19%).

THE NEED FOR PLANNING

The major impediment to establishing successful computer-based applications in schools now is the lack of careful planning. Although some schools have shown progress, others appear to be struggling. Research (Becker, 1994; U.S. Congress, Office of Technology Assessment, 1995) indicates that a substantial percentage of teachers make little or no use of computers in teaching. So although more equipment has been acquired, its effectiveness in the classroom is in question. A major reason for this is that the process of bringing technology to instruction has not been effective and in fact has been described as inefficient, poorly planned, and "incredibly chaotic" (Maddux, Johnson, & Harlow, 1992, p. 119). While problems of hardware cost and software development and acquisition are being resolved, other problems such as curricular integration and staff development remain. Careful planning at both the district and school building levels would more clearly define these problems and provide alternatives for their resolution.

Planning for computer technology requires concentrating on a total application. By choosing an application and asking what is needed to make it successful, educators will naturally have to consider subsidiary questions regarding obvious components such as hardware and software as well as other less obvious components such as staff development, curricular integration, facilities, and ongoing maintenance.

Another important aspect of planning is evaluation and feedback. Although schools have implemented computer applications, few have evaluated them in terms of achieving intended goals or objectives. Evaluation in education is not easy given the variability of human conditions and skills. However, because they are dealing with new approaches, administrators need to assess what works or does not work in their schools. Furthermore, what is successful in one school or district may not be successful in another. Why this happens is the essence of evaluation, a process that identifies strengths and weaknesses in all the various components of an application within a specific operating environment. For example, excellent hardware with poor software will likely not result in a successful application, nor will excellent hardware and software assure success without staff who know how to use them properly. All components depend on each other, and a weakness in one affects all the others. By the same token, a particular strength in one component may disguise or "make up" for weaknesses in another component. For instance, some of the early successes of computer applications in the schools involved teachers and administrators who were most interested in and enthused about using technology. Their basic interests and enthusiasm were strengths that made for apparent successful applications even in cases in which software was mediocre or facilities were inadequate. However, as administrators attempted to replicate these applications with less interested or less knowledgeable staff in other settings, the weaknesses frequently became more apparent and the applications failed.

Planning for technology also requires involvement of the people who will ultimately use a computer application, be they administrators, teachers, or clerical staff. For the many reasons already discussed, educators have been cautious and in some cases even antagonistic regarding computer technology. Top-down implementation of computer applications without consultation and involvement will likely increase resistance among staff and may possibly doom entire undertakings. Involvement is critical, particularly in identifying training and curricular needs and other less obvious components of a computer application, to say nothing of securing the commitment of those who will ultimately influence its success or failure.

In private industry, public agencies, and other segments of society that have been using computer technology for many years, the concept of planning has become widely accepted. For many organizations, planning resulted from trial and error, not unlike what some schools are experiencing today. For others, planning resulted from a gradual change in thinking that evolved as their organizations became more dependent on computer technology. At the same time, systems analysts, software engineers, and information specialists became managers who were increasingly involved in the overall operations. Their prior training in systematic problem solving and analysis allowed them to adapt their analytical skills to broader organizational issues that required planning and evaluation methods and tools.

Conversely, in school systems, with the exception of some larger school districts, systems analysts and designers generally are not present in the administrative hierarchy. As a result, school administrators and teachers must assume the responsibility for planning for technology as they have for the other areas of education.

THE SYSTEMS APPROACH

In presenting any topic, a basic framework for study needs to be established. Systems theory is most appropriate for the major topics of this book: computers in primary and secondary schools and the need for planning for successful implementation of computer applications. The basic systems concepts of "input, process, output" and their interrelationship are generally accepted as fundamental to all aspects of computer technology. For example, the basic configuration of a computer hardware system consists of one input device, a central processor, and one output device. All other hardware configurations are variations of this, whether with multiple input, processor, or output devices or with multiple hardware systems and subsystems working together in some type of planned unison.

The systems approach is also appropriate for studying schools and school processes, including planning. Many social scientists and sociologists would describe and analyze schools as social systems. Basic concepts of input, process, and output are regularly applied to communities, students, teaching, curriculum, and outcomes in describing school "systems." Using systems theory for presenting the technical aspects of computing technology as well as the planning aspects of school administration makes for a consistent, integrated approach for presenting the material in this book. It would be difficult and perhaps impossible to identify another framework that would work as well.

ORGANIZATION

This book is organized into four major sections. Section I introduces basic concepts of computer technology and planning. The foundation of sound planning is conceived as the total application of the technology. Important policy issues in planning for technology are also presented.

Section II presents major applications of technology as used in schools today. A variety of administrative and instructional applications are examined in terms of planning implications.

Section III develops the implementation of each of the five major components of successful computer applications: hardware, software, staff, facilities, and finances. Particular emphases are placed on relating each of these components to an overall application and not as distinct or independent entities.

Section IV reviews many of the important trends that are occurring in technology as related to schools. The section ends with speculation on what the future may provide in terms of educational technology.

The book concludes with three appendices and a glossary of technical terms. Appendix A is designed to provide a review of basic computer concepts. Appendix B is a hands-on activity designed to help the reader become more familiar with commonly used administrative software. Appendix C serves as a checklist to help educators evaluate instructional software. The glossary is a quick reference for providing definitions of technical terms with which readers might not generally be familiar.

SUMMARY

This book offers a foundation on which educators will look ahead to become the agents for realizing the potential of technology in their schools. The current state of the uses of computer technology for administrative and instructional applications has been briefly described in this chapter. While administrative applications have progressed steadily, opinions vary as to the benefits of computer technology in regard to instructional applications. As with other areas of the educational enterprise, administrators need to plan and evaluate carefully the implementation of computer technology in their schools. The chapter also established systems theory as an appropriate framework for examining technology and planning its implementation.

Key Concepts and Questions

1. Schools have not evolved as other organizations have in the use of computer technology.

   Why?

2. Administrative computer applications are different in design and purpose from instructional or academic applications.

   Are there counterparts to administrative applications in organizations other than schools? How are they similar or dissimilar? Are there counterparts to instructional applications in noneducational organizations? How are they similar or dissimilar?

3. Administrative applications have progressed more steadily than instructional applications.

   Why? Is this changing? Will it change in the future? Explain.

4. Planning for computer technology should center on the application rather than on only hardware, software, or other individual components.

   How and where in a district or school should this planning occur? Who should be the major participants in planning for technology? Explain.

5. Systems theory is appropriate to computer applications in schools.

   What is the systems approach? Does it apply only to technology such as computer systems? Identify nontechnical environments in which the systems approach is an appropriate framework for describing and analyzing processes.

Suggested Activities

1. Consider a school district or school with which you are familiar. When did it first become involved with computer technology? What were the first types of applications that were implemented? How advanced is the school or district now in terms of its use of computer technology?

2. Compare a school to a local private business or a public agency in terms of reliance on computer technology for conducting daily operations. Which relies more heavily on technology? If computers were suddenly eliminated, would classes and other activities be conducted as usual in the school? What would happen in the private business or public agency?

3. For students who are unfamiliar with or need a review of computer technology, Appendix A at the end of this book provides an introduction to basic computer concepts.

References

Ballard, R. D. (1992, June). *Living the dream*. Paper presented at the IBM Academic Computing Conference, San Diego, CA.

Becker, H. J. (1991). How computers are used in United States schools: Basic data from the 1989 I.E.A. computers in education survey. *Journal of Educational Computing Research, 7*(4), 385–406.

———. (1994). *Analysis and trends of school use of new information technologies*. Irvine: Department of Education, University of California, Irvine.

Gagné, R. M. (1977). *The conditions of learning.* New York: Holt, Rinehart, & Winston.

Geisert, P. G., & Futrell, M. K. (1995). *Teachers, computers and curriculum: Microcomputers in the classroom* (2nd ed.). Boston: Allyn & Bacon.

Grimm, E. (1988). Coming on fast in the classroom. *Think: The IBM Magazine, 54*(6), 5–8.

Knapp. L. R., & Glenn, A. D. (1996). *Restructuring schools with technology.* Boston: Allyn & Bacon.

Maddux, C., Johnson, L., & Harlow, S. (1992). The state of the art in computer education. In D. Carey, R. Carey, D. A. Willis, & J. Willis (Eds.), *Technology and Teacher Education Annual* (pp. 119–122). Charlottesville, VA: Association for the Advancement of Computing in Education.

O'Brien, J. A., (1989). *Computer concepts and applications with an introduction to software and BASIC.* Homewood, IL: Irwin.

Quality Education Data. (1996). *Education market guide and mailing list catalog 1996–97.* Denver: Quality Education Data.

Robyler, M. D., Castine, W. H., & King, F. J. (1988). Assessing the impact of computer-based education. *Computers in the Schools, 5* (1), 1–149.

Sarason, S. (1995). *Parental involvement and the political principle: Why the existing governance structure of schools should be abolished.* San Francisco: Jossey-Bass.

Sheingold, K., & Hadley, M. (1990). *Accomplished teachers: Integrating computers into classroom practice.* New York: Bank Street College of Education, Center for Technology in Education.

Simonson, M. R., & Thompson, A. (1994). *Educational computing foundations* (2nd ed.). Upper Saddle River, NJ: Merrill/Prentice Hall.

Trumbull, D. J. (1986). Games children play: A cautionary tale. *Educational Leadership, 43*(6), 18–21.

U.S. Congress, Office of Technology Assessment. (1995). *Teachers and technology: Making the connection* (OTA-EHR-616). Washington, DC: U.S. Government Printing Office.

Yates, D. S. (1983). In defense of CAI: Is drill and practice a dirty word? *Curriculum Review, 22*(5), 55–57.

2

Basic Concepts
of Planning

O ne of the most fully treated topics in educational administration is planning. Numerous books, articles, and guides have been written on how to plan and whom to involve in educational planning. Journals devoted entirely to issues of planning are available to enable administrators to keep up-to-date with the most current thinking. Consultants abound at conferences where sessions are routinely dedicated to planning, its theories, and practices. On the other hand, skepticism exists regarding the value of planning in education, particularly during periods of fiscal constraint and "tight budgets" (Engvall, 1995). The major purpose of this chapter is not to review this extensive literature but more to provide a framework for educational planning as related to technology.

First, a generally accepted definition of planning is elusive. In an extensive review of the literature, Adams (1987) provides at least seven different definitions, all of which he considers incomplete. An obvious reason for his conclusion is that planning means different things to different people and is done for different purposes. However, common elements of a definition involve individuals thinking about and developing strategies to prepare their organizations for the future.

Second, planning goes on in all organizations, including schools and school systems, and takes on different characteristics. Planning can be structured, formal, top-down, and nonparticipatory in some cases versus unstructured, informal, bottom-up, and highly participatory in others. These characteristics alternate along a continuum with less or more of a particular characteristic active in the planning process depending on different circumstances. These circumstances can involve complex social and administrative phenomena such as economics, personalities, and individual needs.

Third, schools are social systems that in the course of their activities, including planning, consider the social needs of students, teachers, administrators, and communities within the context of the school and the larger social environment.

These assumptions form the basis for constructing a framework to define and describe planning in educational organizations. They may be considered oversimplifications of a very complex topic; however, because this book is written for all who are involved in school administration and technology, these assumptions recognize and respect a variety of existing situations. The implementation of this framework is left to the judgment of superintendents, principals, assistant principals, and other administrators, most of whom know best what will work in their schools. To emphasize, educational leaders must be endowed with an awareness of the differences that exist within a community and among the individual constituents for planning to be successful in their schools (Engvall, 1995).

SCHOOLS AS SOCIAL SYSTEMS

Various theories and models have been developed to describe and explain the way schools operate in our society. Most of them stem from general organization theory and development. The writings of organizational theorists such as Chester Barnard (1964), Herbert Simon (1945, 1957, 1960), Talcott Parsons (1951, 1958), and Amitai

Etzioni (1961) are cited in basic administration courses and form the foundation of much of our knowledge in this area.

The more recent literature in educational administration deals with topics such as organizational culture, strategic planning, environmental scanning, school-based management, and shared decision making. The common thread throughout this material is the assumption that schools operate, as do most organizations, as part of their larger societies. Teachers, students, and administrators interact with each other in a place called school and also interact individually and collectively with their communities and larger societies. More specifically, schools function as social systems and are part of their larger social systems.

Figure 2–1 is a simplified version of a social process model developed by Getzels and Guba (1957) that is applicable to any social system and easily adaptable to a school. In this model, a school functions as a subsystem (institution) that interacts with the larger environmental social system. The needs of individuals as well as the expectations (roles) of the school (institution) operating within and responding to the values of the culture of the larger environment (community) are the essential elements. Furthermore, processes such as teaching, administering, and planning that operate within the schools are social processes involving people and social interactions. This concept is not complex, but it does provide an important fundamental assumption for understanding educational planning processes.

Applying this model to actual practice, administrators would plan and make decisions based on the human needs of people both inside and outside the school, including students, teachers, parents, and taxpayers. The model also supports the practice of allowing others to participate in administrative processes. Several school systems (e.g., Chicago, Denver, and Miami) have implemented school-based management and shared decision making in their schools; their policies are based on this concept.

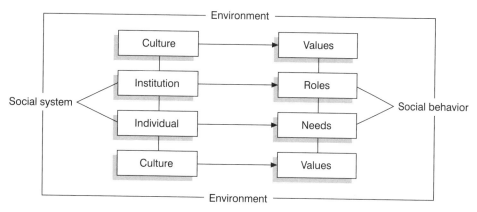

Figure 2–1
General Social Process Model

Source: Adapted from the social process model cited in Getzels and Guba (1957).

As with most theories or models, this one is not perfect. One common criticism is that a social system model is not the most efficient approach for administering complex organizations. Involving many people in administrative processes is time-consuming and leads to more decisions based on consensus and sharing of resources rather than on optimization of resources. Furthermore, people do not always operate in a purely rational manner. They may be focused too much on individual needs and issues and not necessarily on the needs of the school or society as a whole. Indeed, we would be naive to expect a social system model to provide a perfect explanation of how such a complex organization operates. The best way to use this or any other model is to assume that it provides direction focused on a "big picture," will not fit perfectly, and conceptually exists on a continuum.

EVALUATING THE BOTTOM LINE: THE SOCIAL PROCESS AND RATIONAL MODELS

Figure 2–2 represents a continuum with the social process model on the right and its opposite, the purely economic or rational model, on the left. The economic/rational model posits that schools operate similarly to private businesses, with an emphasis on "bottom-line profits." In practice, administering a school and other nonprofit, social agencies strictly according to this model has problems. Unlike businesses, in which one can compare earnings and costs with a common evaluation measure, the dollar, a school's "earnings" are very difficult to define. "Earnings" in education are imperfect. Evaluation measures such as student academic achievement (as a function of student potential), social development, and other student outcomes do not compare or measure well with their costs. Universally accepted measures for student achievement do not exist; standardized tests have been the subject of intense debate regarding their validity, reliability, and cultural bias. Other techniques for measuring student achievement such as portfolios and outcomes-based education likewise are difficult to compare to costs.

Furthermore, human talents and abilities are very diverse. One child may be a poor reader with a talent for mathematics. Another child may perform poorly in mathematics but is a gifted writer. Experienced administrators and teachers would probably agree that the most desirable outcomes would be for these children to achieve their potential in all subjects while recognizing that they will probably achieve much more in their strengths than their weaknesses. However, attempting to measure these outcomes becomes an almost impossible task given existing achievement measures and assessment techniques.

Figure 2–2
Continuum of Economic/Rational and Social Models of Organizational Behavior

Source: Adapted from Luthans (1981).

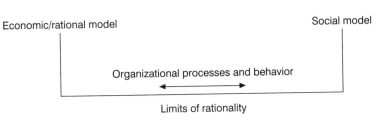

Economic/rational model   Social model

Organizational processes and behavior

Limits of rationality

In addition, given the wide disparity in school district spending even within the same states and counties, municipalities, communities, and boards of education clearly have very different ideas regarding appropriate costs for their children's educations. This further complicates the problem of establishing evaluation measures and attempting to understand and administer school programs according to the economic/rational model.

Instead, what schools do is attempt to serve their children as best they can by offering variety in their curricula and by hiring trained teachers who understand children's diverse needs and talents and can interact with them appropriately. In managing and coordinating schools, administrators interact with teachers and other staff as well as with parents, school board members, state education departments, colleges, and local businesses to try and understand the environment in which these children will eventually use their talents and abilities and in which past graduates are using their talents and abilities. However, administrators and teachers will admit that their understanding of this environment is imperfect. Social interaction is necessary and helps improve our understanding of educational goals and outcomes as well as the problems in achieving them, but it does not perfect this understanding.

As mentioned earlier, these concepts stem from the foundations of organizational theory. An individual commonly associated with them and whose work is highly recommended for further reference is Herbert Simon (1945, 1957, 1960, 1979, 1982). Simon was awarded the Nobel Prize for economics in 1978 for his research on decision making in organizations. His theory on the limits of rationality, later renamed "bounded rationality," has as its main principle that organizations operate along a continuum of rational and social behaviors mainly because the knowledge necessary to function strictly according to a rational model is beyond what is available to administrators and managers. Although first developed in the 1940s, this theory has withstood the test of time and is widely recognized as a fundamental assumption in understanding organizational processes such as decision making and planning (Carlson & Awkerman, 1991; Luthans, 1981; Peters & Waterman, 1982). Interestingly, Simon (1991) has devoted a good deal of his efforts during the past 30 years to examining the role that computer technology can play in expanding the knowledge necessary for administrators to be more effective planners and decision makers.

COMMON ELEMENTS OF EDUCATIONAL PLANNING

In a review of planning processes, Sheathelm (1991) identifies four major elements of successful planning as the four Cs:

- Comprehensiveness
- Collaboration
- Commitment
- Continuity

They are very much worth exploring for developing a framework for planning for technology.

Comprehensiveness

First, planning needs to be comprehensive. A total view of a school and what it is supposed to accomplish for students and the community is an essential element. An important distinction here is the difference between having a total view and necessarily having solutions for everything. Part of planning is examining and understanding both the school and the environment as much as possible with the caveat that they cannot be understood entirely. Likewise, providing solutions for that which is not fully understood becomes imperfect, if not impossible. Nevertheless, administrators need to be aware of the needs of individuals (i.e., students, teachers, other administrators, board members) that may be specific and at times very unique. These needs can frequently be converted into goals and objectives on which a plan is formulated. On the other hand, teachers and staff frequently need to have a better understanding of the total enterprise—overall goals and objectives as well as overall resource availability. The essence of a comprehensive plan links individual needs and objectives into overall institutional goals.

Collaboration

A second element of planning is collaboration. Although administrators generally have a good deal of expertise and knowledge of education, they can never fully know or understand all its aspects. They need to rely on others to provide expertise and help improve their understanding. Specialists such as science teachers or speech therapists know their subjects better than administrators. Business managers, librarians, counselors, school nurses, and other staff have specific expertise that frequently is more complete and more current than that of a general administrator such as a principal or superintendent. This vast pool of knowledge, expertise, and experience needs to be tapped and become a vital part of any planning process.

In addition to the exchange of knowledge, collaboration also allows for greater appreciation of several perspectives of a goal, objective, or need. As Deborah Meier (1995), a nationally recognized school reformer and founder of Central Park East elementary and secondary schools, states, educators need to develop "the capacity to see the world as others might" (p. 40).

Commitment

Through collaboration, securing the commitment of those who are vital in carrying out a plan becomes easier. Commitment is critical because the best-laid plan will not be realized if the people who are expected to implement it are not committed to the task. Commitment comes from being involved both with formulating overall goals and objectives as well as with developing specific courses of action. Collaboration also allows others to understand a plan, a goal, or a course of action and the purposes behind them. Greater understanding generally fosters higher levels of commitment.

The commitment of administrative leaders such as principals and superintendents to planning is also critical. Commitment from teachers, staff, or parents will only come if there is a sense on their part that the administrative leadership is committed to a plan or planning process. Administrators must exercise their leadership skills in securing commitment by offering themselves as examples in sharing knowledge, formulating goals, developing objectives, and implementing courses of action.

Continuity

Finally, every planning process is continuous and never-ending. Societies, schools, and people are constantly changing, and plans must change with them. An organization is like a living organism that continually responds and adjusts to environmental stimuli. As the values of a society change, so must the way schools prepare students to live and function in that society. As new tools and technologies are developed, so should our methods of training students to use these tools and technologies.

In most circumstances, planning usually involves developing a written plan as a result of a series of meetings and committee work. However, planning does not begin with these activities and end with the production of the written plan. On the contrary, the written plan is a guideline for everyday activities. Administrators, teachers, and staff follow this guideline and accumulate information on how well the objectives of the plan are being implemented. This new information (including adjustments to the plan) then becomes input for further planning activity.

PLANNING FOR TECHNOLOGY

An overall model for planning for technology in a school district is shown in Figure 2–3, which is derived from the social process model. This model attempts to show planning for technology as proceeding from values defined by the environment toward goals and objectives formulated primarily at the school district level. To achieve these goals and objectives, computer applications are identified as the main courses of action that in turn require hardware and software, staff needs, facilities, and finances to be implemented or provided for at the school building level. Once implemented, they are subsequently evaluated, and feedback is provided to the planning process for establishing new goals, objectives, and applications and for revising existing ones. Information flows both ways in this process, from left to right as well as from right to left.

The model requires a good deal of information gathering and idea sharing, which may be done formally through committees as well as informally through ad hoc discussions, observations, visits, and reading the literature. This model fits well with and should be integrated with other planning activities in the school district.

An important feature of this model is that it incorporates **external environmental scanning**, which simply means engaging in activities to provide information on the community, state, and society for planning purposes. In addition to understanding societal and community values, environmental scanning is critical for comprehending changes in technology. The fundamental nature of technology includes change and, in the field of electronics and computers, rapid change. For many people involved with technology, this is frustrating but also invigorating. Developing an understanding of trends in hardware and software is important and enables planners

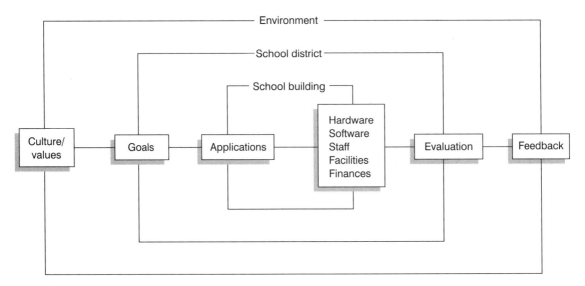

Figure 2–3
Model for Planning for Technology

to implement applications that will progress along with these trends and to avoid technology that will quickly become obsolete. Successful environmental scanning involves establishing and developing contacts with experts in the community, local colleges, and private businesses. District-wide committees for planning for technology are becoming common and can be used effectively as the bridges between school districts and the communities they serve.

A basic assumption of this model is that an administrator, most likely at the district level, provides the necessary leadership in converting environmental values and conditions into district-wide goals and objectives. Committees may be necessary for specific areas such as administrative applications or instructional applications, which allow for participation on the part of administrative staff and teachers. Identifying courses of action and computer applications, in particular, should also allow for input from sources at the building level. In a study of the progress of a technology committee headed by a principal at an elementary school in Boise, Idaho, Keeler (1996) concluded that cooperation and collaboration were enhanced and the principal was viewed more as "a leader and model of lifelong learning than as a manager of a school" (p. 342). A computer teacher or library media specialist can also function as a coordinator who leads a building-level committee for identifying applications that coincide with district-wide goals and objectives. In large high schools with several thousand students, several such committees might exist representing different subject areas or grade levels.

By allowing teachers, parents, and others in a school to participate, those responsible for planning become more knowledgeable and understand better the alternative courses of action and applications that a district might support. On the question of support, financial considerations will quickly rise to the surface. It is thus important to include at various levels the input of a school district's business officer or manager who can provide information on available financial resources. Naturally, planning is easier if the available financial resources can support all the various proposals that might be put forward for consideration. However, if these resources are not available, then administrators will need to draw on their leadership abilities in bringing committees to agreement on which proposals to include in a plan and which to exclude. However, if true participation has been effected, then priorities should become more evident to all participants.

Furthermore, a plan covers a period of time, frequently from 3 to 7 years, which can allow for more inclusion than exclusion. Administrators should attempt to be equitable and to distribute resources among competing participants. If resources are severely limited, then a major goal of the planning participants should be securing more funds rather than developing applications. In this case, the participation of community representatives may help identify and develop financial support from various sources, including governmental (federal, state, local) and private agencies.

A pivotal step in a planning process using the technology planning model depicted in Figure 2–3 is the development of a **written plan**. The purpose here is to provide understanding of the plan to all participants. Just as information flow is critical in the formative stages of planning, a written summary of what has been discussed or agreed on is essential for implementing the plan. Participants and others such as board members, administrators, and teachers need to understand what the goals are and what their responsibilities are in achieving them. School districts, in fact, can be creative in presenting and communicating their goals and objectives (see Figures 2–4, 2–5, and 2–6). Such creativity is desirable and not only helps participants and constituents understand the plan but also builds interest in it. Written summaries also form the basis for the next cycle of planning activities.

As mentioned earlier, planning is a continuous activity that never ends. Evaluation and feedback are critical for continuing planning activities from year to year or from planning cycle to planning cycle. Planning participants need information on how well computer applications are achieving objectives. This can only be provided if mechanisms are established for evaluating applications and generating feedback to the planning participants.

Figure 2–4
Sample Planning Material: Oakland Free School District

> The Oakland Free School District
> Administrators at the Workstation Project
> **Objectives**
> - Implement an integrated office automation system in all schools
> - Expand the regional data communications network
> - Field-test a new attendance monitoring system
> - Assess the effectiveness of the financial accounting system (FAS)

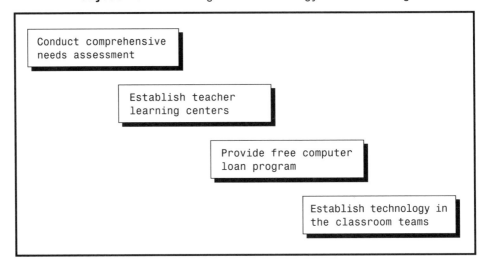

Figure 2–5
Sample Planning Material: Fremont Staff Development Project

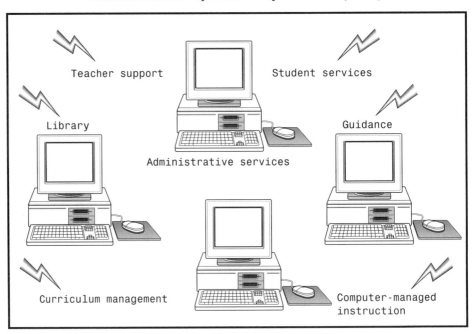

Figure 2–6
Sample Planning Material: North Central School District

TAKING A POSITIVE ATTITUDE TO EVALUATION

Undertaking evaluation with a positive attitude is desirable for all involved in the planning process. Unfortunately, educators approach evaluation with caution or reluctance, especially when it is conducted or administered by others or "outsiders." School and governmental officials have used formal measures such as SAT scores, state competency testing, and other standardized instruments for decades to evaluate school performance. Unfortunately, in some instances, these measures have become politicized to justify criticisms of public education and have come to be viewed as more of a "stick" or "whip." Referring to declines in test scores, political campaign slogans stressing the need "to raise educational standards" are common at all levels from school board to presidential elections and have become "tired clichés" (O'Neill, 1991, p. 4).

Regardless, educators must not abandon evaluation in their planning but instead should attempt to develop nonthreatening evaluation criteria on which all involved (administrators, teachers, parents) can agree. This is especially true for technology planning since resources will be scrutinized even in the most financially able school districts. Large expenditures for equipment, staffing, and facilities, are common when implementing technology and justifiably should be evaluated carefully.

In developing evaluation criteria for technology planning, the measures should be appropriate to the goals. Goals for administrative applications frequently require summative evaluation criteria and the establishment of timetables and milestones for accomplishing certain events. Goals for instructional applications may or may not require standardized measures. However, if an instructional goal is directed to student achievement, then testing or other performance measures are appropriate evaluation criteria and should be considered.

For instructional applications involving student achievement, multiple evaluation criteria are highly recommended. As an example, Rock and Cummings (1994) describe a project designed to evaluate the implementation of videodisc technology in 15 schools in California, Illinois, Missouri, New York, Pennsylvania, Oregon, Texas, and West Virginia. The program was funded by Optical Data Corporation, a leading provider of multimedia software, but school administrators and teachers were free to design their own evaluation criteria. In every school, a standardized test such as the Iowa Test of Basic Skills, the Missouri Master Achievement Test, or the New York State Regents Examination was used in conjunction with some other measure, such as a student attitude questionnaire, portfolio assessment, or classroom observation. Of the 15 schools, 7 used two evaluation criteria, 2 used three criteria, and 6 used four or more criteria. Teachers and administrators reported that the use of videotape to observe and record student involvement and interactivity with lessons was particularly helpful since significant differences were consistently observed between classes using videodisc technology and those not using it.

Educators and policy makers must also prepare for the reality that not every plan and implementation will be successful. However, good technology planning will minimize risks by establishing basic evaluation criteria early on in the process. This is especially important for major technology initiatives involving an entire district. Dick and Carey (1985), Thigarajan, Semmel, and Semmel (1974), and Willis (1993) propose an "instructional development research model" that is appropriate for this type of evaluation. This model essentially recommends developing, implementing, and evaluating technology in small incremental stages until satisfied that the technology is meeting expected goals and objectives on a limited basis before implementing it on a larger scale. Such an approach reduces the risk of making a large investment in technology that may not be beneficial.

ADMINISTRATIVE AND INSTRUCTIONAL APPLICATIONS

The most important characteristic of this framework for planning is the concentration on computer applications as the fundamental courses of action. **Applications** simply are the applying of technology to the goals and objectives of the plan. Most important for our understanding is that the identification of these applications precedes the acquisition of their components such as hardware, software, staff development, and facilities. Applications may use existing hardware and software components, but they should not be determined simply because of these preexisting components. Otherwise, planning becomes the classic case of the "tail wagging the dog."

In general, different types of applications require different components. Administrative applications are different from instructional applications. Within instruction, writing applications are different from science applications, which are different from those for social studies, and so forth. To assume that the same hardware and software can meet these diverse needs is naive.

As an example, when computer technology consisted of large mainframe computers, many users depended on and shared common hardware and software because the costs otherwise would be prohibitive. However, it did not work well then, and it works less well now as more and more applications require specific hardware and software to meet specific needs. Even with present-day microcomputers, less expensive equipment such as monochrome video displays may be appropriate output devices for teaching writing using word processing; it would not be appropriate, however, for desktop publishing, science simulation software, or paint programs that can use high-resolution color and graphics.

Planning for Administrative Applications

Planning for administrative applications is different in several ways from planning for instructional applications. The goals, nature of the applications, participants, and evaluation are different. Environmental scanning is helpful in formulating goals, especially for identifying appropriate technology. State education departments, local governmental agencies, accreditation associations, and professional organizations are valuable sources for helping school districts determine the types of administrative applications that are being used in other school districts. Local businesses such as banks or insurance companies, which frequently use current information technology such as database management systems, can be helpful in identifying appropriate software for establishing and maintaining computer-based information systems. School districts that are part of larger local or state governmental jurisdictions also need to make sure that they understand the information or administrative system requirements of these governing entities. For example, urban school districts frequently have certain administrative systems such as budgeting, payroll, and purchasing provided to them by municipal agencies. Any planning involving these systems should provide for participation by the municipal agents familiar with the future development of these systems.

In planning administrative applications, the goals of a district can be stated in many different ways, and planners are encouraged to be creative to generate interest in a plan. However, as described in the literature (Ray & Davis, 1991; Richards, 1989), administrative applications frequently relate to one or more of the following themes:

- To develop/improve information resources
- To provide/improve new administrative services
- To increase administrative productivity and efficiency

These themes can be stated many different ways as goals, objectives, and applications in actual planning documents.

Information resources are all aspects of the data collection, storage, and retrieval processes and procedures needed by school administrators to monitor, report, and understand what is going on in their schools. The major data collection and record-keeping applications in most schools pertain to students, curriculum, finances, personnel, and facilities. They typically use database management software systems that are maintained centrally at the district level and that can be distributed to the individual schools.

Providing new administrative services is a broad goal with an emphasis on doing or improving that which is not being done or not being done well. Examples might include expanding student grade reports to provide prescriptive information, automating substitute teacher lists, improving general communications to parents and residents, or establishing an on-line student guidance system. These services may use database, office automation, electronic spreadsheet, or desktop publishing software, and they can be developed centrally at the district level or locally at the building level.

Increasing productivity and efficiency in administrative operations is frequently associated with computer technology and refers to improving information and communication flow. For example, database management systems have been particularly effective in improving reporting and reducing redundant data-gathering activities (i.e., having two or more offices collecting the same information). Providing administrative staff with office automation software such as word processing, E-mail, and electronic spreadsheet programs also has been widely accepted in helping these staff become much more efficient in presenting, communicating, and assembling all types of text- and number-based materials.

The major leadership in planning for administrative applications exists centrally at the district level, since applications involving information flow and data management typically are directed and controlled centrally. Building-level administrators and staff should understand and accept the need for central administrative information systems. However, in planning administrative systems, staff at the building level should be involved. They are important resource people who begin the information cycle by collecting source data on students, families, personnel, payrolls, and so on. They will do a better job of data collection if they understand the purposes of their efforts. They will do a spectacular job if they personally can realize some benefits such as less paperwork or less need to do repetitive periodic reports. They can also help planning participants determine staff development and training needs that are as important for secretaries and administrative assistants as they are for teachers and instructional staff.

Developing evaluation criteria as part of the planning process is usually very straightforward for administrative applications. Initially, it involves determining whether certain milestones in developing an application are being met, culminating with the application becoming operational. For example, the evaluation criteria for the development of a new computer-based financial information system might be to establish dates by which certain modules or subsystems are to be operational. Once the system is established, additional evaluation criteria might involve comparing the timeliness and accuracy of critical reports before and after the system became operational.

Figure 2–7 provides a partial example of a school district's plan for implementing a new integrated financial management system. The plan is organized with goals relating well to objectives and the application, and it also shows how planning goals respond to needs emanating from both outside and inside the district. Objectives are clearly stated, and appropriate time frames are established for design, implementation, and evaluation. While focusing on the financial management application, the plan also provides for various components such as hardware, software, and staff development.

Chapter 4 is dedicated exclusively to an examination of the major administrative applications that can exist in a school. Readers will find additional information related to planning for these applications in that chapter.

Planning for Instructional Applications

Planning instructional applications is similar to planning administrative applications, but several differences do exist. Environmental scanning is just as important, and many of the same agencies such as state education departments, accreditation associations, and professional organizations can be excellent sources for information and ideas. In addition, professional organizations such as the National Education Association and the Association for Supervision and Curriculum Development are active in presenting issues on the instructional uses of technology. Local colleges, especially those with teacher education programs, may also possess valuable expertise in developing planning goals and applications.

A school district's goals and objectives regarding instructional applications can be very diverse. Several national studies (Becker, 1994; Sheingold & Hadley, 1990; U.S. Congress, Office of Technology Assessment, 1995) indicate that instructional uses of computers frequently relate to one or more of the following themes:

Background

The following is excerpted from a planning document for implementing an integrated financial management system in a school district. The need for this system occurred because of changes in the way funds were provided by external agencies (i.e., state aid), which increasingly were being allocated later in the school year, requiring the school district to make allocations and adjustments to allocations even later. In addition, demands for fiscal data and accountability had increased significantly from both external funding agencies and internal departments. This application was designed to replace several nonintegrated computer applications that were implemented in the district office in the 1970s.

North Central School District No. 1
Six-Year Technology Plan (1991–97)

Goals (from district's long-range plan)
Improve financial reporting capabilities to external funding agencies.
Improve financial record keeping within the district.
Improve fiscal accountability within each of the schools in the district.
-
-
-

Objectives (1991–92)
Design the requirements of a new, integrated financial management system (FMS).
-
-
-

Objectives (1992–93)
Evaluate computer software products that can meet the design requirements of FMS.
Procure a computer software product that meets the design requirements of FMS.
Evaluate hardware requirements of the central office and schools for implementing FMS.
Evaluate the data communications facilities required to implement FMS in the schools.
-
-
-

Figure 2–7
Sample of Planning Goals and Objectives for an Administrative Computer Application

Objectives (1993–94)
Acquire the necessary computer hardware in the central office to implement FMS.
Implement the financial accounting and budget modules of FMS in the central office.
Train all central office staff in the use of FMS.
Acquire the necessary data communications facilities to implement FMS in all the schools.
-
-
-

Objectives (1994–95)
Acquire the necessary computer hardware to implement FMS in the schools.
Implement the financial accounting and budget modules of FMS in the schools.
Train all school staff in the use of FMS.
Implement the purchasing and accounts payable modules of FMS in the central office.
Continue training staff in the central office in the use of FMS.
-
-
-

Objectives (1995–96)
Implement the purchasing and accounts payable modules of FMS in the schools.
Implement the payroll and personnel modules of FMS in the central office.
Continue training staff in the central office and in the schools in the use of FMS.
-
-
-

Objectives (1996–97)
Implement the payroll and personnel modules of FMS in the schools.
Continue training staff in the central office and in the schools in the use of FMS.
Conduct an in-depth evaluation of the benefits of FMS to the school district.
-
-
-

Figure 2–7, *continued*

- Preparing students to participate in a technically oriented society
- Enhancing/improving learning by using technological tools
- Enhancing/improving teaching by using technological tools
- Providing technology-based curricula for students with special aptitudes or interests in technology

As with administrative applications, these instructional application themes may be stated in many different ways in actual planning documents.

Preparing students to participate in a technically oriented society recognizes that all types of jobs, professions, and everyday routines increasingly use technology. Students should develop basic competency or literacy in using technology during their primary and secondary school programs to function in this society. Accomplishing this may involve taking specific, dedicated courses in computer programming or integrating technology with other courses (such as using databases to conduct research in social studies), or a combination of both.

Enhancing learning by employing technology refers to students' use of technology in general curricular areas. Examples include using word-processing software to teach writing, electronic spreadsheet programs to teach accounting or business subjects, the Internet to learn about other cultures, and electronic encyclopedias to perform research. The list of possibilities is almost endless. Increasingly, integrating technology into the curriculum has became a major goal for many school districts in planning instructional applications (Sheingold & Hadley, 1990; U.S. Congress, Office of Technology Assessment, 1995; Warger, 1990).

Enhancing teaching by making use of technology refers to teachers incorporating technology in classroom presentations and other teaching activities. Specific examples are the use of large-screen monitors and other multimedia (computers and video) in the classroom. The emphasis here is on the use of technology by teachers for teaching more so than by students for learning. A popular element of this theme is staff development and the training of teachers to use technology in the classroom.

Providing technology-based curricula for students with special talents or interests is a rapidly expanding theme for many school districts. This includes special vocational programs such as computer operations, computer maintenance, and data communications. These can be designed to prepare students seeking employment immediately upon graduation from high school as well as to prepare them for 2-year community college programs. High school programs that offer electives in computer programming for students who are considering pursuing a computer science or engineering career also can be included as part of this theme.

The leadership for planning instructional applications should be shared at the district level and at the building level with the teaching staff who possess expertise in the various subject areas. Diverse subject areas and grade levels require different computer hardware and software or specialized staff training. Tens of thousands of instructional software packages are available, which make it increasingly more difficult for central office staff to keep current and maintain a level of expertise. As a result, planning for these applications more frequently allows individual teachers, academic departments, and grade-level coordinators to make specific proposals that might fit an overall planning goal. This process may also involve establishing an ongoing budget and approval mechanism for evaluating, funding, and acquiring instructional software at the building level. In addition to drawing on the expertise of many of the professional staff members, this approach also allows teachers to use technology best suited to their own teaching styles and philosophies. It should also encourage a greater commitment to its successful utilization.

Evaluating the implementation of instructional applications should include a formal assessment. In addition to establishing milestones for implementing instructional applications, a district that uses standardized tests can incorporate these into the overall evaluation criteria. The availability of a good student record-keeping system in a district should easily provide these and other student achievement data such as grades and graduation rates for evaluating an application's instructional effectiveness. Other evaluation techniques that should be considered include portfolios, student and teacher attitude surveys, and classroom observations.

Figure 2–8 is a partial example of a school district's plan for implementing multimedia technology that illustrates several characteristics of a good instructional technology plan. Teachers are actively involved (i.e., Multimedia Coordinating Committee) in planning and implementation. Staff development is continuous and ongoing. Stages of the plan relate to grade levels. It also requires extensive evaluation and review before progressing to each successive stage of the plan.

Chapter 5 is dedicated exclusively to a review of instructional applications. Readers will find additional information related to planning for these applications in that chapter.

CASE STUDY
Place: Lotusville   Year: 1994

Lotusville is a suburban school district in the South with an enrollment of 5,500 students distributed among one high school, three middle schools, and six primary schools. The population has been increasing by approximately 2% per year. The district's tax base has also been rising because of recent commercial development. A formal planning process was implemented in 1981 by the board of education. A district-wide Planning Committee was established and has continued to be active in establishing goals and objectives. The membership of the Planning Committee is as follows:

- Three parents, one of whom is the president of the PTA
- Two school board members
- The manager of the local bank, who is a former school board member
- A teacher who represents the teacher's union and who teaches high school mathematics
- The district superintendent
- The director of pupil personnel services for the district

Background

The following is excerpted from a planning document for implementing multimedia technology in all the schools in a school district. While several isolated uses of multimedia technology had been implemented at the high school level, this plan represents the first district-wide concerted effort. The need for this technology evolved from the recommendations of several teachers at the high school level who had been using videodisc technology since 1988. In terms of equipment, all of the schools had at least one central computer laboratory, and most had also started to put some equipment in individual classrooms. With the exception of two high schools, none of the schools had videodisc equipment. As defined by the Technology Planning Committee, a multimedia workstation consists of a microcomputer and a videodisc player with monitor or CD-ROM. CD-ROM equipment was to be purchased as needed through the yearly computer equipment budget.

South Central School District No. 1
Five Year Technology Plan (1993–98)

Goals (from district's long-range plan)
To improve teaching by making use of multimedia technology.
To enhance learning by making use of multimedia technology.

- •
- •
- •

Objectives (1993–94)
To establish an ad hoc Multimedia Coordinating Committee within the school district.
To conduct exploratory presentations on the use of multimedia in instruction.
To acquire six videodisc players and associated monitor equipment and software for the high schools.
To pilot six multimedia programs in the high schools.
To evaluate the six pilot multimedia programs in the high schools from the teachers' perspective (as teaching tools).

- •
- •
- •

Objectives (1994–95)
To continue to acquire multimedia equipment and software for the high schools.
To conduct staff development programs in multimedia for high school teachers.
To acquire six videodisc players and associated monitor equipment and software for the middle schools.
To pilot six multimedia programs in the middle schools.

Figure 2–8
Sample of Planning Goals and Objectives for an Instructional Computer Application

To evaluate the six pilot multimedia programs in the middle schools from the teachers' perspective (as teaching tools).

-
-
-

Objectives (1995–96)

To continue to acquire multimedia equipment and software for the middle schools.

To continue to provide staff development programs in multimedia for high school teachers.

To conduct staff development programs in multimedia for middle school teachers.

To evaluate multimedia programs in the high schools and middle schools from the students' perspective (as learning tools).

-
-
-

Objectives (1996–97)

To acquire twelve videodisc players and associated monitor equipment and software for the elementary schools.

To continue to acquire multimedia equipment for the high schools and for the middle schools.

To continue to provide staff development programs in multimedia for high school and middle school teachers.

To pilot twelve multimedia programs in the elementary schools.

To evaluate the twelve pilot multimedia programs in the elementary schools from the teachers' perspective (as teaching tools).

-
-
-

Objectives (1997–98)

To continue to acquire multimedia equipment and software for all schools.

To provide staff development programs in multimedia for elementary school teachers.

To continue to provide staff development programs in multimedia for high school and middle school teachers.

To evaluate multimedia programs in all schools from the students' perspective (as learning tools).

-
-
-

Figure 2–8, *continued*

The district superintendent also acts as a resource person for the Planning Committee and has established formal processes for gathering information for the committee's planning activities.

In 1983, at the suggestion of two of the parents, the Planning Committee established an Advisory Committee for Instructional Computing. Although the Planning Committee had always been supportive of computer technology in the instructional programs, the resources devoted to it were increasing. The perception was that a need existed to review more carefully where the district was heading in this regard. The Advisory Committee has the following membership:

- Two parents
- The manager of a local computer hardware distributing company
- One school board member
- A teacher who represents the teachers' union and who teaches science in the high school and was a former part-time computer coordinator
- The assistant superintendent for instruction
- The principal of one of the middle schools

In general, the Advisory Committee has worked well with the Planning Committee and has been effective in expanding instructional computing in the district.

In the entire district in 1983, there were 40 microcomputers in two computer laboratories in the high school. These were supervised by one science teacher who was released from half of his teaching responsibilities. Pascal, BASIC, word processing, and electronic spreadsheets were taught in elective courses within the high school mathematics program. An instructional computing plan was developed in 1984 that called for a significant increase in the number of microcomputers being used for instructional purposes at all grade levels and the hiring of at least one computer teacher for each school by 1987. By 1993, the district had installed 450 microcomputers primarily in central computer laboratories, although some units were being distributed to individual classrooms, primarily in the high school. Each school has at least one full-time computer teacher who supervises the laboratories and teaches computer courses. A full-time computer technician has also been hired who maintains the equipment for the entire district. A wide variety of computer software packages is available for all grade levels, including LogoWriter, simulation programs, desktop publishing, word processing, spreadsheet, database, BASIC, and Pascal. Computer courses are required in several grades in the primary and middle school programs; they are electives in the high school program.

A major issue facing the district's Planning Committee is whether the expansion in instructional computing has been worth the investment in equipment and personnel. Annual standardized test scores indicate that academic achievement has actually been decreasing slightly during the past five years. In addition, the teachers' representative on the Planning Committee has stated that many of the primary school teachers would like to see microcomputers placed in the regular classrooms. The district superintendent has been advised by the assistant superintendent for instruction that locating equipment in the regular classrooms would require a major increase in the number of microcomputers and an extensive new staff development program because many teachers, especially in the primary schools, were not familiar enough with the technology to use it effectively.

Analyze the preceding case study. What observations can you make regarding the effectiveness of the planning process in the Lotusville school district? Do you have any suggestions for improving it? Consider especially the structure, membership of the committees, evaluation, and feedback. Compared with your own environment, does Lotusville appear to be more or less effective in the way it plans for technology? Finally, if you were the district superintendent, what courses of action might you consider or recommend to the Planning Committee to help resolve some of the recent issues identified regarding instructional computing?

SUMMARY

This chapter describes several basic assumptions and concepts regarding educational planning for technology. A great deal of literature exists on educational planning, much of which has roots in organization theory and development. One of the more important concepts is the idea that schools operate as social systems and are part of larger social systems. Individuals (teachers, students), organizations (schools), and larger environments (communities, towns, cities) interact with one another through social processes. One way of describing and understanding organizations is to understand that social processes provide the foundation for how they operate.

In applying the social process model, four common elements are identified as important to effective educational planning. Planning needs to be **comprehensive**, **collaborative**, and **continuous**. In addition, it needs to have the **commitment** of all involved: administrators, teachers, parents, and other community representatives.

Planning for technology can be incorporated into other educational planning activities and processes, following a social process model that involves individuals, the school, the community, and the larger environment. It should allow for participation of administrators, teachers, and staff at the district, school building, and departmental levels. Because of the dynamic and changing nature of technology, planning should extensively use environmental scanning and data gathering on technological trends and developments. Evaluation is critical for determining whether goals and objectives are met, and educators should adopt a positive attitude to using it in planning processes.

In the development of objectives and courses of action, applications become the fundamental building blocks on which hardware, software, staff development, facilities, and financial components depend. Administrative applications are different from instructional applications, and writing applications are different from science applications, which are different from music applications, and so on. Microcomputer technology has matured to the point where specific solutions identified as applications can be provided to meet specific goals and objectives.

Key Concepts and Questions

1. *Planning* is a frequently used term among individuals, schools, organizations, and government agencies.

   How do you define planning? What are its common elements?

2. Much has been written and said regarding what is needed for successful planning to take place in complex organizations such as schools.

   What are the essential elements of an organizational planning process? Are these elements evident in your organizational environment? Explain.

3. Private businesses and governmental agencies use planning processes.

   Are processes developed for these organizations appropriate for schools? Why?

4. Schools can be described and analyzed as social systems.

   How do you define a social system? Who are the major participants in this system? What are their roles, if any, in planning?

5. Planning involves the establishment of goals and objectives. In planning for technology, meeting these goals and objectives should center on computer applications rather than on individual application components.

   What do you consider the essential components of computer applications? Are some components more important than others? Explain.

6. Planning for administrative applications and instructional applications have similarities and differences.

   Compare the two in relation to objectives, participants, and evaluation.

7. *Environmental scanning* has become a frequently used term in planning processes.

   Why is it particularly important when planning for technology?

Suggested Activities

1. Identify how planning is done in a school district with which you are familiar. Who are the main participants in the planning process? What suggestions can you propose for improving the planning process at the district level?

2. Identify how planning is done in a school. How does it integrate with the district planning process? Who are the main participants? What suggestions can you propose for improving the planning process at the school level?

References

Adams, D. (1987). Paradigmatic contexts of models of educational planning and decision making. *Educational Planning, 6*(1), 36–47.

Barnard, C. I. (1964). *The functions of the executive.* Cambridge, MA: Harvard University Press.

Becker, H. J. (1994). *Analysis and trends of school use of new information technologies.* Irvine: Department of Education, University of California, Irvine.

Carlson, R. V., & Awkerman, G. (Eds.). (1991). *Educational planning: concepts, strategies and practices.* New York: Longman.

Dick, W., & Carey, L. (1985). *The systematic design of instruction* (2nd ed.). Glenview, IL: Scott, Foresman.

Engvall, R. P. (1995). The limited value of planning in education: Getting back to basics isn't all about curriculum. *The Urban Review, 27*(3), 251–262.

Etzioni, A. (1961). *A comparative analysis of complex organizations.* New York: Free Press.

Getzels, J. W., & Guba, E. G. (1957). Social behavior and the administrative process. *School Review, 65,* 423–441.

Keeler, C. M. (1996). Networked instructional computers in the elementary classroom and their effect on the learning environment: A qualitative evaluation. *Journal of Research on Computing in Education, 28*(3), 329–345.

Luthans, F. (1981). *Organizational behavior.* New York: McGraw-Hill.

Meier, D. (1995). *The power of their ideas: Lessons for America from a small school in Harlem.* Boston: Beacon.

O'Neill, J. (1991). Drive for national standards picking up steam. *Educational Leadership, 48*(5), 4–8.

Parsons, T. (1951). *The social system.* New York: Free Press.

———. (1958). Some ingredients of a general theory of formal organization. In A. W. Halpin (Ed.), *Administrative theory in education* (pp. 40–72). Chicago: University of Chicago Press.

Peters, T. J., & Waterman, R. (1982). *In search of excellence.* New York: Harper & Row.

Ray, J. R., & Davis, L. D. (1991). *Computers in educational administration.* New York: McGraw-Hill.

Richards, C. E. (1989). *Microcomputer applications for strategic management in education: A case study approach.* New York: Longman.

Rock, H. M., & Cummings, A. (1994). Can videodiscs improve student outcomes? *Educational Leadership, 51*(7), 46–50.

Sheathelm, H. H. (1991). Common elements in the planning process. In R. V. Carlson & G. Awkerman (Eds.), *Educational planning: Concepts, strategies and practices* (pp. 267–278). New York: Longman.

Sheingold, K., & Hadley, M. (1990). *Accomplished teachers: Integrating computers into classroom practice.* New York: Bank Street College of Education, Center for Technology in Education.

Simon, H. A. (1945). *Administrative behavior.* New York: Macmillan.

———. (1957). *Administrative behavior.* New York: Macmillan.

———. (1960). *The new science of management decision.* New York: Harper & Row.

———. (1979). Rational decision making in business organizations. *American Economic Review, 69,* 493–513.

———. (1982). *Models of bounded rationality.* Cambridge, MA: MIT Press.

———. (1991). *Models of my life.* New York: Basic Books.

Thigarajan, S. Semmel, D., & Semmel, M. (1974). *Instructional development for training teachers of exceptional children: A sourcebook.* Reston, VA: Council for Exceptional children.

U.S. Congress, Office of Technology Assessment. (1995). *Teachers and technology: Making the connection* (Report No. OTA-EHR-616). Washington, DC: U.S. Government Printing Office.

Warger, C. (Ed.). (1990). *Technology in today's schools.* Alexandria, VA: Association for Supervision and Curriculum Development.

Willis, J. (1993). Technology in teacher education: A research and development agenda. In H. C. Waxman & G. W. Bright (Eds.), *Approaches to Research on Teacher Education and Technology* (pp. 35–50). Charlottesville, VA: Association for the Advancement of Computing in Education.

3

Technology, Learning, and Equity Issues

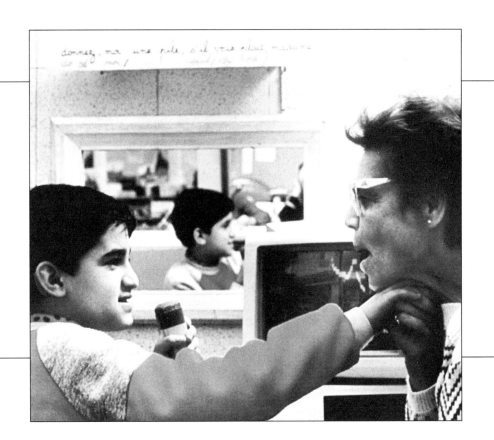

| A | s technology continues to expand in the nation's schools, a variety of associated issues are developing with which administrators should be familiar. Some of these derive from the larger issue of the effectiveness of technology in instruction and learning. Others are equity issues, perhaps involving gender or race, that derive from societal or educational policy issues. Regardless of the type, administrators in all environments should be sensitive to these issues as they plan for and implement technology in their schools. |

This chapter reviews some of the critical issues emerging as technology expands in the schools. Knowledge of these issues is particularly important during planning activities, when they should be discussed and considered frequently.

TECHNOCENTRIC EDUCATION

In *Mindstorms: Children, Computers, and Powerful Ideas*, Seymour Papert (1980) reveals his philosophy regarding the beneficial effects of computer technology on learning. This was one of the first major works to weave an educational philosophy into the development of a computer programming language (Logo). In what is perhaps one of the more controversial passages, Papert says, "I am optimistic—some might say utopian—about the effect of computers on society" (p. 26). He then describes the benefits of the Logo programming language on children's learning and cognitive development.

For many educators, Papert's theories generated unbridled enthusiasm for the use of computing technology in the classroom. Throughout the 1980s, Papert's work and philosophy were the subject of great debate and discussion (Becker, 1987; Davy, 1984; Maddux, 1989; Papert, 1987; Pea, 1983, 1987; Walker, 1987). The debate revolved around a technocentric approach to teaching and learning in which computers would become the vehicles for solving many of the problems in education. Although several educators, including Papert, have since called for a more cautious and deliberate approach in the use of computers in education, the issue remains open.

In a *Computerworld* article, Lewis Perelman (1990), the director of Project Learning 2001, called for computer vendors to seize an opportunity that was presenting itself in American education. Essentially, he described classroom teachers as approaching "rapid obsolescence" and stated that their jobs could be done better by technology. His call was for a major overhaul of the nation's schools that would transform teaching and learning from the traditional, human interactive activity into a machine-intensive one. He is convinced that teachers can be replaced by computers and that the only reason this has not occurred is because the academic establishment and "educrats" are not allowing it to happen. Although many educators consider Perelman's viewpoint extreme, it nonetheless exists and should not be ignored. Surely the use of technology is expanding, and as schools advance, questions are emerging as to how much technology should be employed in the schools. Is more technology better? Can technology replace teachers?

To provide further insight into this issue, an examination of **integrated learning systems** (ILSs) would be helpful. These systems represent the most intensive uses of technology in teaching and learning available today. They integrate hardware, software, and curriculum and also usually provide sophisticated computer-managed instructional techniques that are able to customize or individualize material for each student using the system. They are designed not to be an adjunct to teaching but actually to perform the teaching function. In schools with ILSs, teachers' roles have been transformed to a certain degree from those of instructors to managers of instruction. However, in the vast majority of these schools, instruction is provided on the ILS for a limited period each week.

According to Quality Education Data (1995), approximately 7,022 schools in the United States have installed ILSs. In 1990, the EPIE (Educational Products Information Exchange) Institute of Brookvale, New York, conducted a national study of 24 schools with these systems. Field visits were made to each site, and eight different ILSs were evaluated. In general, administrators, teachers, and students supported the use of these systems (Sherry, 1990). For example, 96% of the teachers and administrators interviewed in these schools recommended that other schools install similar systems, and 99% of the students interviewed indicated that they too would recommend these systems for other schools. Longitudinal student performance data based on grades or standardized tests were not collected. The researchers contemplated collecting this data, but they concluded that the outcomes of ILS use were "too difficult or impossible to measure" at the time. Regardless, the overwhelming support for the ILSs in these schools indicate their general acceptance by all involved. The major benefits of ILSs most often cited by teachers and administrators in this study were the individualization of instruction, the extensive reporting capabilities, and the completeness of content.

Given the results of this study, should all schools acquire such systems, and should schools with these systems expand their use? Because technology is "good," is more technology better? The answers to all these questions are probably no. In addition to careful planning, EPIE recommended caution in investing in ILSs. Administrators, teachers, and students all support and endorsed their use, but their enthusiasm for such systems would not likely endure if ILSs were the primary (or only) teaching delivery system employed in their schools. Although ILSs can be important tools when integrated properly with a district's curriculum, they should not replace that curriculum. Furthermore, teachers must be well trained to use these systems and to integrate them with other teaching activities.

Previously in this chapter, a passage was quoted from *Mindstorms* that gave the impression that technology is a "utopia" for learning and education. However, later on in this same passage, Papert (1980) refers to the computer as "a useful educational tool." Like all tools, the value of computers and other forms of technology can vary depending on who uses them and how they are used. Only when put into skillful hands and integrated with other materials and activities does the value of computers rise, with their potential realized. In providing leadership for their districts and schools, administrators should adopt this "tool" mentality as opposed to a "technocentric" mentality when implementing technology. Though continuing to improve and advance, technology has not yet reached the point of replacing teachers. Administrators should be developing teachers to capture and harness the power of technology so as to integrate it with other teaching and learning activities.

WHEN SHOULD COMPUTER EDUCATION BEGIN?

Patterns of technology acquisition indicate that upper-grade and high school students have more access to technology than early childhood and elementary school children. Studies (Becker, 1994; Picciano, 1991; Quality Education Data, 1996) indicate that junior high and high schools typically have 33% more computer equipment per student than elementary schools. One major reason is that high schools and upper grades adopted computer science and computer literacy courses before the elementary schools did (Geisert & Futrell, 1995). Another reason entails the debate within the elementary schools as to the appropriate age at which to introduce students to technology. Whereas some schools have adopted an "earlier the better" approach, others indicate that there is no need to rush and children can learn it later on in their education.

One side of this issue is based on the concept that technology is good; therefore, the more (and earlier) students can learn it, the better off they will be. The other side of this issue concerns the readiness of children to use technology. Readiness in this regard can relate to a host of subissues including cognitive development, finger dexterity, eye-hand coordination in using keyboards, comprehension of computer instructions, and integration into content areas.

Papert (1980), who lived and studied with Jean Piaget, believes that children are able to benefit from computer technology at a very early age. The fundamental Logo concept of manipulating a friendly turtle icon is directed specifically at the young learner and is derived directly from Piaget's theories on cognitive development. Though children develop cognitively at different rates, Piaget proposed that logical thinking, at least as applied to physical reality, begins in the elementary school years at approximately 7 to 11 years of age. The fact (Quality Education Data, 1996) that 99% of all elementary schools have acquired microcomputer equipment for instructional purposes suggests that educators believe that children are ready to begin using computer equipment at an early age.

Logo, which continues to be one of the most popular instructional software packages ever developed, has been used successfully in many elementary school programs. Offered as a content area in which children learn about computer technology, Logo is also commonly integrated with other curriculum activities such as mathematics and problem solving. The success of Logo and other software packages designed for young children also suggests that many children of elementary school age are indeed cognitively ready to use and benefit from computer experiences.

Young children's finger dexterity is not the critical issue it once was because of recent hardware developments and advancements. Although the keyboard remains the major input device for most computer hardware systems, other devices such as the mouse, joystick, and trackball are available that are relatively easy for children to use and manipulate. Home video games such as Nintendo continue to grow in popularity and expose children to these and other types of input devices. Special instructional input devices such as the Muppet Keyboard, which has oversized letters and keys, have also been designed for use in early childhood education and can be found in prekindergarten classes.

Computer instruction or message comprehension can be a problem in the early years if appropriate software has not been selected. Such errors in selection can result in young children staring at a video screen unable to respond to a command or becoming frustrated because they chose a logic path or continuous loop in a program from which they were unable to escape. Although these frustrating situations can and do continue to occur, even among older children and adults, careful software evaluation combined with proper supervision by teachers can minimize them.

In evaluating software for use by young children, planners should remember that the children's reading comprehension level becomes most critical in determining whether they can follow the software's instructions. Educational software packages routinely include as part of the documentation the necessary reading levels required to use the programs effectively. Teachers evaluating software should match these suggested reading levels against those of their children.

In addition, teachers should not leave young children alone for extended periods of time when using computer equipment. Young children need and appreciate regular assurance that they are doing what is expected of them. This holds true with computing.

Perhaps the most crucial decision as to when to introduce computing into an elementary school program is its placement within the curriculum. When educational software was less abundant, the availability of software almost dictated the content areas in which computing would be used. In most cases, the targeted areas were basic skills, especially reading and mathematics. However, this has changed dramatically, with elementary schools using computers in a variety of content areas including art, social studies, and science. The abundance of quality software across content areas provides many options, and all should be explored in planning sessions at which teachers and administrators can discuss possibilities and voice their opinions. As a guiding principle, the computer should be viewed as a tool that can be integrated into various content areas of the elementary school curriculum, more so than as a subject of instruction in and of itself.

SPECIAL EDUCATION

In the past two decades, American schools have been trying to improve the education of children with special needs. Section 504 of the Rehabilitation Act of 1973 and the Education for All Handicapped Children Act of 1975 (Public Law 94–142) prodded education policy makers to examine more carefully how special education was being provided in the schools. An outcome of this legislation has also been a movement toward mainstreaming special education children. This movement has presented opportunities for educators in preparing these children to participate more fully in American society. On the other hand, it has also presented challenges for educators to provide for the many special needs of these children.

The most fundamental tools used in education are books. Student use them in the classroom and at home to read and write. In addition to the spoken word, they are the primary means of communicating and conveying ideas. Yet, for many special education students, reading a book or writing, even turning a page, may be as formidable an obstacle as ascending a flight of stairs is to a person in a wheelchair. Computers are now being used by children who have difficulty learning through conventional means. Regardless of the impairment, whether hearing, vision, mobility, or learning disability, assistive technology is being used to help provide the links to learning that otherwise might not have been available to these children.

For example, technology provides a variety of voice input and output devices that allow visually impaired students to hear and respond to text stored on a computer disk rather than printed on the pages of a book. In addition, video and text enlargers are available for students with limited vision as are Braille printers, which produce embossed paper output. For students with severe motor control impairments who are unable to use their arms or hands, a variety of innovative input devices have been developed that allow students to control or respond to a computer using other parts of the body. An electronic switch mechanism can be activated by wrinkling an eyebrow, moving one's jaw, puffing on a tube, or making contact with a metal plate. These switches enable students with disabilities to turn to the next page in an electronic book, respond to yes/no questions, and communicate using Morse code, which is instantly converted and displayed on a computer screen.

For a variety of other impairments including hearing, speech, and multiple disabilities, computer technology is also being used to provide the primary means of communication. Special education students are able to have computers in their homes, on their wheelchairs, and in minivans in addition to in the classroom. For many of them, especially those with severe physical disabilities but unimpaired brain functionality, the computer can become the primary means for communicating with the world around them.

The purpose here is not to review completely the various ways technology is being used in special education but to emphasize the concept that technology can be used to provide tools that alleviate the hindrances that many special education children experience in their learning. When integrated with other support services and used by well-trained teachers, technology can be as beneficial to the special education child as the regular education child. Depending on the need or impairment, it may even be more beneficial since the special education child may have far fewer options for communicating and functioning in the regular classroom environment.

Selecting appropriate technological aids for special education children can be complex. Given the limited market, these devices also are more expensive than other forms of educational technology. However, reimbursement for such technology may be available from governmental as well as private insurance agencies. Administrators and teachers involved with planning for technology should make sure that they have access to individuals and sources who can provide the appropriate expertise. Vocational rehabilitation agencies and national and local support groups exist that can provide invaluable advice and assistance. A growing number of organizations (see Figure 3–1) that specialize in assisting and providing technology to persons with disabilities is emerging. The major computer manufacturers such as Apple and IBM also maintain services to guide school districts to information sources.

ACTT (Activating Children through Technology)
WIU, 27 Horrabin Hall
Macomb, IL 61455

ADDS (Assistive Device Database System)
650 University Ave.
Sacramento, CA 95825

AFTA (American Foundation for Technology
Assistance)
Rt. 14, Box 230
Morganton, NC 28655

Alliance for Technology Access
1307 Soans Ave.
Albany, CA 94706

American Foundation for the Blind
15 W. 16th St.
New York, NY 10011

American Printing House for the Blind
1839 Frankfort Ave.
P.O. Box 6085
Louisville, KY 40206

Assistive Devices Information Network
University Hospital, Developmental Disabilities
Iowa City, IA 55242

Braille Institute
741 N. Vermont Ave.
Los Angeles, CA 90029-3594

Center for Special Education Technology
Council for Exceptional Children
1920 Association Dr.
Reston, VA 22091

Closing the Gap
P.O. Box 68
Henderson, MN 56044

Communication Assistance Resource Service
3201 Marshall Rd.
Dayton, OH 45429

Don Johnston, Inc.
1000 N. Rand Rd., Bldg. 115
P.O. Box 639
Wauconda, IL 60084-0639

Helen Keller National Center for Deaf & Blind
111 Middle Neck Rd.
Sands Point, NY 11050-1299

Innotek
2100 Ridge Ave.
Evanston, IL 60204

National Association of the Deaf
814 Thayer Ave.
Silver Spring, MD 20910

National Info Center for Children with Handicaps
P.O. Box 1492
Washington, DC 20013

Figure 3–1
Sources of Information for Technology and Special Education

EQUITY ISSUES

Since the expansion of computer use in the nation's schools in the 1980s, a number of equity issues have emerged that continue to be critical considerations for educational planners. The term **equity**, which refers to qualitative properties (i.e., content or nature of the computer curriculum), is often used interchangeably with **equality**, which refers to quantitative properties (i.e., student access as measured by student/microcomputer ratios). In the following paragraphs, issues of both equity and equality are presented, including gender, minorities, and socioeconomic status.

On-Line Microcomputer Guide and Directory
11 Tannery Lane
Weston, CT 06883

Pass Word
11400 Bacon Rd.
Plainwell, MI 49080

REACH (Rehab/Educ/Advocacy—Citizens with
  Handicaps)
617 7th Ave.
Forth Worth, TX 76104

Research Grant Guides
P.O. Box 4970
Margate, FL 33063

RESNA
1101 Connecticut Ave. NW, Suite 700
Washington, DC 20036

SCAN (Shared Communication and Assistance
  Network)
8605 Cameron St, Suite 406
Silver Spring, MD 20910

SpecialNet
2021 K St., Suite 315
Washington, DC 20006

TADD Center (Technological Aids & Assistance
  for Disabled)
1950 W. Roosevelt Rd.
Chicago, IL 60608

TechLine
Center for Special Education Technology
1920 Association Dr.
Reston, VA 22091

Trace Research Center
University of Wisconsin
Waisman Center
1500 Highland Ave.
Madison, WI 53705-2280

U.S. Society for Augmentative and Alternative
  Communication
c/o Barkley Memorial Center
University of Nebraska
Lincoln, NE 68588

United Cerebral Palsy
1522 K. St. NW, Suite 1112
Washington, DC 20005

Washington Library for Blind and Physically
  Handicapped
821 Lenora St.
Seattle, WA 98129

Figure 3–1, *continued*

Gender Issues

The issue of gender in the use of computers in education can be quite complicated, and to a degree it relates to larger societal issues and sex stereotyping. Women demonstrate their technical abilities in using computer equipment everyday. However, much of the research and literature indicates that differences prevail in the way females and males approach the use of technology during their formative years. Much of this literature comprises two categories, one dealing with the performance of females and males in computer courses, and the other dealing with the attitudes of females and males to computing. Very likely, a relationship exists between the two.

Some studies show differences in the outcomes of males over females in terms of performance and mastery of computer skills (Fetler, 1985; Hawkins, 1987; Martinez & Mead, 1988). Others show no differences (Linn, 1985a; Robyler, Castine, & King, 1988; Webb, 1985). The subject needs additional research and examination.

A possible explanation of the performance differences that found boys performing at higher levels than girls is the assumption that computing is a skill that improves with use. If boys tended to use computers more than girls, then over time they would perform at higher levels or show greater competency, particularly in the upper grades (Sacks, Bellisimo, & Mergendoller, 1994). However, even in studies involving very young children who are first introduced to computer activities, the results are inconclusive. Using preschool samples, Schaefer and Sprigle (1988) found no gender differences in mastering Logo skills. On the other hand, Block, Simpson, and Reid (1987) reported gender differences favoring boys in learning Logo in a sample of kindergarten, first-grade, and second-grade students. Campbell, Fein, Scholnick, Schwartz, and Frank (1986) found gender differences in programming style but not in programming mastery in a sample of kindergarten children learning Logo.

Whereas computer performance research comparing gender differences has been inconsistent, research comparing gender attitudes is more consistent. Many studies involving the optional uses of computers indicate that males tend to favor computer activities and females tend to avoid them. These optional uses of computing included taking elective courses, joining computer clubs, going to summer computer camps, and majoring in computer science in college (Dambrot, Watkins-Malek, Silling, Marshall, & Garver, 1986; Hess & Muira, 1985; Linn, 1985b; Sanders & Stone, 1986). The various reasons for attitudinal differences may relate to larger societal factors including parental influence, subject stereotyping, peer influence, and access to computers (including video games) in the home. Shashaani (1994), in a study involving 1,730 high school students in Pittsburgh, Pennsylvania, concludes that significant gender differences in computer interest, computer confidence, and gender-stereotyped views exist. Furthermore, she states that parental attitudes and influences are directly associated with student attitudes about computing.

In developing computer curricula, planners should keep in mind that these gender-based attitudes toward technology exist and that they most likely were established and reinforced outside the school. Regardless, if technology is to be an important part of their curricula, schools should attempt to overcome these attitudinal problems. In an extensive treatment of this subject, Sanders (1986a, 1986b) and Sanders and Stone (1986) suggest a variety of strategies for educational policy makers:

- Require students to take certain computer courses because girls tend to enroll in much smaller numbers than boys if courses are optional.
- Expand computer curricula beyond mathematics and science courses.
- Integrate computing into the regular academic program.
- Educate parents at parent-teacher meetings to ensure that the home environment does not contribute to stereotyping.

- Educate the staff so that teachers are aware of the issue.
- Establish positive role models in the schools.
- Review and eliminate software and computer literature that might contain stereotypical characterizations or depictions.

Evidence suggests that some schools have indeed begun to make changes in their academic programs to improve access for girls. Kominski (1990), in a comparison of two national surveys conducted in 1984 and again in 1989, reported that, unlike the results of 1984, the 1989 research indicated that males and females were not different in their level of computer use in the schools. However, more research is needed on this issue.

For further information on sex equity and computing, readers may wish to contact the Women's Action Alliance (Computer Equity Program, 370 Lexington Ave., Suite 603, New York, NY 10017) and the Computer Equity Training Project of the U.S. Department of Education (555 New Jersey Ave. NW, Washington, DC 20208-5646).

Minority Issues

Minority access and utilization is probably the most complex of all issues concerning the use of technology in education. The reasons relate to larger socioeconomic issues, school financing policies, and urban school environments. Furthermore, unlike gender issues, on which a great deal more research has been conducted and a corpus of literature is developing, published material on the use of technology by minorities is relatively scarce. Much of this published material tends to focus on three factors: (a) access (i.e., the amount of equipment in the schools or in the home), (b) student performance, and (c) the level of software utilized (i.e., drill and practice vs. higher-level programming).

Computer technology requires substantial financial resources, and those schools that expend less money or have fewer resources have had more difficulty in mounting effective technology programs. Quality Education Data (1991), after conducting three national surveys in 1988 through 1991, concludes that although all school districts had accelerated their acquisition of computers and other technologies, the typical leaders tended to be affluent suburban districts. This point has been a critical part of the problem when discussing minority access to computers. Urban schools, schools in poor districts, and larger schools have less computer hardware per student than other schools; they also enroll much higher percentages of African-American and Latino children. Therefore, in general, African-American and Latino children have less access than do white children. Furthermore, if the premise is accepted that technical skills develop as one uses technology, then simply because of limited access, minority students will have less opportunity to become computer proficient. Since education policy makers consider one of the primary functions of schools is to prepare students for the workplace, a built-in disadvantage exists in the educational system for minority children given the continually growing importance of technology skills in employment.

Although this issue relates to larger school finance problems that require megasolutions on the part of American society, computer access is not related solely to funding. The U.S. Congress's Office of Technology Assessment (1988) reports that even when controlling for socioeconomic factors, school size, and location, predominantly African-American schools are significantly less likely than predominantly white schools to have computer equipment. Exactly why this is so is not explained. However, though many minority schools have less equipment for reasons other than finances, the report also observes that the problem of access is abating in these particular schools, especially for African-American students. In national studies, Becker (1994) and Quality Education Data (1996) conclude that differences among white and minority students in access to computers still exist, but the gap is narrowing. The average African-American student attends a school with 4% fewer computers per capita than does the average white student, while the average Latino student attends a school with 13% fewer computers per capita than does the average white student.

Research on minority student performance vis-à-vis technology is relatively sparse. In an extensive review of the research on equity issues in the use of computers in the schools, Sutton (1991) concludes that the data on "minorities and people of color" were generally lacking and little is known. Perhaps the most extensive study was conducted by the Educational Testing Service in the 1980s. It involved an evaluation of IBM's Writing to Read program and included 10,000 kindergarten and first-grade children in 28 different schools (Murphy & Appel, 1984). The overall performance for all students was positive, but the authors also report that the program worked better with white children than it did with minority children and children from low socioeconomic backgrounds.

Robyler et al. (1988), based on their own meta-analysis of more than 80 studies conducted since 1980, conclude that computer technology might not be as effective as other nontechnical strategies in teaching Spanish-speaking children. However, other research (Gonzalez-Edfelt, 1990; Hess & Tenezakis, 1970) reports that computing is effective in teaching Spanish-speaking children. The inconsistency reported for Spanish-speaking students here may relate more to the limited availability of software appropriate for bilingual students in the 1980s.

Emihovich and Miller (1988) compared African-American and white first-grade children who were assigned either to a Logo, computer-assisted instruction (CAI), or control group class. White students outperformed the African-American children in the CAI and control groups, while the African-American children outperformed the white children in the Logo group. Because of the small sample size ($N = 36$), the researchers recommend further study on larger samples. In addition to the differences in the outcomes between African-American and white students, this study is most interesting because of the comparison of different types of educational software.

Simmons (1987) suggests that in schools where computers are being used in instruction, a level of software tracking is being employed that indicates that minority children make greater use of drill-and-practice software to emphasize basic skills, while white students use computer programming software to develop higher-order thinking skills. The quantitative research on software tracking is negligible and supported more by observations and anecdotes than systematic survey or study. In one survey of 136 schools in the New York City area (Picciano, 1991), such a pattern of inner-city, mostly minority schools using drill-and-practice software and suburban, mostly white schools using higher-level programming software was not found.

This problem may have begun to correct itself as more microcomputer users both in and outside the schools increasingly use tool software such as word processing, spreadsheets, graphics programs, Internet browsers, and databases, none of which require any programming knowledge. Furthermore, by the early 1990s, the educational software industry had begun to develop and market a much broader and "creative" list of products designed especially for the increasing bilingual and especially the Spanish-speaking populations (Smith, 1995). When developing a computer education plan, educators should be cognizant of any bias that might be built into the curriculum favoring particular levels of software for a particular racial or ethnic group.

Minority issues go beyond computer education questions, and educational planners cannot be expected to resolve them simply by virtue of their curriculum and computer access. Nonetheless, educators must be sensitive to these issues as they relate to their schools. They should consider strategies that do not isolate one group from another but instead bring them closer together. Educators should be seeking to provide those opportunities that allow children of all colors and ethnic backgrounds to experiment with technology and experience learning together.

Socioeconomic Issues

Personal socioeconomic situations have always had an effect on education and directly relate to the issue of access to computers outside the school. National surveys of computer use in the United States indicate that the percentage of households owning a computer is doubling every 5 years. The Software Publishers Association (1996) reports that 33.9 million (34%) American households have a computer. Earlier surveys (Kominski, 1990) stated that 15.0% of all households had a computer in 1989, up from 8.2% in 1984.

Various socioeconomic factors contribute significantly to the ownership of a microcomputer in the home. For example, years of education, occupation, race, and income all influence ownership. Perhaps one of the most important factors in ownership of a home microcomputer is whether children are present. Kominski (1990) reports that a computer is twice as likely in the home when children are present, which indicates that parents are increasingly buying computers for their children.

If one assumes that technology is good and can be beneficial in education, then students who have greater access may have an advantage over those who do not. This may be dismissed as just another aspect of the effects of socioeconomics on education in that families with more resources can purchase calculators, typewriters, encyclopedias, or private tutors. However, administrators as part of their planning should consider that the more they implement computer-based education in their schools, the more they should also consider providing access to equipment beyond normally scheduled class periods. After all, access to hardware also offers access to educational tool software programs that can significantly facilitate doing homework and research assignments.

As an example, word-processing software can provide advantages to students doing compositions or essays. Not only does the final paper look neater and cleaner than handwritten or typewritten work, modern word-processing software packages provide spell-checking, thesaurus, and in some cases grammar-checking features. In addition, students using word processors can correct and redo their work many times over without the drudgery of rewriting or retyping it.

Administrators and teachers need to be aware of how many students in their schools have access to computer equipment in their homes and consider doing something for those students who do not. Open access after school to equipment in laboratories, media centers, and libraries is becoming more and more common. However, though an improvement, these facilities are not as beneficial as having a computer in the home. Lending equipment to students, although not as common, is increasingly being considered by school administrators and will likely grow in the future as smaller portable and notebook computers become less expensive. Some school districts already provide computer equipment for homebound students. This equipment is used either stand-alone or interactively over telephone lines so that student work can be electronically transmitted. In adopting any equipment loan program in a school district, administrators should review their states' and locales' legal and insurance regulations.

Administrators and teachers should also consider educating students and parents about the use of computers for schoolwork so that it will be used to enrich learning activities. Home computers used strictly for action games may not be providing as much benefit as they otherwise could. On the other hand, students who do use computers for homework should be advised on the judicious use of spell- or grammar-checking features to make sure that they understand their mistakes and are not simply letting the computer correct their work for them.

Surely with all the concerns that exist in education, access to computers in the home may not be a major consideration. However, with the growing acquisition of such equipment combined with access to the Internet and national networks such as America Online, opportunities exist for educators to use and provide experiences for their students that in the past simply were not possible. By the same token, educators increasingly will have to consider how they supply these experiences to those children who do not have access to such opportunities in their homes.

CASE STUDY
Place: Sojourner Truth High School   Year: 1996

Sojourner Truth High School is the pride of Hewlitt County, a suburban community in the South. The community has grown in the past 10 years as the general metropolitan region in which it is located has increased in population and has attracted businesses relocating from the Northeast and Midwest. The Hewlitt County School District is generally regarded as one of the best managed in the state.

Sojourner Truth High School has an excellent reputation. The principal, Mr. Wells, has spent his entire career in Hewlitt County, where he was first hired as a science teacher in 1971. The entire academic program is highly regarded; in fact, the science and technology programs are considered among the best in the state. Students from Sojourner Truth win both national and state awards each year in a variety of competitions, especially in science. In the past 10 years, several students have won the prestigious national Westinghouse Awards. In terms of computer education, the student/microcomputer ratio is 10 to 1. In addition to three central laboratories, microcomputers are also located in each classroom.

It is Friday, June 7, and Dr. Lewis, the district superintendent, is finalizing the agenda for the monthly school board meeting that will take place Monday night. At the June meeting, Dr. Lewis usually has Mr. Wells give his annual high school report, during which he always introduces one or two students who have achieved some outstanding distinction. This was an especially good year in that four students (James H., Jason K., Roger S., and Miguel P.) won a national science award for developing a computer simulation program to predict drought conditions in the Southwest.

The telephone rings and it is Mrs. Bodine, who wants to discuss a concern she has about her daughter, Caroline, a junior at Sojourner Truth. She says that her daughter would like to join the school's computer club but is reluctant to do so because she would be the only girl. Mrs. Bodine has had at least three conversations with Mr. Wells about this since last January. He promised to look into the matter but, according to Mrs. Bodine, "has not done a thing about it." Although Dr. Lewis promises that he will address her concerns, she informs him that if she does not hear from him with an appropriate solution to her daughter's problem by Monday, she will attend the meeting and bring the issue up before the school board.

Assuming that you are Dr. Lewis, what actions do you take? Do you think it might be appropriate to change the agenda so as not to embarrass anybody? What additional information do you need?

SUMMARY

In this chapter, several issues regarding the use of technology in education are presented. Although perhaps not as obvious as some of the basic hardware, software, and staff development issues, they are nonetheless important. Minimally, educators should be aware of them, but, more important, they should be sensitive to them early in the planning stages when considering the implementation or expansion of technology.

The primary learning issue to be considered is the extent to which technology is desirable in the school. Although enthusiasm is desirable and even beneficial, unbridled, it can be disruptive and do more harm than good.

Technology in and of itself is limited. But as a tool and when placed in skillful hands, it can open new possibilities and enrich learning regardless of grade levels. Elementary, middle, and high school students are able to derive benefits from technologically based teaching techniques. Special education children, who because of various impairments are unable to use traditional educational tools, are using computer aids to provide the necessary links to learning.

In addition to educational issues, a number of equity issues are emerging. Administrators and teachers should be cognizant of gender, minority, and socioeconomic factors in their school districts that may affect the success of their academic computer programs. Some of these issues must be ultimately resolved in the larger society; however, educators should try not to add to the inequity that might already exist and instead employ technology to lessen it.

Key Concepts and Questions

1. Technology is being used in all aspects of our society. Use is growing in business, government, and homes. Many components of our society could not function without computer facilities and information systems.

   Has American education reached the point where teaching should depend more extensively on technology, which, in turn, may form the impetus for school improvement? Or is technology a simple tool that will have little impact on education? Explain.

2. Technology is generally available in high schools and upper-grade levels, but major questions persist as to when it should be introduced in the elementary school.

   What are some of these questions? How would you respond to them if you were involved in planning or implementing technology in an elementary school?

3. Technology is proving to be especially effective for several special education populations.

   Do you agree with this statement? If so, provide examples. If not, what would you consider more appropriate alternatives?

4. Equity issues and the use of technology relate to much larger societal issues involving gender, minority, and other socioeconomic factors that may be beyond the scope of most administrators' duties to resolve.

   What are some of these issues as related to technology in the schools? What strategies would you consider to lessen any inequities that might exist?

5. Computer equipment is increasingly being acquired by Americans for use in their homes.

   Does this pose any special consideration for educators? Is this a problem or an opportunity? Explain.

Suggested Activities

1. Review the educational policies that might exist in a (or your) school district regarding the use of technology in the elementary school program. Has a specific age or grade level been identified as most appropriate? Do you have suggestions for improving these policies?

2. Observe several special education students in a school district. Do they make greater use of technology than other students? If not, do you have any suggestions for improving their learning environment by introducing technology?

References

Becker, H. J. (1994). *Analysis and trends of school use of new information technologies.* Irvine: Department of Education, University of California, Irvine.

————. (1987). The importance of a methodology that maximizes falsifiability: Its applicability to research about Logo. *Educational Researcher, 16*(5), 11–17.

Block, E. B., Simpson, D. L., & Reid, D. K. (1987). Teaching young children programming and word processing: The effects of three preparatory conditions. *Journal of Educational Computing Research, 3,* 435–442.

Campbell, P. F., Fein, G. G., Scholnick, E. K., Schwartz, S. S., & Frank, R. E. (1986). Initial mastery of the syntax and semantics of Logo positioning commands. *Journal of Educational Computing Research, 2,* 357–378.

Dambrot, F. H., Watkins-Malek, S., Silling, M., Marshall, R., & Garver, J. (1986). Correlates of sex differences in attitudes toward and involvement with computers. *Journal of Vocational Behavior, 27,* 71–86.

Davy, J. (1984). Mindstorms in the lamplight. *Teachers College Record, 85*(4), 549–558.

Emihovich, C., & Miller, G. E. (1988). Effects of Logo and CAI on black first graders' achievement, reflectivity, and self-esteem. *The Elementary School Journal, 88*(5), 473–487.

Fetler, M. (1985). Sex differences on the California statewide assessment of computer literacy. *Sex Roles: A Journal of Research, 13*(3/4), 181–191.

Geisert, P. G., & Futrell, M. K. (1995). *Teachers, computers, and curriculum: Microcomputers in the classroom* (2nd ed.). Boston: Allyn & Bacon.

Gonzalez-Edfelt, N. (1990). Oral interaction and collaboration at the computer: Learning English as a second language with the help of your peers. In C. J. Faltis & R. A. De Villar (Eds.), *Language, minority students, and computers* (pp. 53–89). Binghamton, NY: Haworth.

Hawkins, J. (1987). Computers and girls: Rethinking the issues. In R. D. Pea & K. Sheingold (Eds.), *Mirrors of minds: Patterns of experience in educational computing* (pp. 242–257). Norwood, NJ: Ablex.

Hess, R. D., & Muira, I. T. (1985). Gender differences in enrollment in computer camps and classes. *Sex Roles: A Journal of Research, 13,* 193–203.

Hess, R. D., & Tenezakis, M. D. (1970). *The computer as socializing agent: Some socioaffective outcomes for CAI* (Technical Report No. 13). Stanford, CA: Stanford University, Center for Research and Development in Teaching.

Kominski, R. (1990). *Computer use in the United States: 1989* (Current Population Reports Special Studies Series P-23, No. 171). Washington, DC: U.S. Department of Commerce, Bureau of the Census.

Linn, M. (1985a). Fostering equitable consequences from computer learning environments. *Sex Roles: A Journal of Research, 13*(3/4), 229–240.

————. (1985b). Gender equity in computer learning environments. *Computers and the Social Sciences, 1,* 19–27.

Maddux, C. (1989). Logo: Scientific dedication or religious fanaticism in the 1990s. *Educational Technology, 29*(2), 18–23.

Martinez, M. E., & Mead, N. A. (1988). *Computer competence: The first national assessment* (Technical Report No. 17-CC-01). Princeton, NJ: Educational Testing Service.

Murphy, R. T., & Appel, L. R. (1984, November). *Evaluation of the Writing to Read Instructional System, 1982–1984: A presentation from the second year report.* Princeton, NJ: Educational Testing Service.

Papert, S. (1980). *Mindstorms: Children, computers, and powerful ideas.* New York: Basic Books.

————. (1987). Computer criticism vs. technocentric thinking. *Educational Researcher, 16*(1), 22–30.

Pea, R. D. (1983). *Logo programming and problem-solving* (Technical Report No. 12). New York: Bank Street College of Education, Center for Children and Technology.

————. (1987). The aims of software criticism: Reply to Professor Papert. *Educational Researcher, 16*(5), 4–8.

Perelman, L. (1990, October 8). Can technology effectively replace human teachers? *Computerworld,* p. 25.

Piaget, J. (1952). *The origins of intelligence in children.* New York: Norton.

Picciano, A. G. (1991). Computers, city, and suburb: A study of New York City and Westchester County public schools. *The Urban Review, 23*(3), 93–109.

Quality Education Data. (1995). *Education market guide and mailing list catalog. 1995–1996.* Denver: Author.

———. (1996). *Education market guide and mailing list catalog. 1996–1997.* Denver: Author.

Robyler, M. D., Castine, W. H., & King, F. J. (1988). Assessing the impact of computer-based instruction. *Computers in the Schools, 5*(1), 1–149.

Sacks, C. H., Bellisimo, Y., & Mergendoller, J. (1994). Attitudes toward computers and computer use: The issue of gender. *Journal of Research on Computing in Education, 26*(2), 256–269.

Sanders, J. S. (1986a). Closing the computer gender gap. *Education Digest, 10,* 34–39.

———. (1986b). Here's how you can help girls take greater advantage of school computers. In J. C. Arch (Ed.), *Technology in the schools: Equity and funding* (pp. 40–43). Washington, DC: National Education Association.

Sanders, J. S., & Stone, A. (1986). *The neuter computer.* New York: Schuman.

Schaefer, L., & Sprigle, J. E. (1988). Gender differences in the use of the Logo programming language. *Journal of Educational Computing Research, 4,* 49–55.

Shashaani, L. (1994). Socioeconomic status, parents' sex-role stereotypes, and the gender gap in computing. *Journal of Research on Computing in Education, 26*(4), 433–451.

Sherry, M. (1990). An EPIE Institute report: Integrated instructional systems. *Technological Horizons in Education, 18*(2), 86–89.

Simmons, W. (1987). Beyond basic skills: Literacy and technology for minority students. In R. D. Pea & K. Sheingold (Eds.), *Mirrors of minds: Patterns of experience in educational computing* (pp. 86–100). Norwood, NJ:Ablex.

Smith, M. M. (1995). The battle over bilingual education. *Electronic Learning, 15*(1), 30–38.

Software Publishers Association. (1996). *Software publishers fifth annual consumer survey.* Internet uniform resource locator: http://www.spa.org/research/releases/press1.htm

Sutton, R. E. (1991). Equity and computers in the schools: A decade of research. *Review of Educational Research, 61*(4), 475–503.

U.S. Congress, Office of Technology Assessment. (1988). *Power on! New tools for teaching and learning* (Report No. OTA-SET-379). Washington, DC: U.S. Government Printing Office.

Walker, D. F. (1987). Logo needs research: A response to Papert's paper. *Educational Research, 16*(1), 9–11.

Webb, N. M. (1985). The role of gender in computer programming learning processes. *Journal of Educational Computing Research, 1,* 441–458.

Section II

Applications

4

Computer Applications in Educational Administration

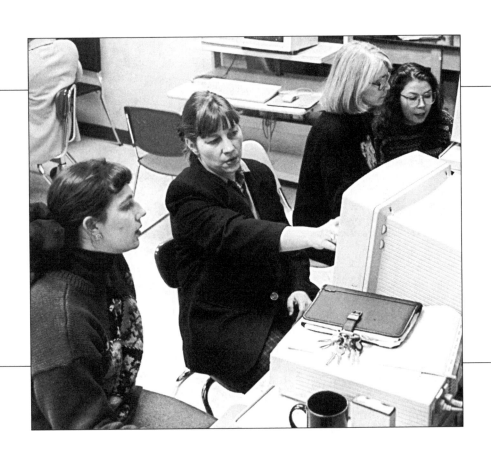

S ince the introduction of microcomputer technology in the late 1970s, the literature on the uses of computers in schools has concentrated on instructional applications in the classroom. Thousands of books, professional journals, magazines, and newspaper articles have been written providing insights into the uses of computers for learning and teaching. However, for superintendents and principals, among the most successful applications have been those that support their administrative operations. While the effectiveness of computers in instruction continues to be debated, the effectiveness of computers to provide information, manage budgets, and improve office operations has been accepted. In this chapter, major applications of computers in educational administration are reviewed, and an integrated framework for planning and implementing them is provided.

KNOWLEDGE IS POWER

History abounds with examples of the concept that knowledge is power: the control of trade routes, the conquest of disease, and the development of the atomic bomb, to name just a few. In organization theory also, the power of knowledge has been well recognized. French and Raven (1959), in a series of studies on administrative management, were among the first theorists to identify "expert power" as a requisite to successful leadership among managers. They defined expert power simply as having access to critical information about one's organization and environment.

This concept that knowledge is power should not be viewed negatively. Because of public control and the number of constituents, schools generally require their administrative leaders to have expert or information power. Parents, teachers, staff, school board members, and the media seek out and rely on administrators to help them understand issues and events in their schools. An important characteristic of the experienced and accomplished administrator is to share freely her or his knowledge with others. Administrators who invest in and develop their information resources are better able to lead and manage their schools in all activities, be they program evaluations, budget presentations, or curricular improvements. Making good judgments in these areas requires accurate information about what is going on both inside and outside the schools.

Furthermore, given the extensive reporting requirements of various governmental agencies at all levels, school administrators need to be able to demonstrate that they have access to and can provide critical data about their schools. Failure to do so can jeopardize budget requests, grant applications, and overall credibility with governmental officials.

Ready access to accurate information is indispensable to the functions of school administrators. Therefore, planning administrative systems for a school district requires the integration of information needs with available computer technology.

THE INFORMATION AGE

In the 20th century, we have witnessed major breakthroughs in humankind's activities and endeavors. Some of these have come to be characterized as periods of time, such as the age of the airplane, the atomic age, and the space age. The period of the past 30 years known as the information age resulted from advances in the use of computer technology for collecting, sorting, manipulating, and reporting information. Corporations, government agencies, and schools have made significant investments over the past three decades to take part in the information age by developing, expanding, and improving their computer-based information systems.

These systems consist of three broad categories of administrative applications: (a) databases to manage data and information, (b) electronic spreadsheets to manage numbers, and (c) office automation, especially word processing, to manage words and communications. Together, these three applications categories form the basis of any plan to develop and improve information systems in organizations.

Databases

Database applications are by far the most important of the three categories mentioned. They involve the management of information about the various activities of a school in the form of data elements, records, and files. Unlike spreadsheets and word-processing applications that became popular with the introduction of microcomputers, database management systems began evolving on large mainframe computers in the 1950s. IBM became a corporate giant in part because it was the first of the major manufacturers to realize the potential of the computer for managing data files rather than for manipulating and "crunching" numbers in scientific research and engineering applications.

In the past 40 years, database management systems have grown in complexity and sophistication, particularly for large organizations. The more data needed to be collected, verified, updated, and reported, the more complex and expensive becomes the task of establishing and maintaining an accurate database. However, the alternatives are unthinkable. Not having access to the data eventually becomes a very serious problem and one that leaves an administration vulnerable. Collecting data manually as needed can also be very expensive and prone to problems of inaccuracy and inconsistency. If they have not already, all school districts, regardless of their level of operation, should have as a priority in their plans the development, improvement, or upgrading of their database management systems.

The terminology used for describing databases has been inconsistent over the years, and certain terms mean different things to different people. Before continuing, identifying and defining some of these terms may be helpful. The general definition of **database** is a collection of files in which data can be created, updated, and accessed. However, a more modern definition requires that data files be interrelated or integrated so that data can be accessed easily across all files and redundancy of the same data be kept to a minimum.

The basic concept of databases involves the management of data in an increasingly more complex hierarchy. The members of this hierarchy, from least to most complex, are the **character**, the **data element**, the **data record**, the **data file**, and the **database**. These terms are defined as follows:

A **character** consists of a single letter of the alphabet (A through Z), a single digit (0 through 9), or a single special character ($, %, +).

A **data element**, also referred to as a **data field**, groups these characters to represent characteristics of a person, place, or thing. Examples of data elements include birth date, gender, father's name, family income, grade, course number, or room number.

A **data record** consists of a collection of related data elements for a single entity (person, place, or thing). Examples of data records include the personal record of an individual employee, the inventory record of a single piece of scientific equipment, or the transcript record of an individual student.

A **data file** is a collection of related data records. For example, the records of all employees would comprise a personnel file, or the records of all students would comprise a student file.

A **database** is a collection of data files and records. The database for a school district would encompass student, personnel, course (or curriculum), financial, and facilities files.

A **database management system** is a package of computer programs that allow the user to create, maintain, and access the data on a database. Examples of database management systems include Oracle for large mainframe computer systems and Ashton-Tate Corporation's dBase for microcomputer systems.

Within a database management system, data should be organized and documented in a **data element dictionary**, which is a table used to identify the content and coding schemes of the database. Table 4–1 is an example of part of a data element dictionary table that would be used to identify the content of a simple personnel record. This table would be stored in a computer file to be used by the database management system software and be included in a documentation manual for reference by the staff and teachers who need to maintain or access this file. Figure 4–1 is a page from a data element dictionary manual that describes the characteristics of one of the individual data elements in the personnel record represented in Table 4–1. Each data element should have a page in a manual similar to this.

As databases grow and become more complex, the task of documenting and maintaining a data element dictionary also becomes more complicated. School systems that operate a dedicated data-processing or computer center frequently have full-time staff functioning as **database administrators** who have these responsibilities. All school districts, regardless of their size, should have someone performing these tasks. Failure to do so may render a database useless after a while because staff will forget how to update or access the files.

Table 4–1
Sample Data Element Dictionary Table for a Personnel Record

Field number	Field name	Type	Width	Decimal	Comments
1	NAME	CHARACTER	25		Last, First, Initial
2	SOC-SEC-NO	CHARACTER	9		Social Security Number
3	SCHOOL-CODE	NUMERIC	2		School Assignment
4	DEPT-CODE	NUMERIC	2		Department Assignment
5	STARTDATE	NUMERIC	6		First Date of Employment
6	TENUREDATE	NUMERIC	6		Date Tenure Awarded
7	BIRTHDATE	NUMERIC	6		Date of Birth
8	GENDER	CHARACTER	1		Female/Male
9	STREET	CHARACTER	15		Street Address
10	CITY	CHARACTER	15		City Address
11	STATE	CHARACTER	2		State Abbreviation
12	ZIP	NUMERIC	5		ZIP Code
13	SALARY	NUMERIC	8	2	Current Salary
14	MARITAL-STAT	CHARACTER	1		Marital Status Code

One of the most important features of database software is the ability to generate reports. Generally, a **query language** is provided that enables users to access data in many different ways. These languages are very powerful for creating customized reports and temporary data files. Designed for nontechnical staff, they give users excellent access to data without having to wait for computer or data-processing personnel to perform the task for them.

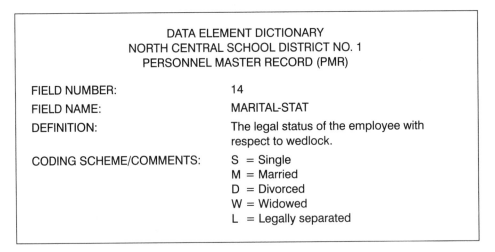

DATA ELEMENT DICTIONARY
NORTH CENTRAL SCHOOL DISTRICT NO. 1
PERSONNEL MASTER RECORD (PMR)

FIELD NUMBER: 14

FIELD NAME: MARITAL-STAT

DEFINITION: The legal status of the employee with
                        respect to wedlock.

CODING SCHEME/COMMENTS: S = Single
                         M = Married
                         D = Divorced
                         W = Widowed
                         L = Legally separated

Figure 4–1
Sample Page of a Data Element Dictionary Manual

The number of software developers providing database management systems has grown over the past 15 years. For microcomputer systems, dBase (Ashton-Tate), Paradox (Borland), PC/FOCUS (Information Builders), and R:base (Microrim) have proven to be very popular and are reasonably priced. For large mainframe computer systems, the selection of a database management system is a serious decision that should be made carefully, with the advice of experienced and trained technical staff. These systems are expensive to acquire and more expensive to implement considering the planning, design, and computer programming required. Some of the major database management systems for large computers are Oracle (Oracle), IDMS (Cullinet), Adabas (Software AG), IMS (IBM), RAMIS (Mathematica), and TOTAL (Cincom).

In reviewing and evaluating information about database management software, administrators will see references to the "data structure" or data organization used. **Data structure** is the method by which one data element relates to other data elements. Many books and articles explore and compare the benefits of the different data structures and approaches taken by software developers. Among the more popular structures is the **relational database**. Although a simple structure, a relational database views all data as being stored as tables or matrices, with each data element having access to the other data elements. Figure 4–2 is an illustration of how a student file and a course file might relate to one another in such a structure. In this illustration, the course codes serve to "relate" or link student records to course records.

Figure 4–3 illustrates some of the major administrative database applications. Each application area has a unique role in contributing to the overall data management resources of a school. The student applications tend to be the most complex because of the amount of data that needs to be collected. In addition, student data are volatile and subject to frequent change. Applications such as attendance reporting and scheduling require extensive data collection efforts and careful coordination.

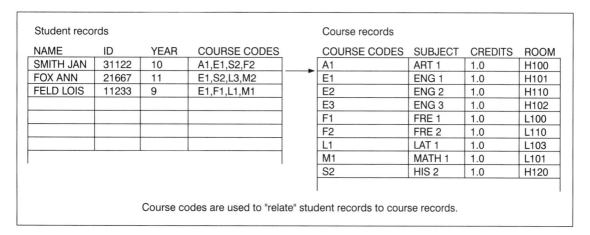

Figure 4–2
Sample Relational Database Structure for Student and Course Files

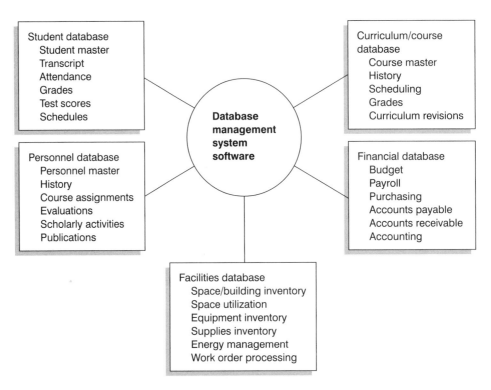

Figure 4–3
Common Database Applications

Student applications are important since certain areas such as achievement and performance come under a good deal of scrutiny, especially from outside the school. Administrators need to have good access to data such as retention, attrition, graduation rates, and test scores. Student enrollment data are also usually critical for various state and local funding formulae, and accurate data on students in attendance become a necessity for various reporting purposes.

Curriculum and course applications are vital for a school's internal academic operations. Curriculum meetings and discussions are, in many schools, the centerpieces of academic planning. Administrators and teachers collect extensive amounts of data to develop new courses and modify existing ones. Data on student performance tied to curriculum and course enrollment become critical for such planning. A good curriculum and course database also is necessary for developing a student scheduling application, one of the most time-consuming activities undertaken in many schools when done manually.

Personnel and financial applications are frequently the first database systems to be implemented. In public schools, they may tie into other local governmental agencies for applications such as payroll, accounting, and purchasing controlled at the municipal or county levels. For any administrator, the management of a budget is a critical responsibility. Access to up-to-date and accurate information on budgets and finances is a necessity and affects all of a school's operations. Personnel files are important complements to the financial data files for purposes of managing a budget, since the major costs in school operations are for personnel items such as salaries and fringe benefits.

Facilities are generally the last of the database applications to be implemented. Facilities data are not as critical or volatile and do not need to be as tightly integrated. However, applications such as space utilization, equipment inventory, and supplies inventory should not be ignored because they contribute to overall effectiveness and efficiency.

In looking again at Figure 4–3, we see that the database management system software is common to all of the applications and serves as an integration mechanism. By developing such a system, schools greatly enhance administrative cohesiveness since offices become more dependent on one another by virtue of sharing common data files. A single system also significantly improves the consistency of information and eliminates issues involving the accuracy of one office's data versus another's.

In developing an overall plan for database management systems, administrators should assess their ability to collect and maintain data in the five major application areas identified in Figure 4–3. More resources may have to be provided for those areas where data collection has been poor or nonexistent. In addition, all database applications, even the most established, need regular modifications and upgrades. In many cases, the ongoing costs for modifying and upgrading an existing database system, particularly when staff time is considered, may be as much as the original implementation. Administrators generally believe that the ability to bring order and easy access to their information resources is well worth the price.

Electronic Spreadsheets

Electronic spreadsheets have grown significantly in popularity for applications that require frequent manipulation of numbers (e.g., budget, accounting, enrollment projections). Increasingly, electronic spreadsheets are becoming indispensable for planning and modeling.

Electronic spreadsheet software is essentially an electronic grid or matrix of rows and columns. It replaces the accounting tablet as a tool for organizing numbers into appropriate boxes or cells, and it performs automatically all of the arithmetic operations that formerly were performed manually or with calculators on each individual cell. VisiCalc was the first popular package developed for use on microcomputers in the late 1970s. Presently, Lotus 1-2-3, Excel, SuperCalc, and Multiplan are among the most popular. Packages such as Microsoft Works integrate spreadsheet software with database and word-processing software. These packages also provide excellent graphics capabilities that enable users to present their worksheets in colorful and interesting ways. After word processing, electronic spreadsheets have become the most frequently used microcomputer software tool ever developed.

Figure 4–4 is an example of an electronic spreadsheet for a school district's yearly budget summary and proposal. This figure shows a grid of rows numbered 1, 2, 3, 4, and so forth, and columns lettered A, B, C, D, and so on. Entries are made onto the spreadsheet by pointing or moving a cursor to the appropriate cell as identified by

	B	C	D	E	F	G
1						
2			North Central School District No. 1			
3			Proposed Budget 1997–98			
4						Approved vs.
5			1996–97	1996–97	1997–98	Proposed
6			Estimated	Approved	Proposed	Budget
7	Category		Expend. ($)	Budget ($)	Budget ($)	Change ($)
8						
9	General support		1,993,500	2,111,500	2,063,500	(48,000)
10	Instruction		19,131,000	19,489,000	20,334,500	845,500
11	Transportation		1,757,000	1,733,000	1,985,000	252,000
12	Plant operations		2,638,000	2,785,500	2,795,000	9,500
13	Employee benefits		3,650,000	3,720,000	4,356,000	636,000
14	Community service		1,543,000	1,613,000	1,569,000	(44,000)
15	Interfund transfer		100,000	100,000	100,000	0
16	Debt service		3,849,750	3,849,750	3,751,750	(98,000)
17						
18	Totals		34,662,250	35,401,750	36,954,750	1,553,000

Figure 4–4
Sample Spreadsheet

grid coordinates (i.e., A1, A2, B4, C6, etc.). Each cell can also have a formula or arithmetic operation that uses data existing in any of the other cells.

The major benefit of spreadsheet software is that these arithmetic operations can be performed automatically so that a change in any one cell will almost instantaneously change all other cells that may be affected. This provides for a very rapid "what if?" facility, as popularized by media advertisements. For example, in doing a school's budget projections, if one wanted to know the effect of some percentage reduction on all the various cost centers or departments, this could be done almost instantaneously by just changing the entry in one cell. This calculation could also be performed over and over again with different percentages. Financial staff who regularly perform spreadsheet-type applications manually can learn to use an electronic spreadsheet in a matter of hours and become proficient after doing a few applications. Once proficiency has been achieved, electronic spreadsheets typically will replace all similar applications that had been performed manually.

Figure 4–5 provides a chart of some of the major administrative applications appropriate for electronic spreadsheet software. It is by no means a complete list of such applications (which easily number in the hundreds). They are grouped according to the major database file applications that are illustrated in Figure 4–3.

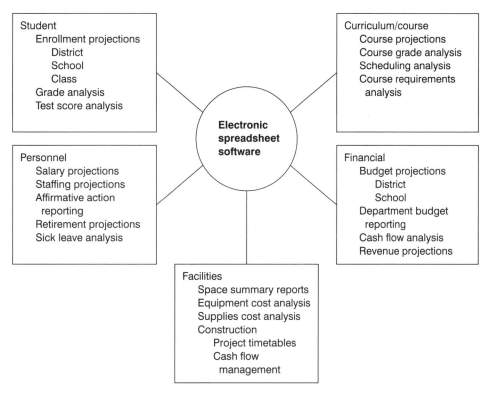

Figure 4–5
Common Electronic Spreadsheet Applications

Because optimum management of information resources requires that all data files and applications be integrated where appropriate, the source data for electronic spreadsheet applications should come from the district's database files whenever possible and not gathered anew from other sources. This is generally referred to as **downloading data** from the database for use by other computer applications. It can be done electronically by creating aggregate data files that can be accessed by the electronic spreadsheet software. Of course, if a database does not exist or if the particular data needed are not available, then they must be gathered from other sources. This is necessary when attempting to do analyses involving phenomena that occur outside the schools. For example, an enrollment projection might require data on birth rates or the number of children under age 4 in a district.

Electronic spreadsheet software is effective in manipulating any aggregate data that are typically presented in tabular form. The number of reports using student data in this fashion is endless. Enrollment projections at various levels, test score analyses, and grade evaluations are common applications. For academic planning and scheduling, electronic spreadsheets can be very effective in doing course enroll-ment projections.

Personnel files are also important sources of data for spreadsheet applications. Staffing projections related to enrollment and course offerings can be routinely done. Personnel costs account for the major portion of the budget, and data such as salary projections are invaluable during budget planning and collective bargaining negotiations.

Designed initially for financial applications, spreadsheets have become commonplace in most accounting and budgeting offices. Entire budget-planning processes are conducted with school board members, superintendents, and others using the printed output from spreadsheets as the basis for discussion. These documents can easily be changed and recalculated many times over the course of the budget negotiation cycle. The graphics capabilities of spreadsheet programs can produce pie charts and bar graphs on budget information (see Figures 4–6 and 4–7). Increasingly, these are being used during public presentations of a budget and in mailings to residents on budget proposals.

Facilities applications such as space utilization reports and projections and equipment and supplies inventory analyses are also commonly done on spreadsheets. Project management timetables, cost projections, and cash flow analysis for capital construction can also be done effectively.

A final comment on electronic spreadsheets: they are important tools in the presentation and manipulation of data and are most effective when integrated with database management systems. When planning these applications, please keep in mind that the benefits of spreadsheet programs will best be realized if they have good data sources from which to draw aggregate data.

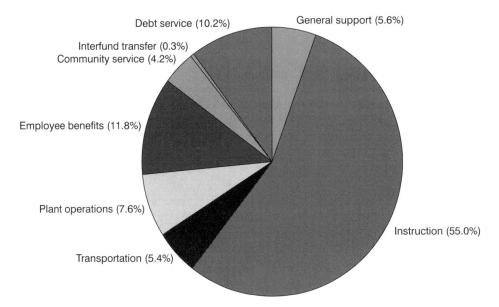

Figure 4–6
Sample Pie Chart Using Data from Figure 4–4

Figure 4–7
Sample Bar Chart Using Data
from Figure 4–4

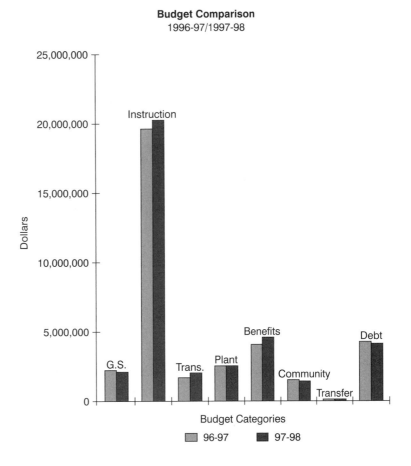

Budget Comparison
1996-97/1997-98

Office Automation

Until a few years ago, the concept of office automation essentially referred to word processing. It was a major step forward when secretaries and other administrators made the change from typewriters to microcomputers. Word processing continues to be by far the most frequently used microcomputer application in the world today. Many people buy microcomputers simply as word-processing tools and rarely use them for anything else.

Developing word processing software has become an industry in itself, with many fine products such as Microsoft Word, WordPerfect, WordStar, and MultiMate on the market. Increasingly, administrators and teachers have learned the basic features of word-processing packages. Although one product might be a little easier to use and another might have a better spelling check, they all do the job very well and certainly much better than typewriters can.

Office automation applications have moved beyond word processing, however, and administrators should be thinking about how to use word processing with overall communications tools and integrating it into a "suite" of administrative software packages. In office automation, word processing is increasingly being used in conjunction with other software such as desktop publishing, electronic mail, voice mail, and databases. Word processing creates and edits text while these other software tools print, report, and communicate the text to others. Furthermore, unlike word processing, which developed essentially as a stand-alone application replacing a typewriter, these other office automation tools require either local or wide area computer networks to be effective. Lotus Notes and Microsoft Exchange are examples of software that link and integrate several office automation packages.

The first use of word processing with other software came with the need to merge data from database management systems with text. The best example is the merging of addresses from a database file with the text of a letter (i.e., mail merge). This not only saved the time that would have been needed to key the addresses but also made good use of the information resources available from the database management system. Today, more and more merging of text with all sorts of data—attendance, grades, test scores, and schedules—that are downloaded from databases is being done. In most cases, this is an attempt to personalize the "form" letter and to relate the contents specifically to the recipients. Figure 4–8 provides a chart of some of the common uses of text with database information that are typically performed in school systems.

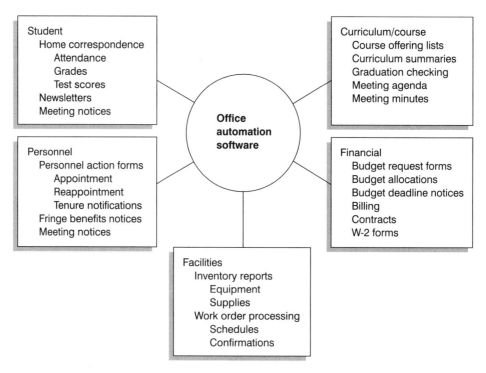

Figure 4–8
Commonly Merged Text and Data Applications

Electronic mail systems to distribute messages are also growing in popularity. These systems concentrate on the distribution of communications throughout an organization by means of **electronic mailboxes**, which are data files containing text data such as messages. These systems also provide software for controlling who can send and who can receive messages and for alerting users when messages are in their electronic mailboxes.

To use these systems, a school district must develop a good data communications network that is used regularly by administrators and staff. Most school districts have begun to establish such systems. In a national survey, Quality Education Data (1995) estimated that more than 13,000 school districts, of the nation's 15,000, had installed either a local or wide area network. Variations of the electronic mail software include electronic bulletin boards and voice mail, which uses digitized voice messages rather than computer text files.

Desktop publishing software is also growing in popularity and is used increasingly by schools to produce their own printed materials such as newsletters, manuals, and other documents. In addition to providing word-processing capabilities, desktop publishing also provides easy-to-use graphics capabilities so that previously simple type-written notices can include illustrations and become more colorful and interesting to the eye. Some of these publishing packages, such as Pagemaker and QuarkXPress, are highly rated and effective in supporting public relations activities. They can also save money by doing printed work in-house rather than sending it to a professional printer.

The development of document storage and retrieval software that integrates computer and microform technologies is also advancing rapidly. Schools and many other people-oriented organizations are tremendous producers of paper documents that need to be stored and maintained for many years, in some cases "forever." Computer indexing systems aid and in some cases replace the extensive paper file systems that are so common in a school's administrative offices. These moderately priced systems provide rapid search capabilities for looking up key identifiers to microform (film or fiche) documents. They assume the existence of a microform system, which would be more efficient if a quick indexing or look-up capability was provided. They should also use existing databases for downloading index keys and other pertinent information.

With the development of optical disc technology, more and more documents that were being converted to microform are being converted to digital form. These systems are presently expensive and are being used mostly in larger school systems that maintain hundreds of thousands of past and current records. However, as this technology becomes less expensive and more readily available on microcomputer systems, with extensive read and write disc storage capacities, more school districts, regardless of size, will start to implement them.

Office support systems that help organize work activities are another type of office automation software. Such systems provide facilities for planning work activities and include electronic calendars, appointment books, address books, notepads, phone lists, and alarm clocks. Several computer manufacturers now include these as part of the standard software package provided on all their microcomputers.

The various programming packages that come under the rubric of office automation are diverse and extensive. Many of these packages perform tasks electronically that in the past were routinely done manually. They generally can be time savers and improve communications in a school district. In planning for such systems, administrators are encouraged to integrate them with other administrative systems, especially their database management systems.

MISCELLANEOUS ADMINISTRATIVE APPLICATIONS

Several additional specialized computer applications should be mentioned before ending this chapter. First, computer equipment increasingly is being used as an external communications tool. With the emergence of the Internet as a major technological communications tool, all organizations including schools are becoming a part of the global digital community. In addition, national and international networks such as America Online, Dialog, Bibliographic Retrieval Services, and Compuserve are now available that provide specialized services at reasonable costs. Via the Internet or specialized networks, administrators can access national databases such as the Educational Resources Information Center (ERIC), which contains the world's largest collection of articles and studies in the field of education; Educational Testing Service Test Collection, which has thousands of descriptions of standardized tests and measures; and NEXIS, which provides access to the full text of articles appearing in all the major newspapers and general-interest magazines. Access to these databases provides administrators with an important research tool allowing them to keep up-to-date on many aspects of the field of education.

Second, statistical software packages such as the Statistical Package for the Social Sciences (SPSS) and the Statistical Analysis System (SAS) can be valuable additions for institutional planning, evaluation, or research offices. They provide inexpensive, easy-to-use programs for doing all types of statistical analyses involving treatments, such as *t*-tests, analysis of variance (ANOVA), correlation, and regression. They are not meant to replace electronic spreadsheet software for doing simple tables and summary totals but rather more to perform the advanced statistical analysis necessary in formal research studies.

Third, test-scoring equipment and software are common in many schools and provide quick marking of objective tests. Many of these systems are on the market and essentially use some type of optical scanner to read the tests and provide the data to a microcomputer, which, in turn, provides the test results in the form of a printed report. The better packages also provide summary statistics such as group results, means, standard deviations, and item analysis. Teachers make good use of these systems in grading and analyzing student academic performance.

Fourth, automatic telephone calling systems that combine computer equipment, stored voice message equipment, and telephones are used in some districts. Originally designed for use in telephone sales or telemarketing operations, these systems have found some success in school districts for monitoring student attendance. Such systems generally require that a disk file of telephone numbers of the children absent from school be provided each day. These are automatically dialed, and a recorded message is played informing the parent that her or his child was not in school that day. These systems can also be used to notify parents of special meetings, school closings, and other news.

Lastly, energy management has become an important means of generating substantial savings through the use of computer technology. Computer applications support energy management in two different ways. One is simply to use a database management system to keep detailed records on energy consumption by heating zones and time of day. Analyzing these data regularly allows facilities personnel to track down and eliminate wasteful uses of energy. A more sophisticated approach requires a computer system that is directly connected to all the physical plant's control mechanisms for electricity, heating, and cooling. These systems can be programmed to control (reduce, increase, shut down) the amount of energy that is being used in all the various zones. Such systems are expensive to acquire and install but should be considered, especially when doing capital improvements.

CASE STUDY
Place: Haltown   Year: 1982

Haltown is a small New England city operating 38 schools with 25,000 students. The population has been declining over the past decade. Its tax base has been stable, and the increases in the school budget for the past five years basically have covered mandatory collective bargaining agreements and inflation. A new district-wide Planning Committee was established in 1981 for instructional computer applications. No formal planning process exists for administrative applications. The school district has had a Data Processing Department for 15 years that has a director and 19 staff members.

The director has been responsible for planning, designing, and implementing administrative computer systems. The major administrative computer applications supported by the Data Processing Department are as follows:

Financial management system—provided by the City of Haltown's Office of Operations

Personnel and payroll system—provided by the City of Haltown's Office of Personnel

Student information system—developed by the Data Processing Department

Course and curriculum system—developed by the Data Processing Department

Facilities and inventory system—developed by the Data Processing Department

In addition to these, the Data Processing Department supports various other smaller administrative applications. All of the applications run on the department's central computer center, which houses a large IBM 370 mainframe computer. Besides the data entry facility at the district's central office, three computer terminals are available at each school for data collection. In general, the superintendent feels that the Data Processing Department does a good job of supporting the administrative computer needs of the school district. She has received a number of letters from several city managers complimenting the Data Processing Department in the way that it has consistently provided timely and accurate data and reports.

In the past three years, the superintendent has fielded many requests from the principals in the schools to purchase microcomputers to support some of their administrative operations. The director of the Data Processing Department has not supported these requests, indicating that he does not have the budget to support microcomputer operations at the schools. Furthermore, the director has made a request to upgrade the existing mainframe computer, which was acquired in 1973.

The superintendent would like to support some of the principals' requests, but she does not want to undermine the good service that the Data Processing Department has been providing for many years. Furthermore, the new district-wide Planning Committee for Instructional Computing is completing its first report. She has seen a draft that includes a significant request for funds to establish microcomputer-based learning laboratories in each school. She has already decided that she must support some of the committee's recommendations because she feels that the district has fallen behind in computer education. Although the high schools have some microcomputers in the science laboratories, there is very little equipment in the primary and middle schools.

Keeping in mind the year (1982), analyze the preceding case study. Assuming that you cannot support all of the requests for new equipment, what alternative courses of action might you suggest to the superintendent? Are the issues facing the superintendent strictly budgetary, or are there other technological, planning, or organizational issues to be considered?

SUMMARY

This chapter reviews the major administrative uses of computer systems. A framework is developed for planning that requires these systems to be integrated with one another as much as possible. Database management systems and the information they provide are critical for this integration; they are the resources on which all the other applications depend.

Database management systems, electronic spreadsheets, and office automation are the major software packages used to perform administrative applications. Extremely sophisticated but easy to use, they are evolving into indispensable administrative software tools. Various examples of the uses of these software packages in educational administration are also presented in this chapter. Finally, several special-purpose applications of computer technology are described, including access to national information networks, statistical software, test scoring, automatic calling, and energy management systems.

Key Concepts and Questions

1. Developing the information resources of a school district is a critical goal of administrative computer systems.

   Why is this goal so important to school administrators? Who are some of the regular recipients of information from a school district? Is developing information resources a common goal in all organizations? Explain.

2. Database management systems, electronic spreadsheets, and office automation are the three major categories of administrative software applications.

   How do you define and compare them? Are they dependent on one another, or do they function independently? Explain. If starting administrative applications from the beginning, what would be your first priority? Why?

3. Database management systems are very complex applications.

   Identify some of the common database applications that exist in a school district. How do they relate to one another? What staff would be involved in designing a new database management system for student records? Personnel records?

4. Spreadsheet applications are used extensively in number manipulation exercises.

   Identify some common uses of spreadsheet applications in a school. How are the data generated for these applications? Who might be the major developers of spreadsheet applications in a school?

5. Office automation at one time referred essentially to word processing.

   How is it changing? What other applications does it include? Who are the major beneficiaries of office automation applications?

6. In addition to database, spreadsheet, and office automation applications, various other special-purpose applications can exist in a school district.

   Identify several special-purpose applications. For each one, consider (a) whether special hardware or software is required, (b) who the individuals in a school involved with developing the application would be, and (c) how important you consider the application to the overall administrative operations.

Suggested Activities

1. Assume that you are responsible for initiating a 5-year administrative computer applications plan for a school district. For the first meeting of the new Administrative Systems Advisory Committee, you are to prepare a brief assessment of the school district's present level of administrative systems development. How would you outline such an assessment?

2. Familiarize yourself with some of the features of the database management, electronic spreadsheet, and office automation software that might exist in a (or your) school.

3. Refer to Appendix B for an introduction to Microsoft Works, versions of which are available on Macintosh and DOS/Windows machines.

References

DATAPRO Information Services Group. (1991). Selecting a database system. In *Managing Information Technology,* Vol. 2 (Section 5060, pp. 1–16). Delran, NJ: McGraw-Hill.

French, R. P., & Raven, B. (1959). The bases of social power. In D. Cartwright (Ed.), *Studies in social power* (pp. 150–167). Ann Arbor, MI: Institute for Social Research.

Luthans, F. (1981). *Organizational behavior*. New York: McGraw-Hill.

Markoff, J. (1996, April 1). New software for business by Microsoft. *New York Times,* p. D1.

Quality Education Data. (1995). *Education Market Guide*. Denver: Author.

Ray, J. R., & Davis, L. D. (1991). *Computers in educational administration*. New York: McGraw-Hill.

Richards, C. E. (1989). *Microcomputer applications for strategic management in education*. New York: Longman.

Schmidt, J. W., & Brodie, M. L. (Eds.). (1983). *Relational database systems: Analysis and comparison*. New York: Springer.

Simon, H. A. (1957). *Administrative behavior*. Upper Saddle River, NJ: Prentice Hall.

———. (1960). *The new science of management decision*. New York: Harper & Row.

———. (1979). Rational decision making in business organizations. *American Economic Review, 69,* 493–513.

5

Computer Applications in Instruction

T | he 1980s and 1990s saw the more than 15,000 school districts in the United States begin to make a substantial new investment in computer technology to support instructional applications. In 1983, the student/microcomputer ratio in all public schools was approximately 125 to 1; by 1995, it was 10 to 1. However, while the investment in hardware continues, the yield in terms of academic benefits is unclear. In some schools, computer applications have been heralded and showcased as models for delivering instruction. In others, computer applications have been a disappointment, not living up to their promises. School administrators can sometimes find themselves caught in the middle as some members of the school community request more resources for expanding instructional technology while others question its value.

This chapter provides school administrators with a balanced assessment of instructional computer applications. The basic concepts of instructional computing that are necessary for doing academic planning are also reviewed.

INSTRUCTIONAL COMPUTING: A NEW BEGINNING

In 1988, the U.S. Congress's Office of Technology Assessment (OTA) conducted a national study on the uses of computer technology for instruction in primary and secondary schools. Extensively researched and documented, the study provided one of the first glimpses of the investment that schools in all parts of the country were making in instructional computing technology. Millions of microcomputers costing billions of dollars had been purchased in the 1980s, and almost every school in the country had acquired some form of computer technology. This study was frequently cited in professional journals as evidence of the "revolution" under way in the schools. In reviewing the data presented in this study, one is left with little doubt that a major new thrust in instructional computing was indeed occurring.

Based on data provided by Quality Educational Data (QED) of Denver, Colorado, Figure 5–1 provides the actual national student/microcomputer ratios in the public schools for 1983 to 1995, with projections to the year 2000. The 10-to-1 ratio in 1995 represents a national average. Among the 50 states and the District of Columbia, the student/microcomputer ratios ranged from a low of 6 to 1 to a high of 16.4 to 1. If the present trend to acquire more microcomputer hardware continues, by the year 2000, the student/microcomputer ratio will be approximately 6 to 1.

In terms of dollars, the public schools spent approximately $2 billion on computer hardware in the 1980s. If the current trend continues, the schools will be spending in excess of $4 billion per year to support instructional technology by the year 2000. These figures are indeed significant considering that in 1975, computers for instructional purposes were nonexistent in many primary and secondary schools, and the expenditures for technology in general were negligible.

Based on the number of machines purchased and the dollars invested, one would assume that computers have become an integral part of instruction in our nation's schools. This is debatable. James Mecklenburger, the director of the National School

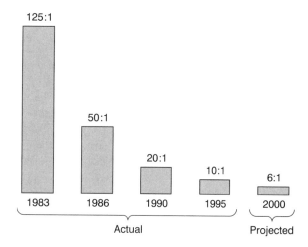

Figure 5–1
Student/Microcomputer Ratios
for 1983 to 2000

Source: Quality Education Data
(1996).

Boards Association's Institute for the Transfer of Technology, saw little evidence of broad-based change. In his words, "No more than 5 percent of schools are truly harnessing the computer's power . . . and in the remaining 95 percent, the impact is nil or next to nil" (O'Neill, 1990, p. 4). In 1995, the Office of Technology Assessment in a national study found that a substantial number of teachers reported little or no use of computers for instruction (U.S. Congress, Office of Technology Assessment, 1995, p. 1).

The question is, Why then do the schools continue to make such a considerable investment in technology? The answer is not simple. If one sees instructional computing as a mature activity with many well-known and well-understood applications, making this investment without substantial results becomes questionable. However, if one considers instructional computing as relatively new and, in many cases, experimental, then this expenditure can be supported as a research or development activity, at least for a while. The presumption is made here that many schools find themselves in the latter situation, still in the developmental stages.

Much of the hardware and software used in the 1970s and early 1980s has little application today. It is true that some of the early pioneers of instructional computing, such as Patrick Suppes, John Kemeny, Donald Bitzer, and Seymour Papert, have seen applications that they designed and experimented with in the 1960s evolve to take a major place in present-day instructional technology. But by and large, they are the exceptions. Computer hardware has changed radically, spurring new approaches to instructional software, most of which has been developed by companies founded after 1980. In a sense, schools are in a new beginning vis-à-vis instructional technology. They are still experimenting with and evaluating different applications, and slowly some of these applications are being accepted and added to the schools' instructional repertoire. Given demands for more technology by parents, the business community, and some teachers, administrators will continue to find themselves in positions of nurturing and helping computer applications to mature.

INSTRUCTIONAL COMPUTING: SOME HISTORY

Most of the instructional applications developed in the early years of computing are no longer relevant to what is going on presently in the schools. However, there are several notable exceptions that are important for an overall understanding of instructional computing in the 1990s.

Patrick Suppes is the individual most associated with computer-assisted instruction, or CAI. Starting in 1959 at Stanford University, he conducted various experiments with CAI and eventually developed software especially designed for teaching basic skills such as reading, writing, and arithmetic. He is still actively involved in computer-based education, particularly with integrated learning systems provided by the Computer Curriculum Corporation in California.

In the late 1950s and 1960s, John Kemeny and Thomas Kurtz were among the first to envision computers in the domain of the common person. The product of their vision was BASIC (Beginners All-Purpose Instruction Code), a programming language that was really a variation of the FORTRAN programming language. The importance of BASIC is that it was the first language designed to be used by anybody. Originally required of all freshmen entering Dartmouth College, with which Kemeny and Kurtz were affiliated, BASIC quickly gained wide acceptance throughout the country. When microcomputers were introduced in the late 1970s, most of the manufacturers decided to provide BASIC as part of their operating systems. As a result, it became the most popular programming language ever developed. Microsoft's Visual BASIC, which is used extensively for programming multimedia applications, evolved from the original BASIC language developed by Kemeny and Kurtz.

Donald Bitzer developed PLATO (Programmed Logic for Automatic Teaching Operations) at the University of Illinois in the 1960s. PLATO was the first popular authoring system for developing instructional applications. Designed to run on a large computer network, it sought to bring quality and innovative instructional material to students over wide geographic areas. One of PLATO's unique features was the use of a plasma display tube for producing exceptionally interesting graphics. Bitzer is generally credited with foreseeing the importance of graphics and sound in developing instructional computer applications.

Probably the best-known developer of instructional computing software for primary and secondary schools is Seymour Papert of the Massachusetts Institute of Technology (MIT). Logo, which many consider the first language developed for children, embodies his philosophy of experiential and discovery learning. Logo, from the Greek *logos,* means word, thought, or discourse. Although developed and well received in the late 1960s, like BASIC, Logo really became popular when made available on microcomputers in the late 1970s and 1980s. Papert has continually improved it, and versions that incorporate word processing (LogoWriter) and mechanical interfaces (Lego-Logo) are commonly used in schools today. Papert's (1980) major book, *Mindstorms: Children, Computers, and Powerful Ideas,* is recommended reading for administrators and teachers interested in instructional computing. It is one of the first books to relate the development of an instructional software package to a particular educational philosophy, namely experiential or discovery learning.

These software developments are well respected among computer educators, but their impact on academic achievement remains questionable. Although hundreds of studies have been conducted, the acceptance of instructional computing as having a definitely positive effect on academic achievement is not universal.

A BRIEF REVIEW OF THE RESEARCH

Some of the most extensive reviews of the research on computer education were conducted by James Kulik and his associates at the University of Michigan. In the 1970s and 1980s, they conducted a series of meta-analyses of hundreds of studies dealing with the effects of computer education at different grade levels (elementary, secondary, college, and adult). Their general conclusion was that computer-based education had a beneficial effect on academic achievement, although it was not uniformly true at all grade levels (Kulik, Bangert, & Williams, 1983; Kulik, Kulik, & Bangert-Downs, 1984; Kulik, Kulik, & Cohen, 1980; Kulik, Kulik, & Schwab, 1986). However, Richard Clark (1983, 1985) refuted the findings by questioning the research controls of most of the studies that were included in the Kulik meta-analyses. Clark further concluded that the computer was basically a vehicle carrying an instructional substance and that real improvement in achievement only comes with improving the substance, not the vehicle.

In the late 1980s and early 1990s, educators saw value in providing instructional computer experiences for reasons other than improving student performance. Benefits such as ensuring computer literacy, providing variety in instructional delivery, or releasing teacher time from record-keeping tasks were considered important enough to continue investing in technology. However, even with objectives that might not directly affect academic performance, schools are having problems implementing and evaluating instructional applications.

Ron Brandt (1994), executive editor of *Educational Leadership,* observed that "most schools lacked the wherewithal to mount major technology-based initiatives" (p. 3). Sheingold, Kane, and Endreweit (1983) from the Bank Street College of Education identified six issues critical to planning and implementing instructional computer applications:

1. Access to hardware
2. New roles for teachers and administrators
3. Integration of microcomputers into the curriculum, especially at the elementary school level
4. Quantity and quality of software
5. Teacher preparation and training
6. Effects and outcomes of the instructional use of microcomputers (p. 426)

These six issues are still appropriate in helping us briefly assess the conditions existent in the 1990s when planning and implementing instructional applications.

Access to hardware, as documented with the previously cited QED data, has improved dramatically. However, improving student access to hardware continues to be a priority in schools. Even in school districts with very favorable student/microcomputer ratios, the priority among computer coordinators continues to be the acquisition of more hardware needed either to upgrade existing equipment or make more machines available to students (Picciano, 1991).

New roles for teachers and administrators have become evident as more and more school districts employ full-time computer coordinators. In districts with many schools geographically dispersed, it is common to have building-level coordinators in addition to district-level coordinators. Graduate schools at many universities across the country have also developed new specialized programs that provide concentrations in computer-related teacher education.

Integration of microcomputers into the curriculum, especially at the elementary school level, is improving but still requires a good deal of attention on the part of administrators. Several studies (U.S. Congress, Office of Technology Assessment, 1995; Becker, 1994; Picciano, 1991; Sheingold & Hadley, 1990) indicate that resources, especially for release time, are needed for teachers and curriculum coordinators to do the detailed curriculum design work necessary for successful integration. This issue also relates directly to the need for more teacher training.

Both the quantity and quality of software has improved. Thousands of instructional software products are on the market, with the number of packages increasing every year. Furthermore, the instructional software industry, which only started in the late 1970s, has grown considerably, and the increased competition has forced improvement in quality. Instructional software is also becoming more specialized as small companies attempt to attract a limited market by meeting the needs of particular applications and subject areas rather than trying to develop general-purpose packages. This specialization also yields a product of higher quality. However, while the quantity and quality of software have improved, as have other aspects of technology, the need for more and better software will continue.

Some colleges of teacher education have begun to make technology a basic requirement; others have not. David Imig, executive director of the American Association of Colleges for Teacher Education, estimates that 20% of all teacher preparation programs are on the cutting edge of technology, 60% offer one or two basic courses, and the remaining 20% are doing very little regarding technology (Nicklin, 1992). Regardless, new teachers entering the education field in the 1990s are more computer literate than their predecessors in the 1980s. However, the existing teacher corps, particularly those who have had very little if any computer training, needs ongoing and systematic training and development in the use of technology. A study by Sheingold and Hadley (1990) indicated that even teachers who take their own initiative in upgrading skills may require as much as 5 to 6 years to master computer-based practices and approaches.

In terms of the effects and outcomes of instructional computing, recent studies and reviews of the literature (U.S. Congress, Office of Technology Assessment, 1995; Becker, 1994; Thompson, Simonson, & Hargrave, 1992; Robyler, Castine, & King, 1988) continue the debate. One of these, a meta-analyses by Robyler et al. (1988), concentrated on more than 80 studies conducted since 1980. Their conclusion probably states best much of the current thinking: "Computer applications have an undeniable value and an important instructional role to play in classrooms of the future. Defining that role is the task [for the future]" (p. 131). Today's administrators are in the pivotal positions in their schools to define that role.

CLASSIFICATION SYSTEMS AND DEFINITIONS OF TERMS

Widely accepted classification systems are elusive in education. This is also true in instructional computing. Although various attempts have been made to establish classification systems for instructional computer software, very little agreement exists. Possibly the best-known classification and the one referenced in many standard computer education textbooks (e.g., Bullough & Beatty, 1991; Lockard, 1992; Merrill, Tolman, Christensen, Hammons, Vincent, & Reynolds, 1992; Simonson & Thompson, 1994) is Robert Taylor's (1980) trichotomy of "tutor, tool, tutee." In **tutor** mode, the computer possesses the information and controls the learning environment. In **tool** mode, the computer is used to assist or act as a tool in the learning activity. In **tutee** mode, the student possesses the information and controls the learning environment. As we shall see in the next few sections, this trichotomy is a flexible system. It lends itself to overlap in which particular software packages might be categorized in more than one of the classifications. Before examining this in more detail, we need to establish some basic definitions of instructional computing terms.

Figure 5–2 summarizes most of the commonly used terms and definitions associated with instructional computing applications. Many of these terms—particularly when used by their acronyms such as CAI, CMI, CBE—have been a source of confusion among educators. In some cases, they are used interchangeably. For example, **computer-based education** (CBE), **computer-based instruction** (CBI), and **computer-assisted instruction** (CAI) are frequently used to refer to any type of learning environment in which a computer is used. Sometimes, the definition of a term has changed over time, such as the use of computer-assisted instruction, which originally was a generic term applied to all instructional uses of computers; now it is used more frequently to refer to tutor-type software. Readers should familiarize themselves with these terms and establish a basic vocabulary in their own environments for use in discussions and printed materials. In this book, the term **computer-assisted instruction** is used to refer to tutor-type applications. Other terms are used specifically as defined in Figure 5–2.

TUTOR APPLICATIONS

Very common today, tutor applications trace their beginning to the 1960s. In tutor applications, the computer has been preprogrammed by educators and technicians. Generally, the computer presents some information or subject matter, the student responds, the computer evaluates the response and presents additional or new

Computer-Assisted Instruction (CAI). The use of the computer to assist in the instructional process. One of the earliest terms used to refer generically to computer applications in education, it is used more frequently now to refer to tutor-type applications such as drill-and-practice and tutorials.

Computer-Assisted Learning (CAL). Similar to CAI.

Computer-Based Education (CBE). Generic term used for the broad array of instructional computer applications.

Computer-Based Teaching (CBT). Generic term for the use of computers by teachers as part of an instructional presentation such as an interactive video.

Computer-Managed Instruction (CMI). The use of the computer in an instructional process in which student progress is monitored and recorded for subsequent instruction and review. Most CMI applications also are able to adjust material to each individual student's level of understanding. A good example of CMI is an integrated learning system.

Intelligent Computer-Assisted Instruction (ICAI). Similar to CAI but also utilizes a substantial database of information for presenting material and selecting instructional paths.

Integrated Learning System (ILS). A single computer package for delivering instruction that combines hardware, software, curriculum, and management components. It is usually supplied by a single vendor.

Integrated Instructional System (IIS). Same as an ILS.

Figure 5–2
Instructional Computing Terminology

information, and the cycle repeats itself. There are four subcategories of tutor applications: (a) drill and practice, (b) tutorials, (c) simulations, and (d) instructional games and problem solving. Figure 5–3 provides examples of some of the popular tutor software programs.

Drill and Practice

Drill-and-practice applications are usually used to reinforce a lesson or material that has already been presented to the student. They have been much maligned as too boring and mechanistic. This view is not entirely unjustified in that many of the drill-and-practice applications developed in the 1960s and 1970s could have been more interestingly designed. However, technological limitations existed in the early years of computing that made some pedagogically important features such as graphics and sound difficult to program. Many of these applications have since been improved by making greater use of graphics, motion, color, and sound to keep students interested in the activity.

Teachers regularly use drill and practice manually (i.e., flash cards, work sheets) as part of their normal instructional repertoire. The benefits of a computer drill-and-

Drill and Practice

Program	Developer	Subject
Math Blaster Plus	Davidson and Associates	Basic mathematics
Fay: That Math Woman	Didatech	Basic mathematics
M_SS_NG L_NKS	Sunburst Communications	Language arts
Magic Spells	The Learning Company	Spelling
Word Spinner	The Learning Company	Spelling

Tutorials

Program	Developer	Subject
Astronomy	Educational Activities	Astronomy
Biology Series	Prentice-Hall Courseware	Biology
Geometry Alive	Educational Activities	Geometry
Earth Science Series	Educational Activities	Earth science
Physical Science Series	Educational Activities	Physical science
Comparison Kitchen	DLM Teaching Resources	Size concepts

Simulations

Program	Developer	Subject
The Oregon Trail	MECC	History
Oh, Deer	MECC	Ecology
Odell Lake	MECC	Biology
Chem Lab Simulations	High Technology Software	Chemistry
The Discovery Lab	MECC	Science
Car Builder	Optimum Resources	Physics
Decisions, Decisions	Tom Snyder Productions	Social studies
S.M.A.R.T. Choices	Tom Snyder Productions	Drug abuse

Instructional Games and Problem-solving Software

Program	Developer	Subject
Muppet Learning Keys	Sunburst Communications	Alphabet
Kids on Keys	Spinnaker	Alphabet/keyboarding
High Wire Logic	Sunburst Communications	Thinking skills
Where in the _____ Is Carmen Sandiego?	Broderbund	Social studies
The Playroom	Broderbund	Thinking skills
The King's Rules	Sunburst Communications	Mathematics
Planetary Construction Set	Sunburst Communications	Science
Factory/Super Factory	Sunburst Communications	Spatial geometry

Figure 5–3
Popular Tutor Programs

practice program can include immediate feedback, automatic adjustment of the level of difficulty depending on student responses, and record keeping on student performance that can be reviewed as needed by teachers. In reviewing and planning instructional applications, administrators should assume that some drill and practice is common in most schools' software libraries; however, it should not dominate the collection.

Drill-and-practice computer applications are used in many learning situations at different grade levels. Much of the earliest drill-and-practice software packages concentrated on basic skills and have continued to evolve as the technology has improved. They are most commonly used in mathematics, basic language skills, grammar, and spelling. They are also popular in special education classrooms where they have been combined with specialized speech and visual equipment.

Tutorials

Tutorial applications are similar to drill-and-practice applications in design and appearance. An important distinction between the two, however, is that tutorial programs attempt to teach something new and are not used specifically for reinforcement of material already presented, although they may be. Tutorial programs have been criticized for the same reasons as have drill-and-practice programs, but they too have improved in recent years. They are used regularly in advanced technologies such as interactive video and integrated learning systems, which will be discussed later in this chapter.

In many schools, the emphasis on using computers has been to try to integrate them into a regular curriculum. When used for stand-alone instruction, tutorial programs tend to keep the computer as something separate; they have not been as popular as other software programs for this reason. Tutorial programs can, however, be very effective in certain situations, such as for students who have missed a good deal of class time because of illness, who are homebound, or who live in rural areas where teachers may not be available to teach certain specialized subjects.

Simulations

Simulations attempt to represent real-life situations on a computer. Generally, the real-life situations or objects of the simulations are impossible to duplicate in most classrooms. Certain scientific experiments, ecological systems, and historical or current events are duplicated by using computer models to represent the real-life situations. Typically, students interact with the simulation and influence decisions and outcomes. Simulation software keeps growing in popularity, and many educators consider it a more effective use of computers than drill-and-practice and tutorial software.

Simulation software is also considered to be appropriate for beginning the teaching of higher-order thinking skills. It can easily be used to supplement a lesson to allow students to apply what they have learned to different situations. Increasingly, simulations are combined with instructional games and problem-solving applications, which are discussed later.

Many popular simulation programs are available today. The Minnesota Educational Computer Consortium (MECC) has been successful in developing a wide variety of stimulating and pedagogically appropriate simulations in social studies (The Oregon Trail), ecology (Oh, Deer), science (The Discovery Lab), and other subject areas. Tom Snyder Productions has also developed a series of excellent simulations called Decisions, Decisions that covers subjects such as colonization, immigration, city management, and teenage drug use. Simulation software is also beginning to be used in developing interactive video programs where the use of motion and sound will add significantly to the pseudo-reality of the computer models.

Instructional Games and Problem Solving

Instructional games software attempts to make learning fun by combining learning, entertainment, and gamesmanship. Competition either between two (or more) players or between one player and the computer is encouraged. Frequently scores are kept, and the object of the game is to win. Although some instructional games continue to be poorly designed, many are well done and have instructional value. Of the various types of instructional software packages, games are frequently successful in using current technology, especially graphics and sound, to keep student motivation and interest in the material very high.

Instructional games should be used to supplement other lessons; they are excellent when used to add some variety to a student's day. This is more important in elementary school programs and especially with younger children. As an example, Sunburst Communications has teamed with Jim Henson Associates to develop a series of software packages that uses *Sesame Street* characters to teach early childhood language arts in a game format and on a specially designed Muppet keyboard.

Problem-solving software is frequently subcategorized with instructional games, although it can also be considered a separate category. Problem-solving software is gaining significantly in popularity because the primary focus is on thinking skills. Students typically are presented with situations in which they use and develop cognitive, analytical, and other thinking process skills. In many cases, the material is presented in game format in which students compete with one another or with the computer. The literature on teaching and learning thinking skills is very extensive and open to much debate. For further reading on problem-solving software and higher-order thinking skills, readers are encouraged to review Vockell and van Deusen (1989) for an excellent treatment of the subject.

Two companies, Broderbund Corporation of San Rafael, California, and Sunburst Communications of Pleasantville, New York, have provided an array of excellent game and problem-solving products. Broderbund's *Where in the ____ Is Carmen Sandiego?* series is perhaps the most popular instructional game software ever developed. In 1991, a television program was produced based on this software; it can be seen regularly on educational television networks. Carmen Sandiego combines geography, history, and adventure with reference and map-reading skills to provide very stimulating instructional experiences. Sunburst Communications has a number of very popular programs that combine the development of thinking skills with mathematics and the sciences.

TOOL APPLICATIONS

Tool applications, comprising the most frequent uses of computers in classrooms, include (a) word processing, (b) spreadsheet, and (c) database software. Although originally designed for purposes other than teaching and learning, tool software packages are being used effectively in enhancing the instructional process. Common examples include the use of word-processing software to assist in teaching writing and the use of electronic spreadsheet programs to assist in teaching scientific formulas.

The popularity of tool software is primarily due to the fact that it is the easiest of all the various instructional software types to integrate into a curriculum. Teachers can use tool software without making major changes to the established curriculum. Also available is commercial software, which has been evolving in sophistication for many years and is also relatively easy to use. Furthermore, as teachers increasingly use tool software packages for their own professional and personal purposes, they are able to draw on their own technical knowledge to use these packages effectively in the classroom. Students likewise increasingly see their parents and older siblings using tool software such as word processing and spreadsheets in their homes and may have already begun to use these same programs themselves.

Figure 5–4 provides a partial list of popular tool software packages used for instruction. The nature of these packages is also presented extensively in Chapter 4, and readers are encouraged to review that material.

Word Processing and Desktop Publishing

Word processing is frequently used to assist in teaching writing, especially in a curriculum that teaches writing as a process in which one writes, revises, rewrites, and revises. Word-processing software makes revisions very easy and avoids the drudgery of handwriting or retyping extensive amounts of text. Commercial word-processing packages such as Microsoft Word and WordPerfect are commonly being used at various grade levels by students to do writing assignments. In addition, some word-processing packages such as Bank Street Writer, Kidwriter, and The Magic Slate have been developed specifically for use by young children in classrooms.

When word processing is implemented as part of a writing program, questions frequently arise regarding the use of spell checking and certain other help features. Some packages such as Rightwriter are available that provide grammar-checking features. In most cases, these features are optional and can be deleted if a decision is made that these aids are not appropriate for teaching writing. Students exposed to word processing early in school generally continue to use it and become more proficient as they grow older, assuming that they have access to computer equipment.

A variation of word-processing software that has grown significantly in popularity is desktop publishing software, which combines standard word-processing features with graphics capabilities to produce visually stimulating print material. Desktop publishing can be used to create professional-quality newsletters, school newspapers, and flyers. It can also be easily integrated into course work and extracurricular activities. Typical applications might be clubs doing flyers on recent activities, social studies classes

Word Processing, Spreadsheets, and Databases

Program	Developer	Subject
Bank Street Writer	Scholastic	Word processing
Kidwriter	Spinnaker	Word processing
Magic Slate	Sunburst Communications	Word processing
Microsoft Word	Microsoft	Word processing
Muppet Slate	Sunburst Communications	Word processing
WordPerfect	WordPerfect Corp.	Word processing
Lotus 1-2-3	Lotus Development Corp.	Spreadsheet
Educalc	Grolier	Spreadsheet
Supercalc	Sorcim	Spreadsheet
Bank Street Filer	Sunburst Communications	Database
dBase	Ashton-Tate	Database
Friendly Filer	Grolier	Database
Appleworks	Apple Computer Co.	Integrated package
Microsoft Works	Microsoft	Integrated package

Desktop Publishing

Program	Developer	Subject
Bannermania	Broderbund	Signs and banners
The Newsroom	Springboard Software	Printing/graphics
The New Printshop	Broderbund	Signs, banners, cards
Pagemaker	Aldus	Printing/graphics
Publish It	Timeworks	Printing/graphics
Superprint	Scholastic	Signs and banners

Figure 5–4
Popular Tool Programs

preparing a newspaper during some important historical period such as the week of the French Revolution or the first landing of men on the moon, or students designing banners for sports and dances. Students usually collaborate on desktop publishing projects, which frequently translates into motivation for completing the final products.

Spreadsheets

Standard electronic spreadsheet programs are being used for a variety of subjects. Mathematics, the sciences, and business education make extensive use of spreadsheet software for all sorts of instructional applications involving the manipulation of numbers. Almost any subject in which mathematical formulas or statistical analyses are used can integrate spreadsheets into the curriculum. Just as word processing takes the drudgery out of typing text, spreadsheets take the drudgery out of doing

Electronic Encyclopedias and Reference Works		
Program	*Developer*	*Subject*
American Encyclopedia	Grolier	General encyclopedia
Bookshelf	Microsoft	General reference
Compton's Encyclopedia	Britannica Software	General encyclopedia
Information Finder	World Book	General encyclopedia
World Atlas	Electromap	Maps
The Works of William Shakespeare	CMC Research	Literature
Audio Notes	Warner Communications	Classical music
Ninth Collegiate Dictionary (Audio)	Highlighted Data	Dictionary with audio pronunciation

Specialized Tool Software		
Program	*Developer*	*Subject*
Adobe Illustrator	Adobe Systems	Art
Dazzledraw	Broderbund	Art
Koala Painter	Koala Technologies	Art
Fantavision	Broderbund	Animation
Color 'N' Canvas	WINGS for Learning	Art
The Music Studio	Activision, Inc.	Music
Music Construction Set	Electronic Arts	Music
Data Insights	Sunburst Communications	Graphs
Easygraph	Grolier	Graphs
Survey Taker	Scholastic	Surveying/graphs
Biofeedback Microlab	HRM Software (Queue)	Biology
Science Toolkit	Broderbund	Science
Playing with Science	Sunburst Communications	Science

Figure 5–4, *continued*

hand calculations. Naturally, they should not be used in courses where it is desirable or necessary for students to do hand calculations as practice in refining their mathematics skills. However, there are many instructional situations where the nature or understanding of a formula is more important than the mathematical practice of adding, subtracting, multiplying, or dividing numbers. In these situations, spreadsheets can be most effective.

Commercial spreadsheet packages also provide easy-to-use graphing features that allow students not only to do a mathematical formula but also to visualize it. Lotus 1-2-3 and Excel are some of the commercial packages commonly used in many schools. Integrated packages such as Microsoft Works also provide excellent spreadsheet programs along with word-processing and database software. These integrated packages can be particularly effective in instructional applications where data collection using a database is combined with data analysis using a spreadsheet. Examples include research activities on voting behavior, economic forecasting, and local census data.

Databases

Database software is also finding its way into a variety of instructional applications. Data-collecting and -searching skills are being taught by having students access national databases maintained by governmental agencies, universities, and research institutions. Research projects also find students building their own databases with information that they have collected on animals, states, famous people, minerals, places, and so forth. A popular long-term assignment is to have all the students in a class contribute to building a database over the course of a semester or year and then to do some type of statistical analysis as a culminating experience.

Standard database packages such as dBase are easy to use and can be learned readily by older students. For younger children, it may be more desirable to acquire database software packages such as Bank Street Filer and Friendly Filer, which have been designed specifically for instructional applications. Some of these packages such as Bank Street Filer provide databases on a variety of subjects in addition to the software for collecting and manipulating data.

In planning the instructional applications of databases, educators interested in building employment skills should recognize the increasing importance of reference and researching skills, as many professions rely more on the ability to access information from a variety of sources. On-line databases are not simply the domain of research organizations and graduate schools but are used routinely in all types of everyday businesses. Students should be prepared to use them along with other standard tool software programs as part of their basic education. Computer literacy, which in the past referred to a simple understanding of hardware combined with a computer programming experience, now includes the basic understanding of the three major types of tool software.

Electronic Encyclopedias and Reference Works

A type of database software becoming standard in most school libraries is the electronic encyclopedia, which gradually is replacing or being used in addition to the standard multivolume printed encyclopedias. Examples include Microsoft's Encarta, Compton's Electronic Encyclopedia, and Grolier's Multimedia Encyclopedia. The popularity of electronic encyclopedias stems from the ease of searching for the required material electronically rather than manually. In addition, they provide excellent graphics, sound, and video clips. Other reference works available on CD-ROM include atlases, dictionaries, literary works, classical music, and the Bible.

Specialized Tool Software

Tool software packages are also being developed for special-purpose instructional applications. In some cases, they combine tool software programs (such as IBM's Writing to Read Program, which uses voice synthesizers and word-processing software) with tutor software to teach writing and reading using a phonics approach. For teaching music, several products such as The Music Studio are on the market for composing and listening to music using synthesizers. Broderbund's Science Toolkit uses a variety of temperature, light, and other sensory probes and instruments to collect data for real-life experiments. The Learning Company has combined word-processing, desktop publishing, and electronic encyclopedia software into a comprehensive package entitled Student Writing & Research Center. As the technology improves, especially in the use of sound and voice, the development and use of specialized tool applications will expand.

TUTEE APPLICATIONS

To develop tutee applications, both teacher and student need to learn to program a computer. In tutee mode, the student programs or teaches the computer to perform some task. Learning computer programming is the best way to develop an understanding of how a computer works. In the tutor and tool applications described earlier, understanding how a computer functions is not the instructional objective. In tutee applications, the computer itself becomes a focus of learning.

Developing computer programming skills provides several worthwhile instructional experiences. Programming languages such as BASIC and Pascal require students to learn rules, syntax, and logic constructs. The nature of computer programming is also one of problem solving and developing plans (programs) for solutions. It is a thinking exercise formalized via programming instructions that can be visualized to a certain degree on a computer.

Debate persists, however, regarding the value of a computer programming exercise in actually teaching thinking skills. Some educators, such as Papert (1980) and Luehrmann (1980), support the use of computers for this purpose. Others, such as Linn (1985) and Pea (1987), accept programming as a thinking exercise but caution that there is no proof that it actually improves the teaching of thinking. Perhaps Vockell and van Deusen (1989) summarize the issue best by making the "chicken and egg" comparison: Do clear and logical thinkers become successful computer programmers, or do people become clear and logical thinkers by writing computer programs? These theorists conclude that computer programming undoubtedly requires and exercises high-order thinking skills, but it is illogical, though tempting, to assume that teaching programming will also teach high-order thinking skills.

In developing a tutee application, administrators and teachers should feel confident that they are providing a high-order thinking and problem-solving experience for their students. They are also offering one of the better experiences for learning about computers. More research is necessary, however, before a firm conclusion can be made that computer programming actually improves thinking skills. In the meantime, educators might consider one of the following tutee programs being used in schools today.

Logo

The most popular programming language taught in elementary schools is Logo, which was designed and developed by Seymour Papert of MIT specifically for young children. Logo can be used in a free-form mode to experiment and explore or to develop very sophisticated computer-programming procedures. A friendly turtle in the center of the screen becomes the focus of children's attention as they learn to master and control the computer by drawing different shapes, developing geometric patterns, or designing a computer game. Logo is especially well suited for continued use at many grade levels.

For educators wishing to provide programming experiences in the early grades, Logo and its derivatives are among the best software packages available. In planning to implement Logo into a curriculum, as with all tutee applications, a good deal of computer access on a regular basis is a necessity.

Beginners All-Purpose Symbolic Instruction Code (BASIC)

BASIC, the most popular programming language ever developed, is a standard feature of many microcomputer operating systems. Usually introduced at the middle and high school levels, a BASIC programming experience combined with a general understanding of computer hardware served to define computer literacy in the schools throughout the 1980s. Recently, this situation has begun to change, as more schools have replaced the BASIC programming experience with tool software packages.

A derivative of the FORTRAN (Formula Translation) programming language, BASIC was used originally for a variety of mathematical, scientific, and engineering applications. It has since been enhanced and now provides a full complement of data management and graphics capabilities. Microsoft's Visual BASIC has evolved into one of the more popular programming languages for doing multimedia programs.

Pascal

Pascal was one of the first programming languages to require structured programming or logic techniques for all instructions. It remains an excellent introductory language for the serious computer science student.

All programming languages require a set logic flow for a program to work, and programmers must learn to write programs in a structured manner to avoid what is referred to as "sloppy" programming—programs that might provide a solution but are poorly designed. Pascal requires programmers to develop their logic constructs as a series of discrete modules within a fairly rigid structure. Professional programmers who develop or modify very complex programs involving thousands of instructions most appreciate the discipline that Pascal instills in beginning programmers. In implementing computer programming courses, particularly at the high school level, educators should consider Pascal over other programming languages for its future usefulness to students.

Authoring Languages

Computer programming over the past four decades has gradually become easier and easier. The computer software industry has been moving in the direction of providing a natural language, comparable to the way people speak and write, to communicate with a computer. Such a language is not commercially available yet, although significant strides have been made in some computer science laboratories. The high-level languages just discussed are easier to use than their predecessor languages, but they cannot in any way be considered natural languages. They have their own special syntax, verbs, and constructs. To fill the gap between these programming languages and natural language, a new type of language called **authoring** has been developed.

Authoring languages are much easier to use than other programming languages and originally were designed to be used for specific applications by people without special computer training or background. For instruction, several authoring languages are available to aid teachers in developing lessons. They are designed specifically to make it easier to present material, ask questions, and interpret student responses. They can also be used to control other equipment such as videodiscs to provide a multimedia presentation.

The first authoring languages such as TUTOR, MicroTUTOR, COURSEWRITER, and PILOT were designed strictly for instruction, and although some teachers were willing to make the effort to use these languages, the time needed to learn to use them effectively proved burdensome. Authoring languages developed in the 1980s and early 1990s such as Apple Corporation's HyperCard, IBM's Linkway, and Asymetrix's Toolbook are appropriate for lesson development as well as other applications such as building databases, maintaining inventories, or keeping a telephone directory. Though easier to use than their predecessors, whether these newer authoring languages will be used by many more teachers remains to be seen. They are not likely to be learned by a majority of regular classroom teachers because they still require a good deal of time and effort to master.

Authoring languages such as HyperCard, HyperStudio, Authorware Professional, ToolBook, and Astound are, however, being used widely by computer teachers who have had more extensive technical training. Using a series of programming objects such as buttons, fields, and graphics, these languages can provide a very stimulating learning environment. They are especially effective in combining graphics and some animation with instructional text and other written material. These languages are fast becoming the basic tools for developing multimedia materials using video and audio. They are also easy enough to use so that computer instructors increasingly are teaching students how to "author" or use an authoring language. Authoring languages will continue to evolve and will play a larger role in the future in computer education curricula.

INTEGRATED LEARNING SYSTEMS

Integrated learning systems (ILSs) are "integrated" systems of hardware, software, curriculum, and management components that are generally marketed by a single supplier. Also referred to as **integrated instructional systems** (IISs), they are probably the most sophisticated examples of computer-managed instructional products on the market. The hardware usually consists of a mini- or microcomputer that can function as a file server in a local area network. The software generally is tutorial and drill and practice. The curriculum provided can range from kindergarten through 12th-grade subjects, although many of the most popular ILSs are used for basic skills instruction in language arts and mathematics.

Critical to all ILSs is a student management system (computer-managed instruction) that tests students, keeps records on their performance, and adjusts lesson material depending on their progress. The management system usually produces automated individual student and group progress reports that can be used by teachers and administrators for instructional planning. (See Figure 5–5 for a list of some of the more popular ILS vendors.)

Many educators consider an ILS as the total solution for implementing instructional computing in their schools. All the major components are provided already integrated. The problems of integrating computer technology into the curriculum are solved because the computer provides the curriculum as well as a major portion of the instruction. Furthermore, some of the vendors, such as Computer Curriculum Corporation, Jostens Learning Corporation, and Wicat Systems, Inc., have a great deal of technical and pedagogical expertise and have been developing and refining their systems for many years.

Why, then, have most school districts *not* acquired these systems? The major reason is their cost. Depending on the number of computer workstations, such systems can easily cost hundreds of thousands and, in some cases, millions of dollars. Furthermore, after the initial investment, there are yearly costs for maintenance and upgrades, which can range from 7% to 12% of the original purchase price. Many school districts simply cannot afford an ILS. Additionally, to be used effectively, these systems require extensive training of the teaching staff and may require teachers to become managers of instruction rather than simply instructors. On the other hand, an ILS with extensive reporting capabilities can be a powerful tool for monitoring student progress and customizing lessons to individual needs.

In planning to acquire an ILS, administrators need to do a very careful analysis to assure that the benefits of such a system will be realized in their districts. Because of the costs, administrators cannot afford to experiment; they must be sure that the curriculum provided is appropriate and consistent with their own curriculum goals and objectives. Most importantly, teachers need to be well trained to take full advantage of the many technological and pedagogical tools that an ILS provides.

Company	Location
Computer Curriculum Corporation (CCC)	Palo Alto, CA
Computer Systems Research, Inc. (CSR)	Avon, CT
Computer Networking Specialists, Inc. (CNS)	Freeport, NY
Ideal Learning, Inc.	Irving, TX
Jostens Learning Corp.	San Diego, CA
New Century Education Corp.	Piscataway, NJ
Wasatch Education Systems	Salt Lake City, UT
Wicat Systems, Inc.	Orem, UT

Figure 5–5
Integrated Learning Systems Vendors

VIDEODISC TECHNOLOGY

Videodisc technology has proven to be a popular technology for delivering instruction. Unlike digital video (discussed in greater detail in Chapter 6), videodisc is an analog technology and may or may not be used with computer equipment. Because of direct access capabilities, videodisc is a much more advanced technology than videotape and other sequential media. Direct access also allows videodiscs to be integrated with computer technology to provide interactive video instruction.

Thousands of videodisc titles are available for purchase, but most are films and television specials primarily produced for entertainment purposes. The number of titles produced specifically for education is far lower, with probably fewer than a thousand interactive instructional titles. However, the educational videodisc industry continues to grow, and more material will be available in the future.

Videodiscs can be used in instruction with several levels of interactivity. Level I provides no actual computer interactivity but assumes that the person using the videodisc has a hand-held controller for directly accessing desired frames or chapters. The simplest controllers are similar to the remote controls used to change channels on television sets. Some textbook publishers such as Prentice Hall and D. C. Heath provide barcode readers that can control a videodisc player. Frames on a videodisc are selected when the barcode reader is passed over barcodes that have been added to the teacher's edition of a textbook. These barcodes have been pre-linked with certain frames on the videodiscs to provide direct access to relevant video material that might be used as a demonstration during a lesson.

A Level II interactive system is a videodisc player with a built-in internal microprocessor. The microprocessor receives its instructions from programs that have to be added onto the discs. These systems have not been very popular for several reasons. For one thing, the videodiscs and players for a Level II system are quite expensive. In addition, the videodiscs are programmed specifically for a particular manufacturer's disc player, which thereby limits their market considerably.

Level III interactivity combines a videodisc player with a standard microcomputer. The microcomputer controls the player using programs available from several sources but usually supplied by the videodisc vendor. Using authoring languages such as Authorware Professional or ToolBook a teacher can develop programs to control a videodisc presentation.

Figure 5–6 provides a list of some of the major suppliers of educational videodiscs. Subjects include the sciences, social studies, literature, art, and music. Optical Data Corporation, in particular, has produced a highly acclaimed Windows on Science series. In one of the first such actions taken by a state board of education, this series was approved in Texas in 1990 for adoption in the science curriculum for grades 1 through 6. Since then, a number of other states have adopted this series.

In planning to use videodisc technology, a common approach is for a school district to start at Level I and gradually move to Level III interactive materials. This is a prudent approach and one recommended for school districts first beginning to use this technology.

Supplier	Sample Titles
ABC News Interactive	In the Holy Land
	Martin Luther King
CEL Educational Resources	Video Encyclopedia of the 20th Century
Mindscape, Inc.	Adventures in Mathland
National Geographic Society	GTV: A Geographic Perspective on
	American History
Optical Data Corporation	Windows on Science Series
	Space Archives
	Encyclopedia of Animals
VideoDiscovery, Inc.	Bio Sci
	Life Cycles
	The Cell Biology Videodisc
The Voyager Company	National Gallery of Art

Figure 5–6
Suppliers of Videodisc Instructional Software

DATA COMMUNICATIONS

Data communications provides facilities for a wide range of instructional applications. **Local area networks** (LANs) are used to support central computer laboratories, integrated learning systems, and other instructional applications mentioned previously in this chapter. Using a file server, the LAN can provide software programs to all the users on the network, which thereby precludes the need to purchase multiple copies of the same software packages for use on stand-alone machines.

Wide area networks (WANs), in addition to offering all of the services of a LAN, allow access to a variety of instructional applications. The Internet, as will be discussed in greater detail in Chapter 7, has emerged in the 1990s as the epitome of the wide area network, providing access to a wealth of resources throughout the world. However, even before the advent of the Internet, several networks were established to supply specific services directed to teaching and learning that involve the sharing of information not ordinarily available at the local school. Either by way of the Internet or as separate entities, many of these networks are still providing specialized instructional resources and applications that are important to educators.

Probably the most common service provided by national networks is access to databases. Students and teachers can access encyclopedias, research databases, information exchanges, and technical documentation. Although somewhat more expensive than manual materials or local computer-based material, using databases via national on-line services provides the most current and up-to-date information. Educational networks such as GTE Education Services provide several services: ED-LINE for general education news, SpecialNet for databases and information exchanges directed to the special education profession, Youth News Service Newsline for news and journalism activities appropriate for primary and secondary school children, and CNN Newsroom for curriculum and other instructional materials based on daily news reports.

Some of these services combine information access with electronic mail and bulletin boards so that students can exchange information with other students across the country and even internationally. National Geographic's Kids Network, for instance, provides services for students to share information about the environment, weather, geography, current events, and so forth. National Geographic even provides curriculum material so that teachers can develop research projects and share reports with other schools doing similar projects.

Possibly the greatest potential for WAN services involves integrating them with television and distance learning technologies. Learning Link and IntroLink, for instance, are designed to be used in conjunction with PBS television. Curriculum information and classroom activities based on current PBS offerings are provided that can expand the uses of educational television for instruction.

Distance learning, which has been emerging as an important educational technology for several years, is greatly enhanced when a two-way communication link is established that allows for interactivity between students and teachers. Many schools originally used distance learning in a one-way or send mode, delivering instruction from a central site to one or more remote sites. Generally, the television transmission used cable television or microwave transmission. Students would view a television lesson and then mail or use the telephone after the lesson to submit written material or ask questions. By combining the three technologies (television, computer, and telephone) into an integrated communications system, distance learning can now provide almost complete interactivity comparable to an instructor's physical presence in a room with the student. The use of such systems has much appeal in rural school districts that cover large geographic areas and whose budgets are limited. However, the costs, expertise, and planning involved in developing interactive distance learning systems are generally beyond the resources of such districts.

State education departments in states like Minnesota, Wisconsin, Alaska, Kentucky, and Iowa have taken the lead in developing distance learning facilities for a number of school districts. Most state education departments, if they have not already done so, are planning to provide distance learning facilities for use by local school districts in the near future.

CURRICULUM INTEGRATION AND PLANNING

Before this chapter on instructional computing applications concludes, some comments on curriculum integration and planning are important. Curriculum integration is a simple concept but is proving difficult to realize with instructional computer applications. Integrating computer tools into the classroom is conceptually similar to integrating other tools such as chalkboards, overhead projectors, or paints and crayons. Teachers and students have few problems using these other, more familiar tools in teaching and learning. Furthermore, these tools have limited application, and mastering them is an easy task.

Microcomputers, on the other hand, are more sophisticated, expensive tools, and mastering them is a more complex and ongoing undertaking. Integrating microcomputers into the curriculum starts with making sure that teachers and students have developed a basic understanding and knowledge of computer use. Once this basic understanding has been achieved, mastery involves developing a knowledge base of the many different ways computers can be used. Teachers need to feel comfortable using computers and developing a repertoire of instructional applications. Integrating technology into the curriculum is therefore closely tied to staff development, which along with hardware, software, facilities, and finances compose the critical components of any technology-based plan.

Integrating instructional applications is not something that can be accomplished overnight. "Quick fixes" in implementing technology usually have very little lasting impact and frequently only delay for another day serious planning activities. Administrators should not be thinking about quick fixes but instead should be evaluating whatever instructional technology is already occurring in their schools and building on that which works.

As mentioned in Chapter 2, planning requires the involvement of those who possess expertise and who ultimately may be responsible for implementing new applications. The fulcrum for curriculum integration and planning instructional applications is the teaching staff. The teachers are critical for identifying applications and evaluating software, hardware, and staff development needs. Administrators must work with teachers to provide leadership in these activities, assuring that resources are available for training, facilities, and staffing as well as for hardware and software.

Finally, because of the many applications and alternatives available, teachers and administrators need to develop a process in which priorities can be established and plans developed for the long term. No school district in the country, even with the best tax base, the most competent teachers, and most enlightened administrators, can afford to do everything it might wish to do; however, every school district can and does do something well. This should be kept in mind when planning for instructional technology.

CASE STUDY
Place: Silicon City   Year: 1994

Silicon City, an urban school district on the West Coast, has an enrollment of 28,000 students in 41 schools. The population has been increasing significantly during the past 10 years, particularly with students needing bilingual education. The voters approved a bond issue in 1989 to build a new high school. As part of the bond issue, $2,900,000 was budgeted for purchasing new instructional equipment, of which $1,500,000 will be used district-wide for computing and newer educational technologies.

A district-wide planning committee was established in 1981 with a standing Technology Subcommittee. This subcommittee has been very effective in securing funds and helping the district implement technology in the schools. Each school has one or more centralized computer laboratories and a building coordinator. A major goal of the district has been to integrate technology into the regular classrooms and not to provide it only in centralized computer laboratories.

The district has a student/microcomputer ratio of 12.5 to 1. Most of the applications use microcomputers, either as stand-alone or networked in LANs. The district has also begun to purchase videodisc equipment. In addition to acquiring basic computer hardware and software for the new high school comparable to that which exists in the other high schools in the district, the Technology Subcommittee would like to use a portion of the instructional equipment budget to make a major thrust into newer technologies that might benefit the entire district. As part of the planning process last year, the Technology Subcommittee asked a group of administrators, teachers, and building computer coordinators to develop proposals to help in this regard.

The subcommittee was provided with three proposals, all of which would cost approximately $750,000 to $1,000,000 to implement initially. They were as follows:

Proposal 1: Establish data communications in the classrooms. This would allow each school to provide telephone access in each classroom. At least one microcomputer in each classroom would also be equipped with a modem and software for tying into the Internet and other national networks. A variety of possible instructional applications were identified, such as accessing databases, teaching weather, monitoring seismographic data, using CNN curriculum materials for teaching current events, and establishing electronic pen pals in Latin America.

Proposal 2: Acquire interactive video equipment. This proposal would provide funds so that each school could be equipped with several large monitors, videodisc players, and a video library appropriate to each school's curriculum. It would build on the video equipment and materials that some of the schools have recently been purchasing. This proposal has been very much supported by the science and social studies departments, which would like to acquire programs such as Optical Data Corporation's Windows on Science and GTV's Geographic Perspective of American History.

Proposal 3: Develop an integrated learning system to teach basic skills. This proposal would use the funds to establish a district-wide ILS. Each school could tie into the system via the computer laboratories at all of the schools. Although the ILS could be used for several instructional applications, it would be used initially for basic skills and bilingual education. One West Coast–based ILS vendor indicated great interest in working with the school district to establish a model for using its products and offered very attractive pricing.

The subcommittee, before it proceeds with making a recommendation to the Planning Committee, has asked the assistant superintendent for curriculum for her recommendation. It is unlikely that the district could afford to fund more than one of these proposals over the next three years.

Assuming that you are the assistant superintendent, analyze the preceding proposals. What observations can you make regarding the appropriateness of the three proposals from technological, pedagogical, and programmatic perspectives? Although you have only been provided with a summary of each proposal, what additional information on each proposal would you consider critical to making a recommendation? Finally, given the information provided and assuming you had to support one proposal, which would you recommend? Why?

SUMMARY

This chapter reviews the development and issues surrounding instructional computing. Almost all school districts have made some investment in instructional technology, with varying degrees of success. According to numerous sources, every indication is that this investment will only increase in the future.

This chapter also attempts to provide administrators with a balanced picture of instructional applications: their problems, benefits, and potential. It is evident that with the emergence of the microcomputer in the 1980s as a fundamental tool in all aspects of businesses, professions, and everyday living, schools throughout the country are attempting to ensure that their students are prepared to use this technology.

The research on instructional computing is conflicting. Some researchers conclude that it is beneficial and improves academic achievement, whereas others dispute these claims. Much of the recent literature also identifies implementation problems such as the unavailability of hardware, the lack of trained staff, and limited resources as the root of many problems. Some of these issues are gradually being resolved. In the 1990s, schools are entering a new beginning in the use of instructional technology mainly because they have made their first investment, have had their first successes and failures, and are now able to plan more properly for the future.

Looking at the evolution of instructional computing applications, much of the work done in the 1950s and 1960s is not relevant because of the radical changes that have occurred in the technology. Several exceptions, though, including the pioneering efforts of Suppes, Kemeny, and Papert, have continued to evolve, and the fruits of their labor can be seen in many schools today.

Instructional computer applications have grown, with tens of thousands of software and media products on the market. Classifying and developing a framework for understanding the various applications is prone to a good deal of overlap. Robert Taylor's "tutor, tool, tutee" approach is recommended. It classifies a computer application as a tutor (computer teaching the student), a tool (computer used as an aid for teaching and learning), or a tutee (student teaching the computer). Major applications within each of these classifications have been described here.

Computer technology is also merging with other technologies, namely video and communications, to create a variety of new instructional applications. These applications are far more exciting and pedagogically more stimulating than anything that the individual technologies alone provided in the past. The potential of these merged technologies is very great and will be more evident as they improve and as educators learn how to use them.

Key Concepts and Questions

1. Schools are investing significant resources in instructional technology.

   How have the schools benefited from this investment to date?

2. Some educators have observed that the computer "revolution" of the 1980s is stalled or "on hold."

   Do you agree with this observation? If so, why? If you do not agree, why are some educators stating otherwise?

3. Instructional technology has been evolving since the 1950s and 1960s. Some computer educators consider that much of the early work has very little application in today's schools.

   Do you agree with this? If so, why? If you do not agree, provide examples of early work in instructional technology that are commonly used in today's schools.

4. In implementing instructional technology, administrators may have several objectives.

   What are some of these objectives? What do you consider the most important objective for using technology in the classroom?

5. Developing a classification system for instructional technology has proven to be an elusive endeavor.

   Why? Are you comfortable with the "tutor, tool, tutee" classification developed by Robert Taylor? Explain.

Which of the three broad types of instructional computer applications do you consider to be the most beneficial for students? Might your opinion change for different age groups?

6. Integrated learning systems are probably the most complete instructional computer applications available.

   If this is so, why have most schools not acquired them? Do you see any change in their acquisition in the near future? Explain.

7. Computer technology is gradually merging with video and communications technologies to provide instructional applications.

   Give examples and discuss the potential of the following: (a) computer and video; (b) computer and communications; and (c) computer, video, and communications.

8. Integrating technology into the curriculum is proving to be a major problem in many school districts.

   Why? How do you see this problem being resolved?

9. Implementing technology in the classroom requires careful planning.

   What are some of the implementation issues common to most schools? Has there been very much progress in addressing these issues? Give examples.

Suggested Activities

1. Examine the types of instructional computer applications that exist in a (or your) school. Classify them according to the "tutor, tool, tutee" system described in this chapter. Evaluate whether any patterns develop according to grade level, subject, or year of acquisition.

2. If you are not familiar with instructional software, consider examining several instructional software packages that might exist in a (or your) school. Try to select a variety (drill and practice, simulations, instructional games) of programs. Take notes on your impressions of these programs regarding their educational value.

References

Becker, H. J. (1994). *Analysis and trends of school use of new information technologies*. Irvine: Department of Education, University of California.

Brandt, R. (1994). Overview, helping professional dreams come through. *Educational Leadership, 51*(7), 3.

Bullough, R. V., & Beatty, L. F. (1991). *Classroom applications of microcomputers*. Upper Saddle River, NJ: Merrill/Prentice Hall.

Clark, R. (1983). Reconsidering research on learning from media. *Review of Educational Research, 53*(4), 445–459.

———. (1985). Evidence for confounding in computer-based instruction studies. *Educational Communications and Technology Journal, 33*(4), 249–262.

———. (1989). Current progress and future directions for research in instructional technology. *Educational Technology Research and Development, 37*(1), 57–66.

Kulik, J. A. (1984). Evaluating the effects of teaching with computers. In G. Campbell & G. Fein (Eds.), *Microcomputers in early education*. Reston, VA: Reston.

Kulik, J. A., Bangert, R., & Williams, G. (1983). Effects of computer-based teaching on secondary students. *Journal of Educational Psychology, 75*(1), 19–26.

Kulik, J. A., Kulik, C., & Bangert-Downs, R. (1984). Effectiveness of computer-based education in elementary schools. *Computers in Human Behavior, 1*(1), 59–74.

Kulik, J. A., Kulik, C., & Cohen, P. (1980). Effectiveness of computer-based college teaching: A meta-analysis of findings. *Review of Educational Research, 2*(2), 525–544.

Kulik, J. A., Kulik, C., & Schwab, B. (1986). The effectiveness of computer-based adult education: A meta-analysis. *Journal of Educational Computing, 2*(2), 235–252.

Linn, M. C. (1985). The cognitive consequences of programming instruction in classrooms. *Educational Researcher, 14*(5), 14–29.

Lockard, J. (1992). *Instructional software*. Dubuque, IA: Brown.

Luehrmann, A. (1980). Should the computer teach the student, or vice-versa? In R. Taylor (Ed.), *The computer in the school: Tutor, tool, tutee* (pp. 127–158). New York: Teachers College Press.

Merrill, P., Tolman, M., Christensen, L., Hammons, K., Vincent, B., & Reynolds, P. (1992). *Computers in education*. Upper Saddle River, NJ: Prentice Hall.

Nicklin, J. L. (1992). Teachers' use of computers stressed by education colleges. *Chronicle of Higher Education, 38*(43), A15–A17.

O'Neill, J. (1990). Computer 'revolution' on hold. *ASCD Update, 32*(9), 1, 3–4.

Papert, S. (1980). *Mindstorms: Children, computers, and powerful ideas*. New York: Basic Books.

———. (1987). Computer criticism vs. technocentric thinking. *Educational Researcher, 16*(1), 22–30.

Pea, R. D. (1987). The aims of software criticism: Reply to Professor Papert. *Educational Researcher, 16*(5), 4–8.

Picciano, A. G. (1991). Computers, city and suburb: A study of New York City and Westchester County public schools. *Urban Review, 23*(3), 93–109.

Quality Education Data. (1996). *Education market guide and mailing list catalogue*. Boulder, CO: Author.

Robyler, M. D., Castine, W. H., & King, F. J. (1988). Assessing the impact of computer-based instruction. *Computers in the Schools, 5*(1), 1–149.

Sheingold, K., & Hadley, M. (1990). *Accomplished teachers Integrating computers into classroom practice*. New York: Bank Street College of Education, Center for Technology in Education.

Sheingold, K., Kane, J. H., & Endreweit, M. E. (1983). Microcomputer use in the schools: Developing a research agenda. *Harvard Educational Review, 53*(4), 412–432.

Simonson, M. R., & Thompson, A. D. (1994). *Educational computing foundations*. Upper Saddle River, NJ: Prentice Hall.

Taylor, R. P. (Ed.). (1980). *The computer in the school: Tutor, tool, tutee*. New York: Teachers College Press.

Thompson, A, D., Simonson, M. R., & C. P. Hargrave, (1992). *Educational technology: A review of the research*. Washington, DC: Association for Educational Communications and Technology.

Turner, S., & Land, M. (1988). *Tools for schools: Applications software for the classroom*. Belmont, CA: Wadsworth.

U.S. Congress, Office of Technology Assessment. (1995). *Teachers and technology: Making the connection* (Report No. OTA-EHR-616). Washington, DC: U.S. Government Printing Office.

———. (1988). *Power on! New tools for teaching and learning* (Report No. OTA-SET-379). Washington, DC: U.S. Government Printing Office.

Vockell, E., & van Deusen, R. M. (1989). *The computer and higher-order thinking skills*. Watsonville, CA: Mitchell.

6

Multimedia in Education

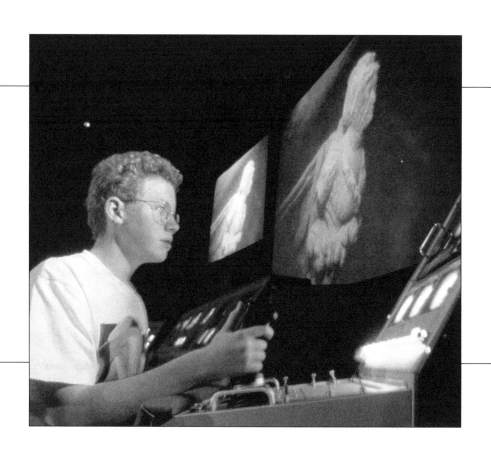

R esponding in a recent interview to a question about a leading soprano's singing and acting talents, James Levine, the artistic director of the Metropolitan Opera in New York City, commented that good music does not need words. His point was that music alone was enough to communicate emotion and beauty between those with talent and those with the ability to appreciate it. However, when a Verdi melody is combined with words, the result is an aria that touches and appeals to many more people who can better appreciate the melody within the context of a story or event. Add actors in colorful dress, a set depicting a quaint mountain village, some graceful dancers, and the result is opera that appeals and communicates to the world.

The expansion of a libretto into an aria and an aria into an opera is an appropriate metaphor for introducing the subject of multimedia as applied to teaching and learning. Indeed, words conveyed by writing and reading alone may not be sufficient to reach all students. Combining words with images, sounds, and movement can extend the teaching/learning process and help communicate a lesson to many more students.

MULTIMEDIA DEFINED

The term **multimedia** refers to many types of communication processes, delivery systems, and events. It is a new buzz word that is used in connection with entertainment, advertisement, museum exhibitions, theme parks, video games, and dozens of other areas of human endeavor. *Multimedia* adds a certain technological "chic" that conjures up images of color, movement, dazzling special effects, and provocative sounds. Because of the variety of ways in which the word has been used, multimedia has come to mean different things to different people.

Generically multimedia can be defined as any combination of two or more media such as sound, images, text, animation, and video. When used with computer technology, multimedia refers to a variety of applications that combine media and that utilize CD-ROM, video, audio, and other media equipment.

In addition to this basic definition, multimedia when used with computer equipment also implies interactive navigational or hypermedia capabilities that can be invoked and controlled by the user. **Hypermedia** is the integration of sights, sounds, graphics, video, and other media into an associative or linked system of information storage and retrieval. It is an extension of the concept of **hypertext**, which links text information in an associative system. Ted Nelson, an engineer, coined the term *hypertext* in 1965 to describe computer-based document retrieval systems that could be used in a nonlinear fashion as opposed to the traditional linear format of other document retrieval systems such as books and microfilm.

Hypermedia allows users to navigate in a nonlinear manner from one topic to another by the use of information linkages built into the associative system. These linkages are usually presented in the form of active screen areas or buttons that when clicked on by a mouse, transfer or link the user to some other material. Examples of these linkage techniques are found in electronic encyclopedias such as Microsoft's Encarta and Grolier's Multimedia Encyclopedia.

For educational technology purposes, then, multimedia refers to computer-based systems that use associative linkages to allow users to navigate and retrieve information stored in a combination of text, sounds, graphics, video, and other forms of media.

MULTIMEDIA FOR MULTIPLE INTELLIGENCES (MI)

For educators, multimedia may seem nothing more than a higher-technological use of sounds and sights to stimulate instruction. Educators have been using slide projection, film, and videotape for decades to enhance student interest in a subject. And recently videodisc equipment has become popular as an audiovisual aide in the classroom. However, in addition to being a point on the media continuum, multimedia also relates to theories of brain functioning and learning theory, especially those that relate learning to sensory stimulation and multiple intelligences (Armstrong, 1994, p. 159).

Since the early 1980s, Howard Gardner, a psychologist at Harvard, has been popularizing a theory of "multiple intelligences" (see Figure 6–1) among educators. He posits that intelligence has been too narrowly defined; it is not a singular entity that can be measured by standard intelligence tests but rather is composed of multiple entities. Gardner (1983) identifies seven basic or multiple intelligences that all humans possess to some degree or another:

- *Linguistic intelligence*—the capacity to use words effectively either orally or in writing (e.g., writers, poets, orators)
- *Logical-mathematical intelligence*—the capacity to use numbers effectively and to reason well (e.g., mathematicians, accountants, computer programmers)
- *Spatial intelligence*—the capacity to perceive the visual-spatial world accurately. It includes the capacity to visualize and represent graphically visual and spatial ideas (e.g., architects, designers, artists).
- *Bodily-kinesthetic intelligence*—the capacity to use one's body to express ideas and feelings and the facility to use one's hands (e.g., athletes, dancers, craftspeople)
- *Musical intelligence*—the capacity to perceive, discriminate, and express musical forms (e.g., musician, composer, singer)
- *Interpersonal intelligence*—the capacity to perceive and make distinctions in the moods and feelings of other people (e.g., counselor, social worker)
- *Intrapersonal intelligence*—the capacity to know one's strengths and limitations and to act according to this knowledge (e.g. psychotherapist, religious leader)

Gardner's theory has been questioned and debated, particularly whether he has really expanded the concept of intelligence(s) or simply extended the concept of intelligence to long recognized talents or aptitudes. Regardless, his theory makes a good case for using multimedia and other multisensory techniques in teaching and learning. Applied to instruction, his theory supports a concern that American education at all levels (primary, secondary, higher) is too linguistically oriented. Teacher

Intelligence	Definition	Learning Needs
Linguistic	Capacity to use words effectively	Books, writing, discussion, debate
Logical-mathematical	Capacity to use numbers effectively	Manipulatives, science puzzles
Spatial	Capacity to perceive the visual-spatial world accurately	Art, video, slides, building blocks
Bodily-kinesthetic	Capacity to use one's body to express ideas	Movement, dance, drama, sports, hands-on learning
Musical	Capacity to perceive and express musical forms	Song, instrumental music, background music
Interpersonal	Capacity to perceive the moods and feelings of others	Group activities, social gatherings
Intrapersonal	Capacity to know oneself	Self-paced learning, quiet time

Figure 6–1
Theory of Multiple Intelligences

talks, students listen; teacher writes, students read; students write, teacher reads; and so forth. If we accept Gardner's theory, or even if we simply accept that people have different talents, aptitudes, or modalities for learning similar to the multiple intelligences, then should we not be teaching in a way that can tap into these multiple intelligences instead of relying on one of them while neglecting the others?

This concept has generated an extensive debate that cannot be treated fairly here. Readers interested in pursuing this topic are encouraged to read Gardner's two primary books on the topic, *Frames of Mind: The Theory of Multiple Intelligences* (1983) and *Multiple Intelligences: The Theory in Practice* (1993). An excellent review of Gardner's theory can also be found in Thomas Armstrong's (1994) *Multiple Intelligences in the Classroom*. The Association for Supervision and Curriculum Development (ASCD) also has provided coverage to Gardner's ideas in its main publication *Educational Leadership* and maintains a Teaching for Multiple Intelligences network.

The application of the multiple intelligences theory to multimedia and other computer technologies is apparent. If materials can be developed and used that extend instruction beyond the linguistic intelligence and make greater use of visual stimulation, sounds and music, logic and mathematics, and so forth, then perhaps a more effective teaching and learning process could evolve. The literature includes many examples of multimedia technology as an outgrowth of Gardner's theory. David Thornburg (1989), who has been involved in designing provocative educational technology such as the Muppet Learning Keys and the Koala Pad, bases much of his application designs on MI theory. Thomas Armstrong (1994) also advocates using multimedia for implementing MI theory in the classroom. Researchers at the Center for Media and Learning at Hunter College likewise have developed interactive video models for teaching history based on MI and modalities of learning (Picciano, 1993).

MULTIMEDIA LITERACY

Fred Hofstetter (1994), professor and director of the Instructional Technology center at the University of Delaware, raised this question for educators: "Is multimedia the next literacy?" It is a serious question not only for the future, as Hofstetter implied, but for the present as well.

The question concerns the manner in which our society receives its information. Essentially, since the advent of television (a multimedia technology in its own right) in the 1940s, Americans have been receiving ever-increasing amounts of their information from the moving images and sounds emanating from their TV sets. In 1991, most Americans did not read about the Gulf War in the Middle East in the morning paper; they saw it on TV in real time. Scud missiles firing, tanks rolling, soldiers running with guns, and reporters ducking for cover were flashed on television sets all over the world by the Cable News Network (CNN). In 1995, the O. J. Simpson "trial of the century" was not read about, either; it was fully covered on a daily basis by several of the major networks. People watched in real time or set their videocassette recorders (VCRs) to tape portions of the trial and watched it at night. For those without VCRs, several stations devoted as much as an hour each night recapping the trial's daily events.

Without question, for the average American, television has evolved into the most powerful information delivery mechanism ever, supplanting newspapers, magazines, and other material meant to be read for this purpose. On the other hand, television can generate so much interest in a subject that viewers actually seek out additional reading. Shelby Foote, playwright and author of a trilogy on the Civil War, was an adviser for and appeared in the award-winning PBS documentary, *The Civil War,* which was viewed by more than 40 million people. In an interview, he commented that in the 15 years before the PBS broadcast, his trilogy sold about 30,000 copies. In the first 6 months after the broadcast, his trilogy sold more than 100,000 copies (Toplin, 1996).

For young people, not only the television but other multimedia technologies have become a fact of their daily lives. Where a generation or two ago music was essentially heard on the radio, the phonograph, or the cassette player, it is now heard and seen on MTV, VH-1, and other cable TV channels. Michael Jackson, Madonna, and other pop singers are not simply heard but are seen in colorful costumes and designer clothes, "moonwalking," dancing, and acting while provocative still and moving images are displayed in the background. Highly sophisticated morphing technology is routinely used in these music videos and motion pictures, too, to dazzle and capture the viewers' imaginations. These displays are dominating how young people receive information and are creating a new generation that increasingly expects and responds to multisensory delivery systems. Competing with such stimulating visual and audio presentations is becoming a challenge for educators.

This challenge has three important components. First, if the American people, especially the younger ones, are becoming a multimedia-dependent society, should schools take advantage of the technology and use it in delivering instruction? Could it be that today's students, who do not read as well and are not as literate in the traditional sense as past generations, are developing a multimedia literacy? If this is the case, educators should begin to capitalize on the state of affairs by channeling their students' multimedia literacy into educational activities. For instance, *Roots* was America's most-watched television special when it appeared in 1977, prompting numerous classroom discussions of slavery and race relations.

The second component of the educator's challenge is more complicated and involves the ability of young people to discern what is real and what is fake. American society has begun to ask, "What is fact and what is fiction?" For instance, are the events depicted in docudramas true or false? Some of them are true and some are false. How do viewers especially young people discern the truth from the false? Oliver Stone's movie *J.F.K.* (1993) is a case in point. Parts were footage or images of the actual assassination of John F. Kennedy and related events. Other images were enactments of a script written by Hollywood fiction writers. However, given the technical superiority of the movie and its extensive treatment of the topic, many viewers, especially those born after the events in 1963, came to accept this movie's version as fact. American educators must consider teaching how media, particularly multimedia, can be manipulated to display events so that fiction appears to be fact.

In addition to television and film, which are nondigital and essentially passive technologies that do not require computer interfaces, young people today are the biggest consumers of video games such as Nintendo, Sega, and others provided on CD-ROMs. These games are highly sophisticated, interactive multimedia computer systems that take advantage of the latest digital technologies to deliver stimulating activities. Go into a neighborhood computer software store and look at the product displays; there will be sections for business software, educational software, and games. Invariably, the sections for games are generally two to three times larger than the others. Young people, especially males, are not only seeing and hearing multimedia presentations but also actually manipulating and interacting with them to create and control outcomes. The third challenge for educators is to develop and provide beneficial content that moves multimedia beyond the action game genre.

Hofstetter, quoted at the beginning of this section, raised the issue of multimedia literacy as a requirement for basic functioning in the evolving American society. He provided examples of how everyday existence will depend on multimedia delivery systems in the form of home shopping, electronic publishing, banking, worldwide communications systems, telecommuting or working from home, and so forth. The future society that Hofstetter envisioned as needing to be multimedia literate is already here for many of the young people in our primary and secondary schools. Surely multimedia will dominate the world in which they will function as adults.

MULTIMEDIA SYSTEMS

In planning for multimedia applications, educators will need to consider specialized hardware and software components. The following sections provide information on some of the technical requirements for developing and implementing multimedia applications.

Basic Hardware Requirements for Multimedia

The hardware requirements for a multimedia microcomputer system are dynamic and rapidly evolving. In addition to a basic computer system with the standard input devices, central processor, and output devices, multimedia systems require additional media hardware such as CD-ROMs, sound boards (or cards), and video boards. Furthermore, because of the tremendous amount of digital storage required for the simplest multimedia presentations, higher-speed central processors and more extensive secondary storage (hard disk) are needed for most applications.

To illustrate how rapidly the hardware requirements for multimedia hardware systems are changing, in 1995 the *minimum* multimedia requirements for a DOS/Windows PC or MPC were as follows:

Processor: 25 MHz with 4-MB RAM (8 MB recommended)
Secondary storage: 160- to 240-MB hard disk
Double-speed CD-ROM
16-bit sound board
Video board
Speakers

One year later in 1996, in addition to the sound boards, video boards, and speakers, the *minimum* MPC hardware system required twice the processor speed and storage capacities:

Processor: 50 MHz with 8-MB RAM (16 MB recommended)
Secondary storage: 240- to 480-MB hard disk
Triple-speed CD-ROM

High-end microcomputers meeting or exceeding these requirements are packaged as "multimedia machines" by several manufacturers including Apple, IBM, and Compaq.

Sound and Video Hardware

Sound and video hardware differentiate multimedia from other computer systems. Sound boards that provide audio/sound capabilities to computers such as those from Creative Labs, Inc. (Sound Blaster boards), Ad Lib Multimedia, Inc., and Tandberg Educational, Inc., are readily available in hardware catalogs and computer stores. Likewise, video boards with full-motion video capabilities such as ones from Creative Labs (Video Blaster boards) and Orchid Technologies (Videola boards) are also becoming commonplace.

When acquiring sound and video hardware, educators should be aware of their technical features and capabilities. In evaluating sound features, CD (regular compact disk) audio quality has become the standard. To attain this standard, two features must be considered:

Bit capacity: The greater the bit capacity, the better (speed and sound quality) the board. For CD quality, minimally a 16-bit sound board is needed.

Sampling rate: The sampling rate as measured in kilohertz (KHz) is the rate at which sound can be recorded and played back. The higher the sampling rate, the better the sound quality. The CD standard requires a 44-KHz rate or higher.

Depending on an application's requirements, other sound features to be considered include frequency modulation, wavetable synthesis capability, and MIDI (musical instrument digital interface) compatibility.

Full-motion video as established by the video and film industries is now the standard for video boards. To meet this standard, the following features must be considered:

Image resolution   The clarity of detail that a video board can store for an individual image or frame. The resolution of video boards ranges from a minimum of 40 × 30 pixels to more than 1,024 × 678 pixels. The higher the resolution, the better the quality of the image. For full-motion video, the minimum resolution is 640 × 480 pixels.

Color capacity   The number of colors a video board can store in each pixel. Sixteen bits per pixel will store 32,000 to 64,000 different colors, which is more than sufficient for full-motion video. At the time of this writing, 24 and 32 bit per pixel video boards were being developed that will be capable of storing millions of colors.

Frame rate   The number of frames or images per second a board can record or playback. Thirty frames per second is the full-motion standard. Slower rated boards will produce video that appears as slow motion.

Depending on the applications being considered, other factors in evaluating video boards include compression formats, audio capture capabilities, video capture, and editing and playback capabilities.

An in-depth knowledge of the specifications described here is essential, particularly if users are interested in developing their own multimedia applications. In all likelihood, multimedia software packages will be acquired rather than developed, in which case users simply need to be generally familiar with the technical requirements of the packages. Packaged multimedia programs will be discussed later in this chapter.

Specialized Multimedia Hardware

In addition to the basic hardware described earlier, development of multimedia applications may also require specialized equipment for video and image capturing, recording, and playback. A brief review of this equipment is appropriate for furthering one's understanding of multimedia applications.

Images, whether still or moving, are a fundamental feature of multimedia applications. Images can be in digital format and ready for processing by a computer, or they can be in analog format. Computer-generated graphics, animations, and digitized photographs are examples of images in digital format. Film, videotape, and videodisc are examples of images in nondigital or analog format. While computer equipment is available to handle either format, educational multimedia development is significantly facilitated when all image handling is done in digital format.

Optical scanners have been available for many years to convert photographs and hard-copy documents into digital images. This equipment continues to become more reliable, easier to use, and less expensive, and it is ideal for simple still-image digitization. Flatbed and hand-held scanners are inexpensive and simple enough to be used by students. For individuals who use 35-millimeter cameras and would like high-quality digital images, film developers such as Kodak will convert 35-millimeter film into digital format for just a little more than the cost for normal film processing. Computer software such as Kodak's Photo-CD is needed to retrieve the images, which generally are provided on a CD-ROM. More recently, digital cameras have become available from major manufacturers such as Kodak, Canon, and Sony. They take the photographs, store them in digital format, and import them directly to a computer for subsequent processing. Once captured in digital format, photographs can be modified, edited, or enhanced through software. Though more expensive than regular cameras, the prices for digital cameras continue to come down as more manufacturers enter this market and increase competition.

For video used in multimedia projects, camcorders, videotape, and videodisc are the major input media. For readers unfamiliar with digital and analog video technologies, a review is provided in Appendix A. The material there is especially helpful for understanding the differences between videotape and videodisc technologies. Video boards (described earlier) are necessary computer components for using any type of video. Hardware and software have recently become available that allow camcorders to connect directly to a computer's video board and subsequently convert the video into digital format. Most of this technology will accept camcorder input from the major manufacturers such as Canon, Sony, and Toshiba. Video cassette recorders and videodisc players can likewise be connected to a computer's video board for subsequent conversion to digital format.

A videodisc player can be controlled by a computer to play video in its original analog format. This technique is desirable if high-quality video is required or if, because of copyright restrictions, a user is not allowed to make a copy of the video material. Converting analog video into digital format is considered making a copy and is thus subject to copyright restrictions. For these reasons, analog videodiscs will continue to be an important technology for multimedia production, although the computer industry is moving toward all-digital formats for image and video handling.

The use of audio and sound equipment for multimedia projects are becoming commonplace in schools and media centers. The most common devices are microphones for input and speakers for output that connect directly to a sound board, as described previously. The microphones and speakers used for multimedia are the same as those used with noncomputer equipment. Prices and quality range broadly for this equipment, which is available in both computer and general electronics stores. For more sophisticated sound input, such as that which might be required for musical instruments, MIDI equipment is available that will connect musical instruments and synthesizers to computers. MIDI equipment can be used to create, record, and play back music. Common in the professional music business for many years, MIDI equipment to control synthesizers and instruments is also growing in popularity in education. Companies that provide MIDI equipment include Sony, Yamaha, and Roland, Inc.

MULTIMEDIA SOFTWARE

Authoring

Authoring languages, as discussed in Chapter 5, are especially popular for doing multimedia applications. Easier to use than traditional programming languages, authoring has become the software of choice for teachers and students developing multimedia. Many authoring languages are now available that allow users to integrate text, images, digital and analog video, sound, and so forth, merely by selecting screen objects such as buttons, fields, and hotwords with the click of a mouse. Authoring languages such as HyperCard, HyperStudio, ToolBook, Linkway, and Authorware Professional are being used by more educators for instructional applications. Although generally platform-specific (i.e., either able to run on a Macintosh or DOS/Windows machine), several companies such as Macromedia (Authorware Professional), and Astound (formerly Gold Disk) Inc. (ASTOUND) have begun to market programs that are cross-platform, with versions available for both Macintosh and DOS/Windows.

In acquiring authoring languages, ease of use should be of paramount importance, as will be discussed further in Chapter 9. Ease of use is relative to the skills and talents of the users, and while designed for the nontechnical individual, a good deal of training and practice is necessary for the average teacher to use this software effectively. However, these packages are easy enough to use so that even students can become proficient in developing multimedia applications. One of the most popular student assignments is to take the traditional composition or essay and make it into a multimedia project that incorporates sights and sounds with the text material. Word-processing and desktop publishing software such as The Print Shop and The Newsroom incorporate pictures and graphics into their programs so that even primary school children are capable of expanding the traditional writing assignment into something beyond simple text.

Image, Video, and Sound Editing

In addition to preparing multimedia presentations using authoring languages, image, video and sound editing software is being used to assist in acquiring and editing visual and audio materials for inclusion into multimedia projects.

Simple image editing such as sizing and cropping a digital photograph is easily accomplished with a wide range of software products such as Adobe's Photoshop, Aldus's PhotoStyler, and Kodak's Photo-CD. Increasingly, simple image editing is being directly incorporated into authoring and other multimedia software packages.

More sophisticated image-editing software packages such as North Coast Software's Photomorph are available that allow users to convert one image into other images using a variety of transitions such as pinpoint size reduction or expansion, color, and special effects. Photomorph can also be used in creating effects on digital video files.

For video projects, video-capturing and -editing software packages such as Adobe Premiere are needed. **Video capturing** is the term used for converting analog video as it exists on a videotape or videodisc into a digital video file. A video board (described earlier) is necessary to accomplish video capturing. Once captured into a digital file, the video material can be edited for subsequent multimedia projects. Likewise, sound-capturing software packages such as Creative Labs' Sound Blaster Pro are available that allow users to capture sound either through a microphone or a MIDI device and save it as a digital file. The digital file is usually stored in a wave format that can be subsequently edited to reduce or expand portions of waves and add echo, bass, and other sound effects.

Digital Animation

Digital animation as a field has grown considerably in the 1990s. No longer are simple movements of a single figure in some "jerky" motion the norm. Digital animation packages have become sophisticated enough to provide animations to multiple objects on a screen, special effects such as three-dimensional images, and high-color resolution approaching photograph quality. Because the animation is all digital, computer processing is simplified and faster. Digital animation is also an important area for future development as major international industries in film, music video, television advertising, and video games continue to invest significant capital and human resources in advancing and perfecting digital animation technology. Disney's popular *Toy Story* (1995) was one of the first full-length feature films to incorporate advanced digital animation techniques. Autodesk's Animator Pro, Adobe's Dimensions/3D, and Macromedia's Swivel 3D Professional are examples of high-level animation packages that can be found in schools today.

MULTIMEDIA FOR TEACHING AND LEARNING

In planning and implementing multimedia applications in schools, a distinction should be made between using this technology for teaching versus learning. For teaching, the emphasis is placed on the presentation of lessons, with the teacher as the center of the lesson delivery and the use of equipment. For learning, the emphasis is on the use of multimedia by students either for discovering learning, accessing information, or developing projects. For the latter, a good deal more hardware and software needs to be acquired, and an investment must be made in class time to train students to use the technology. The possibilities are endless and limited only by the teacher's imagination and creativity. Several common educational uses of multimedia are described here.

Table 6–1
Presentation Multimedia Software Packages

Company	Product
Adobe Systems	Aldus Persuasion
Asymetrix, Inc.	Compel
Astound, Inc. (formerly Gold Disk)	ASTOUND
Lotus Development	Freelance Graphics
Macromedia	Action
Microsoft	PowerPoint
Multimedia Design	mPower
Q/Media	Q/Media
Software Publishing	Harvard Graphics
WordPerfect	WordPerfect Presentation

For teaching applications, many software packages (see Table 6–1) are available that provide templates or ready-to-use models for doing multimedia presentations. Teachers with a basic understanding of computers can learn presentation software relatively quickly given some support by a computer coordinator or other expert. Once the software is mastered, a 50-minute multimedia lesson incorporating images, sound, animation, or video into a text outline can be completed in 1 or 2 hours. Usually, the greatest effort in developing a multimedia presentation is spent in locating appropriate images, sounds, or video. In planning presentations, a large monitor or overhead projection system is necessary so that a class can easily see the presentation.

Teachers may also wish to develop their own custom multimedia programs for use by students in a discovery learning or other pedagogical mode. Authoring languages (see Table 6–2) such HyperCard, Authorware Professional, and ToolBook are ideal for these applications. Teachers will have to devote considerable time to learning these software packages, and although easier to use than other instructional programming languages, they will test the technical abilities and skills of the average teacher. Most likely, custom-designed and developed multimedia programs will require a team effort on the part of teachers and technical support staff. The time required to develop a cus-

Table 6–2
Authoring Software Packages

Company	Product
Apple	HyperCard/HyperStudio
Asymetrix, Inc	ToolBook
Astound, Inc.	Animation Works Interactive
IBM	Linkway
IBM	Storyboard Live
InterSystem Concepts	Summit Authoring System
Macromedia	Authorware Professional
Microsoft	Multimedia Software Development Kit
The Voyager Company	Expanded Book Toolkit
Videodiscovery, Inc.	MediaMax

tom multimedia program will depend on a number of factors, including the scope of the project, whether incorporating digital or analog video, and the availability of video. Such projects usually require several months, if not more, of design and development.

Doing a customized multimedia project should be carefully considered, with serious planning devoted to training, design of the project, and the availability of media. This is especially true if part of the work involves doing video production. Even with the latest editing hardware and software, 30 minutes of quality video can require weeks and weeks of scripting, shooting, and editing. Readers interested in designing such a project are encouraged to refer to Kemp and Smellie's (1989) *Planning, Producing, and Using Instructional Media* or Semrau and Boyer's (1994) *Using Interactive Video in Education*. In addition to technical factors, teachers designing a custom project will also have to consider the abilities and learning styles of their students. Multimedia programs should not be designed for only the higher-ability students but should be easy enough for all students to use. This means that careful consideration is given to "help" features, navigational techniques, and program prompts.

For student learning, the use of commercially developed multimedia is appropriate for many learner-centered activities for studying some topic. Table 6–3 provides a list of commercial multimedia packages that are appropriate for use in classroom activities. Electronic multimedia encyclopedias such as Microsoft's Encarta are becoming prevalent in school libraries and media centers. They incorporate sophisticated but easy-to-use search tools for finding not only text but images, sounds, and video. Custom software products dealing with a specific topic such as A.D.A.M Software's ADAM: The Inside Story (of the human body) or Microsoft's Ancient Lands are available for all the major subject areas. In addition to the appeal of pictures, sounds, and moving images, the benefit of using simple multimedia encyclopedias and programs is that students can begin to learn how to use this technology easily.

A more advanced level of learning applications would be for students to develop their own multimedia project. Examples include:

- compiling a photo essay,
- doing a news report on a event using video,
- collecting oral histories,
- doing a weather report using maps and animations, and
- creating an artistic or musical piece using multimedia.

Planning and implementing these applications require training students to use the necessary hardware and software. Sufficient equipment must also be available for the students to use for extended periods. Because of the amount of preparation and work involved, student multimedia projects are generally group or collaborative activities involving two or more students. One of the benefits of multimedia projects for learning is that students need to use a variety of skills, including reading and writing, in developing the project. Additionally, student-developed projects are excellent for helping children develop multimedia literacy; with guidance from teachers, students can begin to learn how media in general can be manipulated and edited to fit the message that they wish to deliver.

Table 6–3
Educational Multimedia on CD-ROM

Company	Product	Subject
A.D.A.M. Software	ADAM	Human body
Against All Odds Productions	Passage to Vietnam	Culture/geography
Applied Optical Media	Atlas of U.S. Presidents	Social studies
Aris	Tropical Rainforest	Ecology database
Aronowitz Studios	The Animals	Science
Aronowitz Studios	The Coral Reef	Science
Broderbund Software	Alien Tales	Literature
Broderbund Software	Kid Pix	Paint program
Broderbund Software	Math Workshop	Mathematics
Broderbund Software	The Playroom	Early skills
Broderbund Software	Where in the _____ is Carmen Sandiego? Series	Problem solving
Bureau of Electronic Publishing	Multimedia World History	Social studies
Bureau of Electronic Publishing	Great Literature Plus	Literature
Compton's NewMedia	Interactive Encyclopedia	Encyclopedia
Davidson & Associates	English Express for ESL	ESL
Discovery Comm.	Beyond Planet Earth	Science
Discovery Comm.	In the Company of Whales	Science
Discus	Kids Can Read	Literature
Eden Interactive	American Visions	Art
Elliot Portwood Prod.	Widget Workshop	Science
Fairfield Language	The Rosetta Stone	Foreign language
Fife & Drum Software	The Revolutionary War	Social studies
Grolier	Multimedia Encyclopedia	Encyclopedia
Living Books	Just Grandma and Me	Early skills
MECC	Troggle Trouble Math	Mathematics
MECC	The Oregon Trail	Social studies
Microsoft	Bookshelf	General reference
Microsoft	Encarta	Encyclopedia
Microsoft	Explorapedia	Nature studies
Microsoft	Fine Artist	Paint program
Microsoft	Musical Instruments	Music
Microsoft	Ancient Lands	Social studies
Microsoft	Leonardo, The Inventor	Science/biography
National Geographic	Picture Atlas	Geography
Novell Perfect Home	Read with Me 1 & 2	Reading
7th Level, Inc.	TuneLand	Early skills
The Learning Company	Treasure MathStorm	Mathematics
The Learning Co.	Reader Rabbit's Reading Journey	Reading
The Voyager Company	Who Built America?	Social studies
Vicarious Entertain.	CNN Time Capsule	Current events
Warner New Media	How Computers Work	Technology
World Library	Shakespeare Study Guide	Literature

MULTIMEDIA RESOURCES AND COPYRIGHTS

All of the major educational software developers mentioned in Chapter 5 have begun to market multimedia programs that would be appropriate for school use. If a multimedia program is available that meets a school's instructional needs, then certainly it should be acquired. No need exists for teachers to reinvent materials that already exist. Annual catalogs, guides, and compendia are readily available from a variety of sources. These are frequently provided free of charge to educators by journal and other publishers. Highly recommended is the *Multimedia Resource Guide* published by the Educational Software Institute of Omaha, Nebraska, and *The Multimedia Home Companion Guide for Parents and Kids* published by Warner Books, a Time-Warner Company. Keep in mind that commercial multimedia packages are subject to the same copyright stipulations that apply to other software products. Generally, programs and files including image, sound, and video files cannot be copied or used in a manner inconsistent with their original intent.

For those educators who plan to develop their own materials either for presentation or for student use, locating images, sounds, and video in digital format can be very time-consuming. The first source of multimedia materials in digital format would be the files available as part of the authoring or presentation software being used to develop the application. All of the major multimedia authoring or presentation software tools provide "clip media" libraries or files containing materials that can readily be incorporated into multimedia projects. In some cases, a standard version of the package without the clip media and a deluxe or all-inclusive version of the package with the clip media files is available. These deluxe versions are generally worth the additional cost and can save hours of searching for images and sounds. Clip media libraries generally can be used freely by educators without the need to secure permissions for their use.

A second source of digital media would be electronic encyclopedias and multimedia databases. In many cases, the developers allow users to copy a photograph or image for limited use, as would be appropriate in a class presentation. Microsoft and Grolier are two of the major marketers of electronic encyclopedias that allow for a limited amount of copying of their materials, generally through a "copy-and-paste" mechanism.

A third source for digital multimedia materials would be commercially available clip media CD-ROMs. Companies such as Aris Entertainment (Marina Del Ray, California) and Corel, Corp. (Ottawa, Canada) provide clip media libraries of multimedia materials that can be freely used for educational purposes.

The Internet is a fourth source that will be discussed in more detail in the next chapter. Sites around the world make available images, sound, and video that can be accessed and copied by educators for classroom use. The Internet, in fact, will likely be the major source for all types of digitally formatted data in the not-too-distant future.

In addition to digital data, educators may also wish to access analog materials, particularly videotape or videodisc. Local video stores such as Blockbuster Video maintain up-to-date lists and provide search services to locate titles of commercially available materials. Because of copyright restrictions that prohibit copying this material, videotape is difficult to incorporate into a multimedia application. Videodisc, on the other hand, can be incorporated more easily because software exists that allows computers to control and play segments of videodisc materials without the need to make copies.

Taping television programs is also another source of analog video; however, using this material is subject to copyright laws. Discovery Communications (The Discovery Channel) of Bethesda, Maryland, publishes a pamphlet entitled *All About Copyright: Off-Air Taping Guidelines Explained*, which describes the restrictions established by all the major network and cable television stations.

In using any copyrighted materials (text, images, sound, video), educators should be aware of the restrictions on their use. Generally, but not always, educators have a fair or limited use of copyright materials as long as they are used for instructional purposes. However, even here prohibitions exist against the unauthorized use or proliferation of copies. It would be safe to say that any attempt to profit by selling or showing copyrighted materials, even for educational purposes, is generally prohibited. For educators unfamiliar with copyright issues, especially as applied to instructional multimedia, two excellent sources of information are *The Multimedia Legal Handbook: A Guide from the Software Publishers Association* by Thomas J. Smedinghoff (1994) and *Copyright's Highway* by Paul Goldstein (1995).

MEDIA DISTRIBUTION SYSTEMS

Before leaving this chapter on multimedia, readers may be interested in learning about a relatively new type of media system called "media distribution." Media distribution systems integrate several media sources (videotape, videodisc, cameras, computers, etc.) and are able to distribute them to a number of output devices, usually stand-alone monitors. Figure 6–2 shows a flow diagram of such a system developed by Dynacom, Incorporated, of Mishawaka, Indiana, that illustrates a "router" controlling and distributing media from several sources.

These systems are designed to function within a central media center operation so that, rather than media equipment (monitors, VCRs, videodiscs, etc.) being lent out to teachers or students, the media are available for distribution over the system wherever a monitor is connected. One major benefit of these systems is that they can integrate all media sources, both digital and analog. Using such a system, a teacher might present a lesson that integrates several still images, video from a videodisc player, and computer data from the Internet. These systems can also be combined with distance learning facilities so that both the teacher's presentation and the media can be distributed over an entire district or to selected locations within a district.

A good deal of planning is required, particularly in wiring and setting up monitors in various locations. Some schools wire selected classrooms; others attempt to equip all classrooms. Media distribution systems are an expensive technology costing hundreds of thousands of dollars for acquiring and installing the basic routing equipment. However, educators who are making a major commitment to multime-

Media Distribution System

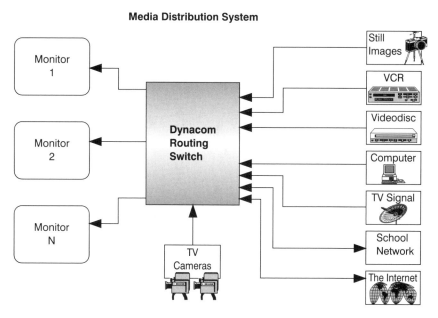

Figure 6–2
Media Distribution System

dia technologies may want to consider them, particularly if substantial funding is available. Whether such systems will become widely used is difficult to say. The hardware system cost along with the cost for wiring classrooms will make them prohibitive for many school districts. In addition, media services that become available on data communications networks such as the Internet will also compete with these systems in the future.

CASE STUDY
Redwood Middle School   Year: 1997

Redwood Middle School is located in an urban center in the Northwest part of the United States. Redwood provides a sixth- to eighth-grade program for approximately 500 students. The school enjoys an excellent reputation in its community, and the administrators and teachers are generally regarded as doing a good job of educating children. Technology is apparent throughout the school, with computer equipment located in classrooms as well as in three central laboratories. The library media center maintains an excellent videotape library and arranges for loans of portable (VCR/large monitor) workstations to teachers. The coordinator of the library media center would like to start a videodisc collection and has been in discussions with the Redwood Site-Based Management (RSBM) Team. An active Parent-Teacher Association has been helpful in securing additional resources for Redwood and has been particularly supportive of instructional technology.

Redwood is one of five pilot schools in the district that plans and administers much of its program under the auspices of a site-based management team. The members of the RSBM Team are

the co-chairs of the PTA (one parent and one teacher),

two teachers elected by the staff,

two parents appointed by the PTA,

a representative from the school district's central office,

a guidance counselor,

a librarian,

the assistant principal, and

the principal.

Decisions are made as much as possible through consensus, with most issues being decided by unanimous vote. When opinions are divided, issues are generally tabled for further discussion.

A special (one-time infusion) city appropriation for the advancement of instructional technology has been made available to all the schools in the district for the 1997–98 fiscal year. Redwood's share of these funds is $75,000. Each school is required to come up with a plan on how it would use these funds. It is October 1997, and all plans for using this appropriation must be submitted by February 1998 for funding in the current fiscal year.

The RSBM Team has been discussing for more than 2 years upgrading its instructional technology equipment, especially with regard to multimedia applications. Several approaches have been discussed, with members of the team leaning to some combination of multimedia systems using both CD-ROM and videodisc technologies. It is estimated that 12 classrooms can be upgraded for approximately $5,000 per classroom. The remaining $15,000 would be used to start a videodisc collection in the library media center. However, the school district representative suggested at the first meeting in September to consider using the entire $75,000 appropriation for wiring all the offices and the classrooms in Redwood with high-speed data communications capabilities. In addition to providing access to the resources on the Internet, district-wide administrative database systems will be more readily available. This would improve information sharing and be helpful for guidance counseling, special education, and transfer student programming.

At a second meeting in October 1997, the RSBM Team seemed evenly split, with most of the administrative members supporting the school district representative's suggestion of wiring the school, whereas the teachers and parents supported moving ahead with upgrading the classrooms with multimedia. It appears that the team will have difficulty reaching a consensus by February 1998.

Assume that you are the principal and have not committed yourself to a position on this issue yet. Given that you are concerned with developing a plan by February 1998 so as not to risk losing the funds, explain what your plan would be for assuring that the team will reach a consensus by February 1998. In developing your strategy, you should have a clear understanding of your own position on the technological merits of the two proposals.

SUMMARY

This chapter reviews the development and use of multimedia technologies in education. Particular emphasis is put on the instructional uses of multimedia. Interest and investment in this technology are increasing, and indications are that it has appeal to both teachers and students.

Multimedia can be defined generically as any combination of two or more media such as sound, images, text, animation, and video. For educational technology purposes, multimedia refers to computer-based systems that use associative linkages to allow users to navigate and retrieve information stored in a combination of text, sounds, graphics, video, and other forms of media.

Howard Gardner's theory of multiple intelligences establishes a theoretical framework for using multimedia in instruction. This theory relates to other widely recognized theories on learning styles and modalities of learning.

Multimedia literacy is a growing concern among educators as American society continues to depend on image technologies such as television, video, and film. Educators need to prepare children to live and function in a society that relies more on multimedia for information storage and dissemination.

Components of multimedia systems have been reviewed. Hardware components include a variety of both basic and specialized equipment. Software components include authoring languages, image handling software, and digital animation packages.

Multimedia can be used in instruction in a variety of creative and stimulating ways. Applications include teacher presentations, student projects, and discovery learning. Although teachers are encouraged to develop their own materials, many excellent educational multimedia products are available and should be considered rather than "reinvented."

In developing multimedia applications, many resources are available to educators. Educators should be aware of copyright issues and infringements when acquiring and using materials, especially video, images, and sound. The chapter concludes with a discussion of media distribution systems.

Key Concepts and Questions

1. Multimedia technology has been evolving slowly but steadily during the past decade.

   How has multimedia affected your daily activities? How do you see multimedia developing in the 21st century?

2. Multimedia means different things to different people.

   How do you define multimedia?

3. Multimedia is frequently used in conjunction with the application of technology for a variety of applications.

   Is multimedia strictly a technological phenomenon? Or does it have some theoretical basis for teaching and learning? Explain.

4. *Literacy* is a frequently used term in education and generally refers to language (reading and writing).

Explain literacy in conjunction with multimedia. Does a need exist for developing multimedia literacy? Explain.

5. Multimedia can include a variety of hardware components.

How are multimedia hardware components changing? Which do you consider the most beneficial for education? Why?

6. Multimedia can be used in a variety of applications.

How would you differentiate multimedia applications for use by teachers for presenting lessons as opposed to use by students in learning?

7. Locating multimedia resources such as video, images, and sounds can be a time-consuming activity.

If you were to design a multimedia project, how would you locate appropriate material? Do you need to be concerned about copyright in using this material? Explain.

Suggested Activities

1. Take an inventory of media (video, film, television) facilities presently being used in a school or school district. Where are they located? When were they acquired or established? How do you see them evolving in the future?

2. Look at your inventory and consider how, if at all, these facilities are integrated with computer facilities. Do you see any trend in this integration?

References

Armstrong, T. (1994). *Multiple intelligences in the classroom*. Alexandria, VA: Association for Curriculum Development and Supervision.

Gardner, H. (1993). *Multiple intelligences: The theory in practice*. New York: Basic Books.

———. (1983). *Frames of mind: The theory of multiple intelligences*. New York: Basic Books.

Goldstein, P. (1995). *Copyright's highway*. New York: Hill & Wang/Farrar, Straus and Giroux.

Hofstetter, F. (1994). Is multimedia the next literacy? *Educator's Tech Exchange,* Winter 1994, 6–14.

Kemp, J. E., & Smellie, D. C. (1989). *Planning, producing, and using instructional media*. New York: Harper & Row.

Levine, J. (1995, September 26). Interview with Charlie Rose, Public Broadcasting System.

Nyce, J. M., & Kahn, P. (1991). *From memex to hypertext: Vannevar Bush and the mind's machine*. Boston: Academic Press.

Picciano, A. G. (1993). The Five Points: The design of multimedia model on teaching social history. *Journal of Educational Multimedia and Hypermedia, 2*(2), 129–147.

Picciano, A. G., Eynon, B., & Vasquez, A. (1993). *Report on the evaluation of Five Points: A multimedia experience in social history, at LaGuardia Community College* (Occasional Paper No. 2). New York: Hunter College Center for Media & Learning.

Semrau, P., & Boyer, B. A. (1994). *Using interactive video in education*. Boston: Allyn & Bacon.

Smedinghoff, T. J. (1994). *The multimedia legal hand-book: A guide from the Software Publishers Association*. New York: Wiley.

Thornburg, D. (1989). *The role of technology in teaching to the whole child: Multiple intelligences in the classroom*. Los Altos, CA: Starsong.

Toplin, R. B. (1996, August 4). Plugged into the past. *New York Times,* Section 2, pp. 1, 26.

7

Data Communications, the Internet, and Educational Applications

V|ladimir Zworykin, the "father of television," invented the iconoscope and kinescope, which became the basic technologies used for broadcasting and receiving television signals in this country. Born in Russia, he emigrated to this country in 1919 and was hired by Radio Corporation of America (RCA) in 1929 to do research and development in communications technology.

In the early years of the development of television, Zworykin envisioned a technology that could be useful in a free and democratic society. He struggled to receive funding for his work and had to "sell" the benefits of his new technology. In later years, even while rising to the position of vice president at RCA, he became concerned, even dismayed, at the commercialization of broadcast television. In 1962, he met President John F. Kennedy, who praised him for his contributions to this country, especially for his invention of the television. Zworykin replied wryly, "Have you seen television recently?" (Negroponte, 1995).

In his later life, Zworykin commented frequently on the commercialization of television as a necessary evil. In an interview he gave in 1975, 8 years before his death, he expressed deep emotion over the "violence and murder" that we teach our children through television. But commercial television was driven by ratings, and the ratings ironically provided the funding for much of his own and others' research and development.

Zworykin's surprise at the direction taken by his own invention serves as an apt vignette to introduce this chapter on data communications and the Internet. The Internet is an infant medium with a potential comparable to television in terms of its societal influence. Observations and concerns already have begun to emerge regarding the content on the Internet. Surely, those involved with its original development had no idea what the Internet would become or will evolve to be in the future.

Without a doubt, the Internet is evolving into the major technology within which a host of information, entertainment, and educational services are being provided. In December 1995, an education advisory council to President Bill Clinton recommended that every school in the United States be connected to the Internet. The basis for this recommendation was a carefully done, 2-year study conducted by McKinsey & Company, an international management consulting firm. The study estimated that every school in the country could establish a new 25-station computer laboratory with connections to the Internet via ordinary telephone lines for a cost of approximately $11 billion. Educators and newspaper editorials (*New York Times*, 1995) praised this recommendation and commented that such an undertaking could "democratize education by bringing the world's best materials into the classrooms of the nation's . . . schools" (p. A20).

This recommendation is worth citing for several reasons. First, its specificity is unusual; recommendations regarding national policies for all schools in the country tend to be very general. Here the recommendation specifies the number of work stations per school, details on the nature of the application, and costs. Second, the recommendation also highlights the importance of the Internet, not simply in terms of teaching and learning but by characterizing its information resources as the "world's best materials." Lastly, as little as five years earlier, such a recommendation would not have been possible in that the Internet as we know it today did not exist; what did exist was being utilized by a relatively small group of academicians, scientists, and government officials.

These developments are indicative of how far communications technologies, especially as integrated with computer and video technologies, have come. The American public is aware of the extensive use that television has made of advanced communications systems to reduce distance between audiences and live events. Major happenings, whether NASA space exploration projects, international crises, or the Olympic Games, are brought into living rooms in real time as they occur. The same advances that have been made in the television or video communications industry are now beginning to be made in the digital or computer communications industry. In the 1990s, terms such as the *Internet,* the *World Wide Web, cyberspace,* and the *information superhighway* became routine terminology for the general populace, whether government officials espousing national policy or children asking parents to subscribe to America Online so they can E-mail their friends. Data communications (i.e., the methods and media used to transfer data from one computer device to another) provides opportunities for a wide range of educational applications. Whether browsing the Internet, using a local area network in a computer lab, or accessing a database on a commercial on-line service, staff and students are discovering that data communications is becoming a major technology to support teaching and learning.

In this chapter, we examine data communications systems in schools, especially those provided by the Internet. Before continuing, readers are encouraged to review the material in Appendix A that covers the basic hardware components of most data communications systems.

DATA COMMUNICATIONS IN THE SCHOOLS

During the past several decades, educators have seen data communications systems and networks expand in size, sophistication, and the ability to communicate over distances. In the late 1970s and 1980s, schools began to install their first **local area networks**, or LANs (see Figure 7–1). The use of these LANs in computer laboratories, libraries, and administrative offices has become commonplace. Quality Education Data (1995) reports that more than 13,000 of the 15,000+ school districts in the country have established one or more LANs. In larger school districts, not only are LANs commonly being used, but **wide area networks** (WANs) are in evidence connecting computers and LANs that are dispersed miles apart throughout the district (see Figure 7–2). The essential concept here involves a large computer network integrating the activities of smaller computer networks. Using district-wide networks, a student in one school can determine whether a library in another school has a particular book, an assistant principal can examine the transcript of a student who has just transferred from another school, or a district business manager can monitor the daily expenditures of several schools.

The data communications technology that enables a computer in one school to communicate with a computer in another school is essentially the same whether the schools are one mile apart or many miles apart. Once a WAN has been established in a locality, the distance between sites does not make that much difference in the abil-

Figure 7–1
Simple Network

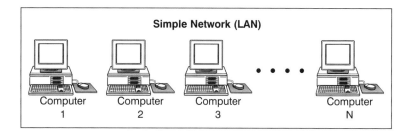

ity of individual sites to communicate with one another. In the late 1980s, this concept was taken a step further as computers in school districts began to communicate with computers on networks outside the school district. A student looking for a particular book was able to use a computer in a school's library to locate the book at a local public library or perhaps even a local college library. A superintendent using a computer in a school district office was able to transfer data on student demographics to a computer located in a state education office.

In the 1990s, data communications technologies have continued to advance to the point where a computer on one network can easily communicate with a computer on another network hundreds and thousands of miles away. The grants officer in a local school district office in Juneau, Alaska, can examine a database of funded programs that exists on a computer network maintained by the United States Department of Education in Washington, D.C. A state education department administrator in Albany, New York, can E-mail a new curriculum proposal to all 800 school district superintendents on a state-wide education network. A social studies teacher in Tulsa, Oklahoma, developing a module in cultural studies can access a database of curricular materials maintained by the National Geographic Society.

With the expansion of data communications' capabilities over the past several decades, networks likewise have expanded to cover greater distances and to link with many other networks. At some point in the future, all of this data traffic occurring on thousands of networks throughout the country and the world might pass over a common universal network.

Figure 7–2
Multiple Networks

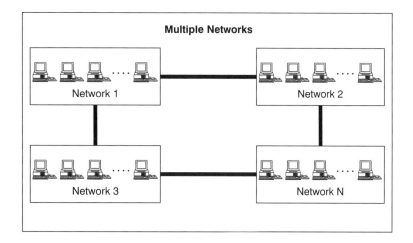

THE INTERNET

The Internet (see Figure 7–3) is an international computer network consisting of tens of thousands of smaller networks that link schools, colleges, government agencies, research organizations, and private businesses through satellite and other high-speed communications facilities. The essential function provided by the Internet is to allow users to transfer and receive data. This data can be a simple, one-line E-mail message, a complex weather map, or a huge subset of the United States 1990 census. The Internet also provides the conceptual framework for a universal computer network and is evolving into a network of networks.

A Brief History

The roots of the Internet can be traced to the U.S. Department of Defense in the 1960s. Concerned about establishing and maintaining a worldwide communications system in the event of a major disaster such as a nuclear war, engineers and scientists from Rand, UCLA, and MIT designed a "doomsday" data communications system that would be decentralized and capable of functioning regardless of whether any single node or point in the network was no longer available. This design was a departure from the common centralized data communications systems that required a hub or center point to control the entire network.

In 1969, the Pentagon's Advanced Research and Projects Agency established the first node of this new network called ARPANET (Advanced Research and Projects Agency Network) at UCLA. Throughout the 1970s, the ARPANET grew but was used essentially by government officials, engineers, and scientists connected with research for the U.S. Department of Defense. In 1983, the military segment of ARPANET developed a separate network called MILNET, and access to ARPANET was expanded to include other computer networks worldwide that used its standard protocol or method of transferring data.

Figure 7–3
The Internet

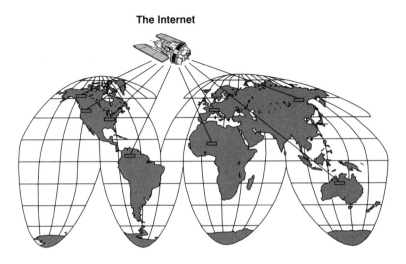

The Internet

Also in the early 1980s, other international networks were being established in the higher education, government, and research communities. Because It's Time Network (BITNET) was established by the City University of New York, Yale University, and IBM to link university mainframe computers. Computer Science Network (CSNET) was funded by the U.S. National Science Foundation (NSF) to provide data communications facilities for industry, government, and university groups engaged in computer science research. Later, several U.S. agencies—namely, the NSF, the National Aeronautics and Space Agency (NASA), and the U.S. Department of Energy—funded and established networking facilities that eventually would be used to enhance the aging ARPANET system. By the late 1980s, all of these major networks were communicating with one another, either using or converting to the standard protocol established on ARPANET; hence the birth of the Internet.

The Internet Today

In the early 1990s, the Internet community grew exponentially as the number of users was estimated to be increasing at the rate of 20% per month or doubling every 5 to 6 months. These numbers were strictly estimates because no one really knew how many people were using the Internet. In 1995, approximately 40,000 computer networks were connected to the Internet, but still no one knew how may users were on each network. Estimates ranged from 30 to 50 million people worldwide.

This growth and popularity are understandable since joining the Internet is relatively inexpensive, voluntary, and service is equitable. The cost of using the Internet is not usage based. For example, sending an E-mail message costs the same whether the message is going 1 mile down the road to a neighbor or halfway around the world. Furthermore, a user incurs very few obligations by joining the Internet and can use its resources as needed. While connecting to the Internet depends on acquiring equipment and on-line services, once on the Internet, all users are equal. A major corporation or government agency does not receive quicker or better service than a group of fourth graders using the Internet to help with their homework.

The type of users on the Internet is changing significantly. In the 1980s, the Internet was dominated by the nonprofit, research, university, and government sectors. Since the 1990s, this has begun to change as many private enterprises, both small and large, have joined the Internet for marketing, sales, and other commercial purposes. Private individuals, likewise, are using the Internet daily for such routine activities as reading the news, checking on the weather, purchasing goods and services, or communicating with friends and relatives around the globe. Although still dominated by users in the more technologically advanced countries, the number of Internet users in developing nations also increased significantly in the 1990s.

This expansion has significant implications. A major issue facing the Internet is in administration; presently, no one organization is really responsible for the Internet. Various government-sponsored arrangements and consortia exist in different countries to administer the Internet on a voluntary basis. In the United States, for instance, NSF sponsors and funds Internet Network Information Center (InterNIC), which maintains information, database directories, and registration services for the Internet.

However, the funding for this center is not guaranteed, and the providers of the services do not accept responsibility for the accuracy of their information and services.

Interestingly, whereas data communications technology usually requires a good deal of precision in developing procedures, protocols, and access, the Internet has evolved with little planning or administrative precision. Some observers (Shirky, 1995; Stoll, 1995) have even referred to this evolution as information "anarchy" and predict that the Internet will shortly outlive its usefulness. On the other hand, others (Ellsworth, 1994; Williams, 1995) consider this voluntary, loosely administered digital community as the very essence of freedom and equality in accessing and sharing information.

The Future of the Internet

Speculation on the future of the Internet is difficult given its dynamic nature. However, the Internet has attracted a good deal of attention, and as planning requires consideration of the future, a few comments and concerns about the Internet in the coming years are appropriate.

The Internet has been perhaps the most dynamic digital technology ever introduced. Computer industry analysts and software developers believe that it set "a new computing standard or platform much as the personal computer did 15 years ago" (Fisher, 1996, p. C15). In a period of a few years, tens of millions of people, most of whom did not even know of its existence as late as 1990, have used its services. Its growth rate in the mid-1990s, doubling the number of users approximately every 6 months, was nothing short of phenomenal.

While this dynamism is stimulating for those who believe in the benefits of technology for the general populace, it is a cause for concern as well. As already mentioned, the Internet is a voluntary community with few rules and little formal administration. In the future, attempts will be made to impose rules and regulations, some of which will require administration and oversight. As an example, the U.S. Congress in 1996 was considering "censorship" legislation for the Internet, particularly as it applied to child pornography and other sex-oriented material. Given the absence of mechanisms in place capable of controlling such activity, combined with the international character of the Internet, such legislation, whether warranted or not, would have limited impact. In the years to come, if the Internet continues to evolve into the network of networks, some international effort will likely be made to administer and to some degree control it. Whether this will be good or bad for the Internet is difficult to predict. Surely, if its growth continues, some technological administration, planning, and funding will have to be implemented. On the other hand, the same forces that provide administration and planning may also bring control, which has the potential of changing the free and voluntary access and sharing of information that has made the Internet so popular.

An issue related to administration and control is the growing commercialization of the Internet. The Internet evolved from the nonprofit (government, research, university) sectors. Commercial use of the Internet is a relatively recent phenomenon; however, much of the growth in the Internet during the past several years has been fueled by commercial activities, everything from private entrepreneurs selling crafts to international corporations marketing goods and services. The Internet was designed primarily for information access and sharing, not for high-volume commercial transaction processing.

Furthermore, security on the Internet is limited. Security breaches happen regularly on many commercial networks, but the Internet is more vulnerable to such breaches because it lacks any security oversight. The protection of common credit card transactions may require security oversight of the Internet that simply is not present. In fact, the possibility exists that the Internet will always be too vulnerable for high-volume commercial transaction processing typically found in banking or financial services and may have to be replaced by some other type of international commercial network that will have security controls in place.

The nature of commercial enterprise and high-volume transaction processing has the potential of significantly adding to the traffic on the Internet. Most nonprofit uses of the Internet, such as information access, do not compare in volume with commercial activity in financial services, retail sales, and marketing. The Internet in the mid-1990s was already suffering from growing pains as access and searches slowed considerably, particularly during the prime business usage hours of 9:00 A.M. to 10:00 P.M. Commercial Internet service providers have already begun to charge differential fees based on peak and nonpeak hour usage. If commercialization of the Internet continues with its concomitant high-volume transaction processing, then access and search speed will slow considerably, changing its character and usefulness.

The basic hardware and software technology that is the foundation of the Internet was conceived in the 1970s and 1980s; the designers, however, were not envisioning a network that would meet the needs of millions of people throughout the world. Data communications, as most technologies, evolved and improved in a steady, predictable fashion. Recently, however, the rapid growth of the Internet has fueled a significant increase in research, development, and new products meant to improve the hardware and software that all data communications systems require. The speed of modem equipment rises every year. The future evolution of Web browser software is impossible to predict as new companies and products such as Netscape seem to appear almost overnight. The speed with which this technology is changing is unprecedented and generating new products with technological life cycles of no more than one or two years. The very nature of the providers of Internet access—whether public or private telephone companies, cable TV companies, or strictly commercial Internet service providers—is not at all settled and can change significantly in the future. Such rapid change requires the most flexible of planning strategies as organizations, including schools, attempt to keep up with and adjust to newer data communications hardware and software technologies.

While considering the future of the Internet, it is most important for schools to provide experiences and opportunities for children to learn to use this rapidly evolving technology. Schools have traditionally prepared children to contribute, work, and play in the larger society, and using the Internet exemplifies the facility that will be required of individuals to function technologically in the future. Nicholas Negroponte (1995) relates a discussion that he had with Jerome Wiesner, the president of MIT, on considering the advances of technology and the evolution of a "digital" society. Although optimistic, Wiesner was concerned that such a society "takes jobs and may have fewer to give back" (p. 233). The Internet and/or its successors will require users in all sectors of society to hone continually their skills as they adjust to rapid advances and changes in using data communications and other technologies. Educators would be wise to include as part of their technology planning the establishment of goals and objectives that require students to be prepared for a "digital" society that will be largely dependent on a worldwide data communications system similar to but more advanced than the Internet of today.

THE WORLD WIDE WEB

Terms for the Internet such as **cyberspace** and the **information superhighway** are designed to provide a descriptive character to this network of networks. Another term that is used in conjunction or interchangeably with the Internet is the **World Wide Web**, or the **Web** for short. The Web is actually a software system that introduced hypertext and multimedia capabilities to the Internet. Originally developed in the early 1990s at CERN, the European Laboratory for Particle Physics, in Switzerland, the Web was designed to provide hypertext and full multimedia support in a relatively easy-to-use language for physicists and other scientists using the Internet. This concept of a hypertext-based software system for the Web is generally credited to Dr. Tim Berners-Lee, who envisioned an Internet that would be much easier to use.

The success of the Web is unquestionable. According to data compiled by Matthew Gray (1996), the number of Web sites with servers was 130 in June 1993; two years later, the number was 23,500; another year later, it was 230,000. Again, because it is impossible to determine how many users are accessing the servers at each site, the number of people using the Web remains unknown.

Hypertext as used on the Web is a nonsequential retrieval system for accessing data on the Internet. Rather than sequential searching, hypertext relies on linkages of data files to one another in a complex "web" of associations. Hypertext is not a new software search concept, having been routinely used in large databases for years. Electronic encyclopedias, for instance, employ hypertext searching when a particular topic or passage has links or "hotwords" that users can click on to jump to a related topic, which in turn has links to other related topics. The same approach is used on the Web to locate data files on the Internet.

Protocols and Client Servers

To understand the nature of the Web in relation to the Internet, a brief discussion of the term *protocol* as used in data communications is necessary. **Protocol** is a general term for a set of rules, procedures, or standards that are used in exchanging data in a data communications system. Examples of these rules would be a code or signal indicating the beginning of a message, a code or signal indicating the end of a message, or a code or signal indicating that a device is busy. Computer and communications equipment manufacturers established different protocols for exchanging data, which complicated the ability of one manufacturer's computer to communicate with another manufacturer's computer. This protocol incompatibility problem was resolved to some degree by the development of protocol conversion software that enabled computers to translate and convert data messages of other computer protocols. The Internet established a standard protocol for all its activity called **transmission control protocol/Internet protocol** (TCP/IP). All computers using the Internet had to exchange data using TCP/IP. The Web's data transfer method or protocol, called **hypertext transfer protocol** (http), was designed to run "over" or in conjunction with the TCP/IP, the standard Internet protocol. Many other protocols have also been designed to run in conjunction with TCP/IP on the Internet; however, because of its hypertext and multimedia capabilities, the Web has become the most popular.

Because of its hypertext facilities, the Web is also an excellent software system to run on a "client-server" data communications system, which is how the Internet functions. In the early days of data communications, the standard network model was for a central computer controlling all the activity on a network and also functioning as the central depository for data files and programs. The client-server data communications model does not require a central depository or controlling computer. To the contrary, the basis for the Internet and its predecessor, ARPANET, was to distribute or share control broadly among the networked computers.

In a client-server model, computers essentially perform two major functions. The client or end-user function makes a request or query for data to a server. The server function, performed by one of many computers sharing network control, processes the request and returns the results to the client. Many computers, not just one, can function as servers and can locate data on a network. Furthermore, servers can forward requests to other servers and create a chain reaction to process the original client's data request.

Uniform Resource Locator (URL)

Within the client-server environment of the Web, the uniform resource locator (URL) is the standard method of accessing the location of information resources on the Web. Uniform resource locators are electronic addresses that identify a unique location of a data file. Conceptually, URLs serve the exact same function as an address in the U.S. Postal Service. If a letter is to be delivered in a timely fashion, an envelope is generally addressed with the party's name on the first line, the house number and street on the second line, and the city, state, and ZIP code on the third. The standard for addressing envelopes is well known and works well. The standard format for entering an address for a URL is as follows:

> **protocol://host/path/file**, where
> **protocol** is the method of transferring data from one computer to another computer (i.e., http),
> **host** is the name of the host computer,
> **path** is the name of the directory on the host computer, and
> **file** is the name of a file in the directory.

For example, the URL

> **http://www.cchem.berkeley.edu/Table/index.html**, where
> **http** is the protocol,
> **www.cchem.berkeley.edu** is the host computer name,
> **Table** is the path or directory, and
> **index.html** is the file name

uses the hypertext transfer protocol to access a file that contains a periodic table of elements at the College of Chemistry at the University of California, Berkeley.

For new users of the Web, the format of the URLs may seem complicated. However, after frequent use, they become second nature. Software browsers that provide the software facilities for locating information on the Web also provide URL address lists that can simply be clicked on to access the data file at the desired host computer or site.

The most commonly used protocol on the Web is the http. Other protocols commonly used are these:

ftp   file transfer protocol

gopher   database and communications software system for searching for data in files

Wais   wide area information system

The host name on many URLs will contain a suffix designating a type of organization. In the previous example, "edu" represents an educational institution Other commonly used suffixes include these:

com   commercial enterprise

gov   government agency

mil   military agency

net   network service

org   non-profit organization

These suffixes are not required but are conventions considered good form when establishing a host name. Figure 7–4 cites examples of the URLs of popular sites on the Web.

Web Browsers and Search Engines

Searching for data and information on the Web using URLs requires software browsers. In 1996, the most popular browsers—Netscape, Mosaic, and Internet Explorer—were available in versions for both Windows and Macintosh computers. It is quite possible that by the time this book is in print, major new software browsers will be in use. However, the basic concept and nature of Web browsing is expected to remain the same.

http://www.altavista.com/
  A popular search engine

http://www.city.net/
  Comprehensive information on all the major cities of the world

http://www.lycos.com
  A popular search engine

http://www.mit.edu:8001/usa.html
  Massachusetts Institute of Technology weather map

http://www.microsoft.com/
  Microsoft Incorporated homepage

http://www.nasa.gov
  National Space and Aeronautics Agency homepage

http://home.netscape.com/
  Netscape Communications Incorporated homepage

http://www.comlab/ox.ac.uk/archive/other/museums.html#LofC
  Oxford University collection of materials on museums of the world

http://thomas.loc.gov
  The official Web site for the U.S. Congress

http://www.census.gov/cdrom/lookup
  U.S. Census Data Retrieval

http://www.w3.org/pub/WWW/
  World Wide Web Consortium

http://www.w3.org/hypertext/DataSources/bySubject/Overview.html
  World Wide Web Virtual Library

http://webcrawler.com
  A popular search engine

http://webcrawler.com/webcrawler/top25.html
  The top 25 sites on the Web as determined by the Webcrawler search engine

http://www.whitehouse.gov
  The official Web site for the White House

http://www.yahoo.com
  A search engine and one of the most popular sites on the Web

Figure 7–4
Examples of Uniform Resource Locators (URLs) of Popular Web Sites

Browsing software is used to access data files that are generally displayed as "pages" on the Web. Figure 7–5 is a sample page from the Netscape Web browsing software. Web browsers generally provide a series of pull-down menus or navigation buttons that allow users to navigate or "surf" the Web. The location where a user starts a Web browsing session is referred to as the user's **homepage**. Beside standard features such as save, copy, paste, and help, the basic navigational functions of browsers are as follows:

Back   returns to a previous page.

Forward   goes to the next page.

Home   returns the user back to the homepage.

Reload   reloads the current page.

Images   sets on or off an option to load images.

Open   opens a URL.

Print   prints current page.

Find   searches for text in the current page.

Stop   stops the current operation.

Web browsers allow users to enter URLs in some designated areas to access the page of the requested data file. Depending on overall traffic on the Internet, the number of users requesting data from the same host computer, and the speed of the telephone lines being used to make the request, requests are usually processed in a

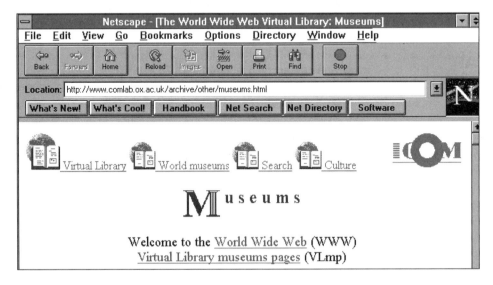

Figure 7–5
Sample Web Browser Page

matter of seconds. If too much traffic exists or if the host does not respond to a request, a message is displayed within some reasonable period of time, giving the user the option of continuing or canceling the request. For readers who have not used a Web browser, an activity is suggested at the end of this chapter that provides practice in navigating to various sites on the Web.

In the mid-1990s, Web browsers relied on software called **hypertext markup language** (HTML) to establish and convert data files. However, other software languages such as Java, developed by Sun MicroSystems, have recently been introduced that will likely enhance the way data are established and displayed on the Internet. Java has the potential of adding a great deal more programmability and multimedia capabilities to data files on the Web. "Filter" or conversion programs are also available that will convert documents produced by word-processing or some other software into a HTML or Web page document.

Without assistance, locating and accessing data on the Web can be a formidable task. An electronic card catalog of all of the Web's holdings does not exist and probably never will, given its dynamic and loosely administered nature. Users can easily spend hours trying to locate some particular data or information. Web browsers have begun to provide keyword search capabilities that work similarly to other database query languages.

In addition, another type of software referred to as a "search engine" is evolving that provides keyword search facilities. These search engines are available at URLs on the Web and can save users a significant amount of time in attempting to identify URLs that contain the information being sought. Several popular search engines (Alta Vista, Lycos, Webcrawler, and Yahoo!) with their respective URLs are included in Figure 7–4. Users should be aware that much of the data searched by these engines have been voluntarily submitted by other users. They are by no means complete searches of all the data resources on the Web.

APPLICATIONS ON THE INTERNET

The Internet is a dynamic communications and information resource. Information of all sorts is constantly being added, deleted, and most importantly shared among millions of people. For educators, the Internet can provide a pedagogically valuable array of skill activities such as writing, reading, and research, as well as a content-rich resource for culture, science, current events, and so forth. The list of possibilities and specific applications is endless, but most of these activities fall into several broad categories.

Global electronic mail is the most popular activity on the Internet. Although E-mail has existed for almost two decades, the Internet has made it available to the masses throughout the world, making it as easy to send and receive messages thousands of miles as for a couple miles. Teachers and students are establishing "pen pal" correspondence with others all over the world. Furthermore, the delay in sending and receiving messages is limited only to the time it takes an individual to collect, organize, and write his or her thoughts; there is no waiting period of days or weeks while paper letters are hand delivered.

The Internet does not provide the E-mail software itself but works through URLs to route messages that have been composed and stored on local E-mail software systems. A school or school district that has established a local E-mail system should continue to use that system and integrate it for use on the Internet.

Discussion groups, also known as **newsgroups** or **listservers** (or **listservs** for short), extend the E-mail concept beyond the individual. Rather than sending mail to individuals, mail is posted to an electronic bulletin board for members of a group to read and to respond as they wish. The messages stay on the electronic bulletin board for a given period of time. Generally, these discussion groups identify a topic of common interest to all members of the group. These topics can be broad or specific depending on the group's interests.

The majority of Internet discussion group activity is conducted on Usenet, which is an electronic bulletin board software system that maintains approximately 10,000 discussion groups at any one time, serving millions of people. To access Usenet, software generically known as **newsreaders** is required.

Electronic bulletin boards exist for all levels of education and in all subject areas. Activity-related bulletin boards on a host of topics sponsored by state education departments, professional societies, museums, and libraries are regularly being established. In addition to supporting discussion groups on the Internet, electronic bulletin boards are also being used by educators on local and commercial computer networks to discuss and keep abreast of locally important issues and topics.

Live conferencing takes the discussion group concept and organizes it into a real-time activity. The Internet provides a software system known as **Internet Relay Chat** (IRC), commonly known as **chat**. On the Internet, text-based "chat areas" or "chat rooms" are available on a host of topics. Live conferencing differs from discussion groups in that the discussion is live and text messages are posted as they are written and answered.

Organizing a discussion group requires familiarity with the IRC software, which can be complicated for the average person using the Internet. However, in a commercial on-line service such as America Online, software facilities for setting up a chat area are easy to use. Administrators and teachers in particular might use this feature to carry out informal conferences or meetings eliminating the necessity of traveling many miles. The nature of live conferencing may also take on another dimension as live audio and video facilities are advanced for use on the Internet. This topic will be discussed further in this chapter in the section on distance learning.

File transferring (or FTP, file transfer protocol) refers to the transfer and receiving of data files on the Internet. These files can include text, pictures, sound, and video. File transfer can occur several ways depending on how a user is connected to the Internet. In some cases, FTP is automatically included as a feature of the E-mail software system in which users send and receive files as attachments to a specific message. In other cases, files are made available for all members of the Internet community to access by invoking specific FTP software. The acts of sending and receiving data files are generally referred to as **uploading** and **downloading**, respectively. The Internet community is generous in what it allows users to access, especially for educational purposes. The National Aeronautics and Space Administration, for example, makes data resources available on many of its active space exploration projects, and the U.S. Weather Service updates on a timely basis data files on weather conditions throughout the world.

In downloading and uploading files, users should be sure to have virus protection software to scan files that are made available to the public. Also when accessing data files, especially images, sound, and video, users should be aware of any copyright restrictions associated with the further use of the data. The copyright guidelines discussed in Chapter 6 also apply to materials downloaded from the Internet.

Theoretically, any computer on the Internet can connect to and use the resources of any other computer on the Internet. Through a software feature known as Telnet, a user on one computer can literally connect to and use the resources of another computer. As an example, rather than downloading a single file from NASA's central computer system, a user might be able actually to connect to and use all the resources available on NASA's computer. Though theoretically possible, most computers on the Internet do not allow outside users to access their computer facilities directly for practical and security reasons. Permission is required along with establishing proper sign-on procedures with user IDs and passwords.

Last but by no means least, and growing daily in popularity, is information navigation also known as "Net surfing" or "cruising" and "Web browsing." Using Web browsing software such as Netscape or Mosaic, as described earlier, users are making their information available to all other members of the Internet community. At the same time, by using these relatively simple navigational software tools, vast amounts of pedagogically valuable instructional information is readily available; how much, no one knows. Students and teachers can spend hours looking up pages of pertinent information on a topic and not even touch the surface of all that is available on the Internet. Reference materials, maps, art collections, frog dissection software, the Periodic Table of Elements, the White House, and the U.S. Congress are all available with a click of a mouse. Never in the history of humankind has such an extensive collection of informational resources been so readily available. However, users need to be educated and need to practice browsing the Web to use it efficiently. Once proficiency is developed in browsing the Web, the informational rewards can be abundant.

THE INTERNET AND EDUCATION

In developing Internet applications for education, administrators should consider how to integrate the Internet with other data communications facilities in a school district. The Internet does not necessarily replace existing facilities such as LANs, WANs, or access to commercial on-line services, but it should be used to enhance them. Schools have begun to establish **intranets**, which are LANs that use Internet software tools such as Web browsers. Also referred to as **mini-Internets**, intranets are useful for controlling access to sensitive data, reducing data traffic, and speeding access to frequently used data files. Generally, the Internet depends on local software systems (i.e., E-mail, file servers, databases, etc.) to accomplish much of its activity. Some of these local software packages may be easier to use than those that exist on the Internet.

Global E-Mail

Global E-mail applications have educational value mainly because they require and aid in the development of basic skills such as reading, writing, and researching. In addition, they can be conducted literally around the world so that electronic cultural exchanges take place with minimal cost or effort. Once a school has access to E-mail, implementing provocative E-mail applications is relatively easy. Examples of E-mail applications abound in the professional literature, including these:

Local news reporters
Have students assume the role of local news reporters and have them swap news stories with students in other locales.

Local weatherpersons
This activity is the same as the previous one, but ask students to report on weather conditions. Expand on this same theme and trace weather patterns (rainfall, snowfall, days over 90 degrees) over the course of a semester or academic year.

Conduct surveys
Conduct surveys with a number of schools around the country or world on a variety of topics (important people, favorite singer, most important event in the 20th century, most important event of the current year).

Problem solvers
Develop a problem (mathematical, scientific, riddle) and solicit opinions for its solution.

Story starters
A very popular activity is to start a story and have others add to it to see how long the story can be kept going.

Organizations such as NASA's K–12 Project and the National Geographic Society's Kids Network provide ideas and limited assistance in helping teachers develop E-mail activities. Several sites on the Internet such as KidLink are set up specifically to facilitate worldwide communications among students through E-mail and discussion groups.

Information Navigation

Navigating the Web for information is becoming one of the more popular applications. Students as well as teachers and the general public do it just for fun. Internet cafes are opening up around the country that provide a social environment in which people "hang out" and surf the Web. For a modest fee, one sits at a computer workstation with a companion or two and looks at interesting sites for hours. Together, they may take a break, sip espresso, and then go back to the workstation for more "Net surfing."

Schools are already providing this type of environment, minus the espresso, in school computer laboratories and libraries. Navigating on the Web can be a significant "time-sink" and is especially enjoyable when valuable informational experiences result. Educators should develop activities that encourage both the fun and the serious uses of the Internet. Ideas for navigating the Web for educational activities should be predicated upon the age of the navigators, subject area, and skill level. Figure 7–6 lists URLs of Web sites that are educationally oriented. This list is provided strictly as a menu of resources and activities to stimulate thinking on using the Web in a variety of ways. Administrators might find interesting information on school policy in The Schoolhouse Project or become acquainted with new grant programs in the NSF database. Teachers can get lesson plans and other teaching ideas from the Clearing House for Networked Information Discovery and Retrieval or the Texas Educational Network. For students, Uncle Bob's Homepage is both fun and educational, the KidLink site is excellent for participating in international discussion groups, and the Teleport site provides "cool" and useful resources for high school students engaged in research projects.

Several sites in Figure 7–6 relate to specific subject areas and disciplines. If a particular subject area is not listed, readers are encouraged to use a search engine such as Yahoo where, in addition to keyword searching, a list of subject categories is provided. Generally, when looking for information on broad subject areas such as history, biology, or mathematics, so much information will be provided that it will take hours to read and consider. Searching for resources on the Internet is like using an electronic card catalogue or database; users need to practice to hone and narrow a request for information. One benefit of using a Web browser for this activity is that users can easily collect useful URLs and store them electronically on address lists. For new users, allow time for practice, and provide instruction on using address lists or bookmarks to save URLs. As with other applications of instructional technology, particularly for new or intermediate learners, collaborative activities should be encouraged.

In developing Internet navigating applications for students, educators must take on some responsibility for screening the materials that students might accidentally or purposefully come across. As mentioned earlier, the Internet is a free and voluntary community with little oversight. Some of the material is unsuitable for children, including child pornography and hate group activity. Children need to be educated about the world around them; however, schools have some obligation to protect children from material that might be harmful. Presently, adults (teachers, parents, paraprofessionals) may simply have to provide guidance and be alert to damaging uses of the Internet. Software such as Surfwatch (Surfwatch, Inc.) and Cybersitter (SolidOak Software, Inc.) has been developed that will assist organizations such as schools to screen some of the material that is delivered from the Internet on their networks.

Creating a Homepage

Growing in popularity as an educational activity on the Internet is the development of homepages. This is not as complicated as one might assume but requires becoming familiar with a programming language such as HTML. Thousands of schools have already begun creating their own homepages. To develop a homepage, a school either has to have its own server with a direct connection to the Internet, generally referred to as a

http://seds.lpl.arizona.edu
> University of Arizona collection of materials on space exploration

http://tism.bevc.blacksburg.va.us/BEN.html
> Bilingual/ESL Network

http://ucmpl.berkeley.edu/
> University of California Museum of Paleontology

http://schoolnet2.carleton.ca/
> Canada's National SchoolNet Project

http://www.ilt.columbia.edu/
> Columbia University's Institute for Learning Technologies

http://edwweb.cnidr.org:90/
> Clearing House for Networked Information Discovery and Retrieval

gopher://digital.cosn.org/
> Consortium for School Networking

http://www.discovery.com
> The Discovery Channel's Homepage

http://faldo.atmos.uiuc.edu/WEATHER/weather.html/
> A variety of class lessons on weather geared to different disciplines

http://galaxy.einet.net/galaxy/Social-Sciences.html
> Galaxy EiNet of Resources on the Social Sciences

http://artsedge.kennedy-center.org/
> The Kennedy Center's Linking the Arts and Education through Technology Resources Page

http://www.kidlink.org/
> Discussion groups, chat areas, and other Internet resources and activities for children. As of 1995, more than 50,0000 children from 77 countries had participated in Kidlink activities.

http://medoc.gdb.org/best/stc/nsf-best.html
> National Science Foundation Grants database

http://quest.arc.nasa.gov/
> National Space and Aeronautics Administration K–12 Project

Figure 7–6
URLs of Interesting Web Sites and Resources for Educators

serial line Internet protocol (SLIP), or, if connected via commercial or public on-line service, obtain permission from the provider to develop a homepage. Many commercial providers make this service available free, but some will charge a modest fee.

Developing a homepage is a stimulating and educationally valuable activity; however, schools must think seriously about how they want themselves portrayed to the Internet community. The major purposes of the Internet are communication and information sharing. When establishing a homepage, schools become information providers and

http://web66.coled/umn.edu
> University of Minnesota, College of Education

http://www.branson.org/mca/
> Multicultural Alliance

http://www.sendit.nodak.edu/k12/
> Hotlist of K–12 Web sites

http://www.pbs.org/
> Public Broadcasting System homepage

http://wwnwrel.org/school_house/
> The Schoolhouse Project–a host of resources for teachers and
> school administrators

http://www.teleport.com/~burrell/
> "Cool" and useful sites for high school students using the Internet
> for research projects

http://www.tenet.edu/
> Texas Educational Network Homepage that provides extensive resources
> for teachers and administrators

http://gagme/wwa.com/~boba/kidsi.html
> Uncle Bob's Web Page for Children

http://www.ed.gov
> U.S. Department of Education homepage

http://george.lbl.gov:80/vfrog/
> Virtual Frog dissection kit

http://www.wentworth.com/classroom/whatnew.html
> The Web and classroom

http://www.csu.edu.au/education/library.html
> World Wide Web virtual library on education

http://www.yahoo.com/Educational/K_12/Resources/
> Yahoo K–12 education resources page

should provide useful information about their students, academic programs, and related activities. Suggestions for developing a homepage abound. As examples:

- Avoid too much clutter per page; this makes it difficult for readers to access important information.
- Avoid electronic vanity plate syndrome via extensive photographs of one or two individuals.

- Highlight the school, not the computer systems or software.
- Keep current events current.
- Assume many home computers have limited-speed modems, so allow for text-only access options when designing a page.

For more information, several sites on the Web provide help in designing a home-page including these:

> http://web66.coled.umn.edu
> http://artsedge.kennedy-center.org/
> http://www.acu.edu/dev/makesaver.edu

The "web66" site at the University of Minnesota also contains a resources page that provides URLs to view thousands of homepages of schools around the world.

Individuals and small groups are also developing their own homepages. A class, an individual teacher, or a student can develop a homepage. In fact, America Online, one of the major commercial on-line service providers, assists all of its subscribers in setting up a homepage. In the years to come, as the Internet evolves, providing information on a homepage will become a routine activity for all users.

Commercial On-Line Services

Schools can connect to the Internet in several ways. They establish their own Internet connection via a slip; they connect via an on-line service provided by a local non-profit organization such as a college, university, or government agency; or they subscribe to a commercial on-line service. For individuals in their homes, most people are connected to the Internet via a commercial on-line service such as America Online (AOL), CompuServe, and Prodigy. As of January 1996, the seven major commercial on-line service companies had approximately 11 million subscribers, many of which represent families with multiple users. Business analysts indicate that commercial on-line service is a major growth industry, and many other companies will be providing commercial on-line services in the late 1990s (Lewis, 1996).

When contemplating connecting to the Internet, educators should consider commercial providers, especially if other nonprofit on-line services are not available or if the technical expertise needed to establish and maintain an Internet connection is limited in the school district. The commercial on-line services provide technical support and are effective in getting new users connected to the Internet. In addition to Internet service, they also provide a host of other on-line services such as access to newspapers, home shopping, financial reports, and so forth. They charge monthly based on usage of their services. Basic rates for individual subscriptions start at about $10 per month and increase depending on usage and connect time. With increasingly heavy usage, flat-rate fees for unlimited access are highly desirable. America Online, for instance, implemented a flat rate of $19.95 per month for unlimited access to the Internet. Group rates for organizations such as schools need to be negotiated. In determining costs, users also should be aware of their telephone access charges. The major commercial providers attempt to make local telephone access available in all major cities and towns, thereby reducing long-distance telephone charges.

If commercial providers are not required for a school's connection to the Internet, educators may still want to become familiar with them for their own professional development and to understand what their students are likely using in their homes. The major commercial providers have not ignored education as part of their menu of services. On the contrary, educational services such as professional homework assistance, educational databases, and standard reference materials are available. Educational discussion groups sponsored by the National Education Association, the United Federation of Teachers, the National Principal's Center, and the Association for Supervision and Curriculum Development are also available via these services and are excellent forums for communicating with other professionals on national issues.

The Internet has been described in this chapter as a dynamic, free, and voluntary community. Commercial activity is still a relatively new phenomenon, but more commercial activity will surely occur in coming years, which will mean that commercial providers will likely have a more significant role in defining the Internet. Based on such speculation, major corporate entities in the telephone, computer, and the television industries have been developing strategies to provide Internet services and are willing to make significant financial investments to corner a substantial part of this growing market (Lewis, 1996). In planning for the future, educators should keep abreast of this activity.

The Internet and Distance Learning

Distance learning has been evolving slowly in the United States for the past 30 years. Early distance learning projects employed passive analog communications such as one-way television. In the past 10 years, two-way analog communications using videoconferencing technologies have begun to dominate distance learning applications. Most recently, data communications facilities as provided by the Internet and other large networks are beginning to redefine distance learning.

Before the Internet, distance learning applications centered on the typical classroom model in which a teacher broadcasts or delivers a lesson at one site and a group of students participates at another site(s). Putting aside cost, technological expertise, and instructor workload issues, the major concern in these applications was meaningful interactivity between teachers and students or lack thereof. The advancement of videoconferencing in the 1980s significantly improved the interactivity and dialogue capabilities between teacher and students in distance learning applications.

Recent initiatives such as the Georgia Statewide Academic and Medical System (GSAMS) are making excellent use of videoconferencing and proving successful in providing highly interactive distance learning activities. Walsh and Reese (1995) describe the GSAMS as the largest interactive distance network in the world, reaching over 200 classrooms and other sites. GSAMS provides an excellent, successful example of the traditional "one teacher delivering to many students" model of distance learning.

The Internet is a fully interactive, digital technology that will eventually redefine distance learning in several ways in the years to come. First, students will no longer have to group themselves together into a common classroom or space to participate. The technology on the Internet is such that students can actively participate in a lesson from any place (schools, day care centers, business establishments, homes) that a computer workstation is connected to the Internet. Second, students will no longer necessarily have to participate at the same time. In digital format, lessons can be delivered and stored and called up by students as needed. Interactivity is achieved asynchronously through electronic bulletin boards, discussion groups, and E-mail. Third, instruction delivery will be an integration of several resources from which students can customize their lesson. While multiple resources may already exist now, students generally need to budget their time and, as a result, schedule their learning in a sequential mode, such as attend a lecture, go to the library, collect thoughts, write a paper, receive teacher comments, and so on. On the Internet, students may have at their immediate disposal a resource that includes the teacher as well as other instructional materials such as videos, computer simulations, and reference works. A student could possibly integrate the sequence by listening to the teacher for a while, consult a reference work, look at a simulation, send an E-mail message, and go back to listening to the teacher. In the not-too-distant future, new digital facilities such as video on demand and split-screen monitors will allow students to do several of these tasks simultaneously.

For the Internet to achieve its full potential in redefining distance learning, more advances must be made in the speed of delivering digital video. The Internet, as it currently is functioning, can already deliver on many of the possibilities described here in a text and still-image mode. This is insufficient for distance learning since important visual contact and clues including the teacher's emphasis through body language are lacking. The same is true for the teacher who is not able to see how students are responding to the material being presented.

Advances in digital technology such as **integrated service digital network** (ISDN) and other higher-speed transmission rates are being made, and in the future, much of what can be done with text on the Internet will also be possible with live or real-time digital videoconferencing. Several applications such as Impact North Carolina: 21st Century Education have begun to use ISDN technology for distance learning. Educators, especially those already investing in distance learning applications, should keep abreast of these and other developments designed to improve the delivery of digital video on the Internet.

SUMMARY

This chapter reviews the state of data communications as applied to education. Specifically, the evolution of the Internet is examined in terms of its applicability for instructional activities. Important concepts associated with global communications, information access, and new learning technologies are considered.

Data communications have been evolving and expanding during the past three decades. In the 1990s, this evolution resulted in the Internet or network of networks. A truly global network that has expanded rapidly in the 1990s and now reaches millions of people worldwide. Every indication is that the Internet will continue to evolve and become a major component of computer and communications applications in all areas of endeavor, including education.

A critical catalyst for the Internet's evolution was the development of the World Wide Web, a hypertext- and multimedia-based software system for establishing and sharing information resources. Through user-friendly Web browser software, users throughout the world can access and share information on a system with standard protocols.

The major applications of the Internet are global E-mail, discussion groups, live conferencing, file transfer, direct access to other computer systems, and information navigation, all of which can be adapted for instructional activities. A list of resources on the Internet is provided so that readers will become more familiar with basic activities. More detailed examples of Internet-based instructional activities for E-mail, information navigation, and information sharing are also presented.

In establishing an Internet connection in a school, educators and planners should be aware of the services of commercial on-line providers. Though still a relatively new industry, recent growth of these services indicates that their potential for shaping and defining the Internet is substantial.

The chapter concludes with a brief examination of and speculation on the role that the Internet will play in defining and expanding the possibilities for distance learning applications. Future advances in digital video communications will significantly expand present concepts of distance learning.

Key Concepts and Questions

1. **Data communications has evolved steadily during the second half of the 20th century.**

   How has this evolution affected your daily activities? How do you see this evolution continuing as we enter the 21st century?

2. **The Internet is a relatively new phenomenon.**

   How do you explain its popularity and growth in the 1990s? Will this popularity and growth continue? Explain?

3. **Many terms are used interchangeably regarding the Internet.**

   How do you explain the World Wide Web in relation to the Internet? Why has the Web become such an important aspect of the popularity of the Internet?

4. **Applications on the Internet are almost endless and depend on users' imagination and creativity.**

   How do you categorize the major Internet applications? Are they adaptable for instructional and other educational uses? Explain. In developing a plan for introducing the Internet into an instructional program, what applications would you consider first? Why?

5. Commercial on-line services have shown significant growth, especially in the home market.

   How do you account for their growth? Should a school consider using them for its Internet connection? Explain.

6. Distance learning has had limited applications in education.

   How do you see distance learning evolving or changing? What role, if any, will the Internet play in changing or redefining distance learning? Explain.

Suggested Activities

1. Take an inventory of data communications networks presently being used in a school or school district. What are the nature of the applications? When were they established? How do you see them evolving in the future?

2. Look at your inventory and consider how, if at all, these networks can be enhanced by connecting them to the Internet. If one or more of these networks are already connected to the Internet, how have they changed or been enhanced?

3. Hands-on activity: Using a Web browser such as Netscape and the list provided in Figure 7–6 as a starting point, visit Web sites and develop lists of useful URLs for the following individuals:

   A school building administrator to help in his or her day-to-day activities

   A district-level curriculum specialist

   A teacher in designing new lessons (Select whatever subject area or level with which you are familiar.)

   A computer coordinator in keeping abreast with the latest developments in integrating technology into the curriculum

References

Browne, S. (1994). *The Internet via Mosaic and World-Wide Web*. Emeryville, CA: Ziff-Davis.

Ellsworth, J. H. (1994). *Education on the Internet*. Indianapolis: Macmillan Computer Publishing.

Fisher, L. M. (1996, January 2). Surfing the Internet sets the agenda for software. *New York Times*, p. C15.

Frazier, M. K. (1995). Caution: Students on board the Internet. *Educational Leadership, 53*(2), 26–28.

Gibson, W. (1996, July 14). The Net is a waste of time and that's exactly what's right about it. *New York Times Magazine*, pp. 30–31.

Gray, M. (1996). *Measuring the growth of the Web*. Unpublished manuscript, Massachusetts Institute of Technology, Cambridge, MA.

Lewis, P. H. (1996, January 2). Rough-and-ready time for the Internet business. *New York Times*, p. C14.

Negroponte, N. (1995). *Being digital*. New York: Knopf.

New York Times. (1995, December 28). Connecting every pupil to the world, p. A20.

Quality Education Data. (1995). *Education market guide*. Denver, CO: Author.

Shirky, C. (1995). *Voices from the Net*. Emeryville, CA: Ziff-Davis.

Stoll, C. (1995). *Silicon snake oil: Second thoughts about the information superhighway*. New York: Doubleday.

Walsh, J., & Reese, B. (1995). Distance education's growing reach. *Technological Horizons in Education Journal, 22*(11), 58–62.

Williams, B. (1995). *The Internet for teachers*. Foster City, CA: IDG Books Worldwide.

Willis, B. (1993). *Distance education: A practical guide*. Englewood Cliffs, NJ: Educational Technology Publications.

Zworykin, V. K. (1975, July 4). [Interview with Mark Heyer and Al Pinsky, Radio Corporation of America, Inc.] Internet Uniform Resource Locator: http://engine.ieee.org/history_center/oral_histories/transcripts/zworykin21.html

Section III

Planning and Implementation

8

Hardware Planning
and Evaluation

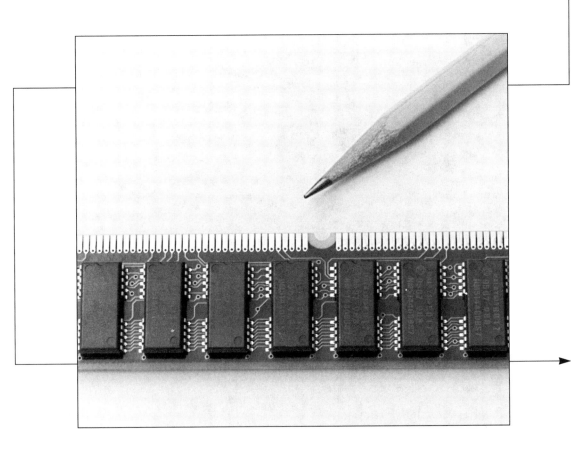

I n the framework for planning for technology described in Chapter 2, emphasis is placed on applications as fundamental building blocks. The components of every application include hardware, software, staffing, facilities, and finances, each of which is crucial to the eventual outcome and effectiveness. Planning the application, therefore, must involve an integrated approach to planning all the components. Detailed evaluations and specifications should be developed for each component that serve to bring the overall application together rather than fragmenting it.

The concept of integrating components such as hardware and software or hardware and facilities is critical, particularly as related to the selection and evaluation of hardware, since too often in the past an overemphasis has been placed on the acquisition of hardware alone. A common assumption was that once the hardware was acquired, the other components (software, staff development, facilities renovation, etc.) would follow. This unfortunately did not always happen, and, as a result, some schools invested in hardware but did not always realize the benefits for which they had hoped. This has become such a recognized problem that many administrators now insist that software and other components be identified and planned for before planning for hardware. Although this approach is prudent, the planning framework of choice remains the holistic one.

This chapter presents the major criteria or factors for evaluating the hardware component, concluding with an examination of some of the special hardware considerations for administrative and instructional applications.

HARDWARE PLANNING FOR THE LONG RANGE

Planning for computer hardware requires planning for the long range. The life cycle of most computing equipment is 5 to 7 years, but it is not unusual to see equipment used 9 and 10 years. In fact, many schools continue to use computer hardware until the equipment literally no longer works. As a result, when acquiring hardware, decision makers should be aware that this equipment may be used for a long time and evaluate it accordingly.

The durability of hardware also tempts administrators and others to look at available hardware that may have been acquired for one purpose and to consider using it for other purposes. This is desirable as long as the hardware is appropriate and can meet the needs of the application. However, the normal modus operandi should not be one of searching for applications for underutilized hardware, which reflects poor planning and an overemphasis on hardware. Planning for hardware should be integrated with the other components of an application. If available hardware is appropriate, then it should be used. Otherwise, new hardware should be considered.

In buying hardware, most schools find themselves making decisions from two different perspectives: when acquiring new hardware for new applications and when replacing hardware for existing applications. In acquiring new hardware for new applications, the purchasing pattern is more varied, with buyers attempting to select the best equipment to meet the needs of the application. When replacing hardware for existing applications, the pattern reveals a tendency to continue with the same manufacturer and upgrade to a newer model with greater capacity or speed. The various reasons for this include familiarity with the equipment and concern about retraining and conversion costs, particularly if larger computer systems are involved.

In many ways, this approach is similar to the way people make most personal equipment purchases, such as home appliances or automobiles. If they have had a good experience with a particular manufacturer, they go back to that manufacturer and buy a newer model when the old one needs replacing. There is one significant difference when it comes to computers, though. Once someone knows how to drive a car, for example, he or she is able to drive a new car of almost any manufacturer with relative ease. With computers, the "driving" is performed via software, and changing the hardware manufacturer may require changing the software, which in many cases means learning to "drive" all over again. The reason for this is that software standards generally do not exist, and software that drives one manufacturer's machine will not necessarily drive another. This is especially true for large mainframe and minicomputer systems and to some degree for microcomputers.

Organizations with large systems have shown a reluctance to change hardware manufacturers even if a better-performing and less expensive piece of hardware may be available because they do not want to have to change or convert the software. Manufacturers of large computers such as Unisys, Control Data Corporation, and Honeywell know this very well. Since the 1960s, proposals to customers who already have an IBM computer include additional software conversion factors for actually doing or assisting the customer in doing the conversion. Because such software conversions are so people-intensive and therefore expensive, they have not been able to compete effectively with IBM's. The same is true if IBM makes a proposal to a customer who already has a Control Data Corporation or Unisys computer. However, because IBM has such a large share of the mainframe and minicomputer market, the other manufacturers usually find themselves in the more disadvantaged position.

With microcomputers, the situation is somewhat different. Although several companies dominate the market, hundreds of microcomputer manufacturers exist, which makes for very keen competition. Many of these manufacturers have designed their products to be compatible with the dominant manufacturers and to use the same software. Another interesting phenomenon unique to microcomputers is the fact that for the first time much of the software being used, including the operating systems, is not being provided solely by the hardware manufacturers. Software companies such as Microsoft Corporation and Novell, Inc., are providing software that runs on a wide variety of microcomputers and is not entirely machine-dependent. These factors have combined to create a more dynamic hardware acquisition pattern than exists with mainframe or minicomputer systems.

The issue of manufacturer dependence will be discussed further in the next section, which deals with various hardware evaluation criteria. The selection of a manufacturer in any equipment acquisition is important; with computers it becomes especially critical because it frequently commits a user to a continuing relationship.

HARDWARE EVALUATION CRITERIA

Evaluating hardware can be a complicated process. For school districts with large mainframe computer systems, acquiring hardware means the investment of millions of dollars for many years to a particular vendor. As an example, Palm Beach County, Florida, a school district of approximately 100,000 students, recently completed a $20 million district automation project that connected all of the district's schools and administrative offices in a wide area network. The planning, evaluation, and selection of hardware took several years and involved awarding contracts to four major hardware vendors. This type of expenditure is not uncommon for large districts with dozens of schools and tens of thousands of students. However, all districts, both large and small, are finding that they are committing more and more of their equipment budgets to computer technology. Making such large investments requires the careful development of specifications and evaluation of equipment. In the public sector, administrators will likely use competitive bidding procedures that may require identifying a formalized evaluation procedure to prospective bidders.

Opinions regarding evaluation criteria vary significantly. One survey of administrators identified 19 different factors used in evaluating hardware (Ferrante, Hayman, Carlson, & Phillips, 1988, p. 36). On the other hand, some administrators simply ask, "How much does it cost?" Figure 8–1 identifies seven important factors for evaluating and selecting computer hardware:

1. *Performance*—how well does the hardware work?
2. *Compatibility*—does the hardware work with other equipment?
3. *Modularity/expandability*—can the hardware grow as applications grow?
4. *Ergonomics*—is the hardware designed with people in mind?
5. *Software availability*—is the software you wish to use currently available?
6. *Vendor*—what is the reputation of the manufacturer in terms of technical support, maintenance, and industry position?
7. *Cost*—what are the costs?

Figure 8–1
Major Hardware Evaluation
Factors

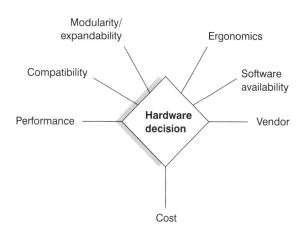

A serious hardware evaluation will take each of these factors into account when comparing different products. As much as possible, quantitative assessments should be developed. Certain factors such as capacity, speed, and costs are easily quantified. However, other factors such as ergonomics or software availability lend themselves better to qualitative assessments.

Site visits or field tests should be part of every acquisition, particularly when purchasing new models. Perhaps the most revealing activities in evaluating hardware are visits to comparable schools or districts that are using the hardware and running similar applications. In addition, popular vendors of both large and small hardware systems are generally most cooperative in demonstrating their products. For larger systems, vendors will also assist in conducting benchmark tests of typical applications. A benchmark test consists of running the same computer program on several different machines and comparing speed, response time, hardware resource requirements, and other factors. For microcomputer systems, local retail businesses are most accommodating in providing demonstrations. Trade journals and consultants should also be employed. Independent research services such as Datapro Research Group of Delran, New Jersey, do periodic hardware evaluation reports and ratings based on national surveys. They can be invaluable starting points in assessing the performance and customer satisfaction with various products.

In conducting an evaluation, one approach is to provide a hardware checklist or evaluation form to assist evaluators. However, the factors that go into a hardware evaluation can be very complex, especially for larger and more expensive systems. Hardware evaluations are not easily reduced to a simple checklist and should have substantial qualitative as well as quantitative back-up material. However, Figure 8–2 does provide a checklist that can be used to summarize and compare hardware evaluation ratings. The most appropriate use of this checklist would be as part of an evaluation summary and a discussion among administrators and teachers.

All of the evaluation criteria identified here are important for an effective evaluation, but in some circumstances one or more factors may carry more weight than others. A brief review of each of these factors will help clarify their general importance in the evaluation process.

Performance

Most hardware performance indicators attempt to assess capacity, speed, or quality of output. Table 8–1 provides some of the common performance criteria in evaluating major computer hardware components.

Large mainframe and minicomputer manufacturers generally customize their central processing units (CPUs), and an in-depth evaluation requires a good deal of technical expertise. For microcomputers, the most commonly used CPU components are provided by Motorola Corporation (for Apple computers) and Intel Corporation (for DOS/Windows computers). Several major attributes of all CPUs can be understood by many nontechnical people. For example, central processing units frequently are compared based on the capacity of the primary storage units as measured in bytes. Generally, the more primary storage a CPU has, the more processing that can be accomplished, assuming other factors such as software and other hardware components are equal.

Hardware description (Type of equipment; identify three manufacturers or models evaluated.)

Manufacturer/model 1 _____

Manufacturer/model 2 _____

Manufacturer/model 3 _____

	Ratings		
Evaluation criteria	*1*	*2*	*3*
Performance (capacity, speed)	_____	_____	_____
Compatibility	_____	_____	_____
Modularity/expandability	_____	_____	_____
Ergonomics	_____	_____	_____
Software availability	_____	_____	_____
Vendor	_____	_____	_____
Costs	_____	_____	_____
Final ratings	_____	_____	_____

Figure 8–2
North Central School District No. 1 Hardware Evaluation Summary Checklist

In terms of processing capacity, one of the most important factors in evaluating a CPU is the size of the data path within the CPU itself. These are usually established in 8-bit increments (8, 16, 32, 64, etc.), each designed to carry instructions or data from one CPU subunit to another. A 16-bit data path (or microprocessor) can carry twice as many instructions or data in the same time as an 8-bit data path, a 32-bit data path twice as many as a 16-bit data path and four times as many as an 8-bit data path. Theoretically, the size of the data path should directly relate to processing speed. In practice, although larger data paths are without a doubt faster, a direct proportion of speed to size is not realized because of software and waiting for other hardware components such as input and output devices.

Evaluating the speed of a CPU can be confusing because different terminology and measures are used. The term **megaflop** is used to compare the processing speeds of different types of computers. A megaflop is defined as a million mathematical calculations per second. This is similar to the commonly used **MIPS**, which means a million instructions per second. However, in comparing CPUs, probably the most common speed measure is **megahertz** (MHz), which is a million machine cycles per second. A **machine cycle** is defined as the number of electronic pulses that a CPU can generate as controlled or timed by its own internal clock. A machine cycle can be compared to a traffic light that goes through a timed sequence of red, yellow, and green signals. When the timing sequence changes (speeds up or slows down), the lights change accordingly. In the case of a CPU, the time pulses control the execution of instructions so that the more pulses that can be generated, the faster the CPU operates.

Table 8–1
Performance Criteria of Major Hardware Components

Component	Criteria
CPU	Capacity of the primary storage unit as measured in thousands (kilobytes) or millions (megabytes) of bytes
	Size of data paths within the CPU as measured in bits (8, 16, 32, 64, etc.)
	Machine cycle time as measured in millions of cycles per second (megahertz)
	Number of input and output devices that can be connected to the CPU
Magnetic disk	Capacity as measured in kilobytes, megabytes, gigabytes, or terabytes
	Transfer rate of moving data from the disk drive to the CPU as measured in millions of bits per second
Video display	Quality of visual image as measured by resolution and color capability
Printer	Print technology (laser, dot-matrix, ink-jet, etc.)
	Quality of print image (letter, near-letter, draft quality)
	Speed as measured by characters per minute, lines per minute, or pages per minute

Performance of various input and output devices is also frequently measured in terms of capacity or speed. Storage capacity of magnetic disk equipment is measured in kilobytes (thousands of bytes), megabytes (millions of bytes), gigabytes (billions of bytes), and terabytes (trillions of bytes). The most important speed measure for magnetic disks and most input/output devices is **transfer rate**, which simply is the speed of moving data from the device to the CPU as measured in millions of bits per second.

These various measures may seem a bit confusing or perhaps even alarming because they involve speeds and numbers that are impossible for most people to conceptualize. However, in evaluations, the relative speeds and capacities are more important than the absolute. A 120-MHz machine is twice as fast as a 60-MHz machine, which is twice as fast as a 30-MHz machine.

For devices such as video displays and printers, the quality of the output is as important as their speed. As an example, many users prefer the quality of a laser printer even though it might be slower than other types of printers. Readers may wish to review Appendix A, which compares the characteristics of various output devices.

Before we conclude this section on performance, two additional factors should receive brief attention. Reliability and durability are important factors but are sometimes overlooked because they cannot be measured with the same precision as other performance criteria. Evaluation of these factors is best handled by contacting other users or research services such as Datapro Research Group. Computer operations managers frequently keep logs of hardware downtime and are willing to share this information with colleagues. In evaluating durability, keep in mind that usage variables may exist that might not apply in all situations. For example, keyboards in a primary school computer laboratory used frequently by many young children might not last as long as keyboards used occasionally by adults. In evaluating reliability and durability, the best approach is to seek information from similar environments.

Compatibility

Compatibility is a common term in technology but is used two different ways. One refers to the capability of one device to work *well* with another device; the other is the capability of one device to work *the same way* as another device. Many smaller hardware manufacturers market their products based on their compatibility (to work well) with other equipment. Manufacturers of peripheral equipment such as disk drives or printers will always identify their products' compatibility with various central processing units. For example, Hewlett-Packard Corporation makes laser printers that are fully compatible with IBM PC and Apple Macintosh microcomputers. As more school districts have become involved in designing wide or local area networks, it has become critical for them to know that the various hardware components (i.e., CPUs, printers, disk devices, etc.) of these networks are compatible and can connect to one another.

The ability to meet compatibility criteria is easy to judge since no relative measures are involved. Either the equipment is compatible or not. Qualified compatibility, percentage compatibility, or other "gray area" compatibility should not be accepted. The vendor should be able to demonstrate to a customer's satisfaction the complete compatibility of the equipment.

For a computing device to work the same way as another means it will execute a program in the exact same fashion. The best example is the number of manufacturers that sell "IBM-compatible" microcomputers. This is critical for any applications that are expected to share the same programs such as a common database system or an instructional local area network. Generally, the hardware products from a common vendor will execute programs in the same way, but this is not always the case. For example, Apple Corporation's two major microcomputers, Apple IIs and Macintoshes, are not compatible, and a program that runs on one machine will not run on the other. Apple Corporation has partially resolved this problem by providing Apple II "emulation" programs for several Macintosh models that allow Apple II software to run on them. For example, an Apple IIe emulator board is available for several Macintosh models. The reverse, that is, Macintosh software executing on Apple IIs, is not available.

In plans for technology at the district level, compatibility is frequently considered as an overall policy issue and one that is not left to individual schools. Many districts establish compatibility guidelines that restrict the types of equipment that can be purchased. It is an excellent discussion item for any planning committee because it leads naturally into long-range thinking about hardware.

Modularity/Expandability

Modularity and expandability are also very important factors for long-range planning. Some hardware analysts consider these to be two different factors that should be evaluated separately. However, they are so similar that they are considered together here. **Modularity** refers to the interchangeability of components or parts of a hardware system. For example, in a CPU can RAMs or ROMs easily be replaced, or can several different types of devices be used or interchanged on an input/output port? **Expandability** is the ability of computer hardware to grow or expand as new applications are developed or as old applications become larger. The importance of modularity frequently manifests itself when considering expansion, and therefore these two features can be evaluated together.

The evaluation of modularity and expandability is critical, especially in the acquisition of large computer systems. Because of the costs involved, computer operations managers tend to develop equipment plans that stagger the replacement of certain components of a large hardware system at set intervals. A simplified example might be as follows:

Component	Replacement Cycle
CPUs	Year(s) 1 & 2
Data communications controllers	Year 3
Secondary storage devices	Years 4 & 5
Input devices	Year 6
Output devices	Year 7

At the end of seven years, the cycle repeats itself depending on application growth, financial condition, and available technology. As a result, large systems are acquired as a series of upgrades rather than as one-time, total system replacement. It would be impossible to function in this mode unless the equipment was both modular and expandable. Hence, in evaluating hardware for large systems, both of these factors must be carefully considered.

Modularity and expandability should also be considered in acquiring microcomputer systems. For example, as with large systems, users should know how many and which type of input and output units can be attached or whether the primary storage can be expanded. Information on these is readily available from manufacturers and retailers. However, these factors are not quite as critical because at some finite point the entire microcomputer system will be replaced.

Modularity and expandability depend to a certain extent on how current or recent the technology that is being used in the equipment is. Technology is constantly evolving. To expand, newly purchased equipment should not reflect old technology being phased out or considered "dead ended." By the same token, some new technology is experimental and may not catch on or may quickly be replaced by newer technology. This is not a common problem, but even the major manufacturers (i.e., IBM PC Junior and Apple Lisa) have had to discontinue products because of changes in technology, design problems, or customer apathy. Information is readily available from user groups and trade journals on the nature of the technology being used on most major manufacturers' equipment. If serious doubts exist about the technology of equipment under consideration and if information is difficult to come by, this might indicate a problem and should be evaluated accordingly.

Ergonomics

Ergonomics describes hardware features directly related to whether the equipment has been designed with the people who have to use it in mind. Is it pleasant to use? Is it easy to use? Most manufacturers of hardware, particularly items like keyboards, video displays, and other widely used devices, do consider the people who have to use their equipment. For example, the basic color patterns for most computer equipment are soft, pleasing to the eye, and blend into office and classroom environments.

For administrative applications, the "feel" of a keyboard is very important to staff who may be using the equipment for many hours at a time. Some of the early microcomputers used what was known as a "chiclet" keyboard, so named because the keys were small plastic pegs that looked and felt like Chiclet chewing gum. Although fine for occasional use, they were a problem for many typists. Their feel was different from a standard typewriter or QWERTY keyboard, and their spacing was more compact, which caused coordination problems. Although they are still available on laptop and portable computers, on desktop microcomputers they have been replaced by the standard keyboard. Several manufacturers also offer keyboards that are designed to reduce stress to ligaments and muscle tissue in the wrists and lower arms. These may be appropriate especially for secretaries and other staff who use a computer for long periods of time.

For instructional applications, various ergonomic features such as video display resolution, color, and sound capability can add significantly to lessons and presentations. However, the potential of these features is generally realized only through appropriate graphics and audio software. Other ergonomic features and options important for instruction include the availability of special hardware features for younger children such as the Muppet keyboard and voice synthesizers, Braille keyboards, and large video screens for special education students.

Software Availability

In evaluating hardware, it is most desirable to identify the software that will meet the needs of an application. A determination can then be made as to whether the identified software can run on the hardware being evaluated. This principle may seem obvious, but earlier in this chapter, situations were described in which schools have acquired equipment without consideration of software. Administrators or teachers then search for applications that in some cases cannot be found or do not exist.

Such situations are typically more a problem with small manufacturers but can arise with the major manufacturers also. A good example of this occurred when the Apple Macintosh microcomputer was first introduced in 1985. In terms of most hardware evaluation criteria such as performance, ergonomics, and vendor, the Macintosh rated very highly. However, very little software was available for it. Although the Macintosh provided a very advanced authoring language in HyperCard, none of the popular software products developed by independent software companies could run on it. As a result, many schools that had invested significant resources into Apple II microcomputers were slow to acquire the newer Macintoshes. Although many instructional software developers have caught up with Macintosh hardware technology in the 1990s, software availability is still an issue especially when one considers the number of software products available for DOS/Windows machines.

Vendor

As mentioned earlier, a hardware investment is usually a long-term one. Through the purchase of hardware, schools are also buying into a long-term relationship with a vendor. This is particularly true for large systems but exists to a certain degree for all hardware acquisitions. The vendor should be evaluated in terms of reputation, technical support, training, hardware maintenance, and industry position.

Most schools find themselves in situations in which they have already had experience with one or two manufacturers. These experiences are valuable and provide the best information regarding a vendor's performance. Additional information is easily gotten from services such as Datapro Research Group, journals such as *The Sloan Report,* directories such as *The Microcomputer Vendor Directory* (Auerbach Publishers), and buyer's guides. However, the computing industry is very dynamic; many new companies have entered it, and many have left. School administrators should be open to and aware of some of these dynamics.

IBM has been a dominant manufacturer of mainframe, minicomputer, and microcomputer equipment for decades. Its reputation for technical support, maintenance, and software availability, among other things, is excellent. For certain segments, especially in private businesses and corporations, IBM has cornered in excess of 70% of the world market. However, IBM has struggled in recent years to keep up with the competition in the microcomputer market and has failed to maintain its base as customers switch from larger to smaller computer systems. As a result, relatively new companies such as Compaq have become the dominant manufacturers of microcomputer systems.

In the primary and secondary school instructional microcomputer market, the market share picture is different. Apple Corporation has come to dominate this market and has provided approximately 60% of all microcomputers used for instruction. The foundation of Apple's success was based on the wide acceptance of the Apple II microcomputers, which were first introduced in the late 1970s, followed by the introduction of the Macintosh in the 1980s. Apple Corporation is a classic example of the dynamics of the computer industry and how a new company that began in 1976 can become a major player in a short time. In the 1980s, Apple was clearly a leader in microcomputer design and manufacturing. In the 1990s, because of increasing competition from new companies, Apple has struggled to maintain its leading position and has begun to lose some of its market share even in primary and secondary schools.

Since the 1960s, many well-known companies such as RCA, General Electric, Osborne, and Coleco have merged, declared bankruptcy, or left the industry. Now hundreds of companies provide computer hardware products; Table 8–2 is a list of some of them.

Table 8–2
Major Computer Manufacturers

Company	Location	Mainframes	Minicomputers	Microcomputers	Other components
Advanced Logic Research (ALR)	Irvine, CA			X	
Apple Computer	Cupertino, CA			X	
AST Research	Irvine, CA			X	
AT&T	Baskins Ridge, NJ			X	X
Atari ST	Sunnyvale, CA			X	X
Commodore International Ltd.	West Chester, PA			X	
Compaq Computer	Houston, TX			X	
Data General Corporation	Westboro, MA		X	X	X
Dell Computer	Austin, TX			X	
Digital Equipment Corporation	Maynard, MA	X	X	X	X
Epson America, Inc.	Torrance, CA			X	
Hewlett-Packard	Cupertino, CA		X	X	X
IBM Corporation	Armonk, NY	X	X	X	X
Intel Corporation	Santa Clara, CA			X	X
Kaypro	Solana Beach, CA			X	
Motorola Computer Systems	Cupertino, CA			X	X
NCR Corporation	Dayton, OH		X	X	X
NEC Technologies	Boxborough, MA			X	
Next Inc.	Palo Alto, CA			X	
Sun Microsystems, Inc.	Mt. View, CA		X	X	
Tandon	Moorpark, CA			X	X
Tandy/Radio Shack	Fort Worth, TX			X	X
Texas Instruments, Inc.	Austin, TX			X	X
Unisys	Blue Bell, PA	X	X	X	X
Wang Laboratories, Inc.	Lowell, MA		X		X
Zenith Data Systems	Glenview, IL			X	
ZEOS International	St. Paul, MN			X	

Cost

School administrators understand the importance of costs as a factor in all equipment acquisitions, including computer hardware. Defining costs for hardware can be complex and involve initial acquisition, yearly maintenance, lease purchases, and a host of other possible arrangements. School administrators, particularly in public bidding situations, find the competition very keen. Many of the smaller companies provide very attractive proposals that can result in substantial savings. All proposals, regardless of the source, need to be very carefully reviewed and evaluated. (Financing computer applications, including hardware costs, is given full treatment in Chapter 12.)

SPECIAL CONSIDERATIONS FOR ADMINISTRATIVE APPLICATIONS

In evaluating hardware for administrative applications, several special considerations need to be mentioned. Because an objective of many administrative applications is developing information resources, certain hardware evaluation criteria such as compatibility and modularity/expandability become critical to ensuring that all equipment can contribute, connect, and grow together. Information needs to flow smoothly up, down, and across the school organization; any present or future incompatibility of hardware can seriously jeopardize this. As a result, school districts tend to establish central district control in developing hardware evaluation guidelines for administrative applications. In many cases, this might mean hardware standardization policies, district-wide procurement plans, or direct approval procedures by a district coordinator.

In school districts with large administrative computer operations, administrators generally do best by relying on their technical staffs. The technology for large systems is very sophisticated, and a trained staff is probably in the best position to conduct in-depth hardware evaluations and to recommend acquisition policies.

Administrative applications such as budgeting, personnel, and inventory control and the hardware used for them are almost identical to those in private industry and public agencies. Administrators and teachers involved with evaluating hardware for administrative applications should take advantage of the extensive data resources available in the private sector in addition to those in the educational sector. Many of the trends that have developed in administrative applications such as data communications, optical disc storage, and laser printers had their first applications in private industry.

Also, in large districts where schools are geographically dispersed, a wide area network likely is or will be put in place to integrate these schools. Data communications continues to be one of the more complex areas of technology. If necessary, consultants should be considered, especially when designing something new or making a major upgrade to an existing data communications system.

SPECIAL CONSIDERATIONS FOR INSTRUCTIONAL APPLICATIONS

Evaluating hardware for instructional applications has evolved differently from administrative applications since many school districts have allowed more control and flexibility at the school level. To a degree, this is the result of differences in the hardware available for different subject and grade levels. Hardware that is appropriate for teaching basic skills in the early grades may not be appropriate for teaching business in the high schools or for doing desktop publishing. Districts will frequently provide guidelines for teachers to recommend equipment that they think will work best in their classrooms. As a result, some diversity of equipment, particularly with microcomputing, can be expected. However, administrators should also be careful to avoid a "technology of Babel" situation in which many different machines have been acquired that cannot communicate with one another.

Software availability is probably the most significant factor in evaluating hardware for instructional applications, since in many cases, teachers tend to identify software first and even consider it a far more important decision than the hardware. Teachers need to be aware of the hardware requirements of any software they are considering. All instructional software developers identify their products' hardware requirements. In addition, certain software packages used to control special-purpose devices such as videodiscs, voice synthesizers, and scientific probes may only work with particular equipment.

Data communications becomes increasingly more important as school districts expand the number of stand-alone microcomputer systems. A major hardware consideration is connecting these systems together in local and wide area networks. Many benefits will derive from networking, but it is also a more complex technology than a stand-alone environment. If the expertise does not exist within the district, administrators should consider using consultant services in designing and evaluating the hardware required for a network.

CASE STUDY
Place: Appleton   Year: 1993

Appleton is a small, suburban school district located in the Midwest with a population of 3,500 students. It operates one high school, two middle schools, and three primary schools. The school population decreased in the 1980s but has stabilized and has been increasing slightly since 1990. The tax base for the school district has been very good mainly because of the relocation of one large corporation into the district in 1980.

The district considers technology important to the instructional program. A district-wide planning committee, established in 1980, has been most supportive of acquiring microcomputer equipment at all grade levels. The student/microcomputer ratio for the district is 11.3 to 1, with the distribution of instructional equipment as follows:

High school—105 units (65 IBM PC-compatibles, 40 Macintoshes)

Middle schools—101 units (60 Apple IIs, 15 Macintoshes, 10 IBM PCs, 10 Tandys, 6 others)

Primary schools—103 units (53 Apple IIs, 20 Tandys, 20 Commodore Amigas, 10 others)

The high school has installed a local area network connecting all of its equipment. Although some serious problems arose in linking different machines onto the one network, they were resolved with the help of a consultant and the vendor supplying the network. All of the machines in the middle and primary schools are being used stand-alone.

A serious issue facing the district as it continues to acquire technology is whether to standardize its equipment for *instructional* applications. The factors involved are varied. First, much of the equipment currently in use, particularly in the middle and primary schools, was acquired in the 1980s and needs to be replaced as the costs of repairs are increasing significantly. Second, administrators in the middle and primary schools have indicated that they would like to follow the lead of the high school in establishing local area networks, mainly to make it easier for the staff to share software. Third, although some teachers would like to be connected to a common network, they have indicated that their major priority is to replace the current equipment with newer but compatible equipment. Lastly, it should be mentioned that for *administrative* applications, the district has purchased only IBM PC microcomputers that are used for local school building applications, district-wide applications, and as communications terminals to a state-wide database system.

Assume that you are the superintendent and have been asked to develop a position paper for the district's planning committee on the issue of hardware standardization for instructional applications. Which options would you consider? Which organizational structure(s) would you recommend for further discussion and for development of a policy on hardware standardization?

SUMMARY

This chapter describes the major factors used in evaluating computer hardware. Because this equipment will be retained for many years, it is critical to approach hardware selection as a long-term investment requiring careful evaluation.

The major criteria to be considered when acquiring computer hardware are these:

Performance
Compatibility
Modularity/expandability
Ergonomics
Software availability
Vendor (support, maintenance, industry position)
Cost

Although some of these factors may be considered more important than others, none of them should be ignored when acquiring equipment.

In selecting and evaluating hardware, administrators need to be aware that the policies of a district might be different for administrative and instructional applications. Administrative applications tend to be controlled centrally at the district level to ensure compatibility and an easy flow of information across the administrative structure. Instructional applications frequently result in more diversity of equipment mainly because of different subject and grade-level needs. Software availability, which may limit the acquisition of hardware to particular manufacturers or models, is especially critical in instructional applications.

Key Concepts and Questions

1. Evaluating and selecting hardware requires a serious consideration of long-range implications.

   Why? What are the characteristics of hardware acquisition and use that tend to make schools dependent on particular machines or manufacturers for many years?

2. In evaluating hardware, the major factors are performance, compatibility, modularity/expandability, ergonomics, software availability, vendor, and cost.

   Are any of these factors more important than the others? If so, why or under what conditions?

3. Performance simply refers to how well a piece of equipment works in terms of capacity and speed.

   What are some of the specific performance criteria used in evaluating computer hardware? Which do you consider the most important?

4. In evaluating hardware, many administrators consider compatibility with other equipment a most critical factor.

   Why? Is compatibility a universal factor that is always important, or can it be more or less important depending on the application?

5. Software availability might be considered the major factor in acquiring hardware. In fact, in many districts, it is common to identify the software to be used before acquiring hardware.

   What are some circumstances or situations in which the software might be the most important factor in selecting hardware?

6. As with most expensive equipment acquisitions (e.g., school buses, maintenance vehicles, air conditioners), the vendor or manufacturer is a major consideration.

   Is this any different with computer hardware? Is it more or less the case? Why?

7. Administrative and instructional applications are different.

   Do these differences affect the way in which hardware is evaluated for them? Should a district establish acquisition policies that recognize these differences? Explain.

Suggested Activities

1. Take an inventory of the computer hardware in a school, or use an inventory that already exists. Identify any patterns regarding year of acquisition, vendor, model, and cost. Do these patterns differ for equipment used for administrative versus instructional applications? Identify and explain any patterns or trends and any differences.

2. Review the policies (if they exist) for hardware acquisition in a school district. Evaluate these policies in light of the material in this chapter. Can you offer any suggestions for improving them?

References

Datapro Research Group. (1995). *Management of microcomputer systems* (Vols. I & II). Delran, NJ: McGraw-Hill.

Dvorak, J.C. (Ed.). (1996). *PC Magazine 1996 computer buyer's guide*. Emeryville, CA: Ziff-Davis.

Ferrante, R., Hayman, J., Carlson, M. S., & Phillips, H. (1988). *Planning for microcomputers in higher education: Strategies for the next generation* (ASHE-ERIC Higher Education Report No. 7). Washington, D.C.: Association for the Study of Higher Education.

Meltzer, K. H. (1990). The district automation project. *Technical Horizons in Education Journal, 18*(4), 84–85.

Pronk, R. (1996). *The Power Mac book*. Scottsdale, AZ: Coriolis Group.

Sales, G. C., & Damyanovich, M. (1990). A model for making decisions about computer and technology implementation. In C. Warger (Ed.), *Technology in today's schools* (pp. 22–31). Alexandria, VA: Association for Supervision and Curriculum Development.

9

Software Selection
and Evaluation

Hardware, with its flickering lights, buzzing circuits, and colorful cabinetry, may seem like the exciting component of computer technology, but among many computer professionals, software is where the action is. A computer cannot perform a single function unless a software program has been developed to provide instructions for the hardware to follow. Some programs can be easily written, whereas more complex programs may require tens or hundreds of thousands of instructions. Programmers who are involved in such large-scale software development are among the most talented and creative in the computer industry. Their completed work can engender feelings of accomplishment similar to those of an artist who has just completed a painting or a chef who has prepared a magnificent meal.

On the other hand, when something goes wrong, when a computer "bug" occurs, feelings of accomplishment can quickly fade. If a program is critical to an operation, a great deal of stress and frustration can develop that evoke mental images of other, more appealing lines of work. These last until the bug is found and corrected, and a sense of accomplishment returns, beginning the cycle again, waiting for the next bug to emerge.

With the proliferation of computing technology over the past decade, this scenario occurs at many levels, perhaps involving a team of software engineers correcting the transmission of data from the Hubble Space Telescope, a staff of computer programmers in a state education department implementing an electronic educational exchange and bulletin board, a secretary experimenting with the new features of the latest version of a word-processing package, a high school class creating a homepage on the Web, or a group of fourth graders completing their first newsletter with a desktop publishing program. Software surely *is* where the action is, where things happen, and where feelings of joy and frustration come and go in relation to successes and problems.

Selecting the software that teachers, administrators, and students will be using may therefore be the most important technical decision made in implementing computer applications. The topic of this chapter is the selection and evaluation of computer software. Commonly used evaluation criteria that are appropriate for both administrative and instructional applications are examined.

DECISIONS, DECISIONS, DECISIONS

Tom Snyder Productions, one of the more successful instructional software development companies, markets a series of excellent simulation programs entitled Decisions, Decisions. These simulation programs require students to make frequent decisions regarding some real-life phenomena. Depending on the decision selected, new situations are created, all of which require the students to make additional decisions. The series' title provides an almost adequate description of the real-life activity of evaluating and selecting software; "Decisions, Decisions, and More Decisions" may be more appropriate. With tens of thousands of software products available from commercial developers and hundreds of thousands available through noncommercial sources, the possibilities are mind-boggling. Even after a software package has been selected, new versions of it quickly appear that require another decision. Software updates, modifications, and new releases are commonplace in computing life and seem endless. In sum, the number and types of decisions related to software have grown considerably in the past 20 years.

Although the basic nature of software has not changed over the past several decades, its acquisition and implementation has changed radically. Through the 1970s, all computer installations required a well-trained software staff to develop application programs using high-level languages such as COBOL, FORTRAN, or PL/1, provided by the hardware manufacturer. Today, in large computer installations, a good deal of application program development still exists, but programmers are also making much greater use of software development tools such as database management systems and communications control software, which reduce the number of high-level language instructions significantly. In some cases, these software tools are provided by the hardware manufacturers, but increasingly they are supplied by software development firms.

In traditional large mainframe applications, users are very dependent on the programming staff for support, documentation, maintenance, and modification of the software. A major application such as a student record-keeping system or a financial management system can have a useful life cycle of 15 years or more. As a result, users and programmers must have good working relationships and procedures for regularly maintaining and upgrading these systems. Clear lines of responsibility may be drawn, with the users identifying needs and improvements, and the programming staff modifying the software. In the most successful situations, the overall software decisions are shared between the users and the technical staff.

The movement to microcomputer technology has changed the technician-user relationship. The vast majority of microcomputer users do not program in a high-level language but instead purchase software packages for word processing, spreadsheets, desktop publishing, and a host of other applications. Most of these packages require a basic understanding of how to load a disk and to respond to a series of menus, prompts, and alternatives. With good documentation and minimal technical support, users are expected to be able to master enough of the features of these packages to do most of what they wish to accomplish. Not unexpectedly, the degree of user success in these environments varies. User aptitude and experience are factors, but the choice of appropriate software is also a critical and determining factor.

For most administrative microcomputer users, the number of applications and appropriate software programs can be narrowed down to database, spreadsheet, word-processing, desktop publishing, and office automation applications. Although many packages exist for these applications, several major vendors such as Microsoft, Lotus, and Novell are beginning to dominate the market. For instructional microcomputer users, the number of applications and appropriate software packages is becoming almost unlimited. Depending on subject, grade level, and student interests and abilities, thousands of software packages exist, and the number keeps increasing every day. Presently, approximately 1,000 companies are marketing educational software products, most of which were established in the 1980s and 1990s. In addition, there are unknown numbers of programmers who work in colleges, school districts, and state agencies who have developed packages, most of which are available free of charge, for use in primary and secondary schools.

School districts have begun to establish instructional software evaluation teams to sort through and evaluate all that is available. Large school systems such as Chicago and New York City employ full-time staffs whose major responsibilities involve evaluating and selecting software for use in their schools. Some states such as California and Texas have established effective state-wide software evaluation services that publish or provide on-line databases of their software reviews (Bakker & Piper, 1994). Despite this centralization, more and more instructional software evaluation is being done at the building level. Frequently, it is an opinion-driven activity, with people liking or disliking certain products based on their knowledge, experiences, or teaching philosophies. Computer coordinators may have the greatest influence in evaluating and selecting software for use in the schools, but committees or teams of teachers and other professionals increasingly are involved in evaluating software as they would any other curricular or academic materials. Involving end-users in software selection may seem obvious, but stories abound of teachers and others questioning the value of software products acquired by somebody else (Pepi & Scheurman, 1996).

Regardless of the process by which software is selected in a district or school, administrators have a responsibility to ensure that appropriate software is selected. Although administrators need not be involved in every software evaluation activity, they should establish procedures that assure that the appropriate technical and application (administrative or instructional) criteria are considered.

SOFTWARE EVALUATION CRITERIA

The most important factor in evaluating and selecting software is determining how well it meets the application's needs. For example, a word-processing package might be evaluated in terms of text manipulation features, spell-checking capabilities, and the number of type fonts supported, whereas a database package might be evaluated in terms of file-handling capabilities such as data merging, query language, and sort features. These evaluation factors can be extensive. In a report issued by the U.S. Congress's Office of Technology Assessment (1988), as a result of a survey of regional educational software evaluation agencies, more than 200 factors (see Appendix C) were identified as being used to evaluate instructional software. All of the factors for every school application will not be reviewed here; however, several major evaluation criteria (see Figure 9–1) are common to all computer software packages:

Efficiency—how well are the programs written?
Ease of use—how easy is the software to use?
Documentation—what are the quality and quantity of the documentation?
Hardware requirements—what hardware is needed to run the software?
Vendor—what is the reputation of the developer in terms of support, maintenance, and industry position?
Cost—how much does it cost?

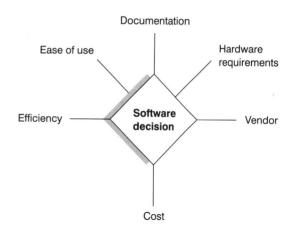

Figure 9–1
Major Software Evaluation
Factors

These factors should be considered in the evaluation and selection of every software product. As is the case in judging hardware, one or more of these factors may be more important depending on individual circumstances and applications. Together with a determination of how well the software meets the needs of a particular application, they form the basis for evaluating all types of software.

Efficiency

Most software efficiency measures relate to the speed with which a program executes. Overall response times, data access or search time, and sort time all relate to the operational speed of a program and are easily quantified. For software packages that are to run on mainframe systems, technical staff are needed to evaluate efficiency. For microcomputer software, users with some assistance from technical staff can evaluate basic speed measures such as response time and access time. **Response time** is how quickly a program responds with the desired computer activity once a request has been made. It can refer to fetching a record from a database, answering a "help" inquiry, or performing a calculation. Data access or search time refers specifically to locating data on a disk file. It directly relates to the number of records on the database and more importantly, to the manner in which they are stored.

In evaluating data access times, the same disk equipment must be used when comparing software, because the speed of the disk hardware can greatly influence access times. In fact, the term **access time** is also used to measure the speed of disk equipment itself in fetching records, and this factor must be neutralized. For large record-keeping applications involving thousands or tens of thousands of records, sort time or the time required to sequence or merge data is also frequently used to test the efficiency of file-handling software.

Professional software research firms such as the Info World Test Center generally use a method of measuring software efficiency called the **benchmark test**. Benchmark tests can be developed by technical staff in any organization, including schools. They consist of identifying tasks that the software being evaluated would be expected to perform, which are then executed on different software packages and measured in terms of speed. For example, in evaluating a sort feature of a database program, an appropriate benchmark test might be to sort the typical number of student records that might exist in a school's student files.

Benchmark tests are easy to perform, but again it is essential to make sure that the hardware, data files, and any other factors that can influence speed are identical. Hardware characteristics, even within a family of computers, are very different, and software will perform differently depending on these characteristics. For example, a software benchmark test comparing two programs by running one only on a Power Mac $6100/60$ and the other only on a Power Mac $8100/80$ is not valid because the inherent CPU speed of the Power Mac $8100/80$ is so much greater than that of the Power Mac $6100/60$. The same would be true if the first program were run on an Intel Pentium 60-based computer and the other on an Intel Pentium 120-based computer.

Efficiency also relates to how well a program is written in terms of structure, logic flow, programming language, and so forth. When the source code (high-level language instructions) is available, it is desirable to have the technical staff evaluate the quality of the programs. This is generally a subjective evaluation dependent on the staff's knowledge and expertise. In cases in which only the object code (machine language instructions) is provided, this type of an evaluation is not possible.

Ease of Use

The software evaluation factor of ascending importance in the past few years is ease of use. With machines being placed in libraries, classrooms, teacher prep rooms, as well as offices, their utilization depends significantly on how easy the software is to use. This factor relates directly or perhaps inversely to the level of knowledge of the intended users. Software that is to be used by a professional technical staff may be more difficult to use and may require a certain amount of training. Software that is to be used by occasional or beginning users such as students should be user-friendly. Menu-driven screens, on-line "help" features, and good supporting documentation are characteristics of user-friendly software and should be evaluated accordingly. These are generally subjectively evaluated, although they can be reduced to a quantified individual or group rating.

In evaluating ease of use, seeking input from the target users is very desirable. Secretaries may be the best choice for evaluating a word-processing package, accountants for an electronic spreadsheet program, teachers for computer-managed instruction, and students for instructional software. This approach is an obvious example of involving users at various levels in a school in technology planning and implementation activities. Not only is their opinion important to the decision maker, but their involvement enhances the environment required for moving ahead with technology.

Documentation

The importance of documentation in software evaluation is consistently recognized regardless of the type of computer being used, the nature of the applications, or the level of expertise of the target users. "What does the software do?" "How does it do it?" and "How do you use it?" are critical questions that should be clearly answered in the documentation. These questions may seem obvious, but teachers have frequently found themselves questioning the benefit of some software and technology with which they are not sure what is supposed to be accomplished. If they are not, the quality of the software is suspect.

Documentation standards have grown considerably since the proliferation of microcomputers; therefore, good documentation is to be expected and should be evaluated most rigorously. Software designed to execute on mainframe computer systems and most administrative software tend to be well documented, mainly because of the competition but also because this genre of software has matured. Surely, word-processing, spreadsheet, and database packages from the major vendors come supplied with a good deal of high-quality documentation. These vendors have learned that to be competitive in these markets, they must have comprehensive, easy-to-understand manuals, and intuitive, on-line help features.

For instructional software, however, the quality and quantity of documentation are more diverse. Some instructional software comes with little more than a diskette and one or two pages of installation instructions. On the other hand, the more established companies will provide a complete set of installation and operating instructions. The best instructional software documentation will also include curricular materials and suggestions for integrating the package into classroom activities. Tom Snyder Productions, Inc., Sunburst Inc., Optical Data Systems, and Minnesota Educational Computer Consortium (MECC) are some of the major instructional software developers that have been attentive to providing good documentation with their products.

One of the exceptions to good documentation standards is software that may be available free from software exchanges and individuals. It frequently may not have high-quality documentation. However, this is to be expected given that the software is usually provided for free or for a nominal fee.

Hardware Requirements

This evaluation factor is the corollary to the software availability criterion used in evaluating hardware. Just as software needs to be available for the hardware, software likewise may have specific hardware requirements. Generally, the hardware requirements for software are

specific computer manufacturer/model or CPU,
minimum primary storage capacity,
minimum magnetic disk space, and
specialized input/output devices.

This information, along with any other specialized hardware requirement, is readily available from the software supplier.

Many software companies will market for a specific computer manufacturer or model. For example, popular administrative software such as Lotus 1-2-3 (Lotus Corporation) and dBASE (Ashton-Tate) require DOS/Windows machines. Some of the earlier desktop publishing software such as Pagemaker (Aldus) would only run on Macintosh microcomputers. Although software companies sometimes will develop a product for a specific machine, if it is successful, they will follow market trends and make the product available for other equipment.

In the early 1980s, most instructional software companies developed their products for the Apple II microcomputer. However, as the microcomputer market share in schools began to change, more of these companies developed versions of their most successful programs to run on Macintosh and IBM PC machines. In any event, the purchaser must have access to or intend to have access to the appropriate computer or model before investing in the software.

All software programs have some minimum primary storage requirements. For very popular software products reissued periodically as newer versions, purchasers should try to determine future primary storage requirements. For example, Version 2.0 of Lotus 1-2-3 required 512,000 bytes of primary storage, while Version 3.0 required 1 million bytes. This practice may seem frustrating and even evoke thoughts of a conspiracy involving artificially created hardware obsolescence. However, the software developers are basically attempting to provide additional options and capabilities to make their products more attractive and competitive. It is highly recommended that extra primary storage space exist on all computing equipment so that this particular requirement can be easily met when evaluating software.

Any software packages that perform some type of file handling will require disk space. As with primary storage, the basic rule is that whatever is needed presently will surely increase in the future. An old computing adage is "You can never have enough disk space." This should be kept in mind when evaluating the hardware requirements of software, especially for administrative applications.

Many software products also identify certain specialized input/output or other peripheral equipment to use all of their features and options. For example, many software packages for microcomputers provide "deluxe" versions that require CD-ROM drives in addition to magnetic disk drives. Many packages providing color images and graphs may require certain levels of screen resolution on video display equipment. Some instructional software packages used in science, music, or art may require sound boards, custom probe, synthesizer, or other specialized input equipment. When these packages are evaluated, this information is generally available and must be considered when selecting software. Failure to do so may result in acquiring software that will not run as planned on a school's hardware or, in the worst cases, not run at all.

In some situations, such as in selecting an integrated learning system, both hardware and software are evaluated together. This is a very desirable situation and streamlines evaluation activities considerably. In general, when the hardware and software can be planned and acquired together, one can expect a smoother implementation of the application.

Vendor

All of the vendor characteristics such as support, maintenance, industry position, and reputation that apply to hardware evaluation also apply to software. However, given that there are over 30,000 software companies, evaluating this factor becomes a more diffi- cult undertaking. Some of these companies consist of one full-time employee; others employ thousands. Microsoft Corporation, one of the world's largest software suppliers, has more than 8,000 programmers and other support and administrative employees. As with many acquisitions, it is important to know with whom you are dealing, particularly if you expect to establish a long-term relationship. In an industry as dynamic as software development, those companies with proven track records should be considered over other companies that may be here today and gone tomorrow.

Track record cannot be considered in isolation, however, since many software com- panies specialize and develop expertise in limited applications. Companies that are the leaders in administrative software such as databases or spreadsheets may have very little expertise in instructional software such as simulations or interactive video programs. As a result, the evaluation of software vendors may require some in-depth exploration.

Software reviews, journal articles, industry research services such as Datapro Research Inc., Auerbach Publishers Inc., and R. R. Bowker's *Only the Best* are excel- lent sources of information regarding vendors. *Technology & Learning* (formerly *Classroom Computer Learning*) includes a software review column in each issue and devotes at least one issue to the "best" instructional software products of the year. Anyone involved with software evaluation, be they administrators or teachers, should use sources such as these to become familiar with the major software suppli- ers. Figure 9–2 lists some of the major sources.

Auerbach Publishers Pennsauken, NJ	*Micro* Florida Center for Instructional Computing University of South Florida Tampa, FL
Datapro Research Inc. Delran, NJ	
Educational Products Information Exchange (EPIE) Water Mill, NY	MicroSIFT Northwest Regional Educational Library Portland, OR
Educational Software Preview Guide ICCE University of Oregon Eugene, OR	*Software Reports* Allenbach Publishers Carlsbad, CA
Educator's Handbook and Software Directory Vital Information, Inc. Kansas City, MO	*Swift's Educational Software Directory* Sterling Swift Publishing Co. Austin, TX
Journal of Courseware Review Foundation for the Advancement of Computer-Aided Instruction Cupertino, CA	Technology in the Curriculum Project California State Department of Education Sacramento, CA

Note: Most state education departments provide educational software review services.

Figure 9–2
Sources of Information for Software Evaluation

Cost

Costs for software vary significantly. On large computer systems, some comprehensive contracts—including software, certain levels of on-site support services, and training—easily can involve millions of dollars over several years. Integrated learning systems that combine software, hardware, and curriculum can easily cost in excess of a million dollars for a large school system. In undertaking evaluations involving software of this magnitude, school districts must be careful and deliberate in making their selections.

On the other side of the spectrum, some instructional software programs for microcomputer applications cost less than $50. Broderbund Corporation's award-winning program *Where in the ____ Is Carmen Sandiego?* normally retails for $49.99 and on sale can be purchased for less than $30. For these acquisitions, the software evaluation procedures are generally less deliberate. In fact, such inexpensive programs may be purchased simply for experimental purposes or as part of a software library without immediate application, which is desirable because it builds expertise and technical knowledge within a school.

However, this approach should not constitute the modus operandi. Whether performed by an individual or, more desirably, by a team, software that is to be used regularly in a classroom should be reviewed and evaluated for both technical and instructional criteria. Simply because a software product might be inexpensive is not sufficient reason to relax or eliminate evaluation activities.

Chapter 12 provides a thorough treatment on finances and cost factors in acquiring technology. Readers are encouraged to review the material there.

ADMINISTRATIVE SOFTWARE EVALUATION FACTORS

As mentioned earlier in this chapter, critical to software evaluation is a determination as to how well the software meets the specific needs of the application through the various features provided. Reviewing all the existing administrative applications software is not possible here, but Figures 9–3, 9–4, and 9–5 list some of the more important evaluation features for the three most popular applications: word processing, electronic spreadsheets, and databases. These features can be considered regardless of whether the specific software product is stand-alone or part of an integrated package such as Microsoft Works.

WordPerfect and Microsoft Word are the most popular word-processing software packages in use today. Originally developed for the DOS/Windows machines, versions are also available for Macintosh computers. Both packages also measure up well against most of the features identified in Figure 9–3. Furthermore, they are regularly upgraded, with versions providing new features issued every year. Microsoft Write, WordStar, and Professional Write are other popular word-processing packages found in many administrative offices.

Figure 9–4 identifies some of the features to look for in electronic spreadsheet programs. Lotus 1-2-3, with the largest share of the electronic spreadsheet market,

Figure 9–3
Features of Word-Processing
Software

Number and type of fonts

Number of type styles (boldface, underline, shadow, etc.)

Footnoting

Wordwrap

Menu-driven

Lengthwise printing

Print preview

Graphics integration

ASCII file conversion

Conversion of other word processing files

Multiple document processing
  (work on more than one document at a time)

Multiple column controls

Spelling checker (how many words?)

Thesaurus

Document security

Grammar checker

Figure 9–4
Features of Electronic Spreadsheet Software

Number of rows and columns

Editing features

Copy features

Lengthwise printing

Multiple spreadsheet processing

Menu-driven

Spreadsheet merging

Spreadsheet security

Graphics integration

Database integration

Types and dimensions of charts (line, bar, pie, etc.)

Types of statistical functions supported
  Basic (summaries, averages, percentages)
  Advanced (standard deviations, correlations, analysis of
    variance)

Figure 9–5
Features of Database Software

Database structure (relational, flat file, etc.)
File security
Menu-driven
Report generator program
Statistical reporting features
Automatic address labels
Query language
Electronic spreadsheet integration
Database restructuring
Sort/merge
Speed
Options (ascending, descending, levels)
Data-sharing features (upload, download)
ASCII file conversion
Conversion of other database files

Microsoft's Excel, and Borland International Corporation's Quattro Pro are among the most popular packages. All of the products provide the standard spreadsheet cell and mathematical features. As spreadsheets advance in sophistication, more importance is being placed on graphics, chart, and other data presentation facilities.

The most important administrative software evaluation decision is the selection of a database management package. Although it is not unusual to experiment with different word-processing and spreadsheet programs, most organizations, including schools, will standardize their database software and once established will be reluctant to change it.

One of the most important features of database software relates to data and file sharing in both local and wide area networks. Given the inherent complexity of networked systems, administrators should rely on the expertise of the technical staff when evaluating the networking capabilities of database software. For many years, Ashton-Tate's dBASE has been the industry leader for database management software for microcomputer systems. However, other database products such as Paradox and FoxPro have begun to challenge dBASE. Furthermore, for mixed (mainframe and microcomputer) environments, products from other companies such as Oracle Inc. (Oracle) and Information Builders Inc. (FOCUS) may be more appropriate.

Before concluding this section on administrative software features, internal software development should be briefly discussed. Many school systems employ technical staff to develop customized programs for various administrative applications. Using high-level languages such as COBOL or PL-1, programming staffs have developed and continue to maintain extensive administrative applications for record keeping and data reporting. In these situations, school administrators make their most important decisions regarding technology when hiring their personnel and should defer to them on most matters of software development. Administrators should be involved in establishing major priorities and in ensuring that a good working relationship exists between the technical staff and the end users. Custom software developed by a district's staff should also be evaluated according to criteria established jointly by the technical staff and the end users. These criteria may vary significantly depending on the nature of the software; however, essentially they should concentrate on whether the specific needs of the application are being met.

INSTRUCTIONAL SOFTWARE EVALUATION FACTORS

Like their administrative counterparts, different instructional applications will have different needs and will require specific software features to meet these needs. As examples, a simulation program such as MECC's The Oregon Trail would be evaluated differently than an instructional tool such as The Learning Company's Student Writing and Research Center. A programming language such as Logo would be evaluated differently than a desktop publishing program such as Broderbund's The Print Shop.

As mentioned earlier in this chapter, the U.S. Congress's Office of Technology Assessment (1988) in a national survey identified more than 200 factors (see Appendix C) that are used in evaluating instructional software. Many of these factors relate to pedagogical and instructional quality considerations (e.g., content, motivation, creativity). Some factors (i.e., simulations, probeware) relate only to a particular type of software. Other factors include the qualifying term "where appropriate" to signify that they are not always to be considered. Appendix C provides a good reference for developing a software evaluation policy in a school district, provided administrators and teachers remain flexible and look to establish a more manageable number of criteria.

Many school districts have adopted an instructional software evaluation form or checklist that generally highlights some of the more important criteria. The form approach does not necessarily provide the mechanism for a thorough evaluation and will not include the hundreds of factors identified in Appendix C. However, the form or checklist does have value; otherwise it would not be employed in so many districts and schools. A software checklist does ensure a record of the opinions of the staff involved in doing the evaluation of some proposed software.

Since major software developers will provide preview copies of programs to a school free of charge and without any obligation to purchase, it is not necessary to purchase a product to do an evaluation. After previewing the software, the evaluators meet and discuss its strengths and weaknesses. Providing a common evaluation form helps focus the discussion.

The criteria can be identified in an open-ended or a check-off format. However, since the nature of these evaluations is subjective, the open-ended format may be more appropriate. It is also relatively simple to provide detailed explanations of the open-ended items in a supplementary manual of procedures for doing software evaluation. Figure 9–6 is an example of an evaluation form combining both the check-off and open-ended approaches. An evaluation form helps define the evaluation procedure itself, and administrators and teachers should work together to develop what they feel will work best in their schools.

Title: _____ Page 1 of 2

    Company: _____

    Subject matter: _____

    Grade level: _____

    Cost: _____
          (Attach additional supporting information if necessary.)

Type: Tutor: Simulation _____ Tutorial _____ Drill/practice _____ Game _____

        Tool: Word processing _____ Database _____ Spreadsheet _____ Other _____

        Tutee: Specify language/title _____

    Computer system:_____

    Special hardware requirements:

Objectives:

Program description:

Evaluation

    Grade (0=lowest; 9=highest)

General characteristics		*Instructional quality*	
Efficiency:	_____	Content:	_____
Documentation:	_____	Pedagogical features:	_____
Ease of use:	_____	Motivational:	_____
Vendor:	_____	Creativity:	_____
		Feedback:	_____
		Evaluation and record keeping:	_____
		Graphics and audio:	_____
		Flexibility:	_____
Overall rating:	_____		

Figure 9–6
North Central School District No. 1 Instructional Software Evaluation Form

Content:

Pedagogical features:

Motivational:

Creativity:

Feedback:

Evaluation and record keeping:

Graphics and audio:

Flexibility:

Reviewer's name: _____ Date: _____

The process of designing an instructional software evaluation form and procedure will provide many insights into the role of technology in the classroom as well as into many other curricular issues. As such, software evaluation should be a rigorous activity comparable to other important curricular and academic decisions. In addition to basic software evaluation criteria, the form in Figure 9–6 devotes an entire page to criteria associated with instructional quality.

For further information on instructional software evaluation, readers are encouraged to review Chapter 5, which includes lists of popular software titles and instructional software developers.

CASE STUDY
Place: Metro High School   Year: 1992

Administered centrally by a city board of education, Metro High School is an inner-city, public high school with 2,900 students. It is a comprehensive high school offering college preparatory and business programs. The school population has been increasing, particularly with Latino students. The school is considered by the board of education and the community as a good school with a dedicated administrative and teaching staff.

Metro High has been very fortunate in securing funds from the central board of education for computer technology. It has approximately 180 microcomputers in the school and a computer science program that has received a good deal of acclaim from the central board of education and parents. The computers are housed primarily in six centralized laboratories. However, in 1990, after various recommendations and discussions with the faculty, a decision was made to place more equipment in individual classrooms.

The computer coordinator has been at Metro High for 19 years; originally he taught mathematics. In the early 1980s, he was instrumental in developing the computer science program and actively sought funds from the businesses in the city and the administration for equipment. The principal has depended on him for making most of the decisions regarding the acquisition of hardware and software.

Although it has been modified several times since its inception in 1982, the present computer science program consists of four half-year courses as follows:

CSC 101: Introduction to Computers
Introduces students to fundamental hardware concepts and provides a beginning programming experience in BASIC

CSC 102: Computer Tools
Introduces students to three major software tools: word processing, electronic spreadsheets, and databases

CSC 103: Pascal Programming I
A first course in programming using the Pascal language

CSC 104: Pascal Programming II
A more advanced course in Pascal programming for the more serious computer science student

All students are required to take at least CSC 101 or demonstrate their proficiency by taking a simple test in BASIC programming. All business students are required to take CSC 101 and 102. CSC 103 and 104 are optional courses and have enough of an enrollment so that at least one section of 103 is offered every fall, and one section of 104 is offered every spring. As a result, 90% of the students who graduate Metro High have taken at least one computer science course, and a little more than 50% have taken two courses.

A major issue facing the school regarding computer technology is integrating it into the curriculum. Several faculty from the social studies, language arts, and science departments have indicated that they need more support from the administration for hardware and software. In 1990, this same group of faculty was instrumental, after several years of discussions and meetings with the administration, in having computers relocated from the centralized facilities into their regular classrooms. Equipment has been moved to the classrooms, but it frequently consists of older models. Furthermore, no provisions have been made for acquiring software.

In a discussion with the principal and the assistant principal for instruction, the computer coordinator indicated that very little additional software exists in the school other than that needed for the computer science program. Furthermore, the computer coordinator sees his major responsibilities as supporting the computer science program and the centralized laboratories. He also suggests that budgets be provided for the departments to acquire their own software because he barely has sufficient funds to support his present operation, which requires buying new equipment, maintaining old equipment, and upgrading the software being used in the computer science program.

The principal is not sure what to do and has asked the assistant principal to review the situation and give her a report with suggestions for improving the integration of computer technology into the school's curriculum. She specifically would like recommendations for establishing new procedures for computer software acquisition.

Assuming that you are the assistant principal, what recommendations do you think you would make? What additional information or data might you need? Who would you involve in helping to develop your recommendations? Lastly, assuming that the overall school budget is very limited and additional funds will not be forthcoming, how would you deal with the computer coordinator's suggestion to establish software acquisition budgets in each department?

SUMMARY

This chapter describes the major criteria used in evaluating computer software. Because software directs or instructs the hardware, many professionals consider software to be the most important component of a computer application. Evaluating software therefore should be a rigorous activity involving both technical staff and end users.

Several factors are common to most software packages and should always be considered when doing evaluations:

Efficiency
Ease of use
Documentation
Hardware requirements
Vendor
Cost

Evaluators should also examine the specific features of software packages in terms of how well they meet the needs of the planned application.

Administrative software such as word processing, electronic spreadsheet, and database management systems each have unique features. Evaluators should be familiar with these features when evaluating and comparing software packages.

The number of instructional software programs has increased significantly since the late 1970s. The sheer number of appropriate packages has made software evaluation a major undertaking. Furthermore, since it frequently involves other curricular issues, evaluating instructional software requires a good deal of time and care. Evaluation teams should be familiar with the many factors that can be considered in evaluating the instructional quality of a software package. Evaluation procedures should be developed that best meet the needs of a school district and that allow for a good interaction of technical and pedagogical considerations.

Key Concepts and Questions

1. **Many computer professionals consider software as where the action is regarding technology**

   Why? Compared with hardware, which do you consider the more important component in planning and implementing computer applications? Why?

2. **In evaluating software, the major factors are efficiency, ease of use, documentation, hardware requirements, vendor, and cost.**

   Are any of these factors more important than the others? Why? And under what conditions?

3. **Efficiency refers to how well a program is written.**

   What are some of the specific efficiency measures used in evaluating software? How would you test some of these measures while doing an evaluation?

4. **With the introduction of microcomputers, people are using equipment for a wide variety of applications.**

   Because so many people have become familiar with computer equipment, has this reduced or increased the need to produce software that is relatively easy to use? Explain. Who are the best individuals in a school to evaluate how easy a software package is to use?

5. **Of the major software evaluation criteria, some computer professionals consider documentation as the most important factor.**

   What questions does the documentation have to answer? As a software evaluation factor, is documentation more or less important depending on the nature of the application or the type of equipment being used? Explain.

6. The relationship between hardware and software is critical in implementing computer applications.

    In terms of software evaluation, provide examples illustrating the importance of this relationship.

7. The number of software development companies has increased significantly since the late 1970s.

    Has this had a positive or a negative effect on the quality of software available? Explain. Does it make software evaluation an easier or more difficult task? Why?

8. Many instructional software programs have become very inexpensive.

    If this is so, is it necessary to establish extensive software evaluation procedures? Or can a school district simply allocate funds each year and let a computer coordinator select a number of packages for each school's software library? Explain.

Suggested Activities

1. Select a software product used with one of the three most popular administrative software applications (word processing, electronic spreadsheet, or database management), and review its common software evaluation features as identified in this chapter. Compare these features with those of a software package used in your environment. Which features are available? Which are not?

2. Review the policies in a school district for evaluating and selecting instructional software. Can you offer any suggestions for improving them?

References

Bakker, H. E., & Piper, J. B. (1994). California provides technology evaluations to teachers. *Educational Leadership, 51*(7), 67–68.

Brown, S., Grossman, G. C., & Polson, N. (1984). Educational software reviews: Where are they? *The Computing Teacher, 15*, 24–29, 38.

Datapro Research Group. (1995). *Management of microcomputer systems* (Vols. I & II). Delran, NJ: McGraw-Hill.

Hannafin, M., & Peck, K. (1988). *The design, development, and evaluation of instructional software.* Upper Saddle River, NJ: Prentice Hall.

James, N. B., & Vaughan, I. (Eds.). (1983). *Evaluation of educational software: A guide to guides.* Chelmsford, MA: Northeast Regional Exchange.

Knapp, L. R., & Glenn, A. D. (1996). *Restructuring schools with technology.* Boston: Allyn & Bacon.

MicroSIFT Project of the Northwest Regional Educational Laboratory's Technology Program. (1986). *Evaluator's guide for microcomputer-based instructional packages.* Eugene, OR: International Council for Computers in Education.

Miller, M. (1990). *The InfoWorld Test Center software buyer's guide* (1991 ed.). San Mateo, CA: IDG Books Worldwide.

Pepi, D., & Scheurman, G. (1996). The emperor's new computer: A critical look at our appetite for computer technology. *Journal of Teacher Education, 47*(3), 229–236.

U.S. Congress, Office of Technology Assessment. (1988). *Power on! New tools for teaching and learning* (Report No. OTA-SET-379). Washington, DC: U.S. Government Printing Office.

10

Staff Development

A n important ingredient for implementing change, improvement, and innovation in education is a knowledgeable and vibrant staff. Studies and research (Fullan & Pomfret, 1977; Huberman & Miles, 1984; Joyce, 1990; Joyce, Murphy, Showers, & Murphy, 1989; Joyce & Showers, 1988; Knapp & Glenn, 1996; Pink, 1989; Sheingold & Hadley, 1990) have consistently supported this concept. Regardless of the nature of change, whether it be introducing a new teaching technique or implementing a major new administrative policy, individuals involved must understand and to a degree accept what is expected and what is going to be done. Neglecting to develop this understanding among the people who ultimately will most influence success or failure will likely jeopardize the implementation of any new project.

In this chapter, staff development is examined as it relates to implementing technology in our schools. Although all school personnel should be participating in staff development activities, particular emphasis is placed in this chapter on teachers' development, since using technology in the classroom has become and will continue to be a critical need in most schools.

A LONG WAY TO GO

Practically all schools in the country have acquired some computer equipment (Quality Education Data, 1996), and every indication is that the hardware acquisition trend that began in the late 1970s and grew significantly in the 1980s is continuing in the 1990s. Using surveys and field visits, governmental agencies, industry analysts, and academic researchers are monitoring the number of computers and types of components acquired and the dollars schools have expended (Becker, 1994; Quality Education Data, 1996; U.S. Congress, Office of Technology Assessment, 1995). These important activities have helped administrators develop computer facilities and support services in their schools.

On the other hand, "hard" data on the actual use of this equipment, particularly in classroom activities, is difficult to come by. In fact, a growing concern is that much of the computer equipment is underutilized. Many anecdotes have been told of microcomputers sitting unpacked in locked closets or in the back of a classroom where they are rarely turned on because the teacher does not know how to use them. Throughout the 1990s, studies and observations (Becker, 1994; Goodson, 1991; Northrup & Little, 1996; U.S Congress, 1995) consistently report that most teachers are not using computer technology in their classrooms. They suggest a situation in which hardware and software are being acquired at an escalating rate in the schools, and yet many teachers appear not to know how or are otherwise unable to use it.

If administrators are to develop strategies for correcting a serious imbalance between computer acquisition and technical knowledge, some background information on the causes would be helpful. One fundamental reason for the imbalance is that the majority of today's teachers, especially those trained before the early 1980s and before the proliferation of microcomputers, were not exposed to technology as part of their preservice teacher training programs. As a result, they did not include it as part of their teaching repertoire. Schools of education, as well as state education departments (which are responsible for certifying teachers), generally had not required competency in technology as part of a teacher preparation program.

Fortunately, this situation is beginning to change, and the problem is alleviating as colleges and some state agencies have begun to recognize the importance of a technologically literate teacher corps (Northrup & Little, 1996). More and more teacher preparation programs are requiring minimal computer proficiency, if not a complete methods course in educational technology. David G. Imig, executive director of the American Association of Colleges for Teacher Education, estimates that approximately 20% of the nation's teacher training programs are on the cutting edge of technology, and another 60% offer at least one or two courses in educational technology (Nicklin, 1992). School administrators are finding that recent graduates are more familiar with computing equipment and need ongoing training to keep their skills honed rather than an introduction to basic computer literacy.

A more difficult problem is an attitudinal one. Many teachers are uncomfortable and lack confidence in using computer technology. For some it is an extension of the basic "computerphobia" that exists in the general population. In the extreme, some teachers feel threatened by technology and fear losing their jobs. Many educational leaders dismiss the idea that teachers can be replaced by computers, but the natural evolution of technology is such that the nature of people's jobs will change. In schools that use technology extensively, teachers, in addition to their teaching role, must also adopt a managerial role in providing instruction. In environments where advanced computer-assisted instruction techniques such as integrated learning systems are in operation, teachers are required to spend more time monitoring student progress and prescribing appropriate curriculum materials rather than teaching the subject matter. Shifting roles certainly cannot be equated with replacing teachers, but for many of them these changes are threatening.

In planning staff development activities, administrators should be prepared to deal with these attitudinal issues. Assuming that attitudinal concerns will go away simply by exposing teachers to the benefits of technology is a fallacy. Educators need to convey that computer technology, while becoming an important tool in the teaching process, is not close to being used as a substitute for caring, talented human beings. Given the social responsibilities such as parenting, nourishing, and nursing that schools have been assuming, "real" teachers are needed now more than ever.

One of the most important reasons that teachers do not use technology is that it is not easy to implement in the regular classroom. In schools where teachers have received training, many other problems such as the lack of enough hardware, poor support services, or inappropriate software have hindered teachers' ability to use technology effectively in the classroom. Administrators and teachers find they spend a good deal of time on solving basic logistical and technological problems associated with implementing effective computer applications. Additionally, even in school districts where training and staff development activities are provided, teachers need to continue to invest time and effort to feel comfortable using computer technology routinely in their classrooms.

Sheingold and Hadley (1990), in a national study of teachers who were identified as experienced and accomplished in integrating technology into their teaching, found that it took five to six years of practice to master computer-based teaching approaches. Furthermore, although these teachers were supportive of staff development programs that have enabled them to use computer technology, they also cautioned against one-shot approaches or "quick fixes." A major recommendation of this study was that there should be ample support and time for teachers not only to learn how to use technology but also to plan carefully for its use in the classroom. This may even require fundamental changes in the way teachers teach.

THE STAFF DEVELOPMENT PLANNING MODEL

Figure 10–1 is a schematic for a staff development planning model that can be integrated with the general planning for technology model discussed in Chapter 2. A basic assumption is that the initial component (staff development) is a product of the larger technology planning model. The major components consist of these:

Staff development—planning activity that integrates staff development with other planning activities

Assess needs—identifies the staff development needs of a district

Design program—meets the needs

Provide incentives—for staff to participate

Implement program

Evaluation and review

This model forms the framework for most of the discussion in the remainder of this chapter.

WHO LEARNS?

In planning staff development activities, the critical question is, Who learns? The simplest and broadest answer is everybody: administrators, teachers, clerical staff, and so forth. However, a more specific answer to the question should be related directly to a district's planning objectives.

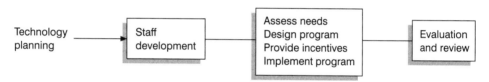

Figure 10–1
Staff Development Planning Model

Assessing staff development needs is a logical outgrowth of the computer applications that a district or school wishes to implement. In addition to identifying hardware and software, planning computer applications should also inherently determine the users and developers of these applications and therefore also identify the targets for staff development. If a district is planning to implement a new financial management system, it would be appropriate to assess the needs of financial managers, accountants, and clerical staff in using databases, query languages, or electronic spreadsheet software packages. If a district is planning to begin using word processing as a tool for teaching writing in the elementary school curriculum, it would be appropriate to assess the needs of the elementary school teachers in using word-processing software. Once identified, the personnel (administrators, teachers, or clerical staff who will be using the actual applications) should be included in the process of determining needs and designing appropriate staff development activities.

As much as possible, staff development should relate to a planning objective and, in the case of technology, to a computer application. Although some school districts adopt staff development as a planning objective in and of itself, this should be the exception and not the rule. Planning that continually identifies staff development as an objective without relating it to an application is indicative of a planning integration problem and should be reviewed. Just as hardware and software should relate to the applications a district wishes to implement, the staff likewise should be trained to implement or use these same applications.

Finally, the importance of principals, superintendents, and other leaders in participating in staff development activities should not be underestimated. The example set when a school leader participates in staff development or when she or he begins to use some new technology is extremely powerful. A clear and direct message is sent that will be picked up by staff and others that developing staff and implementing technology are important.

By the same token, high-level administrators who appear technologically illiterate or provide staff development activities for others and consistently avoid participation send the opposite message. Many administrators rely very heavily on some other person(s) to buffer them from technology. Such situations are very common and also unfortunate. In most cases, these administrators would love to use the available technology but "just have not had enough time to learn it." In their schools, you will find that many of their teachers and other staff "have not had enough time to learn it," either.

DIFFERENT ALTERNATIVES FOR DIFFERENT NEEDS

Designing a staff development program should be done in a systematic way so that the proposed program relates closely to the district's overall technology plan. Simply offering several workshops each year that may or may not be relevant to a district's goals and objectives will not be effective. A major requirement in planning a staff development program is identifying what a district needs to do through a needs analysis. If a district has not provided very much staff development in the past, an in-depth or comprehensive analysis may be in order. On the other hand, if a district has been active in providing staff development and is experienced in using technology, then the analysis can be targeted to specific applications and educational objectives.

Doing a comprehensive needs analysis for the purpose of designing a staff development program for technology requires an in-depth examination of all existing and proposed computer applications, both administrative and instructional, followed by an evaluation of all staff (administrative, teaching, clerical, etc.) in terms of their technical knowledge and their abilities to develop, implement, or use these applications. The needs that are identified become the targets of the staff development plan.

Although some districts are able to do comprehensive needs analyses, most limit them to specific school populations, categories of applications, or specific applications. For example: Doing a needs analysis and designing a training program for all science teachers in the use of videodisc technology involves a category of application for a specific school population; a needs analysis and training program for middle school science teachers in the use of Optical Data Systems' Windows on Science videodisc series involves a specific application for a more specific school population. Some districts may start with broad training of many teachers or staff and work to more specific applications; others might experiment with a smaller group and, if successful, expand the program for larger groups and categories of applications. Both approaches can and do work. Which approach should be taken is best determined by the district as part of the overall planning activities.

When identifying and targeting staff development to specific applications, planners should keep in mind that the common or unifying goal should always be to build and expand on the accumulated mass of technical knowledge and expertise (see Figure 10–2) in the district. This accumulated mass of technical knowledge is most important for a district to accomplish planning goals and objectives. As districts attempt to do more, a correspondingly larger accumulated mass of technical know-

Figure 10–2
Accumulating Mass of Technical Knowledge/Expertise

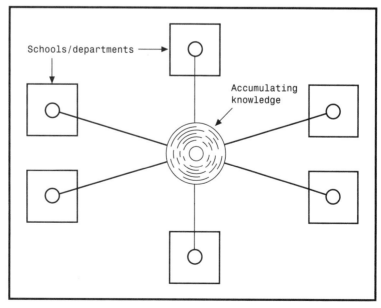

ledge is required. An interesting characteristic of technical knowledge is that it grows almost naturally as a district implements more technology. Diane Ravitch (1992) refers to this phenomenon by describing educational technology as difficult and costly to initiate, but once established it has a "relentless forward momentum" (p. 7). This occurs because a good deal of knowledge is gained as one uses hardware and software. Therefore, the more teachers and other staff use technology, the more they learn and the more capable they become of expanding to newer technologies.

As a result of staff development, a threshold or level of technical confidence is reached in most organizations that acts as a driving force from within for further technological enhancement and development. At this point, much staff development will evolve into a self-driven activity, with many staff members seeking out and learning a great deal on their own through contacts with colleagues both inside and outside the school or district.

DESIGNING AND IMPLEMENTING EFFECTIVE STAFF DEVELOPMENT PROGRAMS

Designing and putting into practice effective staff development programs is a complex undertaking. In designs for these programs, the input of the target groups is most important and will provide many suggestions for the nature of the development activities. As much as possible, programs should be designed that provide some variety of activities (i.e., lectures, demonstrations, discussions, hands-on workshops, etc.) and that take place over an extended period of time to allow participants to practice and experiment. Staff development programs also require resources, and budgets need to be allocated as part of the design and implementation.

School districts use a wide-ranging assortment of staff development activities. Workshops (on- and off-site), large conferences, small seminars, and user group activities abound. All the modes and characteristics of a good staff development program will not be reviewed here, but we can identify common elements (see Figure 10–3) considered especially effective for technology training:

Hands-on activities
One-on-one coaching
Training the trainer
Equipment availability

Hands-on Activities

A fundamental tenet of staff development for technology is the concept that one learns by doing; therefore, a portion of any technical training program should include hands-on activities. Participants can listen to and read about technology, but not until they use it will they develop an understanding. Consider how one learns typing or keyboarding. A teacher may lecture on how to type or a student can read

Figure 10–3
Elements of a Staff Development Program for Technology

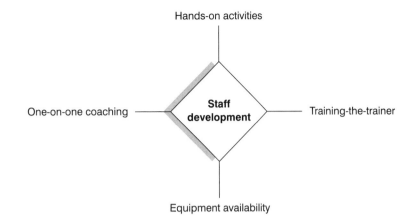

about typing, but until the student actually types, he or she really cannot develop the skill of typing. The same is true with computer technology. To understand computer technology, one needs to use hardware and to experiment with software, and the more one practices, the greater will be one's proficiency and knowledge development. This holds true whether the target populations are high-level engineers and computer scientists, teachers, secretaries, students, or principals.

One-on-One Coaching

Individualized training or coaching is another characteristic of many staff development programs. If a district has support staff who can function as individualized trainers or coaches, they should be used. If not, then coaching should be provided by outside experts or consultants. Regardless of who provides the individualized training, short (1 or 2 hours), one-on-one coaching sessions are more effective than longer, large-group activities. A common format is a large-group, information delivery session followed by much smaller coaching sessions in which participants can practice or experiment with the assistance of a coach who customizes the training to individual needs.

Training the Trainer

A certain amount of outside expertise and consulting is required for many staff development activities, but relying extensively on external trainers can become costly over the long term. A popular approach is to have outside consultants train a cadre of trainers who in turn will train large numbers of the staff. This "train the trainer" approach can be most effective in developing a core group of in-house experts who become actively engaged in sharing their knowledge with others.

Earlier in this chapter, reference was made to an accumulated mass or threshold of technical knowledge that a district should seek to develop. A cadre of trainers can be a critical component that drives the entire staff development activity for a school or district. Such a group can begin with computer teachers, media specialists, and representatives from every department or grade level in a school who have shown a particular interest in technology.

Deciding whether to convert numbers of present employees into full-time trainers depends on the size of the district and the number of people to be trained. Large districts with thousands of employees would probably find that a group of full-time trainers would be less expensive than large-scale use of outside consultants. On the other hand, small districts might make training a part-time or add-on responsibility (for extra compensation) for existing full-time staff who have an aptitude for technology training.

Using existing staff versus outside consultants for training also can provide many attitudinal benefits. Teachers, for instance, might relate better to colleagues who are a few steps ahead of them in using technology in the classroom. A sense of "If they can do it, so can I" frequently develops. This approach also can be very effective in fostering a team or "We are in this together" attitude. If successful, it helps build an esprit de corps among the teaching staff that begins in the technology area and carries over into other areas of the school, such as implementing collaborative learning, reviewing a writing program, or expanding the teaching of process skills in science instruction. Given the many problems involved with integrating technology into the curriculum, training a group of trainers may be one of the most effective ways of resolving them.

Teachers Need Equipment Too!

The design of a staff development program that includes hands-on activities implies that equipment, software, and other facilities are available for the participants' use. Along with other factors such as costs and travel arrangements, access to equipment becomes a critical consideration. Frequently, the number of participants may be limited by the availability of equipment.

Administrators understand the need to acquire equipment for instruction and student use, and providing this same equipment for teachers to learn and to use is also a necessity. Whereas secretaries and other administrative staff are routinely given equipment to take advantage of standard office automation applications such as electronic mail, word processing, or electronic spreadsheets, teachers frequently are the last group to receive equipment from the district and in some cases even expected to acquire it on their own. Given the premise that one learns technology by doing, attempts to integrate technology into the classroom are likely to fail if teachers are not able to practice, to experiment, and "to do computing."

The most common approach to resolving this problem is to set aside a teacher's area (laboratory, library, media center, lounge, study room, etc.) where equipment is provided exclusively for teachers' use. This approach is effective because it provides access to equipment and also allows for the informal exchange of information and ideas among peers. Teachers can work together on common computer applications, and a good deal of technology sharing can occur. Again, a sense of teamwork and camaraderie can develop that can be extremely beneficial to fostering positive attitudes to technology. For this reason, schools that have progressed and moved away from central computer laboratories and provide equipment for individual teacher use in each classroom should also consider offering or maintaining a small central training area for teachers.

Some school districts have begun to adopt policies that aim at supplying every teacher with a microcomputer. Though costly, this may be the best approach for providing teachers with access to equipment and ultimately for using technology in instruction. The Shoreline School District in Seattle, Washington, was among the first to adopt such a policy in 1989, and it provides a microcomputer for each of the district's 600 teachers (Schlumpf, 1991). Although the district owns the equipment, teachers are free to bring computers home or wherever. Administrators report that not only has this approach been effective in terms of staff development and the use of technology, but it also has unleashed a "mass of creativity" and has given the teachers a sense of technological empowerment. Other districts implementing "a computer for every teacher" policy have reported similar results (Buckley, 1995).

In looking at the proliferation of microcomputers in the larger society, before long every teacher will likely have a computer on her or his desk and probably even one at home. Some administrators and teachers have doubts that this will happen, but a simple look at the desks of stockbrokers, insurance salespersons, department store cashiers, attorneys, and others suggests otherwise.

Incentives

Staff development programs should also consider providing incentives for teachers and others to ensure active participation. Both intrinsic and extrinsic rewards need to be considered for staff who become substantially involved with developing staff and implementing technology in their schools. Professional growth, stimulating involvement with instructional innovations, experimentation with different teaching styles, and other intrinsic rewards may be the most important reasons that teachers become involved with technology. However, because of the time and effort involved, particularly in districts that have fallen behind technologically, more extrinsic incentives such as extra compensation, release time, or gifts of equipment are also needed.

Staff should be compensated for attending workshops, seminars, and other activities conducted in the summer or on weekends. Tuition reimbursements or sabbatical leaves should be considered for teachers who upgrade their skills by taking college courses. Teachers who agree to be trainers should receive extra compensation for assuming additional responsibilities. Those involved with developing a major new curriculum using technology or some other innovation should be provided with release time to evaluate and plan their materials carefully. Faculty involved with evaluating software (which if done properly can take hours and hours of viewing, discussing, and reviewing) should be compensated. Recognizing faculty who make a major contribution to staff development, maybe in the form of a cash award or a gift of a personal computer, can be a very strong inducement for others to participate.

The possibilities for providing incentives are extensive, and administrators should be attuned to offering those that would be most appropriate for the staff involved and for the nature of the contribution. In developing an incentive program, administrators may have to conform to existing employee compensation poli-cies within the district. Schools that have advanced technologically develop a cul-ture that lends itself more to incentives involving recognition and professional acknowledgment. Schools that have to catch up with technology or are planning major leaps forward should consider more direct rewards such as extra compensa-tion and release time. Regardless, administrators should be able to identify incen-tives to which a school staff will respond, and provisions for them should be made accordingly.

Evaluation and Review

As with any other technology planning activity, staff development should be evalu-ated and reviewed. Participants in workshops or demonstrations should evaluate the effectiveness of these activities, with suggestions for improvements if need be. Sim-ple evaluation questionnaires distributed and collected at the end of a staff develop-ment activity are common practice. Depending on financial resources, external eval-uators might also be considered. Since a major purpose of staff development is to have teachers and others using technology in their classrooms or offices, evaluation should also provide for some follow-up to determine whether participants have in fact been able to transfer their training to actual application.

Evaluation and review activities should not be considered the end of staff develop-ment. To the contrary, as with other planning activities, evaluation should naturally start the process of assessing needs and designing new staff development programs.

A Continuous Process

Planning a staff development program for technology should be a continuous process, primarily because technology is constantly changing and new equipment and software are regularly being introduced. Mechanisms should be in place for eval-uating and sorting out new technology to determine appropriateness in a district. Some individuals must be provided with the resources to visit other schools or attend vendor meetings and specialized workshops that enable them to keep up with the technology. Determining who these individuals are is best decided as part of an overall planning activity. Obviously, computer coordinators and trainers are the most likely candidates; however, teachers who show an interest in or have an apti-tude for technology should also be included.

The need for continual staff development will become apparent as planners review and evaluate their activities. Whether it be the evaluation of a single work-shop or an entire year's program, the most common suggestions and requests from participants are for additional staff development opportunities and activities. Besides the enjoyment they have in attending such activities, staff should quickly recognize their need to learn and advance, advance and learn. As planners look at the broader staff development picture, they will see different individuals functioning at different levels along the process. The essence of their staff development planning will be to keep all these individuals moving along this process.

RESOURCES

Figure 10–4 lists organizations and other resources that might be helpful in planning, designing, and implementing programs. Although the emphasis in this chapter has been to develop and use in-house staff as much as possible, outside expertise and consultants should also be considered, particularly if a new or inherently complex technology is being considered.

American Association of School Administrators
1801 N. Moore St.
Rosslyn, VA 22209

American Federation of Teachers
555 New Jersey Ave. NW
Washington, DC 20001

American Society for Training and Development
1640 King St.
Alexandria, VA 22313

Association for Computers in Mathematics and
    Science Teaching
P.O. Box 4456
Austin, TX 78765

Association for Supervision and Curriculum
    Development
Curriculum/Technology Resource Center
1250 N. Pitt St.
Alexandria, VA 22314

Bank Street College of Education
National Center for Technology in Education
610 W. 112th St.
New York, NY 10025

Computer Learning Foundation
P.O. Box 60007
Palo Alto, CA 94306-0007

Computers, Reading, and Language Arts
P.O. Box 13039
Oakland, CA 94661

International Society for Technology in Education
University of Oregon
1787 Agate St.
Eugene, OR 97403

Minnesota Educational Computer Consortium
3490 Lexington Ave. N.
St. Paul, MN 55126

National Association of Elementary School
    Teachers
1615 Duke St.
Alexandria, VA 22314

National Association of Secondary School
    Administrators
1904 Association Dr.
Reston, VA 22901

National Council for the Social Studies
Instructional Media Advisory Committee
3501 Newark St. NW
Washington, DC 20016

National Education Association
1201 16th St. NW
Washington, DC 20036

National School Boards Association
1680 Duke St.
Alexandria, VA 22314

Optical Data Corporation
30 Technology Dr.
Warren, NJ 07060

Technical Education Resources Center
8 Eliot St.
Cambridge, MA 02138

The Thornburg Center for Professional
    Development
P.O. Box 1317
Los Altos, CA 94023-1317

Figure 10–4
Resources for Design and Implementation of Staff Development Programs

Consultants abound in every state and most urban centers since the need for technical training is broad-based and exists in all types of commercial enterprises and public agencies. Before contracting with any consultants, whether they be private individuals, state agencies, or divisions of large corporations, administrators should do a careful review of their expertise and track record in providing the type of training or development that the district or school is seeking. Local colleges and universities, particularly if they have a school of education, generally are helpful resources for providing staff development expertise. Most states fund some type of assistance to school districts in the use of technology. User groups based on vendor hardware, special interests, common software, or subject matter, among other things, are excellent sources of information and can be extremely valuable in helping keep school personnel current on technological developments.

Vendors know their products better than anybody else, and if they provide training services, which in many cases may be free or at a discount for customers, school districts would be wise to take advantage of them. Major technology corporations such as Apple, Microsoft, and IBM provide a wide range of training services and facilities. Major educational software suppliers such as Broderdund, Tom Snyder Productions, and the Minnesota Educational Computer Consortium provide many excellent curriculum materials to help teachers use technology in the classroom. Vendors who specialize in particular products such as Optical Data Corporation (videodiscs) and Novell, Inc. (local area networks), have extensive expertise that they routinely provide to their customers and potential customers. As mentioned in previous chapters, in acquiring computer products, a vendor's background and reputation regarding support services, including training, should always be considered. In most cases, an additional cost or higher price may be well worth it, if the staff's ability to use the product is facilitated.

CASE STUDY
Place: Learning Town   Year: 1991

Learning Town is an urban school district in the farm belt of the country. It has 41,100 students and operates 75 schools. The board of education created a Planning Committee in 1978 that regularly establishes a broad set of goals and objectives for the district. The Planning Committee relies heavily on subcommittees to study issues at length and make recommendations, most of which it accepts. In terms of instructional technology, the board of education has been supportive. In 1983, a major procurement was made to equip the schools with microcomputers. Since then, the board has regularly allocated funds to allow each school to make incremental improvements in equipment and software. As a result, all of the schools have computer laboratories, a variety of software, and at least one computer coordinator. The overall student/microcomputer ratio is 15 to 1. Some schools have begun to place equipment in individual classrooms, but most of the equipment is located in centralized facilities.

Last year a proposal was made to the board of education by the chair of the Middle School Principals Association that the district consider making a major new thrust in the use of technology as a teaching tool. Specifically, she recommended that the district make an investment in interactive video technology and that each classroom be equipped with a teacher workstation that would consist of a microcomputer, a videodisc player, and a large-screen (36-inch) monitor. Such a workstation would allow teachers to take advantage of new multimedia materials combining sound, pictures, and the programming power of the computer. Teachers would be able to use new authoring languages such as HyperCard and ToolBook to enhance classroom presentations. She concluded her presentation with the success stories of several of the schools in the district that have begun using interactive video technology on a limited basis.

An ad hoc subcommittee of the district-wide Planning Committee has met six times in the past 5 months to study the feasibility of implementing this proposal. Members of the central administration have been supportive, providing a variety of data and analyses for the subcommittee members. Initial hardware costs for each workstation have been estimated at approximately $11,000. Costs for software and supplies would vary depending on the size and level of the school.

The subcommittee appears split in terms of recommending this proposal to the Planning Committee. Whereas some members view interactive video as an exciting and stimulating instructional technology, others do not feel that the district can afford it for all the schools at this time. The subcommittee has nearly completed its work for the year and would like either to recommend this proposal or table it for reconsideration next year. The chairperson of the subcommittee also has just received a memorandum from one of the committee members who represents the Teachers' Association. It indicates that the Teachers' Association discussed this proposal at its last two meetings and is very supportive. However, it expressed one concern that most of the teachers were not familiar with using this technology and would need training. The head of the subcommittee, a supporter of the proposal, has asked the superintendent to do a quick analysis of the training needs of the district regarding the proposal before the next, and last, meeting of the year, which will be in two weeks.

Analyze this case study assuming that you are the superintendent. What course of action do you take? Keep in mind that you would like to see the subcommittee recommend the proposal to the Planning Committee rather than table it until next year. However, you also recognize that the Teachers' Association has raised an important issue, and you do not have any data at this time to provide to the subcommittee. If your decision is to do a quick analysis, what information would you need?

SUMMARY

In this chapter, staff development is examined as a critical component for implementing technology in a school district. National estimates and other indications are that most schools have a long way to go to train their staffs, particularly teachers, in the use of technology. The reasons for this involve lack of preservice training, attitudinal concerns, and lack of support services, which together have made it difficult for many teachers to use technology effectively.

Planning a staff development program should be integrated with other planning activities and should relate to the objectives that a district hopes to achieve. The key elements of a staff development planning model include assessing needs, designing programs for specific applications, providing incentives, and doing a review and evaluation. In designing a program, a unifying goal is the expansion of the mass of technical knowledge and expertise that exists in a school district. Staff development techniques proving to be most successful include hands-on activities, one-on-one coaching, in-house trainers, and ready access to equipment. Because of the time and effort required to implement new technology, administrators should be prepared to provide incentives such as extra compensation, release time, and recognition awards for staff who actively participate and make significant contributions to staff development activities.

Lastly, staff development is a continuous process. Technology changes and so do the people who use it. Planning staff development requires a long-term commitment that aims to upgrade technical skills gradually and continually rather than on a short-term or one-shot basis.

Key Concepts and Questions

1. Staff development for technology has been a major issue in the nation's schools for many years.

   Why? What are the factors that have made staff development such an important issue? Is it likely to be resolved in the near future? Explain.

2. Staff development should be integrated with other planning activities.

   Why? What planning objectives should be considered in designing a staff development program for technology? Who are the personnel within a school district who should participate in staff development?

3. Identifying the needs of a school district for staff development should be a careful and well-planned activity.

   What are some of the critical questions to be answered in a needs analysis?

4. As a district develops its technical resources and capabilities, a mass of knowledge and expertise develops.

   How does this mass of technical knowledge relate to staff development?

5. Designing a staff development program for technology can consist of many different activities.

   What are some of the common characteristics of a staff development program? Why are they effective?

6. Equipment availability for participants in staff development is important for the success of a program.

   Why? What does it provide? Is it essentially a short-term or long-term requirement? Explain.

7. Staff development is described as a long-term, continuous process.

   If this is so, why do so many staff development activities consist of relatively brief workshops and seminars?

Suggested Activities

1. Review the planning that goes into staff development in a (or your) school district or school. What suggestions, if any, would you make for improving it?

2. Review the incentives that are provided in a (or your) school for participating in staff development activities. Are they intrinsic or extrinsic? Which do you think are the more effective?

References

Becker, H. J. (1994). *Analysis and trends of school use of new information technologies*. Irvine: University of California.

Buckley, R.B. (1995). What happens when funding is not an issue? *Educational Leadership, 53*(2), 64–66.

Fullan, M., & Pomfret, A. (1977). Research on curriculum and instruction implementation. *Review of Educational Research, 47*(5), 335–397.

Goodson, B. (Ed.). (1991). *Teachers and technology: Staff development for tomorrow's schools*. Alexandria, VA: National School Boards Association.

Huberman, M., & Miles, M. (1984). *Innovation up close*. New York: Plenum.

Joyce, B. (Ed.). (1990). *Changing school culture through staff development*. Alexandria, VA: Association for Supervision and Curriculum Development.

Joyce, B., Murphy, C., Showers, B., & Murphy, J. (1989, March). *Reconstructing the workplace: School renewal as cultural change*. Paper presented at the annual meeting of the American Educational Research Association, San Francisco.

Joyce, B., & Showers, B. (1988). *Student achievement through staff development*. New York: Longman.

Kinnaman, D. E. (1990). Staff development: How to build a winning team. *Technology and Learning, 11*(2), 24–30.

Knapp, L. R., & Glenn, A. D. (1996). *Restructuring schools with technology*. Boston: Allyn & Bacon.

Nicklin, J. L. (1992). Teachers' use of computers stressed by education college. *The Chronicle of Higher Education, 38*(43), A15–A17.

Northrup, P. T., & Little, W. (1996). Establishing instructional technology benchmarks for teacher preparation programs. *Journal of Teacher Education, 47*(3), 213–222.

Pink, W. (1989, March). *Effective development for urban school improvement*. Paper presented at the annual meeting of the American Educational Research Association, San Francisco.

Quality Education Data. (1996). *Education Market Guide & Mailing List Catalog 1996 & 1997*. Denver: Quality Education Data.

Ravitch, D. (1992). TECHNOS interview. *TECHNOS Quarterly for Education and Technology, 1*(3), 4–7.

Schlumpf, J. F. (1991). Empowering K–12 teachers. *Technological Horizons in Education, 18*(9), 81–82.

Sheingold, K., & Hadley, M. (1990). *Accomplished teachers: Integrating computers into classroom practice*. New York: Bank Street College of Education, Center for Technology in Education.

U.S. Congress, Office of Technology Assessment. (1995). *Teachers & technology making the connection* (Report No. OTA-EHR-616). Washington, DC: U.S. Government Printing Office.

11

Computer Facilities

A n important aspect of planning and implementing computer systems is the establishment and management of computer facilities, an area that generally did not receive enough attention in the early days of computer acquisition. Schools purchased equipment and housed it as best they could. Classrooms were converted into laboratories overnight by simply putting microcomputers on available desks, running additional electrical cables, and assigning release time to one of the teachers who was most interested in technology to "manage" the facility. This approach enabled schools to get their programs started, but soon they ran into many problems as computer acquisitions increased, more space was needed, and the management of equipment, software, training, and so forth, became a full-time job. In this chapter, the planning and management of computer facilities is examined, with various issues including space utilization, personnel, and security presented.

GETTING BIGGER

As late as the 1930s, airplanes were regarded with a certain awe, the way people view the space shuttle today. However, now airplane travel is routine and among the safest ways to travel. In the next 20 to 30 years, space travel, at least as provided by a space shuttle, will also become more routine, and its mystique will disappear. So too with computers. The mystique behind computer technology is gone because computer equipment has become so commonplace. The days of huge blue and gray boxes in temperature-controlled computer centers have given way to the nearly ubiquitous presence of microcomputers. Cash machines, checkout counters, exercise equipment, and hand-held games are some examples of computers that we see and use in everyday life. In schools, too, we are beginning to come across computers just about everywhere: in laboratories, classrooms, and libraries and on the desks of secretaries and administrators.

Because of their convenient size and propensity to become smaller, microcomputers are fitting into almost any available open space. However, although computer equipment has become remarkably smaller in the past 15 years, the number of machines has increased dramatically, and the job of managing this equipment is getting bigger and bigger. School administrators should be planning for computers to exist nearly anywhere in their buildings. At the same time, they need to establish larger support services to assure that this equipment is being used effectively.

STAFFING AND ADMINISTRATION

Though getting easier to use, computer technology will require more and more management in the foreseeable future for both administrative and instructional applications. More resources and support will likely be needed to help in planning hardware, software, and physical environments; to provide maintenance; to establish data communications systems; to distribute and maintain documentation; and to assist in training. This will be true regardless of where equipment is located. However, the nature of the resources and support will change depending on the applications and to some degree the location of equipment.

For administrative applications, the need to establish highly efficient information systems tends to support a strong centralized approach. Major databases are implemented and maintained centrally by well-trained technical staff and distributed as needed throughout the district. This operation is housed in a central computer facility, the size of which depends on the size of the district in terms of both enrollment and geography. The informational resources are distributed throughout the district through a data communications network. Secretaries and administrators use microcomputers both to access database information and to perform tool applications such as word processing and electronic spreadsheets. This approach is not unique to schools but is common in businesses and governmental agencies and has been evolving over the past 30 years.

The staff requirements to manage these applications again depend on the size and geographic distribution of a district. Larger districts with tens of thousands of students will need larger and more technically sophisticated staffs to develop and maintain systems and to distribute them over data communications networks than will smaller districts with 2,000 or 3,000 students. The staffing for administrative applications in schools has been evolving similarly to other noneducational environments such as private businesses and governmental agencies. Typically, a staff of computer programmers, computer operators, data communications specialists, and other technicians is established at a central location. In districts governed by municipalities, a certain amount of support may be provided by local governments, particularly for financial and payroll applications. In general, the staffing and management for administrative applications is better understood and in many districts has matured as the applications have developed and grown.

For instructional applications, the use of computing technology is still a relatively new phenomenon, becoming more widely used in the early 1980s as microcomputer technology became available. The nature of instructional applications is somewhat different from administrative applications. Whereas administrators need efficient and accurate information flow, teachers and students need variety, stimulation, and ease of use in their applications. Administrators find rewards in using computers because they reduce manual efforts and are able to produce accurate and timely reports for use both inside and outside the school. Teachers and students, on the other hand, require pedagogically appropriate software perhaps designed more to meet individual needs. The applications needed for language arts, for example, frequently are different than those needed for science and mathematics or the fine arts.

These requirements tend to support a more decentralized environment unique to educational institutions. The staff to support these applications need to be not only technically knowledgeable but also pedagogically knowledgeable. The key to effectiveness is being able to integrate computing into the regular curriculum. In the 1980s, schools generally established centralized laboratories mainly because of the limited amount of equipment on hand and because there was a tendency to follow the administrative approach with which most district administrators were more familiar. However, although centralized facilities will continue to play a major role in supporting instructional applications, the general thinking is that more equipment has to be placed in the regular classrooms to be effective. The staff needed to support these facilities are computer teachers who have received both pedagogical and technical training. In addition to teaching responsibilities, they also frequently function as coordinators for the computer program in each school and work with regular classroom teachers. Their main roles are to help other teachers use computing equipment and provide basic computer instruction for the students. As equipment continues to be acquired for instruction, schools increasingly will have to have at least one staff member who will serve to coordinate computer activities. Schools with an extensive amount of equipment (i.e., several hundred microcomputers) may have many staff members coordinating activities.

To manage computer facilities throughout the district, school superintendents must decide on an appropriate administrative structure. Two common organizational models (see Figure 11–1) for managing administrative and instructional computing are (a) one central computing administration managing both activities or (b) separate administrations for administrative and instructional computing, respectively. Either model works.

The single administration model (model A) can provide significant economies in terms of technical knowledge and maintenance services. Certain applications such as computer-managed instruction that require good student record keeping might be easier to establish if both administrative and instructional computing report through the same administrator. Data communications systems for applications such as Internet access also are probably better planned and implemented from a single administrative source. However, the director in this model needs to make sure that both administrative and instructional computing are equitably provided for in terms of philosophy and share of resources. Hardware, software, and training decisions may be very different for administrative and instructional applications, and an effective administrator has to develop different procedures and processes for the two areas.

Organizational model B, which separates the administration of computing services into two separate entities, generally will produce more philosophically appropriate computer applications and will ensure a more equitable distribution of resources. On the other hand, certain economies may not be realized, particularly for basic hardware acquisitions and maintenance. Regardless of the model being used, a district administrator or superintendent will attempt to make sure that economies are realized where appropriate while allowing differences in philosophy, staffing, and approaches to occur. Furthermore, planning and policy committees for the two activities would remain separate and have different participants. Committees for instructional applications need to involve greater participation at the building level to ensure that various academic departments and disciplines are represented. Committees for administrative applications need to involve administrative and clerical staff for analyzing the system and for using the centralized applications effectively. Finally, budgeting for the two areas should be kept separate mainly because the sources of funds generally are quite different. Administrative computing usually relies on the local school district operating budget for funds, while instructional computing can pursue a variety of funding sources including not only the operating budget but gifts and grants, special state appropriations, and so forth.

Figure 11–1
Organizational Charts

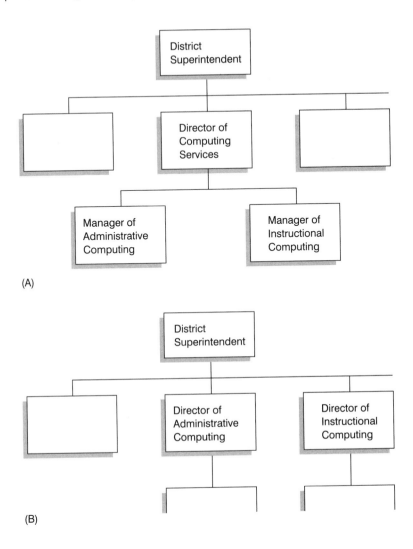

(A)

(B)

CENTRAL LABORATORIES

A major issue in facilities planning and management is the establishment of central-ized laboratories for instructional applications. Although mentioned in other parts of this book, this topic requires attention here, especially in relation to instructional effectiveness. If a school district had the funds to purchase an unlimited amount of equipment, convert all facilities, and train all the teachers, such a district would locate computers where learning occurs—that is, in the classrooms. Computers would routinely be available as tools to be used as needed by teachers and students. However, school districts do not have unlimited funds; therefore, alternative loca-tions for computer equipment must be considered.

Centralizing computers is appropriate when the supply of equipment and the supply of technically trained teachers is limited. A central facility allows for greater access to equipment and staff. The familiar approach of moving students to a central laboratory for several periods per week is effective given limited resources, but it is not ideal. In addition to disrupting the schedules of both students and teachers, a central facility can tend to separate computers from the learning that goes on in the regular classroom. On the other hand, many teachers are not able yet to use computer equipment effectively in their instruction. In this case, the centralization at least guarantees that students will have some computer experience, and it benefits especially those students who are more interested in or able to use computer technology. The solution is to compromise and provide for some mix of centralized and decentralized facilities depending on the amount of equipment available and the technical training of the teaching staff.

The location of central computer facilities can be a significant decision. The choices typically are between developing a dedicated central computer laboratory or becoming part of another centralized instructional support center such as a library or media facility. Either approach works and depends essentially on the skills and knowledge of the personnel supervising the areas. If library and media staff are knowledgeable about the technology, then housing a computer facility as part of these centers is appropriate. If staff in these areas are *not* knowledgeable, then the tendency has been to set up a separate computer laboratory.

In examining this decision, one is tempted to look at other organizations such as colleges and universities that have had to make similar decisions. The major tendency there has been to establish dedicated computer centers rather than integrate them as part of a library or other instructional support activity. However, instructional computing in colleges has evolved differently than in primary and secondary schools. Higher education, particularly research universities and schools of engineering, were at the forefront in the early years of computing in the 1950s and 1960s when computer centers were all centralized and staffed by highly trained technicians and faculty from the science and technology departments. Primary and secondary schools did not become involved with computing until the late 1970s and 1980s with the introduction of microcomputers, which physically did not require a central facility and could be housed almost anyplace and operated by most teachers interested enough in using the equipment in their lessons. Colleges in the past 10 years have been making major strides in distributing equipment very widely throughout their campuses, and microcomputers can now be seen in dormitories, libraries, and hallways as well as in classrooms. In the 1990s, colleges and universities have begun to examine the organizational structure of information services. Computer centers, library services, and media services in particular are now being examined in terms of greater organizational integration.

Primary and secondary schools likewise should be focusing on how to distribute and integrate computers into everyday instruction by physically locating equipment where teaching and learning occurs. Where centralization is necessary because of equipment or staff limitations, locating computers where staff can assist teachers and students makes good sense. If library or media personnel are capable, they should be employed. If not, a separate computer laboratory would probably be more effective.

PHYSICAL ENVIRONMENT

The physical environment in which computer equipment is located, regardless of whether centralized or not, is very important and should be well planned. Ergonomics, floor layouts, furniture, electrical precautions, and security requirements are critical. School districts in which some degree of administrative computing exists probably have technical staff who can be helpful in planning physical facilities. However, there are certain factors in designing space for children and learning that are not the same as designing work spaces for adults.

Facilities for Administrative Applications

For administrative applications, expertise in designing the physical environments is readily available both inside and outside the district. In establishing or expanding a central mainframe computer facility, usually the technical staff, with assistance from a computer vendor, is able to design an efficient and pleasant work environment.

In facilities for office staff, computer workstations should be comfortable and blend into the office environment. Desks and chairs with adjustable heights are readily available and help make it easier for staff to use their keyboards. Wall space should be used to reduce the amount of electrical cable and wires that have to be distributed onto areas where people might walk. Even when covered by floor strips, cables can be serious tripping hazards. For administrators or secretaries who are expected to spend a great deal of time using a workstation, glare on a video screen can be annoying and lead to eyestrain. Situating workstations to minimize glare is common practice, and using polarized video shields is also effective. Most districts may call on the expertise of their professional computer and architectural staffs to design pleasant and safe workstation layouts to provide comfortable work environments.

Administrative applications (i.e., office automation, database, Internet access, etc.) increasingly are relying heavily on a high-speed data communications network. Careful planning should be done at the district level in developing the physical requirements of such a network. This will be discussed further in the section on information infrastructure.

Facilities for Instructional Applications

For instructional applications, the physical layout should be conducive to learning and meeting the requirements of children of different ages, sizes, and understanding. For a central laboratory or a computer classroom, the location of workstations should be carefully evaluated.

Figures 11–2 through 11–4 provide several floor plans for a 20-station computer facility. These figures assume that each station at least has a keyboard and video monitor resting on top of the processor and disk drives, as is typical for Apple Macintosh and DOS/Windows machines. Additional equipment such as printers, video players, and CD-ROMs can be added as needed. Most of these peripherals can also be shared

Figure 11–2
Floor Plan for 20 Workstations:
Rows

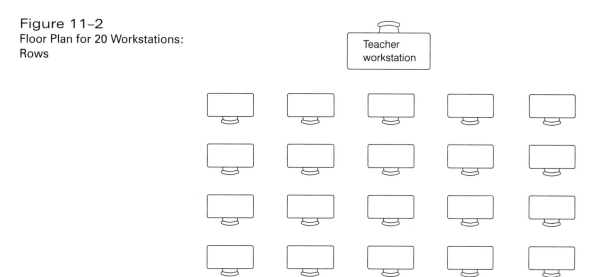

and stacked one on top of another to use the available space efficiently. Local area networks also fit into this basic workstation configuration without any problem.

The row design (Figure 11–2) is a common layout for a computer facility and represents an efficient use of floor space. It is conducive to teaching, with the teacher in the front of the class delivering lessons and instructions. However, a drawback involves the distribution of electrical wires and computer cables, which can become tripping hazards if not hidden or entrenched in conduits. In computer instruction, a good deal of time is needed for hands-on use of the equipment by students. Most teachers during this time move from workstation to workstation, providing advice and helping children with their computer work. Teachers may also encourage other students to look at what one of their peers has accomplished for both demonstration and recognition. This is especially true in the younger grades. For both teachers and students, this configuration is not the ideal and tends to create barriers that inhibit free movement around the room.

Figure 11–3 is a cluster design with four student workstations grouped together. It makes efficient use of available floor space and reduces some of the tripping and mobility problems by locating most of the computer cables in the back of the equipment away from where teachers or students might walk. The cluster design provides open spaces for teachers and students that are effective for group and collaborative learning environments, especially if large tables are used for the workstations. If this floor plan is used in an instructional resource room where students are expected to work alone, a recommendation is that carrels be used for the workstations.

Figure 11–4 is a horseshoe design that places workstations along the walls of the room. This approach is the least efficient in terms of the use of floor space, but it may be the most conducive to teaching and encouraging free movement. In this configuration, all wiring and cables are located along walls away from walking areas. Teachers can choose to be either in the front or right in the middle of the class. Stu-

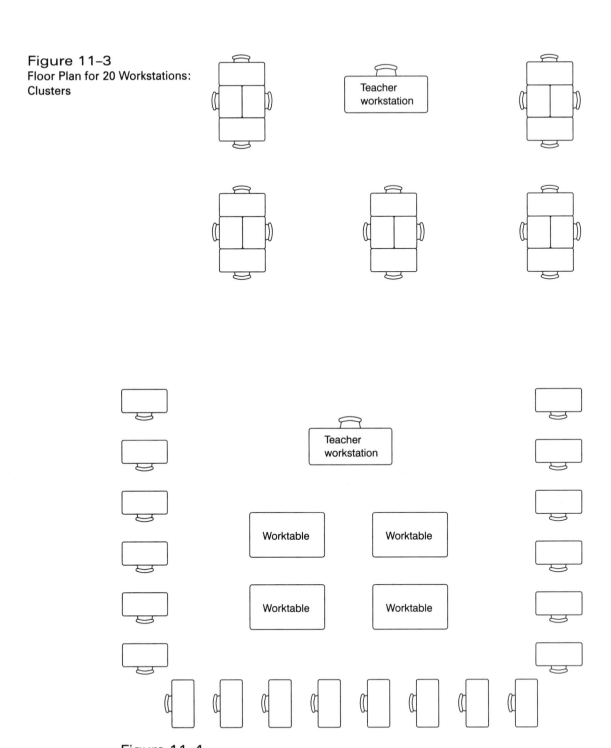

Figure 11–3
Floor Plan for 20 Workstations:
Clusters

Figure 11–4
Floor Plan for 20 Workstations: Horseshoe

dents will never have to have their backs to the teacher, and they can easily and safely move about the room. Variations of the horseshoe approach are used in some schools to allow students to work in teams, with each station providing equipment and chairs for two or more students.

Regardless of the configuration chosen, in planning the facility, some considerations should also be given to furniture that will be comfortable, useful, and conducive to learning. Large open work tables allow for greater sharing and group activity, whereas carrels are more appropriate for individual activity. Light colors are more cheerful than dark colors and blend better with the equipment, most of which is beige, light gray, or white. Glare, especially natural light coming in from windows, can be a serious distraction for students using video monitors. In planning the placement of monitors, some evaluation should be done as to whether certain stations would have a glare problem. One solution for this might be the installation of vertical blinds, which are very effective in shutting out natural light.

Physical planning for the teacher's workstation also requires special consideration and should be designed to maximize learning. Large monitors (i.e., 36 inches) and video projection systems increasingly are becoming the standard demonstration vehicles for computer-based lessons. Many products are available, and improvements in resolution and image quality are being made every day. In general, a large monitor provides better image quality than an overhead projection system, but it is also more expensive. Light switches or controls should allow teachers to dim all or part of the room so that students can view a monitor free from glare. If an instructor likes to move about a great deal while teaching, consideration should be given to situating the keyboard on a high stand rather than on a standard-height desk so that commands and other keyboard operations can be executed standing up rather than bending over. Simple overhead projectors and whiteboards using dry markers should be provided rather than chalkboards, which generate dust, a potential problem for the equipment.

In designing spaces for standard classrooms where only a limited amount of equipment is provided, many of the considerations mentioned still are appropriate. If two to five workstations are to be provided, consider setting them up in a computer corner to take advantage of the wall space for wiring and cables. In classrooms with only one computer, give consideration to providing a large monitor so that several children can participate and view what is happening. This can be especially effective when used in conjunction with group or cooperative learning exercises where the large images can make an activity seem to come to life. For readers wishing additional information on teaching with limited equipment in a classroom, Dockterman (1990) provides many useful suggestions in *Great Teaching in the One Computer Classroom*.

DATA COMMUNICATIONS FACILITIES AND INFORMATION INFRASTRUCTURE

As discussed in Chapter 7, computer applications are using data communications facilities for teaching and learning. Internet access, LANS, are WANS are becoming common wherever computing is taking place. As a result, administrators should consider developing an overall planning and support mechanism for providing "connectivity" throughout a district for both administrative and instructional applications. Such plans should consider not only the local school needs but may be integrated with the larger community's planning and requirements. Furthermore, these plans can take into consideration all aspects of information processing including telephone, fax, video, and computer. Other key factors such as the geographic distribution, size of population, and the reliance on public or private telephone and cable systems should be evaluated and understood.

Of all the areas of information technology, planning and implementing a data communications network combining computer, telephone, and video technology is probably the most complex. Even districts with experienced staff frequently require the services of consultants in planning a new data communications system or making major revisions to an existing one. Investing funds to hire a good consultant for this planning is generally very well worthwhile. Such planning can take into consideration the cooperation of local utilities and businesses, especially telephone, cable television, and other technology-based enterprises.

In the 1980s, planning and implementing communications systems usually focused on the wiring of buildings and rooms to be able to receive digital transmissions. Modern communications systems require a far more careful analysis and design. Carlitz, Lentz, and MacIlroy (1995) recommend a "layered" approach that considers data communications networks in three basic layers: physical, protocol, and applications. The physical layer contains all aspects of the media and devices through which data or signals will pass. Discussions regarding physical transmissions using copper wire, fiber optic, or wireless transmission are critical. Whereas school districts can control to some degree the physical medium within their buildings and campuses, outside connections are totally dependent on local utility providers—hence the need to involve these providers in planning this aspect of the system.

An example of an issue discussed within this layer would be bandwidth. The frequency with which signals can be transmitted and received directly affects the speed of a network and is dependent on the medium. Lower bandwidth, as is available over standard telephone lines, is fine for simple data transmission, and many existing networks use telephone lines for their outside connections. However, applications requiring high speeds, such as video transmission, will need much larger bandwidth than generally provided through standard telephone connections. Identifying how higher bandwidth can be provided at a reasonable cost is a serious issue that is and will continue to be discussed in many school districts and communities.

The protocol layer refers to the rules or standards that enable one device to send and receive signals to other devices on a network. Although the Internet has provided an overall standard protocol (see Chapter 7), most LANs and WANs are using machine- and manufacturer-designed protocols for local signal processing. In the past, planning the protocol layer would involve determining whether and how the protocol from one LAN or WAN would interact with the protocol from another LAN or WAN. This has begun to change as more schools adopt the Internet protocol as the standard protocol for their networks, especially their WANs. In a sense, schools are developing Internet-based protocol networks—or intranets—within their districts.

However, because of the extensive communications systems using several different protocols already in place, school districts cannot change these quickly and generally will have to plan and implement such changes in phases over a number of years.

The application layer refers to all the existing and foreseeable applications that are expected to run on computers connected to the networks. At this third layer, it is especially important to identify how data are to be transferred from one network to another and from one program to another. School districts might adopt tool applications such as electronic spreadsheets and may establish one of the popular software packages such as Lotus 1-2-3 or Excel as the district standard for use on the network, thereby assuring easy transfer of spreadsheet data. The same would be true for other commonly used applications such as word processing, data bases, electronic mail, virus detection, and so forth. Some applications, however, such as multimedia and digital video, are still evolving as software technologies and generally accepted standard packages and formats are more difficult to establish throughout a district.

Because of the phenomenal growth of the Internet in the 1990s, all organizations, including school districts, are rethinking their data communications systems. Schools, private corporations, and government agencies at all levels are examining their information infrastructures to determine whether they are poised to use the evolving resources on the Internet. This type of facilities planning will be the focus of district-wide planning discussions for many years to come. Readers may wish to refer to Rothstein and McKnight (1996) who, as part of their work with the National Information Infrastructure initiative, provide an excellent summary including detailed cost analysis for school districts developing information infrastructure plans.

HARDWARE MAINTENANCE

As more and more equipment is acquired, maintaining it in good working order becomes a bigger and more complex job. The three major components of hardware maintenance are repairs, preventive maintenance, and upgrading.

Making Repairs

Computer hardware, because it has mostly electronic components rather than mechanical parts, is not prone to breakdowns. This is especially true of the main processor components but less true of printer and disk devices, which do have mechanical and moving parts. However, when repairs are needed, they have to be performed by someone with the appropriate knowledge and training. For large mainframe computer systems, a district should have a comprehensive service contract with an outside vendor that provides for quick response by field engineers to correct any hardware problems. Generally these contracts also offer a certain number of preventive maintenance visits involving testing, cleaning, and making minor repairs to the equipment. Most major mainframe manufacturers are responsive in accordance with the stipulations of their service contracts and do a good job of keeping their equipment functioning.

Also available are third-party repair companies whose service contracts are usually less expensive than those provided by the manufacturer. The services from these companies vary significantly. Before entering into a contract with a third-party vendor, evaluate carefully the company's service record, particularly with other organizations in the immediate geographic area. The qualifications of local repair personnel, response times, the availability of parts, and attention to preventive maintenance schedules are critical evaluation criteria.

Large mainframe computer systems that are providing networking services throughout a school district are expected to be functioning every day. Administrators, teachers, and other staff who use such systems expect them always to be available; when they are not, the day's planned activities can be seriously disrupted. Extensive downtime due to repairs can be costly in terms of human resources, and good operations management should be able to keep it to a minimum.

For microcomputer systems, several options for handling repairs are available. First, service contracts similar to those used for large mainframe computers are available from both manufacturers and third-party vendors. This tends to be the most reliable but also the most costly approach.

Second, because microcomputer systems are much simpler in their design than large mainframe computers, more and more school districts are developing their own hardware maintenance staffs. The size of these staffs depends on the number of machines that need to be maintained. Major manufacturers such as Apple and IBM will train staff and provide various diagnostic tools to help identify and locate hardware problems. Less expensive parts can be kept on hand to make repairs, and more expensive parts can be ordered and generally received within 24 to 48 hours from manufacturers. Several extra back-up computers can also be kept on hand and substituted during repairs. Serious problems beyond the skills of a district's staff may require packing the problem computer and bringing it to a manufacturer's local outlet for repairs. As more and more microcomputers are being acquired, the trend in school districts is increasingly to do their own repairs.

A third alternative is a combination of the two options already cited, with the district handling certain usually simpler repairs and an outside service company, either the manufacturer or an independent, addressing more complex problems.

Providing Preventive Maintenance

Regardless of the approach a district takes in handling repairs, attention should always be given to preventive maintenance. The old adage that an ounce of prevention is worth a pound of cure is appropriate for computer hardware. Procedures should be in place and documented for caring for equipment. These include daily routines and periodic examinations.

Students should be taught to respect the equipment and should be involved with its care. Basic rules such as no eating or drinking anywhere around computer equipment should be strictly enforced. Dust covers should be used and kept in place, especially for equipment such as printers with mechanical and moving parts. School districts may draw on their own high school students to help in doing repairs and in providing periodic preventive maintenance services such as cleaning and testing equipment. This is especially true if the school district has vocational programs in electrical or mechanical technology.

Upgrading

Hardware upgrades and replacement plans are also important as school districts become more dependent on computer technology. After a while, computer equipment needs to be replaced because of extensive repairs or obsolescence. Hardware replacement plans should be in place that assume a certain life cycle for equipment, generally five to seven years depending on use and function. For large mainframe computer systems that are critical to the administrative functioning, upgrades may be necessary to keep up with current software and available technology rather than repairs. Microcomputer systems, especially those used by students, may need to be replaced because of wear and tear and accidents that can occur in an instructional environment.

Regardless, equipment will need to be replaced on some regular basis. Administrators need to be aware of the replacement schedule so that budgets and resources can be secured and disruption of services minimized.

SOFTWARE MAINTENANCE AND DISTRIBUTION

Computer software, like hardware, needs to be maintained. Depending on the nature of the computer applications, the manner in which software maintenance is provided can vary significantly. Large administrative software systems require a great deal of maintenance. In large administrative computer centers, a substantial portion of the programming staff will be dedicated to software system maintenance. Studies tend to indicate that the people resources devoted to software maintenance generally exceed those devoted to new system development.

Maintenance involves correcting problems, modifying the software because of changes in policies or procedures, or upgrading it to take advantage of newer technology. School districts are particularly cognizant of making modifications due to changes in policies because they are dependent on various governmental bodies for funding. These bodies tend to increase their demands for data and accountability as they establish new programs or make additional budget allocations.

A current trend in instructional software is to acquire proprietary products from companies such as Broderbund, Inc., and Sunburst, Inc., that cannot be modified by teachers or academic support staff. Assuming users know how to run the programs, most instructional software will operate without problems, and generally it is not subject to changes in policies or procedures.

When software manufacturers do upgrade their software, they generally will supply a completely new version of the package to replace the old. As a result, maintenance per se is not as significant a problem for these products. On the other hand, software distribution and lending is requiring more attention as software packages are used by more students and teachers. Again, questions of centralization and decentralization arise. Some control may be maintained by having a central software library that might be located in the school's library; software may be borrowed in the same fashion as books. In addition, a central software library can provide basic services such as testing newly acquired software; cataloguing, securing, or making back-up copies; and establishing standard software documentation manuals. However, because so much instructional software is customized for specific subjects, departments will also acquire it for the use of their own teachers and students. This reduces the amount of software that can be shared throughout a school and leaves most of the responsibility for software maintenance to the individual departments.

Both centralized and decentralized approaches are used in the schools. As with hardware, the trend again is to adopt a decentralized approach, with departments and teachers acquiring software specifically for their classes much like other instructional supplies and materials. However, a compromise approach may be to have a central library for software that can be distributed throughout the school while allowing departments to keep a limited number of specialized packages.

Particularly effective in solving software distribution problems is the use of local area networks in which a software library is kept on a central file server (high-capacity disk drive), with users throughout a school being able to access the software they need through the network. This is a major benefit of using LANs to distribute computer services, both hardware and software, throughout a school.

In managing software distribution, school districts should adopt certain policies to protect their software and ensure compliance with vendor contracts and other legal stipulations. Software and files that are used regularly need to have current back-up copies. For administrative software, this should be done routinely on a cyclical basis (daily, weekly, etc.), with back-up copies kept in protected areas such as a magnetic tape vault. Instructional software likewise should be backed up if the vendor allows copies of the software to be made. In many cases, this is not true, and a back-up copy of the software needs to be purchased, usually at a nominal price.

There is a temptation to make copies or at least to try to make copies of software even when a vendor prohibits it. This is against the law and should not be encouraged. The Computer Software Copyright Act, passed by Congress in 1980, affords considerable protection to software vendors for their products. School district administrators should acknowledge this law and should make sure that their students, teachers, and other staff are aware of it by prominently posting notices in computer areas against illegally making copies of software.

Software vendors generally will make available site licensing arrangements or quantity discounts to address the need for additional copies. Site licenses allow customers to make unlimited copies of packages. Modified site licenses allow customers to make some specified number of back-up copies. Generally, they are very attractively priced, and school districts intending to use a particular software package extensively should acquire a site license.

Some vendors do not provide site licenses but instead offer quantity discounts in the form of "lab packs." These are discounts for purchases of certain quantities, usually the number that would be needed for a single class. In addition to price discounts, vendors such as Tom Snyder Productions, Inc., and Logo Computer Systems, Inc., encourage the acquisition of lab packs by including curricular material that may be helpful to teachers in preparing their lessons.

PROCEDURES AND DOCUMENTATION

Written procedures and documentation are critical to the effective use of computer technology. **Procedures** are the overall manner of doing things. They are frequently developed in conjunction with policies and form the framework within which an organizational entity operates. Procedures should be developed for all the basic operations that can occur in a computer facility. Examples of procedures include

backing up files and software,
using facilities (access, hours of operation, priorities),
scheduling preventive maintenance,
evaluating software,
testing software,
distributing and lending software, and
distributing and lending hardware.

Procedures should be well communicated so that everyone using the facilities knows them. A procedures manual that is regularly updated, reviewed, and distributed to users of computer facilities can be very effective in this regard.

Documentation refers to applications and describes how to use specific computer programs or sets of programs. All applications, administrative and instructional, require some documentation. Organizations that do not devote enough attention to documentation are vulnerable should key staff persons who know a great deal about the software applications leave. Written documentation must be maintained and made easily accessible for every program used in a school. For simple instructional software packages, it may consist only of the documentation that the vendor supplies. Teachers who use computers occasionally especially need documentation to understand how to use the software. The best software packages will not result in the best applications if teachers do not understand how to use them. The reverse is also sometimes true; that is, some mediocre software packages result in successful applications mainly because good documentation was provided and teachers understand how to use them.

For complex administrative applications, the standard operating procedure should require up-to-date, detailed descriptions and maintenance histories of all the programs that comprise the software system. For major administrative applications, the basic documentation should include for each program

program specifications and design,
program description,

logic flowcharts,
operations documentation,
samples of output and input formats, and
maintenance documentation and history.

In addition, user manuals for the overall application have to be developed for administrators and staff who are expected to maintain and use it. User manuals may be supplemented by on-line help facilities that assist users in "navigating" through a computer application. These are very helpful but should not replace a written document; it may be stored in a text editor file.

School administrators should not underestimate the importance of documentation when dealing with computer technology. Generally, computer center staffs are more conscientious in developing documentation than are other departments mainly because of their training and because they understand the vulnerability should key staff persons who know a software application leave. However, technical staff will also admit that more documentation is needed. In decentralized environments, procedures for monitoring documentation are rare and difficult to implement. Furthermore, with instructional applications, the wide variety of available software packages from many different sources makes it difficult to require documentation standards. As a result, documentation tends to be inconsistent and, in some cases, poorly done or nonexistent. Regardless of the degree of centralization or decentralization in a district or school, administrators should develop a minimum documentation standard and require it for all computer applications.

SECURITY

Computer security refers to procedures for protecting software and sensitive data files. Issues of security are of growing importance to schools as well as many other organizations. In corporate America, there have been many cases of unauthorized access via computer to customer bases, research and development test results, and financial accounts. Two well-publicized cases (O'Brien, 1989) involved major thefts from Wells Fargo ($21 million) and Security Pacific Bank ($10.2 million). Federal laws such as the Computer Fraud and Abuse Act (1986) provide severe penalties for persons convicted of computer crime.

Schools do not maintain data subject to regular, high-volume financial transaction processing as is common in banks and brokerage houses. However, a school's payroll or accounts payable files can be vulnerable to abuse if security procedures are lax. Other files such as student records must also be protected. They contain sensitive information about individuals and must not be readily available except as needed for legitimate educational purposes.

Data security minimally involves establishing password protection to access a computer system. Additionally, it entails devising access codes that allow certain individuals to access particular files and data. All commercially available database management software packages routinely provide password and access code protection and should be used as standard operating procedures. Written policies should be developed citing which offices and individuals have the authority or need to access specific data. Part of these policies also establishes the degree of access, that is, whether an individual can simply view data or change or update data.

In developing and monitoring data security, school administrators should be particularly concerned with students. Although a more common problem at the college level, there have been many cases of high school computer "hacks" with the talent to break through a password system to access student data such as grades and test scores. Just one or two such individuals can cause havoc to the integrity of data files. A solitary breach of the security system may require major review and verification of the violated data files to determine the extent of the damage. This process can take a great deal of staff time; more important, it can also leave users feeling insecure and wondering about the integrity of the data files.

In recent years, another form of unauthorized access to data files has emerged in the form of "viruses" that are designed to spread from one central processing unit to another. Whereas some viruses are harmless and simply generate annoying messages on a video screen, others are destructive and designed to erase data files, especially disk directories and operating system files. The concern for the destructive power of a computer virus was evident in 1992, when headlines worldwide reported the spread of the Michelangelo virus designed to attack on the anniversary of Michelangelo's birth (March 6).

To protect against viruses, software products, referred to as "antiviruses" or "vaccines," are available that will scan a disk for a virus. Antiviruses are prudent investments for all computer operations but especially in network environments in which viruses can easily spread from one computer to another. The Norton Antivirus from Symantic, Inc., and Virex from Microcom, Inc., are two popular products available for DOS/Windows and Macintosh computers.

In addition to data security, some schools, especially those in high-crime areas, should plan to expend resources on physically securing computer equipment and protecting it from theft and vandalism. As computer equipment becomes smaller, lighter, and more easily disposed of, this need increases. A variety of measures can be taken to secure computer equipment. Anchor pads, which bolt the main computer components to a desk or table, are commonly used and effective in most areas. Electronic security systems for doors and windows can also be used in centralized computer facilities and likewise are effective.

For schools and, again, particularly for those in high-crime areas, security becomes a more serious problem when distributing equipment throughout a school and into the classrooms. Anchor pads should be used in the classrooms; they may be the most cost-effective security measure that can be taken. Electronic security systems can become very expensive depending on the physical distribution of equipment and the accesses to a school building, which for fire code and ergonomic reasons tend to have many more doors and windows than other facilities.

In planning computer facilities, security issues should not be underestimated. To ignore them leaves a school or district vulnerable and subject to major setbacks in their computer development should a breach in security occur.

THE HELPING PLACE

One of the most important responsibilities for those who manage computer facilities is to develop the proper school-wide attitude to technology. Earlier in this chapter, the external elements (i.e., hardware maintenance, room organization, security) were presented, all of which, if done well, will contribute to the overall success that a school will have in using computer technology. However, critical to this success will be the development of a positive attitude or a computer culture that is supportive and nonthreatening to the teachers and staff who are expected to use the technology.

The concept is not a new one and should be familiar to many administrators and teachers. In some schools, "helping places" have been established to provide support services to students who need them. They may be extensions of a guidance office or a tutoring program. They are usually friendly places staffed by teachers who smile easily, have positive dispositions, and will go out of their way to help a student with a problem. Computer facilities likewise should be helping places. In addition to the popular "What if?" questions, staff need to be available to answer the "What happened?" and "How can I do it?" questions. Given the wide disparity in training and understanding that exists regarding computer technology, computer center staff need to be oriented to respond to simple as well as complex questions.

Computer educators (Sheingold, 1991) have espoused establishing computer environments in which children have free and open access to equipment so that it becomes a basic and routinely used tool for learning. This concept also applies to teachers, secretaries, and clerical staff who are called on to use computing systems. Furthermore, they need access not only to equipment but, just as important, to the expertise and knowledge necessary to use it. Managers of computer facilities need to provide both equipment and expertise in a friendly, helpful manner.

Formal staff training sessions are a good beginning, but continuous, ongoing, support services are what will make for a positive computer culture. Hotlines or help phones, staffed by knowledgeable personnel, are extremely effective for answering questions. User groups that meet regularly are helpful in establishing relationships among users and technical staff. Newsletters providing suggestions and hints for using hardware and software are effective communication vehicles for keeping staff informed. These are all excellent examples of ways of establishing a positive computer culture in a school or district. In the final analysis, however, the most important element for building such a culture will be the positive attitude of the people providing these services.

CASE STUDY
Place: Watson Middle School   Year: 1994

The Watson Middle School is an alternative program for bilingual students. It shares facilities with an elementary school located in an inner-city neighborhood in a large metropolitan center. The program was started in 1987 with 100 students. It has grown consistently and is regarded as a major success in the district. The current population is 300 students.

Watson is administered by a director who reports directly to a district superintendent. Thirteen teachers are assigned to the school. The director, who started the school, feels very strongly that the success of the program can be attributed to its small size. Though very supportive of the district establishing similar programs in other schools, she does not feel the program should grow any further at Watson.

The director has been very supportive of computer education and established a central computer laboratory when the school first opened. Presently it houses 25 microcomputers. One teacher who previously taught mathematics has served as the computer coordinator and has done an excellent job. The computer facilities are well integrated into mathematics and science instruction, and all students receive some computer instruction at least twice a week. The average class size is 25 so that during computer instruction, students are able to work individually on a computer. The director feels that the major problem with the central laboratory is that it is simply a large classroom that was converted into a computer laboratory by rearranging desks and tables. Renovations have never been made to the area although renovation funds have been requested in each of the last three years. While generally supportive of most of her budget requests, the district superintendent has not been able to allocate funds for a renovation.

After attending a city-wide workshop for administrators on integrating computing into the curriculum in spring 1994, the director has been considering putting equipment into the regular classrooms. After discussing the idea with the teaching staff, she detected a good deal of support and enthusiasm on their part, especially since she has indicated that she is committed to continuing and expanding several staff development workshops that focus on computer education. The computer coordinator also backed the idea of putting equipment into each of the classrooms, but he raised several legitimate concerns regarding the physical facilities, security, and the overall management of the hardware and software. The coordinator further suggested that maybe the best approach would be to have both a central facility and some equipment in each of the classrooms.

It is May 1994, and the district superintendent has just informed the director that he is confident that approximately $40,000 may be available for renovating the computer facilities, of which $20,000 could be used for equipment and furniture. He would like a proposal from her regarding how she would use these funds. He wants to present it to the district's equipment and facilities planning subcommittee on June 1.

Assuming that you are the director of the Watson Middle School, what would you include in your proposal? To help you with this, further assume that you would like to maintain a smaller central computer facility and to provide equipment in each of the 12 classrooms in the school. However, critical decisions need to be made regarding the number of microcomputer stations to be kept in the central laboratory, the number of stations to be established in each classroom, security, and other physical requirements. Lastly, you are also concerned that if you radically change the nature of your previous request, which was to renovate the central facilities only, you might jeopardize receiving any of the renovation funds.

SUMMARY

In this chapter, the basic elements of planning and managing computer facilities are presented. Space utilization, personnel considerations, security, and hardware and software maintenance are examined. As more and more equipment is acquired, the task of managing it enlarges. Increasingly, school districts are establishing larger technical support groups to support technology in their schools.

Several major issues such as the centralization and locations of computer support facilities are examined. The evolution of the Internet and the demand for more extensive data communications systems is specifically identified as a major issue in facilities planning. Documentation and security are also discussed. Finally, the chapter concludes with a call for establishing a positive computer culture in the school directed not just to students but to teachers and other staff as well.

Key Concepts and Questions

1. While computer equipment is becoming increasingly easier to use, managing computer facilities in schools is becoming more complex.

   Is this situation likely to change in the near future? Does it depend on the nature of the applications? Explain.

2. Various organizational models exist in school districts for managing computer facilities.

   Which model do you think is most appropriate? Why?

3. Centralized computer facilities are common in many schools.

   What are some of the major considerations in managing centralized versus decentralized facilities?

4. Ergonomic factors in the design of computer facilities are critical for the comfort and safety of users (teachers, students, and staff) in schools.

   What do you consider some of the most important ergonomic considerations? Do they change depending on the users? Explain.

5. With the proliferation of microcomputers throughout the schools, maintenance of hardware and software is becoming more difficult.

   Why? Is it simply a matter of more equipment and software requiring more maintenance? Explain.

6. The concept of developing a positive culture in a school or any organization is a recurring theme in many discussions about leadership and administrative style.

   Borrowing from this theme, what are some of the techniques that can be developed to promote a positive computer culture in a school?

Suggested Activities

1. Identify the organizational structure for managing computer facilities in a (or your) school district and in a school. Evaluate the structure(s) in terms of effectiveness. What suggestions, if any, do you have for improvement?

2. Evaluate the computer culture that has evolved in a (or your) school. What factors do you feel have contributed to this culture?

References

Carlitz, R. D., Lentz, M., & MacIlroy, A. (1995). Standards for school networking. *Technological Horizons in Education Journal*, *22*(9), 71–74.

Conway, K. (1990). *Master classrooms: Classroom design with technology in mind*. Chapel Hill: University of North Carolina and Chapel Hill Institute for Academic Technology.

Dockterman, D. A. (1990). *Great teaching in the one computer classroom*. Cambridge, MA: Tom Snyder Productions.

Harris, D. P. (1990). Developing a comprehensive microcomputer lab for small- to medium-sized campuses. *Technological Horizons in Education Journal, 18*(3), 80–84.

O'Brien, J. A. (1989). *Computer concepts and applications*. Homewood, IL: Irwin.

Ritterspacher, P. (1990). The home-based middle school: Implications for facility design. *Technological Horizons in Education Journal, 17*(6), 61–62.

Rothstein, R. I., & McKnight, L. (1996). Technology and cost models of K–12 schools on the National Information Infrastructure. *Computers in the Schools, 12*(1/2), 31–57.

Sheingold, K. (1991). Restructuring for learning with technology: The potential for synergy. *Phi Delta Kappan, 73*(1), 17–27.

12

Financial Planning

I n the previous chapters of this section, emphasis was placed on the need for planning the various hardware, software, and people components of proposals to implement computer programs in a school or district. However, these proposals cannot move forward without the necessary financial resources to initiate them and to maintain them in the future. In this chapter, the financial side of planning is examined, with emphasis on evaluating costs for computer technology and on seeking funds to support it. In developing examples for this chapter, several of the ideas and approaches discussed in previous chapters are considered again from a cost perspective.

TECHNOLOGY CAN BE EXPENSIVE

The U.S. Congress's Office of Technology Assessment (OTA), in a comprehensive report issued in 1988, estimated that as much as 32% of the average school district's instructional materials budget will be devoted to computer technology by the year 2000. In terms of dollars, this represents an expenditure of more than $4 billion *per year* for the country's 15,000-plus school districts. Quality Education Data (QED), Inc. (1991), supported the OTA estimate. Based on actual 1990 expenditures of $1.4 billion for instructional technology, QED projected an increase of $800 million through 1994–95, or $2.2 billion. Projecting QED figures through the year 2000 would generate an estimate of almost $4.5 billion.

However, both estimates have proven to be too low. QED (1996) reported that the actual expenditures for instructional technology among the nation' schools had already exceeded $4 billion by 1995. Present projections of school expenditures for technology for the year 2000 based on an 11% increase per year are now almost $7 billion (QED, 1996).

Becker (1994) conducted four national surveys of American schools in the 1980s and early 1990s and concluded that the nation's schools were acquiring approximately 300,000 to 400,000 microcomputers per year. Becker sees this trend maintaining itself, if not accelerating, well into the next century. Looking to the future, Rothstein and McKnight (1996), in a study for the National Information Infrastructure Initiative, estimated that the cost for putting a microcomputer on the desk of every student and teacher in the country, with high-speed connection to the Internet, could be as much as $145 billion for the first year and $11 billion per year thereafter. Considering that as late as 1980 the spending for computer technology in education was negligible, these projections indicate that American education is making a substantial financial commitment to technology.

School administrators will need to plan wisely to meet the funding requirements of computer technology and to make sure that they have the resources to maintain computer-based programs. Rare are the administrators who have reduced expenditures for computer technology once it has been established in their schools. In some years, they may "hold the line" because of some budgetary problems, but these measures tend to be temporary, and the overall pattern is to increase funding.

This escalating pattern of increased expenditures for technology is not unique to the field of education. It is typical in private corporations, governmental agencies, and most other organizations that have been using technology since the 1960s, well before technology became popular in schools. Once a computer-based program is established, in addition to maintenance, the normal pattern has been to expand and provide additional services and to upgrade it with newer technology when necessary.

THE COST-EFFECTIVENESS OF COMPUTERS

A common assumption among some administrators is that computers can be cost-effective and save money in the long run. This complicated issue greatly interests many people, including school board members, teachers, union representatives, and taxpayers. The simple but popular notion that machines can replace people and thereby save money has yet to be proven in an educational setting. This idea was often promulgated by computer salespersons as a marketing or sales strategy; indeed, in other industries, such as automobile assembly lines, telephone communications, and printing, jobs have been lost to automation. This has not happened yet in education, and cases in which computers have replaced teachers are practically nonexistent.

Regardless of costs, many teachers and administrators do see the computer as making them more effective in their daily activities. Albert Shanker, the president of the American Federation of Teachers, has spoken and written extensively on the potential benefits of computer technology in the classroom and sees it as a tool to be integrated into the learning process by the teacher. As early as 1989, Shanker had indicated that the installation of computer equipment in the nation's classrooms should be education's top priority in the 1990s. The National Education Association (NEA) has released reports and statements declaring that computer technology holds great promise for enriching classroom instruction and management. The NEA has further recommended that a computer be installed on the desk of every teacher (National Education Association, 1989). This has not happened, but the recommendation indicates the positive attitude of a major teacher organization to technology in the classroom.

Although many educators are enthusiastic regarding the potential of computer technology, the cost-effectiveness is still open to debate. That is, will the funds expended for it yield improved learning? As an example, Levin and Meister (1986) conducted a series of studies from 1978 to 1984 comparing four cost-effective strategies: computer-assisted instruction, peer tutoring, increased instructional time, and reduced class size. They concluded that peer tutoring was the most cost-effective approach in terms of improved reading and mathematics scores on standardized tests. Computer-assisted instruction was the second most cost-effective strategy, followed by reduced class size and increased instructional time. These studies were later challenged by Niemiec, Blackwell, and Walberg (1986), who in reviewing Levin and Meister's methodology concluded that computer-assisted instruction was more cost-effective than peer tutoring.

Given the inherent difficulties in educational evaluation, the debate on cost-effectiveness will probably continue for some time. As referenced in earlier chapters, readers are directed to some of the excellent literature reviews conducted in the past by Kulik (1984), Robyler, Castine, and King (1988), and Clark (1989), to develop an overall opinion of the merits of computer-based education. In general, though positive to the use of technology, they do not agree that computer education leads necessarily to improved student performance. However, even in these reviews, cost-effectiveness is rarely examined in any depth.

A TIME LINE FOR FINANCIAL PLANNING

With the introduction of microcomputers in the late 1970s, a major breakthrough was realized in the costs for computer technology, comparable to the introduction of the Model T automobile by Henry Ford, which made a car affordable for practically every American family. Before the Model T, cars were viewed mainly as luxury items affordable only by somewhat wealthy people. Within a few decades, and even with the depression of the 1930s and World War II in the 1940s, cars became indispensable, and the multicar family has now become commonplace. So too with microcomputers. However, the rapidity with which the microcomputer has become a basic tool in all types of endeavors is impressive.

The major catalyst for this phenomenon was the cost, as much if not more so than the need. In the 1960s and 1970s, computers were not items that the average person felt they needed to live from day to day. As late as 1977, Ken Olsen, the president of Digital Equipment Corporation, the leading manufacturer of minicomputers, stated publicly that there was no need for any individual to have a microcomputer in their home (Stoll, 1995). As a matter of fact, with the exception of some video games and very rudimentary home applications such as balancing a checkbook, calculating mortgage payments, and estimating a grocery bill, there were very few applications for the average person. In the late 1970s, most people purchased microcomputers because the cost, typically under $1,000, was attractive. Large quantities of computers were purchased, and this trend has continued into the present. In the meantime, computer vendors and software firms have been catching up with the availability of hardware by developing tens of thousands of computer programs to meet all kinds of interests and needs. While basic applications such as word processing, Internet access, and electronic games tend to be the most common home uses today, microcomputers routinely touch our daily lives in the form of cash machines, checkout counters, and telephone information services.

Primary and secondary schools are among the last organizations to become dependent on computer technology. With the introduction of microcomputers, this has begun to change, mostly because schools are now able to afford to purchase this equipment. Furthermore, the trend is clear, and in the future, computer equipment will become indispensable in many schools as it has in many other individual and organizational activities. Educational applications have been developed and will continue to be developed to meet the demands of the education market. Administrators will be devoting more and more of their budgets to computer technology even though the unit cost of a microcomputer has been very stable and will not likely increase in the future; it may, in fact, decrease.

To understand this situation better, review Table 12–1, which provides a time line of the trends in computer technology with their respective costs from the 1960s through the 1990s. This time line illustrates the characteristics of the major cost categories for implementing computer-based educational applications, namely hardware, software, and personnel.

In examining hardware costs, computing equipment has evolved from the expensive mainframe computers of the 1960s, to the minicomputers of the 1970s, to the

Table 12–1
Time Line for Financial Planning, 1960s–2000

	1960s →	1970s →	1980s →	1990s → 2000
Hardware				
Type	Mainframes	Minicomputers	Microcomputers with limited storage	Microcomputers with extensive storage
			Local area and wide area networks (introduction)	Multiple networks and the Internet
				Computer/video workstations
				Hand-held/superlight microcomputers
Cost	$500,000–$1M	$75,000–$300,000	$1,000–$2,500	$1,000–$2,500 (Workstation)
				$500–$750 (Hand-held)
Software				
Type	BASIC	BASIC/Pascal	Packages	Packages
	FORTRAN	Word processing (Introduction)	Tool software	Tool software
		Logo	Logo	Logo (enhanced)
		PLATO	Authoring languages	Advanced authoring languages
		CAI	Integrated learning systems	Integrated learning systems
				World Wide Web
Cost	Bundled with hardware	Inexpensive/ expensive	Inexpensive/ expensive	Inexpensive/ expensive
Personnel				
Type	Technicians	Technicians	Computer teachers	Computer and regular teachers
Cost	Highly paid	Highly paid	Average to highly paid teachers	Average to highly paid teachers

inexpensive microcomputers of today as characterized by Macintosh and DOS/Windows machines. These are high-speed microcomputers with limited disk storage capacities in the range of 100 million to 1.6 billion bytes. The 1990s also saw the introduction of hand-held data organizers and other superlightweight microcomputers. By the end of the 1990s, microcomputers will continue to evolve, especially with advances in data storage capabilities. Manufacturers will continue to develop and enhance magnetic disk and CD-ROM (compact disc-read only memory) technology and provide virtually unlimited on-line storage with both read and write features. In addition, video technology using both CD-ROM and videodiscs will be more widely used. CD-ROM and digital video provided by the Internet will compete with videodiscs as the primary media for integrating video applications with computers. Internet access and networking capability via high-speed modems have had phenomenal growth in the 1990s and will continue to increase. Educational workstations that combine computing, video, and networking will be more prevalent, and all components (computer, video, and data communications) will be available from a single manufacturer. Schools will be more fully equipped by the year 2000, with student/microcomputer ratios approaching 6 to 1.

In terms of cost, the unit price of computer hardware has fallen dramatically from the typical $1 million large mainframe systems of the 1960s to the $1,000 microcomputer systems of today. While unit prices of microcomputers have been stable throughout the 1980s and 1990s, even decreasing, performance (speed, primary storage, and secondary storage capacities) continues to expand and improve. Through the year 2000, the typical microcomputer system will continue to range between $1,000 and $2,500 depending on options such as CD-ROMS, printers, and other peripheral equipment. Hand-held and other limited application microcomputers will sell for as little as $500. Larger-scale integrated learning systems that provide hardware, software, and curriculum material in one package will steadily grow in popularity. However, because of the cost (which can easily involve hundreds of thousands of dollars), they will not replace microcomputer workstations as the basic educational computing equipment in American schools but will be integrated with them.

The time line indicates that the evolution of software has not been as dramatic as that of hardware. Although much easier to use, software is still viewed by many educators as the impediment to the effective use of technology in instruction. Two of the most popular programming languages still used today in instruction are BASIC and Logo, yet BASIC was developed in 1964 by John Kemeny at Dartmouth University, and Logo in 1967 by Seymour Papert at MIT. With the exception of Logo, programming will be reserved for more advanced or elective classes. The development of authoring languages such as HyperCard began in the 1980s, and more advanced versions will evolve that will be easier to use, particularly for accessing video media. Inexpensive, simple-to-use software packages, which became very popular in the 1980s, will continue to proliferate. Interactive video packages, introduced in the late 1980s, will be easier to use and more generally available, especially if the cost for producing these materials can be reduced. The cost of software will vary significantly, from as little as $30 to $40 for simple packages to as much as hundreds of thousands of dollars for integrated learning systems that also provide extensive curriculum databases. The Internet will continue to grow as a major, if not *the* major source of software and media.

The people needed to support computer applications have been and will continue to be the crucial factor in providing computer-based education in the schools. The time line shows major changes in the salary structure, caused by the changing nature of the people directing computer activities, as well as an evolution from the highly paid technicians of the 1960s to the computer teachers of today.

Teacher education programs in colleges have expanded and are now providing specializations in computer education that combine technical training with teaching and learning. In addition, many teacher education programs are beginning to require all students to have some computer literacy and to take course work in educational technology. By the year 2000, schools will depend on computer teachers assisting regular teachers who already have some basic technology training. Staff development will continue to be a serious need, and resources will be devoted not only to educate those who require basic technical training but, more importantly, also to maintain the skills of those who already have had some training.

With this time line providing the necessary background plus a glimpse of the future direction of computer-related costs, we are ready to consider a budgeting process for funding technology.

THE BUDGET WORKSHEET

Financial planning supports the overall planning processes of a school district. It should not dominate the process but be integrated as needed. As with many aspects of administration, a proper balance must be achieved so that those doing the educational planning are not stifled by budget considerations and at the same time are cognizant of the costs of what they are proposing to do.

As mentioned in Chapter 2, in planning for computer-based education, the first step is to develop a planning process that yields worthwhile proposals for consideration for possible implementation. Each of these proposals should include a budget worksheet identifying the major costs associated with the application (see Figure 12–1). Information is required for the major components (hardware, software, personnel, etc.) of each computer planning proposal.

This worksheet serves several purposes. First, it requires those making a proposal to identify the necessary costs for implementation. Although this may be a routine procedure in some schools, administrators frequently face situations in which the cost of a project or proposal has not been carefully determined. A common example in many computer-based education proposals is that emphasis is placed on hardware costs alone, which frequently may account for only a fraction of the total cost. The use of a budget worksheet requires an examination of all the costs associated with the proposal.

Second, the worksheet initiates important information-gathering activity for those making a proposal. Collecting information on costs requires administrators, teach-

Please complete all sections as best asyou can. Include the costs
for consultants within the categories of hardware, software, personnel, and so forth. Attach additional pages if necessary. If you need
help in completing this worksheet, feel free to contact _____ .

Hardware (Identify the type of equipment and its cost.)   Subtotal $ _____

Software (Identify the software needed and its cost.)   Subtotal $ _____

Personnel (Identify any staff requirements including training
and release time for curriculum development.)   Subtotal $ _____

Repairs/upgrades (Estimate any projected costs for repairs and
upgrades to equipment.)   Subtotal $ _____

Supplies (Estimate the annual costs for supplies.)   Subtotal $ _____

Facilities (Identify where equipment is to be located and any
special requirements for electricity, security, etc. Also include
any requests for new furniture.)   Subtotal $ _____

                                                Grand total $ _____

Figure 12–1
North Central School District No. 1 Budget Worksheet for a Computer-Related
Planning Proposal

ers, library media personnel, and other staff to seek out computer vendors, salespersons, suppliers, and others who can provide important information not only about
costs but also about new models of hardware, educational discounts, and demonstration opportunities. The inclusion on the budget worksheet of the name of a person in the district who functions as a computer coordinator is also very helpful. Such
a person can be an important source of information about what already exists in the

district and bring individuals together who may have common purposes, which is especially effective in larger school districts where interaction between schools may be limited. Such an individual can also be effective in encouraging teachers and other staff to share equipment and facilities.

Third, the use of a budget worksheet makes it easier to coordinate the costs of all proposals into one overall financial plan. With the cost information readily available, summarizing and approximating all costs is much easier for determining the total budget request. This, in turn, can be compared to the existing or projected availability of funds, and the process of evaluating what is to be funded can begin.

A BUDGET MODEL

In developing an overall financial plan, much time is spent in determining the component costs of the various proposals. The budget worksheet is helpful in providing the approximate costs for all the requests. However, administrators will need to refine these requests because rarely are there enough resources to fund all proposals. As part of this refinement, administrators will ask teachers and administrators to reduce or sometimes to expand their requests and very frequently to pool or share resources. With computer technology, the pooling of resources to acquire hardware, software, supplies, and so forth, can result in substantial economies. Essentially, this was one of the most important reasons that schools centralized rather than decentralized computer facilities when they first began new computer-based education programs.

In developing the overall financial plan, administrators should make sure the proposals presented have accurately projected all the various costs for implementing a plan and have considered sharing and other means to achieve the greatest benefit from available resources. For applications that may be implemented over several years, the costs likewise should be projected accordingly. Figure 12–2 provides a simple modification of the budget worksheet for doing multiyear projections.

Table 12–2 illustrates a composite budget model of an overall financial plan that might be used to fund computer-based education. The major cost categories of hardware, software, and personnel comprise 72% of the total, with other items such as staff training, repairs/upgrades, supplies/furniture, and miscellaneous categories accounting for the remaining 28%. These percentages are meant to provide a general direction and can vary depending on the computer applications being supported.

Also provided in Table 12–2 are three other models that illustrate the differences in trying to establish average cost percentages for computer expenditures. Many of the differences in these models can be attributed to how school districts identify different cost categories. For example, some school districts include part or all of "Repairs/Upgrades" and "Supplies/Furniture" with "Hardware." School districts also frequently include computer supplies in the general supplies budget or repairs in a general administrative repairs budget. Where these items are budgeted is not important as long as they are included somewhere.

These models, all of which come from published material, indicate that variability in funding computer technology exists. In the final analysis, school administrators

Please complete all sections as best as you can. Include the costs for consultants within the categories of hardware, software, personnel, and so forth. Attach additional pages if necessary. If you need help in completing this worksheet, feel free to contact _____.

	Year 1	Year 2	Year 3
Hardware (Identify the type of equipment and its cost.)	Subtotal $ _____	Subtotal $ _____	Subtotal $ _____
Software (Identify the software needed and its cost.)	Subtotal $ _____	Subtotal $ _____	Subtotal $ _____
Personnel (Identify any staff requirements including training and release time for curriculum development.)	Subtotal $ _____	Subtotal $ _____	Subtotal $ _____
Repairs/upgrades (Estimate any projected costs for repairs and upgrades to equipment.)	Subtotal $ _____	Subtotal $ _____	Subtotal $ _____
Supplies (Estimate the annual costs for supplies.)	Subtotal $ _____	Subtotal $ _____	Subtotal $ _____
Facilities (Identify where equipment is to be located and any special requirements for electricity, security, etc. Also include any requests for new furniture.)	Subtotal $ _____	Subtotal $ _____	Subtotal $ _____
Total requested for all years $ _____	Total $ _____	Total $ _____	Total $ _____

Figure 12–2
North Central District No. 1 Budget Worksheet for a Multiyear Computer-Related Planning Proposal

Table 12–2
Composite Budget Model for Computer-Based Education

	Hardware	Software	Personnel	Training	Repairs/ upgrades	Supplies/ furniture	Miscellaneous
	35%	10%	27%	7%	9%	6%	6%

Other budget model comparisons							
	Hardware	Software	Personnel	Training	Repairs/ upgrades	Supplies/ furniture	Miscellaneous
Public sector	41%	7%	33%	NA	NA	7%	12%
OTA report	37%	12%	27%	9%	9%	6%	NA
Two-Percent solution	50%	17%	17%	8%	NA	NA	8%

Source: Public sector model based on a 1988 survey by *Datamation* magazine of public sector organizations, including schools (Hodges, 1988); OTA model based on data for primary schools (U.S. Congress, Office of Technology Assessment, 1988); 2% solution model based on the work of Moursand (1986).

Here is a sample cost analysis for implementing a minilab of 10 computers networked together (LAN) with access to the Internet. The basic hardware configuration would be as follows:

> 10 PCs with 16-MB RAM, 1.6-GB hard drive, 15-inch monitors, OR:
>
> 10 Macintosh Power PCs similarly equipped
>
> Local area network cables, cards, and server
>
> 1 flatbed scanner
>
> 1 laser printer
>
> Beginning set of application software packages, authoring tools, LAN software, and supplies

The total cost for above would be $28,000 initally plus $2,000 per year thereafter for maintenance and basic upkeep.

Connecting to the Internet via a high-speed ISDN line would require the following:

> 1 Internet router
>
> Monthly ISDN connect charges

Cost for this service would be $9,700 for the first year and approximately $6,700 per year thereafter.

Personnel costs for this proposal would be the salary of one person to serve as the system administrator or coordinator. Depending on this person's technical experience some outside assistance/consulting may be required for system installation, training, and maintenance. Assume $6,500 for the first year and $4,000 per year thereafter.

The overall costs would be as follows:

	1st Year	2nd Year →
Basic hardware, software, and supplies	$28,000	$ 2,000
Internet connection/communications	9,700	6,700
Outside assistance, training, maintenance	6,500	4,000
Total	$34,200	$12,700

Figure 12–3
Sample Cost Analysis for a Networked Minilab

Source: Natuzzi (1996).

will establish an affordable funding model with which they are comfortable. What is most important to financial planning is that administrators be aware of all costs and not just the obvious or direct items.

Figure 12–3 is an abbreviated cost analysis for establishing a 10-station minilab with a connection to the Internet. In addition to hardware, other costs for networking, maintenance, and personnel are identified.

SPECIAL CONSIDERATIONS OF BUDGETING
FOR COMPUTER APPLICATIONS

Although budgeting for computer applications, whether administrative or instructional, is similar to other budgeting exercises, administrators should be aware of several special considerations unique to technology.

Opting for Centralized or Decentralized Computer Facilities

The decision to centralize or decentralize computer facilities has significant budgetary ramifications. As discussed in Chapter 11, a centralized computer laboratory can be far more efficient than decentralized facilities. Sharing technical support—whether it be the expertise of laboratory personnel, back-up maintenance equipment, or a software library—is much easier to accomplish in a central facility. Other considerations such as physical security, accidental breakage, and renovation costs also contribute to the efficiency of central facilities.

On the other hand, the trend with microcomputing has been toward decentralization, with more and more equipment being acquired and placed where the activity occurs. For administrative applications, microcomputers are placed on the desks of administrators and secretaries. Likewise, for instructional applications, microcomputers are more and more being placed on the desks of students and teachers. Decentralization is desirable to resolve problems of ready access to the equipment, to integrate computing with other instructional activities, and to avoid the logistics of scheduling and moving children to the central laboratories. Administrators should be planning for a more decentralized computing environment than presently exists in most schools.

That is not to say, however, that the concept of sharing resources should not be entirely abandoned. A common hardware maintenance contract for all equipment is far more economical than having each computer location handle repairs on an individual or as-needed basis. The sharing of software through site licenses is very cost-effective. The use of networks at the building level to share software, data, and documentation can also be very efficient. Some centralization also can and should continue to exist for certain applications, and the movement toward decentralization should not be viewed as completely incompatible with centralized facilities. Such a combination of centralized and decentralized facilities sharing certain resources is commonly described as **distributed**. Schools are moving in the direction of distributed systems. Typically, these systems are centrally coordinated, and hardware and software is shared by way of computer networks.

Hiring a Consultant

Routinely used in the fields of education and technology, consultants are readily available for assisting in the design or implementation of computer applications. School districts that have been late in developing computer facilities and are just beginning to invest significant resources should consider the use of consultants to help avoid common pitfalls and costly mistakes. In the budget model provided, consultant costs are not specifically identified but should be included within specific budget categories such as hardware, software, and personnel if they are required.

Technical expertise is becoming more specialized, so a consultant who is very effective in recommending and guiding a district in one aspect of technology may not be as effective in another. For example, an expert in the hardware and data communications requirements of a local area network may not be effective in helping launch a comprehensive teacher training program. Generally, as districts or schools do more, internal expertise develops and accumulates, which lessens the need for outside consultants.

However, even in districts where a good deal of expertise exists, administrators should not rule out the need for consulting services, particularly if considering some new or inherently complex technology. For example, integrating voice and data communications in a wide area network is not a simple task, and many school districts, regardless of their staffs' expertise, would probably seek outside technical advice to help them plan and implement such a project. In some states such as California, Kentucky, Minnesota, New York, and Texas, educational cooperatives and technical centers are supported by the state education departments and may be good starting points for seeking assistance.

Standardizing on a Common Vendor

The question of standardizing on some common hardware vendor and thereby realizing efficiencies in terms of quantity acquisitions, software development, hardware maintenance, or staff training should be addressed. Before the microcomputer explosion, school districts and most other organizations attempted to standardize on a common hardware vendor for these purposes. However, with the advent of microcomputer technology, this has changed. For administrative applications, the tendency is still to acquire compatible equipment, if not a common vendor. The use of common hardware will allow for the sharing of software and, most importantly, the sharing of common databases (i.e., student, personnel, scheduling) for various administrative applications within the school, which is highly desirable. In addition, in large urban school districts and districts governed by municipalities, schools may have to acquire equipment that is compatible with the local government's administrative systems so that common data systems such as financial accounting, census, and payroll can easily be used.

For instructional applications, this is not necessarily the trend or the desired direction. Presently, a variety of equipment is being used in the classrooms, and every indication is that this will continue in the future. Surely, Apple Corporation with the Macintosh computers along with Compaq, Dell, and IBM, among other firms, are all providing excellent pieces of equipment. School administrators should allow for variety as long as it can be justified because of the needs of the proposed application. If the proposed application requires specialized software that is only available for a particular model of computer, then this might be a justifiable reason for acquiring that equipment. For instance, some excellent educational software packages using videodiscs are written in specific authoring languages such as Hyper-Card or HyperStudio, which are only available on Apple Macintosh computers. This should not preclude a school from considering acquiring this software and the requisite Macintosh hardware because the standard in the building or district might happen to be another manufacturer. The same would be true if the authoring language was LinkWay or ToolBook, both of which only execute on DOS/Windows machines.

Hardware First, Other Needs Later?

A common practice in acquiring computer equipment is to buy as much hardware as possible up front and plan to take care of the other costs later on. This approach is becoming more common as competition among hardware vendors grows, and significant savings may be realized by taking advantage of special, limited-time discounts. Buying equipment first is acceptable as long as the equipment meets the needs of an overall plan and funds for the other costs will in fact be provided. However, given the "up and down" budget cycles in some states and school districts, this is not always the case. Unfortunately, some administrators find themselves with equipment that is not fully used because the proper software is not available, teachers have not been trained, or electrical upgrades in the computer facilities have not been completed. The recommended approach is to plan for an application that includes planning for all the component costs, not just hardware.

Choosing a Purchasing Plan

Purchasing plans vary with the vendor and type of equipment. The choice of a plan was much more significant before the introduction of microcomputers when the purchase prices of large mainframe and minicomputers were substantial. School districts as well as most other organizations wanted to spread costs out over a period of time. Spreading costs through a lease-purchase agreement rather than paying full price, for example, is still recommended for districts making large acquisitions such as integrated learning systems.

The main reason for this approach is to reduce the budget impact in any one given year and to spread the costs out over several fiscal years. Another reason is to build a base budget for computer hardware, which makes it much easier to replace or upgrade equipment without having to request funds for a major new acquisition every 5 to 7 years. The yearly lease-purchase allocation can simply be continued with small percentage increases for upgrading or adding on to the original configuration. Regarding the acquisition of microcomputers, the vast majority of educational users purchase this equipment outright. However, administrators should also build an equipment replacement plan into their base budget to make sure that they can replace units that will become damaged or technically obsolete.

SOURCES OF FUNDS

Once a number of worthwhile planning proposals have been received and consolidated into an overall financial plan, an examination of the sources that will finance the plan is now required. The four major funding sources are the school district budget, bond issues, governmental entities, and gifts and grants.

The School District Budget

The school district budget generally is the primary source of funds for implementing computer applications. If not already in place, two base budgets for computer technology need to be established: one that will support administrative applications and a second that will support instructional applications.

Administrative applications are almost always supported entirely by a school district's tax levy budget. In general, boards of education are cognizant of the need for timely and accurate data and the efficiency of office operations utilizing basic computer technology; hence, they tend to be supportive of providing funds for administrative applications. School boards also tend to be very demanding in terms of receiving data about their school districts, and they are receptive to technology that improves their information delivery systems. In some cases, other governmental agencies may provide funds because of a special initiative or a mandatory reporting requirement that exists outside the school.

Instructional applications, on the other hand, because there are perceptions that funds can be provided from a variety of other sources, may require more negotiation and justification to be funded fully by the school district's tax levy budget. This situation varies significantly from district to district depending on the wealth, tax base, and financial personality of a district.

Both budgets, administrative and instructional, should have an established minimum base within the district's budget because all computer applications require some ongoing cost items, such as maintenance, supplies, and upgrades. How much is needed for a base budget depends entirely on the goals and objectives that a district has identified in an overall technology plan. There are no fixed percentages of a total budget for funding computer-related programs. According to the U.S. Congress's OTA (1988), by the year 2000, the average school district will be devoting at least 32% of its instructional materials budget for computer-related items such as hardware, software, and direct computer repairs. Additional budget allocations will be needed for personnel costs, training, and facilities.

In seeking funds from boards of education for instructional applications, school administrators should consider drawing support from parents, many of whom want their children learning about and using computer technology. Many parents use computer equipment in their jobs and see computer literacy and competence as important if not necessary for career success. They can be very helpful in securing budgetary approvals from elected school officials.

Bond Issues

Bond issues for the purpose of some major capital improvement, such as the construction or renovation of a school building, can be an important source of funds, because equipping and furnishing the building is generally an accepted part of the project. These funds, sometimes quite substantial, provide a school district with an infusion of dollars to launch major new technology programs. Of course, many districts are not necessarily building new facilities, and capital construction funds may not be available. If this is the case, administrators might ask the board of education or the governing board of the municipality to consider a special bond issue for major equipment purchases and upgrades for the entire district or for the schools that are not targeted for any capital improvements in the near future.

If a school district does acquire a significant amount of new equipment as a result of a bond issue, the necessary funds to maintain this equipment in the future should immediately be built into the operating budget. The understanding should be that bond or capital funds will be used for significant and not simply incremental acquisitions. In general, a school district should not rely on bonds for equipment and other needs that normally should be provided for in an operating budget.

Governmental Entities

Governmental entities at the federal, state, and local levels may also be the source of funds for instructional computing programs. Although subject to changing political and financial climates, various governmental agencies have demonstrated interest in technology and responded accordingly. State education departments throughout the country increasingly are providing support for technological improvements. Statewide resource centers such as the Minnesota Educational Computer Consortium and Pennsylvania's Information Technology Education for the Commonwealth (ITEC) centers have been established for these purposes. Federal programs administered by the U.S. Department of Education and the National Science Foundation have provided funds to acquire computer equipment for educational programs, usually directed for specific populations and purposes. Chapter 1 (Aid for Disadvantaged Children) and Chapter 2 (Block Grants for Innovative Projects) funds have especially been useful for acquiring technology.

All levels of government are aware of pressure from the business community, which has been influential in calling attention to the need for a well-educated and well-trained work force. For example, the New York City Partnership, an organization of business and civic leaders, issued a report in 1989 indicating that New York City's position as a world financial center was threatened because of a shortage of workers with technical skills. The report went on to cite the theoretical loss of tens of thousands of jobs, recommending that the state consider revising its curricula to ensure that all students develop computer and other job readiness skills as part of their basic educational programs. In part, because of the importance of technology and information services to their economies, both New York City and New York State have set aside special budget items to be used to support technology-related instructional programs.

Several excellent sources of information regarding federal grants and funding include these:

- *The Federal Register,* Office of the Federal Register, National Archives and Records Administration, Washington, DC 20408
- *Education Daily,* Capital Publications, Inc., 1101 King St., Alexandria, VA 22313-2053
- *Federal Grants and Contracts Weekly* (also published by Capital Publications, Inc.)

Gifts and Grants

Gifts and grants can also be a significant source of funds to implement computer applications. A certain aggressiveness on the part of administrators is required to seek out potential donors, foundations, and other grant agencies, but the rewards can be quite substantial. Individuals, parent-teacher organizations, small local businesses, and international corporations contribute hundreds of millions of dollars each year for improvements in schools, and computer technology has particularly benefited from this generosity.

One of the most dramatic gifts for technology occurred in the state of Mississippi in 1990 when two businessmen, Richard Riordan and Richard Dowling, donated $7 million for a 5-year program to improve reading and writing skills. The gift required that the state contribute $6 million to the program, which entailed establishing IBM's Writing to Read computer program in kindergartens and first grades in all public schools.

Although the amount of this gift is very unusual, it exemplifies several common characteristics of gift giving and grantsmanship directed to education. First, the gift required a matching contribution. Many donors, individuals as well as foundations, prefer to give to those who are willing to invest some of their own resources in a project as evidence of its need and validity.

Second, the gift required that a certain computer program be implemented. Attaching certain conditions to a gift or grant is not uncommon, but the specificity of the condition in this case, however, is unusual and raised questions about the influence of the donors on the educational philosophy and approaches in the state's schools. Although schools had the option of not participating in this program, none refused.

Third, the donation was targeted specifically for a computer-based program, which is indicative of the belief held by an increasing number of businesspeople in the benefits of technology. Although donors willing to give $7 million to education are rare, many businesspeople in school districts and localities are willing to make more modest donations. Banks, insurance companies, and department stores are enormous users of computer information systems and need to employ local people to operate these systems. They may be willing to make small donations to ensure that their future employees have familiarity with technology.

Three excellent sources for information on grants from private corporations and foundations are these:

- Sloane Reports, Inc., P.O. Box 561689, Miami, FL 33256
- The Foundation Center, 79 Fifth Ave., New York, NY 10003-3050
- The Grantsmanship Center, P.O. Box 17220, Los Angeles, CA 90099-4522

Lastly, no discussion of gifts and grants to schools would be complete without mention of the work and generosity of parent-teacher associations throughout the country. In the area of technology, many school districts have received gifts of computer equipment from these associations. Imaginative fund-raisers such as bake sales, collection of grocery market receipts, and craft fairs have been used to acquire modest amounts of equipment. Administrators should encourage these activities because, in addition to acquiring funds, they also generate interest and enthusiasm for computer education.

CASE STUDY
Place: Mount Hope School District   Year: 1992

The Mount Hope School District is located in a suburban city in the northern midwest section of the United States. It operates 37 schools for 33,000 students and is considered a model school system within the region in terms of student performance, innovative teaching, and a progressive administration. An active planning process involving teachers, parents, and local businesspeople has been instrumental in helping Mount Hope achieve this distinction.

Mount Hope has been most active in providing and using technological tools for instruction. A carefully developed technology plan has evolved from the district's planning process that has kept the city in the forefront. The current inventory includes approximately 2,600 microcomputers being used in the schools for instructional purposes. In the primary and middle schools, most of the microcomputers are Apple IIs and Macintoshes, whereas in the high schools IBM PCs/PSs and Macintoshes dominate. In 1990, the district adopted a hardware acquisition policy that established Macintoshes and IBM PCs/PSs as the standard machines for the district. The extensive number of Apple II microcomputers in the district are gradually being replaced by Macintoshes.

Possibly the most important element of Mount Hope's success in terms of computer education has been the emphasis on involving teachers in the planning process, especially in selecting software and other educational materials. A district-wide Technology Planning Committee has eight members, two of whom are teachers. Another district committee, the Software Review Committee, has 12 members, eight of whom are teachers or computer coordinators. This committee prides itself on putting the needs of students first, and it diligently reviews all software packages before approving their use in the classroom.

The economic base in Mount Hope in 1989 received a needed boost when a major developer of business software for IBM PC and PC-compatible microcomputers, 1st-ONE Inc., established its national headquarters in the town. With 1st-ONE have come the development of other very desirable support companies, increased tax revenue, and well-paying jobs. On May 1, 1992, the president of the company announced a new venture to develop educational software. Furthermore, the company was also entering into an agreement with a manufacturer, TopXXX Products Inc., of IBM PC-compatible microcomputers to market jointly some of their products.

On June 15, 1992, the president of the Mount Hope Board of Education, who is a vice president at the Mount Hope Bank and Trust Company, received a phone call from the president of 1st-ONE indicating that the company was considering making a large donation to the school district over the next three years in the form of new equipment with a market value of in excess of $1 million. The equipment would be IBM PC-compatible and supplied by TopXXX Products. Each microcomputer would also come with several new educational software products that 1st-ONE had just developed and was beginning to market.

On June 16, the president of the board of education mentioned at an executive work session that 1st-ONE would like to offer the school district a most generous gift of computer equipment and software. Three of the board members were ecstatic about the president's announcement, but others expressed some reservation about the nature of the gift. In response to several questions from these board members, the superintendent indicated that he knew very little about either 1st-ONE educational software or TopXXX products but that he would be happy to discuss both with his staff and the chairpersons of the district's technology committees and report back to the board at its next meeting, which was in one week.

On June 17, the superintendent asked his assistant to schedule a meeting the next day with his staff and the chairpersons of the district's technology committees. At 11:00, he received a telephone call from a reporter for the *Mount Hope Gazette* inquiring about a gift that 1st-ONE was about to make to the school district. The superintendent told her that it was too premature to make any comments. In the afternoon edition of the *Gazette,* on page one of the business section, the headline "1st-ONE to Donate $1,000,000 to Mount Hope Schools" appeared.

Assuming that you are the superintendent, what are your concerns about the headline? What actions do you consider taking? How do you prepare for your upcoming meetings with the chairpersons of the district's planning committees and with the board of education? Please keep in mind that at this time you do not have any information about the quality of the hardware or software.

SUMMARY

This chapter presents the background and several issues associated with financial planning for computer applications. Technology can be expensive, and even more so if not planned properly. Cost considerations for an entire computer application should be identified and go well beyond the direct hardware and software costs. Trend data indicate that although the unit cost for computer technology has decreased, the overall expenditure for computer technology is increasing each year in both primary and secondary schools.

A review of the literature on the cost-effectiveness of computer-based education leads to inconclusive results. Most of the major reviews of the effectiveness of computer technology in education tend to ignore the questions of cost. Regardless, schools are well on their way to implementing new systems and expanding existing ones.

A procedure for gathering budget information using a budget worksheet should be integrated into the overall computer technology planning process within a school district. A composite funding model suggesting percentage distributions of the various costs associated with computer applications has been presented. However, school districts will likely fund according to their own goals and financial abilities. Several major issues associated with computer technology costs such as centralization, shared resources, single vendor procurement, and use of consultants are presented, with suggestions for possible courses of action.

Finally, in funding computer technology, school districts should establish base budgets and seek the support of their boards of education. Administrators should also be aggressive in seeking funds from other sources such as local businesses, governmental agencies, parent-teacher groups, and individuals who might be interested in providing funds for computer technology.

KEY CONCEPTS AND QUESTIONS

1. Financial planning for technology requires an understanding of changes in component costs that have occurred over time.

   Identify some of these changes, explaining how they have affected financial planning for educational technology.

2. Financial planning for technology requires a consideration of all the component costs of an application.

   What are the major component costs of a computer application? Are some more important than others? Explain.

3. Centralization and decentralization of computer resources is a recurring issue in education.

   Review this issue from a financial perspective for administrative applications. Do the same for instructional applications.

4. School administrators have been struggling with the standardization of hardware for many years.

   What are some of the factors that administrators should consider when establishing a policy regarding hardware standardization?

5. Securing resources for technology is a critical part of financial planning.

   What are some of the common sources of funds? On which should an administrator most rely? Why?

6. Financial planning, like planning in general, is an ongoing activity requiring a good deal of careful analysis.

   How might an administrator involve others, including teachers, in financial planning for technology?

Suggested Activities

1. Review the financial expenditures/budgets for computer technology in a school or district for the past three years or more, if data are available. Try to isolate different component (hardware, software, maintenance, etc.) costs. Can you identify any clear trends?

2. Identify the policies in a school or district regarding standardization of computer hardware. Have these policies been formalized, or are they an informal understanding? Do you have any suggestions for improving them?

3. Look again at the Watson Middle School Case Study in Chapter 11, and cost out your proposal using the budget worksheet (Figure 12–1) introduced in this chapter.

References

Arch, J. C. (Ed.). (1986). *Technology in the schools: Equity and funding*. Washington, DC: National Education Association.

Becker, H. J. (1991). How computers are used in United States schools: Basic data from the 1989 I.E.A. computers in education survey. *Journal of Educational Computing Research, 7*(4), 385–406.

Becker, H. J. (1994). *Analysis and trends of school use of new information technologies*. Irvine: Department of Education, University of California, Irvine.

Chira, S. (1989, June 19). Action urged to retain jobs in finance: New York task force warns of heavy losses. *New York Times, 139*, pp. B1–B5.

Chira, S. (1990, January 24). Electronic teacher: A Mississippi experiment. *New York Times, 140*, pp. A1, B5.

Clark, R. (1989). Current progress and future directions for research in instructional technology. *Educational Technology Research and Development, 37*(1), 57–66.

Hodges, P. (1988). Budget surveys: More for your money. *Datamation, 34*(7), 80–83.

Kulik, J. A. (1984). Evaluating the effects of teaching with computers. In G. Campbell & G. Fein (Eds.), *Microcomputers in early education*. Reston, VA: Reston.

Kulik, J., Bangert, R., & Williams, G. (1983). Effects of computer-based teaching on secondary students. *Journal of Educational Psychology, 75*(1), 19–26.

Levin, H., & Meister, G. (1986). Is CAI cost effective? *Phi Delta Kappan, 67*(10), 745–749.

Moursand, D. C. (1986). The two-percent solution: Funding for the use of computers. In J. C. Arch (Ed.), *Technology in the schools: Equity and funding* (pp. 12–16). Washington, DC: National Education Association.

National Education Association. (1989, July). *Report of the NEA special committee on educational technology*. Paper presented at the 127th Annual Meeting of the National Education Association, Washington, DC.

National School Boards Association. (1989). *ON LINE financing strategies for educational technology*. Alexandria, VA: Author.

Natuzzi, J. (1996, May). *The hype and reality of the Internet: Implementation strategies for K–12 science and math teachers*. Paper presented at New York University's Teaching and Technology Conference, New York.

Niemiec, R., Blackwell, M., & Walberg, H. (1986). CAI can be doubly effective. *Phi Delta Kappan, 67*(10), 750–751.

Quality Education Data. (1989). *Microcomputer and video purchasing and usage plans: 1989–1990 school year*. Denver.

Quality Education Data. (1991). *Technology in the schools: 1990–91 school year*. Denver.

Quality Education Data. (1996). *Education market guide & mailing list catalog 1996–1997*. Denver.

Robyler, M., Castine, W., & King, F. (1988). Assessing the impact of computer-based instruction. *Computers in the Schools, 5*, 1–149.

Rothstein, R. I. & McKnight, L. (1996). Technology and cost models of K-12 schools on the National Information Infrastructure. *Computers in the Schools, 12*(1/2), 31–57.

Shanker, A. (1989, December 24). Technology holds the key. *New York Times, 139*, p. E7.

Stoll, C. (1995). *Silicon snake oil: Second thoughts on the information superhighway*. New York: Doubleday.

U.S. Congress, Office of Technology Assessment. (1988). *Power on! New tools for teaching and learning* (Report No. OTA-SET-379). Washington, DC: U.S. Government Printing Office.

A Look to the Future

13

Trends and the Future

This book opened with a look at the work of Dr. Robert Ballard, whose JASON Project allowed children to participate in controlling the operations of a deep-sea robot as it explored the ocean floor. What started as an experiment in 1989 now reaches more than a million children, and Ballard has received national awards for his innovative approach to bringing "real-life" science into classrooms around the world. When asked about the future of his work, Dr. Ballard quoted his grandmother, who told him, "Great is the person who plants a tree, not knowing whether he will sit in its shade." When he started, he was not sure whether the JASON Project would be a success but was willing to take a chance on something in which he believed. He was confident, however, that with hard work and by assembling good people who shared in his dream, the JASON Project would touch the lives of children for many years to come.

Planning has been the basic emphasis of this book, and fundamental to planning is thinking about and developing strategies for the future based on an understanding of the past and the present. In the previous chapters, the background, history, and current issues associated with the developments in the use of computer technology in education were discussed to help administrators conduct planning activities. With 100,000 schools in the United States at various stages of technological development, one school's present might be another's future, or, conversely, one school's present might be another's past. Planning for the future, therefore, may mean different things to different people.

In this chapter, several technological trends are examined that have likely affected all schools at one time or another. Particular attention is paid to those trends that show strength and are likely to continue into the future. For the purpose of this examination, the future is defined as the early part of the 21st century. Naturally, predictions of the future are based on an imperfect knowledge of the past and present, and they are prone to modification by unforeseen developments as well.

MAJOR TECHNOLOGICAL TRENDS

The Merging of Technologies

The technological trend that has had the most obvious, recent impact on education is the merging or integrating of three technologies: communications, computer, and video/image handling. The merging of these technologies has occurred to meet the needs of other industries and enterprises, but it has also had an effect on schools. Communications encompasses all forms of information (voice, text, images, signals, etc.) transfer, including telephone, television, radio, and satellite. Computer technology entails all forms of programmable, electronic devices that accept input, process it, and produce output. Video/image handling includes all forms of technology involved in the production and storage of images.

The communications and computer technologies have been merging since the 1950s and now have reached a mature state. National and international enterprises such as the military, aviation, and large corporations required the ability to move data in computer storage devices around the country and the world. Telephone companies and the computer manufacturers have developed and will continue to develop equipment that makes the transference of data over distances easier and faster. Wide area networks (WANs) are now commonplace, representing the success of these two technologies in meeting industry needs and improving the sharing of information across distances. The maturity of this trend is also evident in the number of local area networks (LANs) that are routinely installed in buildings and schools throughout the country so that data can be shared and accessed more efficiently within limited distances. In addition to networks, the merging of these technologies is evident in simple, everyday devices such as telephone answering machines that use a microprocessor to control the recording and storage of messages.

Communications and video technologies also have been merging successfully since the 1950s. The popularity of television does not need any elaboration; however, new strides were made in the 1980s by introducing television into the schools using cable services. In the 1990s, tens of thousands of schools were receiving and using broadcasts from Cable News Network (CNN) Newsroom and Whittle Communications' Channel One. In addition, thousands of school districts began to install satellite dishes to receive television and radio signals. In addition to television, the recent introduction and proliferation of facsimile or fax machines, which are capable of transferring both text and images over ordinary telephone lines, have affected daily life.

In the 1980s and 1990s, computer and video technologies began to make important strides toward merging, particularly in the development of digital video production and storage. Digital video is capable of being produced and stored using computer equipment such as CD-ROMs and other optical disc equipment. Presently, the majority of all video production and storage uses an analog or frame format, the best examples being videotape, videodisc, and 35-millimeter film. In schools, digital video as well as videodisc (analog) technologies are growing in popularity as new products such as electronic encyclopedias, atlases, and interactive video materials are developed specifically for educational purposes.

As important as each of these paired technological trends has been in the use of technology in the schools, the merging of all three technologies promises to be even more significant. Each of these technologies provides a unique component important for teaching and learning. Communications provides the ability to transfer information; computers offer interactivity, control, and storage of information; and video uses images and sound as well as text to enhance information. General-purpose microcomputer workstations have become available that integrate all three technologies; however, further development is needed to make the transfer and storage of data, particularly video, more efficient. Workstations integrating the three technologies will be the fundamental, conceptual prototypes for much of the hardware designed and developed for use in all organizations, including schools.

In education, such design and research is being conducted at the Edison Project, a for-profit private school venture led by Christopher Whittle of Whittle Communications. In addition to Whittle, investors and partners include Time-Warner, Inc., Philips Electronics N.V., and Associated Newspapers of Britain. A major feature of these schools is expected to be an electronic teaching aid or "learning partner" that would be available both in the school and at home. This learning partner would integrate the capabilities of a computer, a VCR or videodisc, a printer, a fax machine, and a stereo (Kleinfield, 1992). Via this partner, students would have access to an electronic library of reference and other books, films, lectures, and educational software, as well as the ability to communicate with teachers and fellow students. Whittle refers to this electronic learning partner and library of materials as "America's new textbook industry." The first school opened in the mid-1990s, and the major goal of the Edison Project is to have approximately 1,000 schools using this technology by the year 2010.

Whether the electronic partner will actually evolve in the manner described here cannot be certain. All of the technological components are presently available from different sources and manufacturers; however, additional research and development needs to be done to integrate these components and build a comprehensive electronic library that can be used extensively at a reasonable cost. As the overall merging of the three technologies continues, an integrated hardware system providing all the communications, computer, and video capabilities described should be realized. The precursor for this system is the Internet. It provides the starting point from which the future of instructional technology can be discussed.

Communications: The Link to the Universe

William Gibson (1996), the futurist who coined the term *cyberspace* in 1981, sees the Internet as being in its "larval stage," a "test pattern" for whatever will become the dominant global medium in the 21st century. In the meantime, the Internet will remain in its present state until much higher speed data transmission is available routinely in homes, schools, and businesses. A major development in communications related to data transmission will be the conversion of all telephone and other communications systems that use copper and coaxial cable wire (i.e., Cable TV) to fiber optics. Land-based fiber optics systems will be linked with satellite receivers and transmitters to provide rapid long-distance (national, international, and beyond) services.

In addition to the benefit of speed, fiber optics carry digital signals capable of easy integration with computer equipment, are almost impervious to interference, and have much larger data- and signal-carrying capacities. The capacity of fiber optics is approximately 30,000 times greater than copper and approximately double that of coaxial cable. Copper cable can carry voice and data but cannot presently carry a television transmission. Coaxial cable, used for common cable TV services, can carry 54 channels; fiber optics can carry several hundred channels plus voice and data. As with most technologies, research is continuing with all of these communications modes. Enhancements in data transmission and compression are announced regularly, so these comparison figures will change over time.

Henry Geller, a former Federal Communications Commission general counsel and professor of telecommunications at Duke University, predicts that the conversion of America's 200 million miles of copper telephone wire will take 20 to 30 years and cost approximately $100 billion to $1 trillion (Ramirez, 1991). Bill Gates (1995), founder and president of Microsoft, Inc., does not see a "full information highway" functioning for at least a decade or more when the fiber optic infrastructure, more sophisticated high-speed digital switches, and new software platforms are available.

In the meantime, users including schools do not have to wait to take advantage of fiber optics. Telephone or computer networks designed in new buildings can have fiber optics installed rather than copper wire or coaxial cable. Old buildings, likewise, can be rewired to utilize fiber optics and local telephone companies have begun the process of converting their systems.

National and international educational networks such as National Geographic's Kid's Network and Learning Link as well as the Internet already exist and will provide more services as fiber optics become more readily available. Eventually, high-speed access to such networks will be as common in homes as in business organizations and schools. Because of their speed and data capacity, fiber optics will also allow for the rapid transmission of video and images stored in digital format. This same technology will also allow telephone companies to deliver television transmission services and in effect compete with cable TV companies. In sum, using fiber optics, especially in combination with satellite systems, the three major forms of information transfer (voice, data, and video) will be delivered rapidly on one integrated system everywhere in the world.

The task of the 1980s was to develop and begin the process of converting to fiber optics technology, whereas the task of the 1990s and the first decade of the 21st century will be to complete the conversion and to develop applications. A good example of a creative, exciting use of this technology, the JASON Project represents a glimpse into the future. How far away are applications that bring into our living rooms a space shuttle mission, a visit to the Louvre, an exploration of a rain forest in the Amazon, or a microscopic probe of the human body? Keep in mind that in addition to seeing, children and adults together would be able to be involved with these activities as if they were actually present. Applications of this nature will bring a much broader perspective to present concepts of distance learning.

Computers and CD-ROM: The New Papyrus

Computing equipment undoubtedly will continue to advance, particularly in terms of speed and storage capacity, but for impact on educational applications, the two most important developments are CD-ROM technology and portability. Established as significant trends in the 1980s, they will continue into the 21st century.

CD-ROM technology, or "the new papyrus," has been described as the "summation or combination" of all other media including television, books, movies, and audio by Bill Gates (1986). The fundamental attributes of CD-ROM technology are high storage capacity, high speed, low cost, portability, and most importantly, digital formatting. Text, audio (including music and dialogue), and images (both still and moving) can be stored in a digital format and thereby accessed and used by common computer equipment. The 1980s and 1990s saw the emergence of this technology in the form of electronic books, music, and reference materials, but the technology is still evolving. CD-ROM has the potential of being as revolutionary a medium for people in the 21st century as papyrus was for the ancient Egyptians.

In its present state, CD-ROM is optical disc technology that provides "read only" capability; it is already being heralded as the ultimate storage medium. However, research and development in erasable optical discs is well under way in providing significantly greater optical storage capabilities that can both read and write or play back and record. Though presently available, when erasable optical discs become less expensive and more portable, the ultimate storage medium will have arrived. Magnetic disk technology will become obsolete since optical discs are faster and have greater capacity. Optical discs will also challenge other audio and video storage technologies that rely on analog formats. Although digital audio is already widely accepted, video technology (i.e., television transmission, videotape, and videodisc) has not accepted the digital format yet. This changeover promises to be one of the most interesting technological phenomena in the early 21st century.

CD-ROM technology also provides a high degree of portability that allows it to challenge books and other print material as the major information transfer medium. As other components of computer equipment continue to become smaller and more powerful, CD-ROM technology can provide a degree of compactness comparable to the popular Walkman audio devices. The production of hand-held computers has already begun and is expanding rapidly in applications such as engineering, science, and mathematics. Apple Inc. introduced the hand-held Newton computer in 1992. General consumer electronics companies such as Sharp Electronics and Casio, Inc., also market hand-held microcomputers. In addition, as telephone and computer technologies continue to merge, portable hand-held devices that provide voice, data, and even video will be common. In the not too distant future, teenagers may have strapped to their waists a Walkman- or cellular phone–sized computer/receiver/transmitter capable of providing telephone, music, video, and electronic textbooks. They will also use these devices to do homework as well as to access MTV and a variety of other services on the Internet.

Video/Image Handling

Video production and storage were discussed briefly earlier in this chapter. Critical to an understanding of the future impact of this technology on education is the relationship to and integration with the digital-based computer. The Internet and erasable optical disc technology may be the stimuli that move the video industry to change from the present analog, frame-format technology to a digital format. Although the computer industry naturally favors the move to digital, the speed with which the video industry will move to digital is not clear. The reasons for this deserve some attention in a discussion about the future of these technologies.

First, the quality of the image and motion on analog video media such as videotape and videodisc is better than on digital video such as CD-ROM. The highly competitive television and film production industries are very much aware of this and will not quickly give up the high quality of analog video production to which they are accustomed, and which is continually improving. However, the quality of digital video is improving also and should become a less significant issue by the early 21st century or sooner.

Second, because digital video is a new technology, standards have not been set for storing data (images) in digital format. Various hardware and software developers of digital video materials are establishing different formats, and users are generally reluctant to commit themselves or their organizations to a format that is limited to a particular manufacturer. Many video media users remember the confusion of beta versus VHS formats when VCRs were first introduced in the late 1970s. Furthermore, the competition among developers in the area of digital video formatting is very keen and has been likened to a "war" (Van Horn, 1991, p. 108). When the issue of standards will be resolved is not certain. However, several cooperative ventures among major hardware and software developers are emerging that may alleviate the problem. (This topic is discussed further in a later section on multimedia software.)

Third, a good deal of material including videotapes, videodiscs, and films exists in frame or analog format. Schools and many other organizations have already built extensive libraries of such material and are unable to convert these libraries to another format quickly and affordably. The highest-quality video material produced by major film and television companies is copyrighted and subject to royalties. Converting or copying this material is against the law until the appropriate approvals have been secured and royalties paid. This is a major issue that not only remains unresolved but is becoming more complex as owners of copyrights become more attentive and aggressive in pursuing any infringements. In the meantime, the video production industry continues to develop high-quality material in frame format that keeps being added to libraries and requires continuing investments in videotape or videodisc equipment.

Fourth, videotape and videodisc are relatively easy-to-use technologies. VCRs are common in homes and schools. Videodisc players are also growing in popularity and can provide interactivity with computer equipment. Playing back or reading from a CD-ROM is simple to learn, but recording or writing is more complex and still evolving; this skill will require a more extensive development of one's computer skills. Likewise, accessing digital video on the Internet requires some familiarity with computer hardware and software. Furthermore, the data speeds necessary for transmitting good quality digital video is not available in the vast majority of homes or schools yet. As discussed in Chapter 10, staff development in the use of computer technology remains a serious issue in many schools, and technologies that are easier to use will have an advantage over more complex ones.

Fifth, and perhaps most illuminating, a good deal of evaluation by major international companies is presently being undertaken regarding digital versus analog video technologies. Digital will be the way of the future, but defining when that future begins is problematic. An article (Pollack, 1992) regarding the development of high-definition television reported that Japanese research and development favor the analog format, whereas American companies prefer digital video. Hiroschi Fujiwara, senior vice president of GC Technology Corporation, a maker of computer chips used to transmit video images, summed up the future of digital versus analog formats:

> It is a very delicate time. . . . [That] the future belongs to digital television is the substantial consensus of the world including Japan. But officially nobody can tell you [when] the future is going to digital because we Japanese [have] spent much money to develop analog HDTV. (Pollack, 1992, p. 31)

Given the past success and influence that Japanese manufacturers have had in electronics, a good deal of credence can be given to Fujiwara's statement. The confrontation of these two technologies promises to continue into the 21st century and will have an impact on many aspects of life well beyond entertainment.

Educators should follow the development of video technology closely. Several schools will invest in both digital (computer and CD-ROM) and analog (videotape and videodisc) equipment. Multimedia and interactive video—whether delivered digitally on the Internet, on CD-ROM, or in analog format with videodisc equipment—have the potential of being the most creative educational applications ever developed. The use of both digital and analog technologies will be common at least through the beginning of the 21st century.

In addition to the traditional producers of educational video materials such as the Public Broadcasting System, National Geographic, and Time-Warner, Inc., other major companies have become active more recently in educational multimedia, including Microsoft, Inc., and Lucasfilms, Inc. The nature of these companies and the resources they can invest indicate that a good deal of high-quality, educational video material will readily be available in the near future.

SOFTWARE TRENDS

Hardware Integration and User Friendliness

Software trends generally can be identified as following and supporting hardware trends. During the past decade, hardware has been merging or integrating with other technologies. As a result, software is being made available to support this integration. The 1980s and 1990s have seen the development of major new software products from companies such as Novell, Inc., which facilitated the establishment of high-speed, reliable data communications networks. In the early 1990s, software products such as HyperCard, Authorware Professional, and ToolBook were significantly enhanced to develop multimedia programs integrating computer and video technologies. More recently, a host of newer software products such as Netscape and Java have come on the scene to support the ever-growing needs of Internet users. The computer industry well understands the concept that new software must be continually provided to support new hardware.

Software is also responding to the new capabilities that faster and higher-capacity hardware has provided. One result has been the integration of programs into single-application packages. Integrated administrative software packages combine office automation, word processing, spreadsheets, database management, and data communications. Operating systems such as the Macintosh and Microsoft Windows provide various applications software such as notepads, schedulers, and word processing as well as software to access the Internet. For instructional applications, the epitome of integrated software is the integrated learning system (ILS), which combines hardware, educational software, a curriculum database, and a student database in one product. The trend to more integrated software will continue as hardware allows for larger programs to be stored and rapidly executed. As an added bonus, integrated software meeting several different application needs is also less expensive and easier to manage.

Another software trend affected by hardware has been the evolution of **user-friendly** products. The introduction of microcomputers in the late 1970s was followed by a proliferation of **user-friendly** programs as software developers attempted to provide products for a large number of first-time computer owners. To develop user friendliness, several new software features were designed such as graphical user interfaces that can be controlled by a mouse, menu-driven screens that anticipate commands and instructions, and on-line "help" facilities. User friendliness is critical to the success of many computer hardware and software products and will remain a very strong trend and requirement well into the 21st century.

To cover the entire universe of software possibilities for the future would take volumes. For purposes of educational planning, an examination of several critical, specific software developments is in order.

Authoring Languages

Authoring languages have been among the most important new software tools for teachers since the 1970s. Early products such as PILOT, Coursewriter, and PLATO were designed specifically to put the power of computers into teachers' hands. However, for several reasons, including the need for other software development resources such as dollars, time, and teacher training, early authoring languages met with limited acceptance and success.

In the 1980s, authoring languages such as HyperCard, which was easier to use and made available on every Macintosh computer, greatly expanded the number of users who took advantage of authoring. In the late 1980s and 1990s, the major trend of authoring languages was to provide multimedia capabilities. Existing languages such as HyperCard, LinkWay, and ToolBook were greatly enhanced to interface audio and video equipment into teacher presentations. Newer products such as Astound and PowerPoint were developed specifically for multimedia lessons and presentations. The 1990s also began to see authoring languages integrate multimedia capabilities with the Internet and World Wide Web. However, the average teacher still finds authoring software difficult to implement in lesson planning without specific technical training.

For the future, the evolution of authoring languages will continue. While a major breakthrough in the ease of using authoring languages and other software products would be well received in the educational community, in all likelihood the change will be slow and evolutionary. Even so, the capabilities of existing authoring languages are impressive. In the future, assuming that teachers are provided with ongoing technology training, the impact on education will be dramatic and clearly visible as authoring software tools advance.

In addition to teacher and student, a third partner, "technology," will become tightly integrated into educational endeavors. Just as other enterprises such as banks and hospitals have come to use computers routinely in the basic delivery of their services, schools likewise will come to depend on this technology as the major teaching tool. Computers, especially when integrated with video and communications, can potentially replace chalkboards, overhead projectors, VCRs, and reference books.

Software Standards and Corporate Alliances

Multimedia have been discussed many times throughout this book and deservedly so, as their educational potential is significant. However, despite this potential, multimedia may be impeded because of a lack of software standards. The authoring languages mentioned previously are excellent products that can make multimedia easier for the average teacher to use. However, these languages are unique to particular computers, models, and types of video or audio devices. In addition to the decades-old, basic problem of software that what executes on one computer may not execute on another computer, format standards for new multimedia storage technologies such as CD-ROMs, digital video, and digital audio do not exist as mentioned earlier. The result is that administrators and teachers have difficulty in selecting and using many multimedia products. In the future, a possible solution to this problem exists if major hardware and software developers could agree on standards.

In 1992, Apple and IBM announced an alliance for the development of several software products (Guarino, 1992). This alliance brought together two fierce competitors in the computer industry. Several joint projects are being designed to allow hardware manufactured by these two companies to share common software. This would eliminate entirely the software incompatibility that currently exists between Apple Macintosh and IBM PC/PS microcomputers, and schools will no longer have to purchase separate versions of programs to run on these two popular machines. Part of this alliance was also an agreement to design and develop multimedia format standards, common authoring tools, and packaged application software that will run on both companies' equipment.

At the time of this writing, these projects were still evolving, but in looking to the future, products that might result from these or similar ventures should be considered and evaluated by educational planners. If successful, these projects could establish the future path for computing in general and for multimedia software in particular.

In communications, the Internet has already provided the network software standard for computers to communicate with one another. Internet software products are evolving that will set the standard for not only the Internet but also local and wide area networks. In a sense, schools and other organizations will design their local networks as "intranets" to look and function like the Internet. Although the conversion of existing networks to Internet standards and products will not happen immediately, Microsoft, the world's leading software developer, has already begun to integrate Internet tools into its basic operating systems to facilitate this conversion.

In addition to establishing a data communications standard, the Internet or its progeny will evolve into the major information medium in the world and will merge with telephone and television services in the future. Existing computer hardware and software enterprises will have to expand into other communications services to compete effectively. The mid-1990s saw the emergence of a number of alliances among computer, communications, and video production companies. Examples include Microsoft and DirecTV; TeleTV, a joint venture of Bell Atlantic, NYNEX, and Pacific

Telesis; Novio, an alliance made up of Netscape, IBM, Oracle, and four Japanese electronics companies; Microsoft and MCI Communications; and so forth. These alliances and closer working relationships bode well for the future and promise to provide the connections through which technologies will further merge, thereby alleviating the problem of conflicting standards. Educators, in considering the future for their schools, should keep abreast of these alliances in that they portend important technological developments that are evolving in this country and the world.

Special Education Software

Speculation about future educational software trends would not be complete without some consideration of special education software that can be used to help students with disabilities communicate and function in learning environments. As discussed in Chapter 3, computer technology for special education students has progressed steadily and is becoming an important means of communication for people with disabilities. Given the advances in biotechnology combined with the advances being made in computer hardware, particularly in terms of miniaturization and data storage capacities, the possibilities for lightweight, unobtrusive, portable devices that can be used by people with disabilities in the 21st century are endless. Just as the general population uses eyeglasses or hearing aids to overcome modest disabilities, children with more severe disabilities will be able to use computer devices routinely to help them overcome their disabilities.

Critical to the development of new aids and devices for people with disabilities is the need for software in the areas of speech synthesis and audio response. Although software research and development has been progressing for almost five decades in speech and voice applications, improvements have been slow and evolutionary. Enthusiasts of this technology will admit that "imminent success has been wrongly predicted many times in the past" (Bradsher, 1992, p. D6). However, even if continuing on an evolutionary path into the early part of the 21st century, significant progress will have been made in improving speech and voice synthesis software.

Impressive new products are beginning to make an appearance that 10 years ago might have been considered futuristic. In 1991, Bell Laboratories conducted a three-month experiment in California during which deaf residents successfully used computer synthesis for telephone conversations with people with full hearing. Franklin Electronics Publishing Company markets several inexpensive "talking dictionaries" that translate English into other languages and vice versa. Texas Instruments and Tandy Corporation market a variety of educational toys using speech synthesis. Although presently limited to specific applications, these examples hold great promise for the development of affordable technology that will make communication for many children with disabilities easier.

NEW COMMUNITIES FOR LEARNING

In response to a question about his vision of the typical school at the end of this century, Gary Watts of the National Education Association indicated that he hoped that *school* and *classroom* would become obsolete terms, replaced by **learning communities** (Hoffman, 1990). Watts envisions places where teachers, students, administrators, and parents come together as a community to learn and share. Developing such communities will not be easy and will require changes in many aspects of the way present-day schools function. No single school reform promises to revolutionize all education along these lines, but technology will play a significant role, especially when integrated with other reforms.

Several educational reformers, including Knapp and Glenn (1996) and Sheingold (1991), have posited that the major means for improving education for the 21st century are a move to more active learning and teaching, school restructuring, and technology. Furthermore, although any one of these components can be a powerful vehicle for changing schools, the three should be integrated and pursued concurrently to be maximally effective. Technology has been examined extensively in this book; the other two components, active learning and teaching and school restructuring, have not. These deserve some brief discussion because, as general terms, they may convey a variety of meanings.

Active learning and teaching is a movement away from passive, simple information transfer from teacher to student or textbook to student toward a joint seeking of knowledge and understanding on the part of students and teachers. Activities include solving open-ended problems with multiple routes and multiple solutions. Group projects are emphasized. Students engage in learning because they want to understand and see a purpose in what they do. Teachers participate, facilitate, and share knowledge and power with students as they learn together. Collaborative learning is raised to the next level as teachers, students, and even parents become true partners in education.

Restructuring schools assumes that fundamental, systemic change is necessary for reforming schools and that administrative structures at both the district and building levels must foster this change. Administrators may have to share power and decision making with teachers and parents; establish new goals, objectives, and performance criteria; consider different grade patterns, class schedules, and calendars; or provide new incentives for students and teachers to reach their potential. As with teaching, administering schools becomes a collaborative and sharing activity. Though easy to discuss, restructuring is difficult to accomplish and requires competent, creative administrators and educational policy makers committed to making major changes in their schools.

When integrated with active learning and school restructuring, technology can provide critical tools. Whether using problem-solving software, establishing instructional or administrative databases, sharing information, or improving communications across a room, building, or neighborhood, educators will find technology an important part of overall school reform. Technology's greatest potential may be as the instructional and administrative synergist that moves schools to become true communities of learning. The basic nature of technology is to change and evolve. As such, it can continually provide new stimuli and common environments in which all can grow and learn. In the 21st century, through vision, sharing, and planning, administrators are in pivotal positions to introduce and nurture the use of these tools and to help their schools become communities of learning.

CASE STUDY
Place: Futuretown Learning Center   Year: 2025

Futuretown is a planned community built in the year 2002. Everything about Future-town is well organized and modern; it is the epitome of efficiency. High technology is a critical component of life. Shopping, banking, and entertainment rely on an extensive Communications and Computer Services Utility (CCSU) that provides ready access in all homes and buildings to an integrated network of facilities including computer, tele-phone, television, electronic mail, funds transfer, and so forth. The CCSU is the main hub for Futuretown's connection to Universal Network (UNIVET), which replaced the Internet in 2007 as the main Earth-based communications facility.

Futuretown's education system is highly regarded in the state and country. Students completing the program do very well on the national competency examinations and go on to many of the best colleges and universities in the country. The board of educa-tion and the administrative staff credit as the cornerstone of this success an active Par-ent's Advisory Committee (PAC) that is involved in all planning, budgeting, and curricu-lum matters. New and creative approaches to learning have been carefully planned and implemented. For example:

- school is a year-round activity;
- the academic program is centered on developing skills as well as mastering content areas;
- the curriculum integrates the concept of the Earth as a global village and makes extensive use of UNIVET for engaging in a host of international instructional exchanges;
- learning centers in which children and teachers work together have replaced schools and classes (Futuretown eliminated the grade structure in 2005); and
- learning activities are integrated with home and family activities and rely on ready access to electronic mail, databases, educational software, video libraries, and so forth, that are provided by the CCSU and UNIVET.

The CCSU is especially important to education in Futuretown. Students, teachers, parents, and administrators regularly use this facility to communicate with one another. Teachers send notes to parents, students complete assignments, and adminis-trators send memos almost exclusively via electronic mail. The CCSU also works closely with the board of education to provide a series of video specials (documen-taries, multimedia productions, etc.) each month on the education channels; these shows coincide with different projects on which children and teachers are working. These materials are readily available in the video library, and broadcasting them encourages parents to be involved with the projects.

An important issue is facing the board of education regarding the creative arts learning projects, including visual art, creative writing, and music. Originally these pro-jects were designed so that children could feel free to express themselves through var-ious media and forms and through text and word expression. However, teachers observe that most student projects, though rich in images, sound, and color, are lack-ing in text expression. Despite discussion with parents and attempts to encourage and reinforce the activity, a clear trend has developed indicating that Futuretown children are becoming unable to express themselves well with text or words.

At a joint meeting of the board of education and the PAC, the issue was discussed, and several suggestions were made for modifying the creative arts learning projects. However, the most controversial suggestion was made by Mr. Leland, a creative arts and word expression learning partner (teacher). He suggested that Futuretown modify its use of electronic mail and word-processing software as the only means of developing word expression skills in the learning centers. Instead, he suggested using the "old-fashioned" or "hard way" of writing with fountain pens and paper. His rationale was that children might enjoy developing their own letters of the alphabet and making them into words and sentences rather than composing them electronically. When asked where he got such an idea, he indicated that he recently visited a library in one of the "old" cities. On display was a Bible that was so beautifully written that the words just seemed to jump out at him.

After the meeting, a small group of board members and parents approached Ms. Colthrane, the senior learning partner in Mr. Leland's center. They suggested that maybe she should have a discussion with Mr. Leland for making such a ridiculous suggestion.

Assuming that you are Ms. Colthrane, how would you handle this situation? (You should know that Ms. Colthrane keeps a Parker Brothers fountain pen in her desk at home that her grandmother gave her when she graduated from college in 1984.)

SUMMARY

This chapter presents several of the fundamental trends occurring in technology that have had a particular impact on education. These trends are examined in an attempt to predict their future directions and how they may affect teaching and learning in the early 21st century.

The major trend that has affected all technology in schools and other organizations is the merging or integrating of communications, computers, and video. Advances in communications technology by way of fiber optics and satellites provide the link with the world and beyond. Computers using optical media such as CD-ROM continue to advance as the tools for developing, storing, and disseminating information. The form of information itself is also changing as video/image handling equipment is used with the other technologies to provide pictures, sound, and motion. The Internet, presently in its "larval" stage, provides the prototype for a system in which all three technologies will merge.

Software is attempting to keep pace with advances in hardware that the new technologies are providing. Integrated packages, authoring languages, and multimedia programs are among the trends that continue to advance. Although software tends to evolve slowly, progress is steady. New levels of user friendliness have been reached. The issue of software standards, an ongoing problem for many years, may be moving a step closer to resolution as several leaders in the technology industry begin to develop joint projects. Technology and software is also advancing in the development of new communication aids for children and adults with special needs.

The chapter concludes with a look at schools of the future developing as true communities of learning. Technology can play a critical role in the development of these communities as a synergist for change that supports sharing and partnership approaches to teaching, learning, and administration.

Key Concepts and Questions

1. Trends provide important frameworks for understanding the past and present and for predicting the future. Educational technology can be better understood if one is aware of major trends.

   Identify several trends in educational technology. Consider whether they have benefited education and, if so, how.

2. A major trend is the merging or integrating of several different technologies.

   What are these technologies? Why are they important to education?

3. Hardware and equipment are usually the demonstrative examples of changes in technology.

   Identify several specific devices commonly found in the home or school that exemplify the merging of technologies described in question 2. What, if any equipment, have they replaced? How have they improved home or school life?

4. In addition to hardware, software has been evolving.

   Identify several software trends. How do they relate, if at all, to hardware trends?

5. William Gibson describes the Internet as being in its "larval stage."

   How do you see the Internet evolving? Do you see it as *the* future or a prototype of the future? Explain.

6. Educational planning for the future means different things to different people, depending on what stage of technological development their school system has reached.

   How do you see the early part of the 21st century in terms of educational technology? Is there a clear future in which several present trends will surely continue and evolve, or is the future wide open, with almost anything possible in the next 10 or 15 years? Provide examples.

7. Gary Watts of the National Education Association has stated that he hopes *schools* and *classes* become obsolete terms and that they are replaced by *learning communities*.

   Describe a learning community. Do most schools function as learning communities? Explain.

8. Some educational reformers have identified three major components for changing learning and improving schools.

   What are these components? Which do you consider the most important? Why?

Suggested Activities

1. Identify a present-day, technology-based learning activity in a school. Consider how this activity functioned 10 years ago. Speculate on how it will function 10 years from now. Do the same for a present-day, technology-based administrative activity.

2. Consider a school with which you are familiar, and identify any developments, activities, or policies that suggest a "learning community" is evolving. How do you see this learning community five years from now? Ten years from now?

References

Bradsher, K. (1991, January 2). Computers, having learned to talk, are becoming more eloquent. *New York Times,* p. D6.

Gates, W. H. (1986). Foreword. In S. Lambert & S. Ropiequet (Eds.), *CD-ROM: The new papyrus* (pp. xi–xiii). Redmond, WA: Microsoft.

Gates, W. H. (1995). *The road ahead.* New York: Viking.

Gibson, W. (1996, July 14). The Net is a waste of time, and that's exactly what's right about it. *New York Times Magazine,* pp. 30–31.

Guarino, R. A. (1992, June). *IBM strategic alliances.* Paper presented at the IBM Academic Computing Conference, San Diego.

Hoffman, D. (1990). Technology, trends, and gizmos: A timeline for the '90s . . . and beyond. *Technology & Learning, 11*(1), 92–98.

Kleinfield, N. R. (1992, May 26). Plan for high-tech private schools poses risks and challenges. *New York Times,* p. B8.

Knapp, L. R., & Glenn, A. D. (1996). *Restructuring schools with technology.* Boston: Allyn & Bacon.

Lambert, S., & Ropiequet, S. (Eds.). (1986). *CD-ROM: The new papyrus.* Redmond, WA: Microsoft.

Pollack, A. (1992, July 4). Technology shift blurs future of Japan's new TV system. *New York Times,* pp. 31–32.

Ramirez, A. (1991, November 17). Fiber optics at home: Wrong number? *New York Times,* p. D18.

Sheingold, K. (1991). Restructuring for learning with technology: The potential for synergy. *Phi Delta Kappan, 73*(1), 17–27.

Van Horn, R. (1991). *Advanced technology in education.* Pacific Grove, CA: Brooks/Cole.

Appendix A

Basic Concepts of Computer Technology

Computer science, like other disciplines, has developed a language of its own. *Hardware, software, icons, LAN, bytes, videodiscs, modems, RAMs,* and *CD-ROMs* are just some of the terms that are heard more and more in everyday school affairs. These are common words for the technologically trained but can evoke insecurity and frustration among even the most experienced school administrators. When faced with making major decisions such as purchasing new computer equipment for the science laboratories, providing a library with Internet access, or acquiring a database management system for student records, administrators must quickly learn as much of the technology as they can, relying extensively on the advice and recommendations of others. An administrator should not become the top technician in a school to manage technology. However, an acquaintance with commonly used terms as well as an overall conceptual understanding of computer systems will help administrators plan for and incorporate technology.

The Concept of System as a Starting Point

The starting point for the conceptual understanding of computer technology is that it is a system. A **system** is defined as a group of interrelated parts that are assembled to achieve some common goal or end. The three basic parts of any system are **input**, **process**, and **output** (see Figure A–1). Specifically, a computer is a system of interrelated input, processing, and output devices that are assembled for the processing of data (characters and numbers). This is true whether we are talking about a single microcomputer located on a secretary's desk or a national network of large mainframe computers that might consist of thousands of devices connected by telephones or satellites. The major difference is in the number of devices, not the basic operating concept.

Figure A–1
Basic System Design

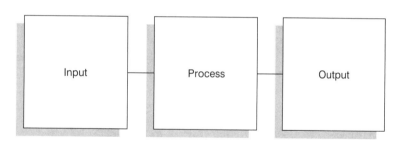

Input — Process — Output

Figure A–2
Microcomputer System
Configuration

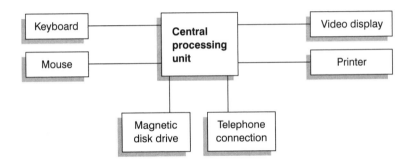

The minimum configuration of a computer system is best exemplified by the common microcomputer, which consists of at least a keyboard or mouse for input, a central processing unit for process, and a video monitor or printer for output. In addition, it usually has a secondary storage device such as a magnetic disk drive for storing data and instructions and a single communications interface or modem for establishing a telephone link (see Figure A–2). Larger computer systems are simply variations of this same basic microcomputer configuration. The major differences are that the larger systems are capable of having many input and output devices, multiple processors, and several additional secondary storage and other special function devices (see Figure A–3).

An important characteristic of systems is that multiple systems can interact with one another. Furthermore, some systems can function within other systems as subsystems. This interactive quality also applies to computer technology. A microcomputer on a secretary's desk is a system unto itself with input, processing, and output devices, and it can also be used to connect to a larger computer system that, for example, might be housed at a district office. Under this circumstance, the microcomputer functions as a part of the larger system or as a subsystem.

Hardware and Software

In the preceding discussion, the references are to the physical devices that comprise a basic part of any computer system. However, all com-

Figure A–3
Large Computer System
Configuration

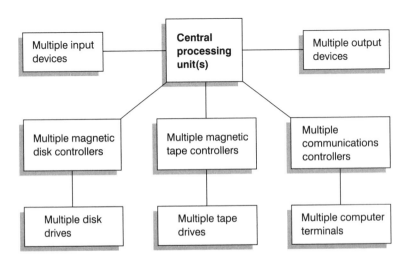

puter systems must include two fundamental components: hardware and software. **Hardware** is the physical component such as keyboards, video monitors, and disk drives. It also includes the wiring, circuit boards, and cabinetry that we can see and touch. **Software** is the nonphysical component or instructional component that directs the hardware. It consists of computer programs or sets of instructions communicated to the physical devices via electronic media such as magnetic disks and tapes. Critical to an understanding of computer technology is the fact that the physical devices are unable to perform any task without being directed to do so by software (computer programs).

The nonphysical aspect of software is sometimes difficult to understand for people who are not technically trained. Even trained technicians tend to refer to the computer as making the decisions and generating instructions. This is not the case.

To clarify this point, a comparison may be helpful. Imagine one person giving another person directions on how to get to the Grand Canyon from Chicago. The basic instructions might go something like this:

Take Airport Car Service to O'Hare International Airport.
Board American Airlines flight 999.
Fly to Phoenix.
Rent a car.
Drive north on Route 17.
Decide to go to the North or South Rim of the Grand Canyon.
If going to the South Rim, drive north on Route 64.
Check in at the Bright Angel Lodge.
Enjoy!

To make sure that the traveler does not get lost or forget a point, the directions might be written on a piece of paper. In this example, the plane, car, and roads represent the computer hardware; they are the physical things that enable the traveler to get from one place to another. The directions are similar to computer software; they instruct the traveler in using the hardware to get to a destination—in this case, the Grand Canyon. These directions are not something physical; they are a logical plan of instructions that provide guidance to the traveler. Computer software is composed of the many logical plans of instructions called **computer programs** that guide physical devices to achieve a desired result. The piece of paper on which the directions to get to the Grand Canyon are written is similar to computer media such as magnetic disks and CD-ROMs that are used to communicate with the physical devices. The piece of paper can be referred to or read over and over again as can computer media.

Although we can understand how one person communicates with another person as long as they both speak the same language, understanding how the software communicates with the hardware is difficult to comprehend. Does the hardware actually interpret and understand instructions? The answer is that it does so electronically.

The Central Processing Unit

The most important piece of hardware in any computer system is the **central processing unit** (CPU). This unit is composed of vastly sophisticated, high-speed circuits that are capable of transmitting electronic impulses at speeds measured in terms of nanoseconds (billionths of a second) and picoseconds (trillionths of a second). The exact nature of these circuits differs from one computer manufacturer to another, and one would need several courses in electrical engineering to comprehend the finer points of modern CPUs.

Conceptually, CPUs generally consist of three basic subunits: a **control unit** (CU), an **arithmetic-logic unit** (ALU), and a **primary storage unit** (PSU) (see Figure A–4). Each of these subunits has a very specific function and purpose. The CU interprets instructions and directs the processing of the other physical devices. The ALU performs all arithmetic operations, including comparisons. The PSU stores instructions and data. Physically, these subunits can be either separate components or integrated. Many computers use an integrated circuit or microprocessor that combines the control unit and the arithmetic-logic unit on a common chip, which is a thin wafer of silicon or other type of semiconductor material. The primary storage units generally are separate components within the CPU that can be replaced and enhanced as needed.

The control unit is the most sophisticated component of the CPU. It is capable of interpreting instructions that have been converted into electronic impulses or codes and directing the physical operations of all of the other devices in the computer hardware system. The control unit alone determines the sequence of tasks performed by the physical equipment. Before assigning new tasks, it verifies that the preceding tasks have been satisfactorily completed.

The arithmetic-logic unit performs all arithmetic operations such as addition, subtraction, multiplication, and division. It can do this because all data are converted into numeric codes in the CPU before they are received by the ALU. Data used in computer systems consist of all the letters of the alphabet, the digits 0 through 9, and commas, periods, exclamation marks, and so forth, which are called **special characters**. Each of these has a unique numeric code that enables the arithmetic-logic unit to manipulate them as numbers. Because all characters are converted into numeric codes, operations that usually might not be considered as arithmetic, such as alphabetizing or sorting a list of names, becomes an arithmetic operation in a CPU. Alphabetizing or sorting actually becomes a series of "less than/greater than" or subtraction operations.

The primary storage unit stores instructions and data; thus, it is also referred to as the **memory unit**. There are generally two types of PSUs: random access memory (RAM) and read only memory (ROM). **Random access memory** stores instructions and data temporarily as needed to perform a specific computer operation. It is used to store instructions (portions of computer programs) at the time they are to be processed by the control unit. It is never used to store instructions or data permanently. **Read only memory** is used to store permanently a set of instructions that are to be used over and over again. Once a set of instructions has been stored on a ROM, it generally cannot be changed—hence the term "read only." Special versions of ROM do exist that can be changed but are not regularly used in computer systems. **Program-**

Figure A–4
Conceptual Design of a Central Processing Unit

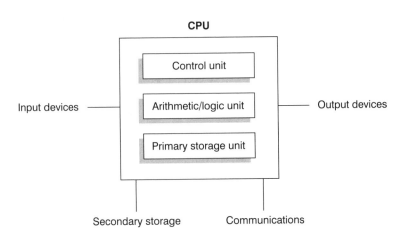

mable read only memory (PROM) and **erasable programmable read only memory** (EPROM) are examples.

All CPUs must have RAM for the temporary storage of instructions and data. Those that have only RAM store instructions and data permanently on other non-CPU storage devices such as magnetic disks or tapes. From the 1950s through the 1970s, the type of primary storage generally being used in CPUs was RAM.

The primary storage or memory capacity of a CPU is measured in terms of characters, or bytes. A **byte** is the minimum amount of memory needed to store a character of information and is made up of binary digits, or bits. A **bit** is a single electronic circuit capable of being in either the "on" or "off" position, conceptually similar to an ordinary light switch. When it is on, the electrical current is flowing; when it is off, the electrical current is stopped. Eight of these bits comprise a single byte or the amount of memory needed to store one character of data (i.e., letter of the alphabet, digit 0 through 9, or special characters).

An important characteristic of all CPUs is the memory capacity of the primary storage unit. The earliest computers in the 1950s had memory capacities measured in thousands of bytes. Modern computers are measured in millions of bytes. Most microcomputers purchased today will have a minimum of 1 to 32 million bytes of primary storage. Large mainframe computers easily may have many millions of bytes of primary storage.

The number of bytes of primary storage available in a CPU determines the size and the number of computer programs that can be resident (running) at any one time. Therefore, the larger the primary storage capacity, the more computer programs that can be running and hence the more computer processing that can be performed. Although not as critical on microcomputers, which usually run one or two programs (i.e., word processing, database management, electronic spreadsheet) at a time,

memory size is very critical on large mainframe computers, which are designed to run hundreds of programs simultaneously.

Before concluding this section on central processing units, a brief introduction to data representation may be helpful for visualizing how characters are actually stored in the primary storage unit of the CPU. The two basic coding schemes for storing characters are **American Standard Code for Information Interchange**, or ASCII (pronounced "as-key"), and **Extended Binary Coded Decimal Interchange Code**, or EBCDIC (pronounced "ebb-sih-dick"). Table A–1 provides the actual coding schemes used in primary storage units. Notice that each individual character code is eight binary digits (bits) long or the length of a single byte. These bits represent individual circuits that can be turned "on" or "off." A bit turned on is represented by a 1, and a bit turned off is denoted by a 0. For example, the ASCII codes for the first three letters of the alphabet are as follows:

A = 0100 0001
B = 0100 0010
C = 0100 0011

The vast majority (99%) of people who use computers do not need to know these codes. However, knowing that they exist provides a broader understanding of how computers operate. A fundamental characteristic of all "digital" computer systems is that data be converted into a series of bit patterns or codes to be processed. The frequently used term *digital* as applied to computer systems means the numerical representation of data in bit format.

Earlier it was mentioned that the control unit interprets instructions that have been converted into electronic impulses or codes. As with data, the various instructions that a computer can execute, such as reading a file from an input device or displaying a data record on a video monitor, are coded as a series of bit pat-

Table A–1
ASCII and EBCDIC Data Codes

Character	ASCII	EDCDIC
0	0011 0000	1111 0000
1	0011 0001	1111 0001
2	0011 0010	1111 0010
3	0011 0011	1111 0011
4	0011 0100	1111 0100
5	0011 0101	1111 0101
6	0011 0110	1111 0110
7	0011 0111	1111 0111
8	0011 1000	1111 1000
9	0011 1001	1111 1001
A	0100 0001	1100 0001
B	0100 0010	1100 0010
C	0100 0011	1100 0011
D	0100 0100	1100 0100
E	0100 0101	1100 0101
F	0100 0110	1100 0110
G	0100 0111	1100 0111
H	0100 1000	1100 1000
I	0100 1001	1100 1001
J	0100 1010	1101 0001
K	0100 1011	1101 0010
L	0100 1100	1101 0011
M	0100 1101	1101 0100
N	0100 1110	1101 0101
O	0100 1111	1101 0110
P	0101 0000	1101 0111
Q	0101 0001	1101 1000
R	0101 0010	1101 1001
S	0101 0011	1110 0010
T	0101 0100	1110 0011
U	0101 0101	1110 0100
V	0101 0110	1110 0101
W	0101 0111	1110 0110
X	0101 1000	1110 0111
Y	0101 1001	1110 1000
Z	0101 1010	1110 1001

terns referred to as the **instruction set**. The instruction set for each manufacturer's computers is different, and there are no generally accepted standards. Like data, every single instruction has to be converted into an appropriate bit code before being interpreted by the control unit.

Micros, Minis, and Mainframes

Classifying or categorizing computer systems is not an easy task. In some ways, it is like trying to hit a moving target because as technology improves, the classification systems keep changing. The simplest classification system is based on the physical size of the equipment. **Microcomputers** are considered small systems because they may take up a small amount of space on top of a desk, **mainframe computers** are large systems that may take up as much as several thousand square feet of space, and **minicomputers** are something in between. However, with a technology demanding precision, these classifications are very inexact. For example, microcomputers can be the size of a credit card, a small briefcase (as in laptops), or a standard typewriter. Some minicomputers are available that are larger than mainframe computers. Even some supercomputers (the most advanced mainframes) of the 1990s are about the size of the minicomputers of the 1980s.

Another way of differentiating computers is the speed of the central processing unit as measured by **megaflops**, or millions of mathematical calculations per second. For example, an Apple Macintosh IIfx microcomputer can execute 0.23 megaflops; a DEC Vax 8800 minicomputer, 1.3 megaflops; and an IBM Risc System/6000 mainframe, 62 megaflops. Some supercomputers (very large mainframes) are measured in billions of mathematical calculations per second. Though impressive to computer engineers and scientists, these speeds do not hold much significance for everyday computer users, most of whom are satisfied if their computer systems provide an acceptable level of response time. Furthermore, because computers are continually becoming faster, any classification system based on the speed of the CPU would be subject to continual revision.

The storage capacity of the CPU as measured by millions of bytes (characters) is also frequently used as a way of differentiating computer systems. Large mainframe computers may be able to store hundreds of millions of bytes, whereas the average microcomputer is able to keep 1 to 32 million bytes in primary storage. However, as with speed, primary storage capacity regularly increases. For example, as late as the middle 1970s, most large mainframe computers only

had 1 or 2 million bytes of primary storage, and microcomputers had only 16,000 to 32,000 bytes. In general, the primary storage capacities of computers are doubling every one or two years.

Possibly the best way of describing the differences among micros, minis, and mainframes is based on the number of physical devices (input, output, storage) that can be controlled by their CPUs. Microcomputers generally consist of one CPU or microprocessor that is capable of controlling several other devices, usually less than a dozen. The CPU on minicomputers generally contains multiple microprocessors that are capable of controlling dozens of other devices. In most such systems, each microprocessor has a control unit and an arithmetic-logic unit, with separate primary storage units being shared by all the microprocessors. Large mainframe computers, including the largest supercomputers, have hundreds of microprocessors that are capable of controlling hundreds and in some cases thousands of other devices.

A most practical way of differentiating computer systems is by their unit costs. Microcomputers generally cost from several hundred to several thousand dollars, minicomputers from tens of thousands to hundreds of thousands of dollars, and large mainframes from hundreds of thousands to tens of millions of dollars for advanced supercomputers. However, costs are also constantly changing as manufacturers attempt to remain competitive with one another. In general, the cost of computing decreases as demand and competition increase.

The final assessment of computer classification—specifically the micro, mini, and mainframe schema—is whether it has become obsolete. The technology has changed and will keep changing so as to make any classification subject to constant revision.

Input Devices

The central processing units of all computers receive instructions and data through input devices. The keyboard and the mouse are probably the most familiar. However, in the past 15 years, an assortment of other input devices (touch-sensitive screens, light pens, Koala pads, joysticks, etc.) have evolved that are appropriate for educational applications. They may be a bit more expensive now or require special software, but they will likely play a more significant role in the years to come.

The basic input device for computers is the **keyboard**, which has been the mainstay for all types of computer systems since the 1950s and continues to be so today. Whether used for developing software, maintaining records, or doing word processing, the keyboard is the essential input device for computer systems. The key arrangement is the same as a typewriter keyboard. When a key is depressed, an electronic signal is sent to the CPU with the code of the respective letter, number, or special character. In addition, keyboards have special function keys that can be programmed to perform certain tasks automatically, such as transferring the contents of a video screen to a printer or saving a file on a disk. Many keyboards will also have a number pad, which simulates a calculator and is an important time saver for users such as accountants, bank tellers, and bookkeepers who manipulate numbers extensively.

Increasingly becoming standard on microcomputers, the **mouse** is a hand-held, input device electronically connected to a video screen. The mouse is used to position a pointer on the screen, then the user presses a button to select options depending on the software used. For example, Macintosh and Windows-based microcomputers allow users to choose basic computer operations such as shutting the computer down, formatting a new disk, or discarding an old file, simply by pointing the mouse to the desired option and clicking. For young children, the mouse is an especially attractive input device and easier to use than a keyboard.

A **touch-sensitive screen** performs the same function as a mouse but allows users to point to one of the options provided on the video screen. Although similar to a mouse, a touch-sensitive screen provides a more natural connection between the person and the machine. However, the options provided must be displayed in areas large enough to be easily discriminated by the size of one's finger. For this reason, the mouse may be more appropriate for certain applications because it allows for very small objects to be available for selection. A touch-sensitive screen is also more expensive than a mouse and requires a special monitor.

Light-sensitive pens likewise can be used to point to options provided on a video screen. They are versatile, allowing for a great deal of interaction between user and machine. Of all the various input devices, light-sensitive pens permit the greatest accuracy when pointing or selecting an option. They also may be used for painting or drawing on a screen and so have significant potential in educational applications. They require special software that may be expensive depending on the application.

Graphics tablets such as Koala pads are electronic surfaces connected to a CPU and include software that allows instant display of the surface on the video monitor. They come with a pen, stylus, or arm that is used to manipulate or alter the image on the tablet and simultaneously on the monitor. Depending on the accompanying software, they can also perform other functions. They are very popular for electronic drawing applications and are very easy to use.

Joysticks, **track balls**, and **game paddles** are the commonly used input devices for computer and video games. They allow for faster manipulation of the pointer and other objects on the video screen. Track balls, in particular, have become popular in the 1990s and are being supplied as standard input devices on some laptop computers such as the Macintosh Powerbook.

Voice recognition devices allow users to speak to input data or instructions to a computer via microphones that convert human speech into electronic impulses. This technology has not achieved its original promise but continues to improve. Because speech is the most natural way for people to communicate, voice recognition devices eventually will likely be the major way of communicating with computer systems. Various voice recognition devices are on the market and working well in limited applications. In education, these devices are being used more and more in special education classes whose students may have limited hand dexterity.

Optical scanning devices, which include **optical mark recognition** (OMR), **optical character recognition** (OCR), **hand-held wands**, and **digitizers** have been available as special-purpose input devices for many years. They are used for scoring tests, reading bar codes on labels, and converting paper images into electronic impulses or digital form. A number of machines have come on the market in recent years securing the future of optical scanners as important input devices because they can be significant time savers in converting printed and graphic materials into digital form, which thereby obviates the need to key in manually extensive amounts of data.

Output Devices

The major purpose of most computer systems is to produce various types of output so that users can see or read the results of their input and computer applications. The two basic output devices are **video displays** and **printers**.

Cathode ray tubes (CRTs) are the most common type of video displays. They generally use an electron gun that generates a light beam that can be scanned across a video screen. These beams are displayed as a series of picture elements, also known as **pixels**, that appear as single dots of light in horizontal and vertical patterns. A pixel (derived from the words *picture* and *element*) is very small. For example, on a medium-resolution video monitor, 128 pixels are needed to display a single character of

data. Generally, the quality of a picture on a video display is directly related to its **resolution**, which is the number of pixels that can be displayed on the screen. The resolution of video monitors ranges from tens of thousands to more than a million pixels per screen. In addition to the number of pixels, the number of colors that can be displayed is also a significant factor in terms of image quality. For example, an image displayed on a video monitor with 300,000 pixels and 16 colors may not look as sharp as the same image displayed on a monitor with 60,000 pixels and 256 colors.

In selecting monitors, users generally have a choice of monochrome (one color) or color. The tendency in education is to acquire color monitors to take advantage of the vast array of graphics software that is available. In evaluating color monitors, the choices are extensive, and options include standard color, RGB (red, green, blue), CGA (color graphics adapter), EGA (extended graphics adapter), PGA (professional graphics adapter), and VGA (video graphics adapter). These options all refer to resolution and number of colors available. For most student uses, a standard color monitor is sufficient. For classroom presentations, the higher-quality color monitors should be considered. This is especially true if a CRT is to double as both video monitor for a computer and as a television receiver for viewing educational TV programs. Receiver/monitors are the most versatile video devices available and also the most expensive. Nevertheless, they are becoming widely used for classroom presentations. Software packages, particularly those that require a certain level of resolution or color, will indicate their requirements in their brochures.

In addition to CRT displays, there are plasma display and liquid crystal display (LCD) devices. **Plasma displays** use neon and argon gas to produce a very high-quality and bright image. They were used extensively with the PLATO educational software systems. **Liquid crystal displays** or **flat-panel displays**, which are used in watches and calculators, are also being used as monitors. Most portable and laptop computers have switched to LCD technology. A good deal of research and development has gone into improving the quality of the images produced on LCDs, and in years to come, this technology may replace CRTs as the major video output devices for computer systems.

Computers' ability to generate paper has become legendary. Stories abound about reams of computer-generated reports "drowning" their users in paper. Despite the jokes, the popularity of printed material in computer technology and the importance of printer output devices cannot be denied. Many types of printers are available, differentiated by the technology used to generate characters and images on a page. For microcomputers, the basic types are dot-matrix, daisy-wheel, ink-jet, and laser printers. For large mainframe computers, a basic type is a line printer. Laser printers are also used on large mainframe computers to produce high-quality print output.

Dot-matrix printers are the least expensive and commonly used with microcomputer systems. They generate a series of small dots to form images and characters. The quality of images produced on dot-matrix printers ranges from poor to near-letter quality.

Daisy-wheel printers use a wheel with all the characters appended to them. They get their name from the fact that the appendages look like daisy petals. The wheel spins at very high speeds, and the appropriate character appendages strike a ribbon similar to a typewriter. Daisy-wheel printers are considered letter quality, which means that the image is comparable to that produced by a standard typewriter.

Ink-jet printers use tiny droplets of ink sprayed from a nozzle to produce images. They are considered letter quality, are very quiet, and are capable of producing color. If an application requires good color output, ink-jet printers are probably the best solution.

Laser printers are letter-quality printers that use laser technology to produce whole images on a page similar to a photocopying machine. The fact that they are page printers is an important distinction from the other printers that produce a character at a time along a print line. An important feature of some laser printers is their ability to be programmed to produce different size and style images including print fonts. For this reason, they are extremely popular with desktop publishing applications. Because of their advanced technology, laser printers are also more expensive than other printers. However, as the technology improves and production becomes cheaper, they are becoming less expensive. Laser printers for microcomputers can range from several hundred to several thousand dollars, depending on features and options. For large mainframe computers, they can easily cost hundreds of thousands of dollars.

Line printers are commonly used on large mainframe computers. They are very high-speed devices, printing at speeds in excess of 3,000 lines per minute. They print a line at a time using little hammers to strike characters through a ribbon onto continuous sheets of paper.

Plotters are a special type of printer designed to draw graphic displays on paper. Plotters are available for all types of computers (micros, minis, and mainframes). They are extremely useful for applications in art and drafting for which high-quality and color images need to be produced.

Voice output or **audio-response units** use speech synthesis to replicate the human voice. Most examples of voice output are for special and limited-purpose applications such as toys, games, and telephone answering systems. Like voice recognition units, which are input devices, they represent the most natural way for humans to communicate, and for this reason, their future is assured as an important part of computer technology. However, the technology still needs to improve to be used routinely and to become a standard component of most computer systems. In education, their application in special education classes, especially those for the visually impaired, shows great promise.

Secondary Storage Devices

Secondary storage devices are used to store data and instructions permanently or at least until the application no longer needs them. They are called secondary storage devices to distinguish them from the primary storage devices that are part of the central processing unit. They are also referred to as **input/output** (I/O) **devices** because they are capable of reading data and instructions (input) and writing them (output). The major types of secondary storage devices are magnetic disks, magnetic tape, and optical discs.*

Today, **magnetic disks** are the most common type of secondary storage devices and include floppy disks, hard disks, and fixed-head disks. They all use a similar technology that stores characters of data or instructions electromagnetically on disks or platters. These disks can be **hard** or rigid (i.e., composed of a metallic material) or soft or "**floppy**" (i.e., composed of a plastic material).

The **disk drives** (see Figure A–5) on which the disks rotate are spindles similar to a phonograph player. They use microscopic read/write heads, rather than a stylus (phonograph needle), that are capable of electromagnetically decoding and encoding data in digital format (bit patterns) on the disks' surface. These read/write heads are mounted on an extension arm that can extend itself across the radius (from the center to the outer edge) of the rotating disk. Data and instructions are stored on

the disk in a series of concentric circles called **tracks**. Through software instructions, the read/write heads can move across the rotating disks and directly access any information stored on the disk. For this reason, magnetic disks are also referred to as **direct access storage devices**, or DASD (pronounced "dazz-dee"). The fact that the read/write heads actually move or extend themselves has led to their being called **moving-head disks**.

Another type of magnetic disk has a series of stationary read/write heads, one for each of the tracks on a disk. Because the heads do not have to move to access any of the information stored on the disk, these disks are referred to as **fixed-head disks**. Their major advantage over moving-head disks is that they save time by not having to extend the read/write heads across the radius of a rotating disk. But because they have a read/write head for each track (as many as 200), they are much more expensive than the single, moving-head disk drive. However, some extremely high-volume, high-speed applications require the additional speed, which makes these disks worth the additional cost.

An important characteristic of magnetic disks is their storage capacity. The smallest disks (5.25 or 3.5 inches in diameter) can store 160,000 to 3.5 million bytes of data. These are the familiar floppy disks commonly available on microcomputer systems. Hard disks may be as large as 14 inches in diameter and can store from millions (megabytes) to billions of bytes (gigabytes) of data. Most mainframe computers use disk drives that can operate on a number or "pack" of disks stacked one on top of another. A stack of disks used for this purpose is referred to as a **disk pack**. On most microcomputers, there is a limit as to how many hard disk drives can be attached to a CPU. On large mainframe computers, many disk drives can be attached, which thereby increases a computer system's storage capacity to billions and trillions of bytes (terabytes).

Magnetic tape drives were the original secondary storage devices used on all computer

---

*According to the *Microsoft Press Computer Dictionary* (1991), "It is now standard practice to use the spelling *disc* for optical disc and the spelling *disk* in all other computer contexts (p. 1009). This approach is used throughout this book.

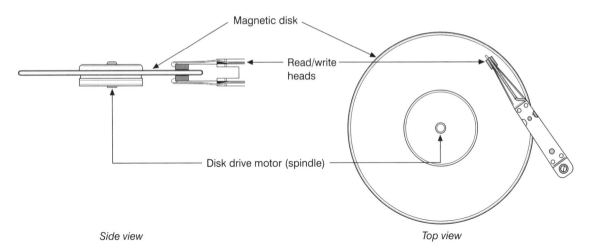

Side view   Top view

Figure A–5
Magnetic Disk Drive Operation

systems. They operate similarly to a tape recorder; that is, a length of tape passes through an electromagnetic read/write (play-back/record) head as it moves between two reels. Magnetic tapes were the major secondary storage devices used on large mainframe computers through the early 1970s. However, as magnetic disk technology developed with faster and greater direct access capability, magnetic tape (a device requiring the physical reading of all data records in sequence to reach the desired record) became too slow a processing technique for many high-volume computer applications. As a result, the computer industry has gradually moved to the use of disk equipment for most secondary storage needs. Magnetic tape is now used primarily to back up (make copies of) disk files and to transport large data files from one location to another.

The newest type of secondary storage is the **optical disc**. The term *optical* is used because the still-evolving technology depends on laser light for reading data from the disc surfaces. CD-ROM (compact disc–read only memory), WORM (write once, read many) discs, erasable optical discs, and videodiscs are examples of the variety of devices available using laser technology for storing data. An important distinction among these different devices is the method of encoding data. They use either digital format—that is, bit patterns (on/off or 1 and 0) similar to all other digital computing equipment—or analog format similar to a series of video frames and sound tracks. Digital format can be directly accessed by CPUs and easily manipulated. Analog format cannot be directly accessed by CPUs and must pass through an analog to a digital converter or a video digitizer.

Optical discs that use digital format are already having a significant impact on secondary storage technology. Devices such as **CD-ROMs** are becoming more common on microcomputer systems. Although read only, they are relatively inexpensive and capable of high storage capacities of 500 to 600 million bytes. They look like and are similar in size (4.75 inches) to compact discs used for audio players. Compared with other secondary storage devices, they have high storage capacity for their size. For example, CD-ROMs can hold as much data as 3,600 of the original floppy disks (5.25 inch with a storage capacity of 160,000 bytes).

Presently, the most common computer applications used with CD-ROM equipment are reference works such as electronic encyclopedias, training manuals, and textbooks.

WORM devices were the first attempt to develop a writing capability for optical discs. They are high capacity (200 to 600 million bytes) and are similar in appearance to CD-ROMs. However, they provide the user with the ability to record or write data once on a disc surface. Data can then be accessed or read over and over again but can never be erased from the disc. This feature is acceptable for applications in which the data will remain static and never change, but it becomes a serious limitation for most administrative and instructional applications in which data must be updated or changed regularly. Various types of WORM devices are on the market, but they are unlikely to evolve to dominate secondary storage technology.

Erasable optical discs are beginning to become available but need a bit more research and development. Their potential is significant, so much so that they may become the dominant secondary storage devices used on all computer systems provided the technology for writing and erasing can be improved and the cost of manufacturing can be reduced.

Video Technology

Any discussion of optical disc equipment generally raises the question of whether most computer users have a need for equipment capable of holding billions or trillions of bytes of data. This is a legitimate question because most users do not need such capability for many computer applications. However, to use a common phrase, we live in the information age, and the desire of American businesses, public agencies, and schools to collect information appears unending. The more they collect, the more they want. This has been essentially the case with character (letters and numbers) information. However, we are also becoming an increasingly image-dependent society, as more people are getting information from television than they do from newspapers and other print media.

Designers of computer technology have supported this trend and have gradually been integrating computer and video technologies over the past decade. In addition to characters, computer systems can provide pictures and other graphics in their basic applications. More research and development is still needed especially for digital video, but the potential is staggering for educational applications where graphics can add significantly to both the presentation and understanding of material.

In the previous section, most of the equipment described uses a digital (bit pattern) format for storing data. Television and most high-quality video production involving motion pictures do not use digital format for storing images but rather a simple concept called **analog frame format**. The moving pictures produced for video are not actually moving at all but are a series of still pictures or frames shown at rapid speeds (30 frames per second). Slower speeds appear as slow motion; faster speeds appear as hyperactivity.

Storing video in this format requires a significant amount of storage capability. For every second of video, 30 frames of color and positioning (vertical and horizontal lines) information must be stored. A 30-minute video, then, requires approximately 54,000 frames.

In an ideally integrated situation, these frames would exist as digital information; however, present technology requires as much as 1 million bytes in digital format to store one frame with high resolution and good color. Thirty minutes of video would require 54 billion (54,000,000,000) bytes. For effective storage and handling, secondary storage devices will have to have far greater capability than they do currently. As combined computer and video applications develop, the demand for greater and greater storage capacity will increase significantly. Researchers are actively engaged around the world in developing alternative digital formats for storing video information on optical disc devices such as CD-ROMs. Through hardware and software techniques that use highly efficient data compression algorithms, technology is being developed that reduces the digital storage requirements for high-quality video.

Many applications are being developed that already use computers and analog video together in what are popularly referred to as interactive video programs. In general, the video portions of these applications depend on videodisc players that continue to store video information in frame format and not digital format; however, a microcomputer is used to control the videodisc player. More specifically, the microcomputer is used to control which specific frames are shown. Therefore, an interactive video program can be developed that engages the user with questions and prompts interactivity via the computer software. When required to show a video segment, the computer gives a signal to the videodisc player to show or play the desired frames.

In these applications, the video information from the videodisc does not pass through the computer system at any time. However, video digitizers do exist that are able to capture small amounts of analog, frame-formatted information from a videodisc and convert it into digital format. Presently, this technology is limited and is used more for capturing and manipulating small portions of a video segment. However, as the technology improves and expands in storage capacity, digital video will replace analog or frame-format video.

Many educators are curious as to why videodiscs are more appropriate for instruction than other analog media. After all, educational films, filmstrips, and videotape are used regularly in many schools. The difference is that none of the equipment that uses these media is able to interact effectively with a computer. Earlier, the difference between magnetic disk and magnetic tape was discussed. Once the major storage medium for many years in computer applications, magnetic tape has been almost completely replaced by magnetic disk equipment since magnetic tape cannot provide direct access to information that is being stored throughout the length of the tape. Magnetic disks, on the other hand, are able to provide direct access to any information stored on the disk, much more rapidly as well. Within a span of approximately 20 years, magnetic disks became the basic information-processing technique used in all computer applications.

Videodisc likewise is a direct-access medium similar to magnetic disks. Frames are stored on a series of concentric tracks on 12-inch or 8-inch disks. Any individual frame or segment of frames can be accessed directly and played. The older video equipment (film, filmstrip, videotape) can only be used sequentially. If integrated with computer technology, the time required for video segments to be accessed and shown would be much too long. When videodisc players are integrated with computers, any individual segment or frame can be accessed in less than two seconds. This easily allows for educational interaction directed to specific material of interest or need.

As an example, a videodisc that contains the movie version of *Moby Dick* by Herman Melville could be shown sequentially in a literature class. After the showing, a teacher may wish to show particular segments over again to demonstrate character or plot development. Although this could easily be done with a videodisc, it would not be possible on a videotape or film unless one engaged in a slow and clumsy fast-forward and rewind operation.

Data Communications

Although the integration of computer technology and video technology is a relatively new development, computers have been routinely integrated with communications technology since the 1960s to provide an array of applications that transcend physical distance. **Data communications** simply refers to the transfer of data between two or more digital devices over some physical distance. This distance may be several feet or thousands of miles.

The interconnection or "connectivity" of computer equipment transferring the data is called a **data communications network**. The most common interconnections use cable for short distances and telecommunications (i.e., telephone) for longer distances, although telephone systems can also be used for short-distance communications. Interconnecting computer equipment over some limited distance such as a room, building, or campus is commonly referred to as a **local area network** (LAN). Interconnecting equipment over longer distances such as throughout a large city, across a state, or spanning a nation or continent is called a **wide area network** (WAN). The 1990s saw the phenomenal growth of the Internet, which is the epitome of a wide area network.

Usually LANs use coaxial cable to connect various computer devices together, especially when confined to a single room, floor, or building. In addition to connecting the equipment physically, LANs also require specialized software to handle the transferring of data from one device to another. The sophistication of the software needed to control the network depends on how much interaction is required between the various devices.

Along with the number and type of devices, the amount of data to be transferred and the speed needed for transferring data are important factors in determining the software requirements. Central computer laboratories in many schools use a LAN to distribute instructional software. A typical network might consist of 20 or 30 microcomputers in a single room, with one microcomputer functioning as the **central file server** for the other microcomputers. The central file server usually has added hard disk storage so that it can contain a library of all the various software programs acquired by the school. Teachers or students using the other microcomputers access the central file server directly to select the individual program(s) needed. The central file server then downloads or sends a copy of the program over the network to the microcomputer that requested the program.

Although conceptually similar, WANs are more sophisticated networks than LANs because of the distances involved, the number of users, and the large amounts of data that can be transferred. However, the most important difference between WANs and LANs is that WANs require telecommunications or telephone facilities to connect the various devices on the network. In a LAN environment using coaxial cable, all the data transferred are in digital (bit pattern) format, and conversions are not required as the data pass from one device to another. In a WAN environment using telephone lines, this is not possible because telephone communications are not in digital but analog frequency format. This analog frequency format is a varying electric current that is generated from or converted into sound (i.e., human voice) by telephone transmitters or receivers, respectively. For computer equipment to use a telephone line, the computer's digital format must be converted into a frequency format and vice versa. To do this conversion, special equipment called **modulator-demodulators**, or **modems**, are needed. These are relatively inexpensive devices when used to connect a simple computing device such as a microcomputer. In fact, most manufacturers are now providing modems as standard devices on many microcomputers. For larger computing systems, modems may be combined with other communications control equipment such as multiplexors and communications controllers, which in addition to modulating and demodulating signals are also able to perform complex message handling, protocol, and queuing operations.

The speed of modems as measured in bits per second (bps) varies significantly. Most microcomputers are being equipped with modems in the range of 2,400 to 28,000 bps.

Modems for larger computer systems can be acquired that are measured in millions of bits per second. The growth of the Internet has generated a good deal of research and development in improving the speed of modems and other data communication devices.

Although WANs were originally designed and used by large corporations and public agencies for long-distance transaction processing such as making airline reservations and transferring funds, they are increasingly being used by everyone for a host of different services. National networks such as America Online, Prodigy, and Compuserve provide electronic mail and shopping, reference, and financial services for modest fees to the general public. Many state education departments and large school districts have established WANs for record keeping and other administrative services such as reporting attendance, purchasing, and making library exchanges.

In view of the proliferation of WANs, the telecommunications industry has recognized the need for facilitating the integration with computing equipment and is beginning to provide digital data services that do not require modems. In the future, this will be greatly enhanced as fiber optic cable, which uses digital format, becomes more widely installed.

The Internet is a WAN that established a standard protocol so that networks throughout the world could communicate with one another. The Internet promises to be the major source of all digital information as we enter the 21st century.

Computer Software

Computer software is the instruction component of a computer system that directs the physical devices (hardware). Sets of instructions are called **computer programs**. These instructions may be communicated to the CPU through input devices such as keyboards, whereas instructions and programs that are executed over and over again are usually stored on storage devices such as magnetic disks.

There are two broad categories of software: system software and application software. **System software** directs, supervises, and supports the computer hardware system and all the tasks that are to be executed on it. **Application software** consists of all the computer programs "applied" to specific computer user activities such as word processing, record keeping, computer-assisted instruction, and so forth.

The relationship of system software and application software is an important one for understanding how computers perform tasks. For clarification, compare two components of an automobile assembly line plant. In the plant, the people who work directly on the assembly line are actually accomplishing the task of building cars. This is the application. However, for the assembly line workers to complete their task, other workers must supervise and coordinate activities such as making sure that resources (i.e., raw materials) are available in sufficient quantities, that basic utilities (i.e., electricity) are functioning, and that certain tasks are completed satisfactorily (i.e., quality control) before commencing a new task. These activities are comparable to system software functions.

System Software

The most common example of system software is the **operating system**, which is a set of programs that all computer manufacturers provide for their computer systems. The operating system supervises and controls the activities of the physical devices and the application software. It is the master control program on which all computer processing depends. On large mainframe computers, the operating systems are the most complex and sophisticated software programs being used, and the computer programmers who develop and maintain them are generally the most talented people on the technical staff.

Some computer manufacturers (e.g., Burroughs Corporation) have actually named the operating systems used on their computers the **master control programs**, or MCPs. IBM has used names such as OS (operating system), DOS (disk operating system), and VS (virtual system). One of the most powerful and one of the few machine-independent operating systems is UNIX, developed by AT&T Corporation. The Unix operating system has proven to be especially effective in network environments and functioning as the "server" in client-server applications as are common on the Internet.

On microcomputers, the operating systems are complex yet much easier to use and understand. Examples include Microsoft (MS)-DOS, XENIX (microcomputer version of UNIX), OS/2, and Microsoft-Windows. The Apple Corporation popularized the concept of windows or a menu-driven operating system on its Macintosh computers. The menu can be displayed as small pictures or icons representing the available programs. Using a mouse, users simply click on the icon of the program or command they wish to execute.

Although operating systems differ from one manufacturer's computer system to another, almost all provide several fundamental programs or commands (see Table A–2). The three most important are supervisor programs, utility programs, and language translator programs.

Supervisor programs include job management, resource management, and data management programs. **Job management programs** allow users to execute their programs or tasks. They set job priorities and queues when there are multiple requests. Such ordering is critical especially on large mainframe computers capable of executing hundreds or thousands of programs simultaneously. **Resource management programs** allocate physical resources (devices) to programs and determine whether they are available. The greater the number of physical devices that a computer system has, the more sophisticated the resource management programs that control them must be. **Data management programs** allocate and retrieve data and programs on input/output devices such as magnetic disks. Because a major function of computer systems is to store data and programs, data management is critical on all computer systems.

Utility programs that are used repeatedly are generally supplied in the operating system. Examples include programs for copying data files from one storage area to another, sorting data into alphabetical or numerical order, making back-up copies of storage media such as magnetic disks, and preparing (formatting) new disks to store data.

Language translators, also referred to as **compilers** or **interpreters**, are programs that convert or translate commands into machine-readable or bit pattern instructions. Hundreds of programming languages are being used today. However, to use a particular language on a particular computer, a language translator program must be part of the operating system to convert instructions into a form that can be interpreted by the control unit of the CPU. The major language translator programs being used today are these:

BASIC (Beginners All-Purpose Symbolic Instruction Code)—the most commonly

Table A–2
Basic Functions of Operating Systems

Supervisor programs	Utility programs	Language processors
Job management	File Copy	Assembler
	Disk Copy	BASIC
Resource management	Disk Format	COBOL
	Sort Files	FORTRAN
Data management	Merge Files	Pascal
	Display Files	PL /1

used programming language available on microcomputers; developed by John Kemeny at Dartmouth University

COBOL (Common Business Oriented Language)—one of the first languages to use words (English) as the primary method of providing commands; the most commonly used language for business applications

FORTRAN (Formula Translator)—one of the oldest programming languages and used mostly for scientific and mathematical applications; replaced by BASIC as the most commonly used programming language

Logo—a language designed for teaching young children how to program a computer; developed by Seymour Papert at MIT

Pascal—a highly structured language that is very popular for teaching proper programming style and techniques; developed by Niklaus Wirth in Zurich

PL/1 (Programming Language 1)—a language designed originally to provide the best features of COBOL and FORTRAN

Most of these languages use English-like words such as *print, read, input,* and so forth, or arithmetic operators such as "+" for addition to provide instructions. These words or operators must be converted into a series of bit patterns (on/off codes) similar to the ASCII codes discussed earlier in order for them to be executed by the control unit. Simple programs may consist of several hundred instructions; more complex programs may consist of tens of thousands of instructions, all of which are translated before they are executed.

DOS, Macintosh, and Windows

DOS is probably the most widely used operating system ever developed. Developed for IBM

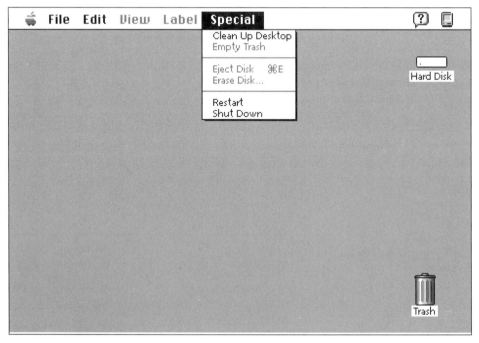

Figure A–6
Macintosh Special Menu

Screen capture used by permission of Apple Computer Corporation.

machines by Microsoft, Inc., DOS is referred to as **PC-DOS** when used on IBM PC/PS microcomputers and as **MS-DOS** (the "MS" stands for Microsoft) when used on IBM-compatible computers. It was considered the standard operating system for most microcomputers through the 1980s, and many other manufacturers besides IBM used it or something very similar on their own equipment.

DOS is a command-driven operating system, which means the user keys in a command on the keyboard to invoke a particular function. For example, the user would key in the command "copy" to copy a disk file. Users are expected to commit these commands to memory or at least be able to look them up in a user's manual.

The Macintosh operating system (see Figure A–6), developed in the mid-1980s, is radically different from DOS. Though performing most of the same functions, the Macintosh is a menu-driven operating system that provides the user with a series of window selections from which a particular function can be invoked. Rather than key in a command on a keyboard, the user employs a mouse to select or click on a selection on a menu essentially by pointing to it. The Macintosh operating system also introduced the extensive use of picture representations or icons to represent functions, files, and other system facilities rather than words or file names. The use of icons and menus that open as electronic windows is also referred to as a **graphical user interface**, or GUI (pronounced "gooey"). Other microcomputer operating systems have begun to move to the GUI style. The popular Microsoft Incorporated Windows operating system (see Figure A–7), for example, uses the GUI style as a shell or interface for DOS on IBM and IBM-compatible microcomputers.

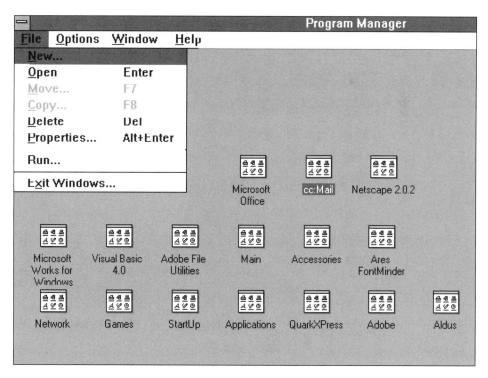

Figure A–7
Microsoft Windows Menu

Application Software

Application software is the programs that actually perform the specific user tasks for which the computer system was acquired. In a bank, they would involve the financial record-keeping applications. In a hospital, medical record keeping and patient monitoring would be common applications. In a school, administrative and instructional applications are the two major categories; Chapters 4 through 7 are devoted entirely to the nature of these applications. Readers are also encouraged to review Appendix B, which provides specific, hands-on activities that use some of the major application software being used in schools today.

Summary

This appendix introduces the basic concepts of computer systems. Covering the entire field of computer science is not possible here, so instead only the major concepts and developments in hardware and software of importance to school administrators are included.

In terms of hardware, the computer system is made up of input, processing, output, and storage devices. The central processing unit (CPU), which includes control, arithmetic-logic, and primary storage units, is the fundamental hardware component of every computer system. Input devices such as keyboards provide data and instructions to the CPU. Output devices such as printers receive data and instructions from the CPU. Storage devices such as magnetic disk drives both provide data and instructions and receive them from the CPU. All of these physical devices work together as a common hardware system to provide computer services to users. These are sometimes connected through data communications systems called wide area networks (WANs) and local area networks (LANs).

The physical devices or hardware can only respond to instructions that have been provided in the form of a computer program. Computer programs, developed by people, are communicated to the CPU by way of keyboards, magnetic disks, and other computer media. The two broad categories of computer software are system software and application software. System software is all the programs and instructions that control, supervise, and coordinate the physical devices and the application software programs. Application software is all the other programs that actually accomplish the specific tasks for which the computer is being used. In schools, the two major categories of application software are administrative applications and instructional applications.

Key Concepts and Questions

1. A computer system is made up of interrelated hardware and software components.

   How does one distinguish hardware from software? What are some of the major hardware components? Are they essentially the same in all computer systems? Explain.

2. The central processing unit (CPU) conceptually is divided into three subunits: control, arithmetic-logic, and primary storage.

   How do these subunits differ? What is a microprocessor, and what is its relationship to the CPU? What is the difference between primary and secondary storage?

3. The terms *microcomputer, minicomputer,* and *large mainframe computer* are used to classify types of computer systems.

   How appropriate are these classifications? What are some of the characteristics on which these classifications are based?

4. Computer systems can include a variety of different input and output devices.

Identify those devices that are appropriate for only specialized applications. Which are common to all applications?

5. Secondary storage devices have advanced significantly during the past 30 years. In particular, storage technology has favored direct access processing like that provided by magnetic disks.

Why is direct access processing beneficial? What types of applications are dependent on it? What is sequential processing? What secondary storage device is most associated with it? What does the future hold for secondary storage technology?

6. Computer technology is gradually becoming integrated with other technologies such as video and communications.

How has the integration of these technologies been progressing? What are the future implications?

7. Computer software is categorized as system software and application software.

How do they differ? Is one dependent on the other? Explain. Are they different depending on the type of computer equipment being used? Explain.

Suggested Activities

1. Familiarize yourself with a microcomputer hardware system. Identify the physical components. Practice using the hardware by keying in or clicking on simple commands, inserting and removing disks, and generating output on a video display or printer. If you can gain access to a minicomputer or mainframe computer system, compare and contrast the basic hardware components, especially input, output, and secondary storage devices. Try to identify the operating system(s) that are available on these computer systems. For minicomputer and mainframe computer systems, you will probably need to discuss this question with a member of the technical staff.

2. Review the basic functions provided by the Macintosh or Windows operating system. If not familiar with an operating system, take the on-line tutorial that is provided with most microcomputer systems. Practice using some of the basic utility programs such as copying a file or listing a directory.

References

Dvorak, J. C. (Ed.) (1996). *PC Magazine 1996 computer buyer's guide*. New York: Ziff-Davis/Macmillan.

Forester, T. (Ed.). (1985). *The information technology revolution*. Cambridge, MA: MIT Press.

Kurzban, S. A., Heines, T. S., & Sayers, A. P. (1984). *Operating systems principles*. New York: Van Nostrand Reinhold.

Lambert, S., & Ropiequet, S. (Eds.). (1986). *CD-ROM: The new papyrus*. Redmond, WA: Microsoft.

Markoff, J. (1991, June 5). Computer said to be fastest. *New York Times, 140*, p. D1.

Markoff, J. (1991, May 31). Supercomputing's speed quest. *New York Times, 140*, pp. D1–D6.

Microsoft Press Computer Dictionary. (1991). Redmond WA: Microsoft.

O'Brien, J. A. (1989). *Computer concepts and applications with an introduction to software and BASIC*. Homewood, IL: Irwin.

Paske, R. (1990). Hypermedia: A brief history and progress report. *Technological Horizons in Education Journal, 18*(1), 53–57.

Paske, R. (1990). Hypermedia: A progress report. Part 2: Interactive videodisc. *Technological Horizons in Education Journal, 18*(2), 90–94.

Paske, R. (1990). Hypermedia: A progress report. Part 3: CD-ROM, CD-I, DVI, etc. *Technological Horizons in Education Journal, 18*(3), 93–97.

Pronk, R. (1996). *The PowerMac book!* Scottsdale, AZ: Coriolis Group.

Van Horn, R. (1991). *Advanced technology in education*. Pacific Grove, CA: Brooks/Cole.

Warger, C. (Ed.) (1990). *Technology in today's schools*. Alexandria, VA: Association for Supervision and Curriculum Development.

Appendix B

An Introduction to Administrative Software

This appendix provides an introductory workshop activity for readers who are unfamiliar with the common administrative software features available in an integrated package. For this purpose, Microsoft Works has been chosen. Microsoft Works is an integrated software package that provides five components: word processing, database management, electronic spreadsheet, graphs and charts, and communications. Originally developed to execute on DOS/Windows computers by Microsoft, Inc., in 1986, Works is now also available in a version for the Apple Macintosh.

The popularity of integrated software stems from the ability to share data and files easily among components so that a spreadsheet can be easily converted into a graph or a letter merged with a database address file. The sharing and integration of data have a great deal of appeal for administrative applications where the goal may be to provide common data throughout a school district. In addition to application packages such as Microsoft Works, operating systems such as Microsoft Windows and Macintosh have begun to provide integrating features that allow data such as text and graphics to pass from one program to another. As these features continue to evolve, users may rely more on the operating systems to provide integration features.

The commands shown in the workshop activities will execute on a DOS/Windows microcomputer. Readers wishing to use a Macintosh microcomputer for these exercises will have to make several adjustments. Although the menu-driven styles of both DOS/Windows and Macintosh versions are similar, the following differences should be noted especially for these exercises:

Print Commands
Provided as a separate menu item on the DOS/Windows version.
Provided as a submenu within the main File menu on the Macintosh version.

Charts and Graphs
Provided in the View menu on the DOS/Windows version.
Provided in the Chart menu on the Macintosh version.

Placeholders for Integrating Data across Modules
Provided by the INSERT commands in the main Edit menu on the DOS/Windows version.
Provided by the Prepare to Merge and Show Field commands in the main Edit menu on the Macintosh version.

Works Tutorial

Because of the size of the program, Microsoft Works is usually loaded onto and executed from a hard disk. This tutorial assumes that Works is loaded on your hard disk. If you are using a network or floppy disks, please refer to the user manuals for the appropriate program loading instructions.

After turning on the machine, if you are using the DOS operating system, set the date and time. Most hard disk–based DOS systems will respond with the "C:\>" prompt to indicate that they are ready to accept commands. To execute Microsoft Works, change the directory with

C:\>CD WORKS

and then

C:\WORKS>WORKS

If you are using the Windows operating system, after turning on the machine, select the Works icon in the opening Windows Program Manager.

Microsoft Works supports both pull-down menus as well as keyboard commands. Throughout these exercises, pull-down menus will be provided followed by the corresponding keyboard command in parentheses such as (ALT H) or (W). Users may choose either method for entering instructions.

The Microsoft Works Opening Screen menu (Figure B–1) will appear on your video display screen. Pull down the Help menu (ALT H) and select the Works Tutorial (W). Once in the Works Tutorial, type in your name and follow the instructions. The Works Tutorial is an especially well-written introduction to this package. Before continuing with this workshop, complete all components of the tutorial.

Spreadsheets

After completing the tutorial, return to the Opening Screen menu (Figure B–1), pull down the File menu (ALT F), and select "Create New File" (N). Works will respond with a menu requesting you to select the type of file you wish to create; select "Spreadsheet" (S). A blank spreadsheet (Figure B–2) will appear on the screen. From the tutorial, you should be familiar with the basic concept of a spreadsheet as being a grid of cells that are referenced by letters to represent rows and numbers to represent columns. For instance, the upper left-most cell is referred to as A1. The cell to the right of

Figure B–1
Opening File Menu of Microsoft Works

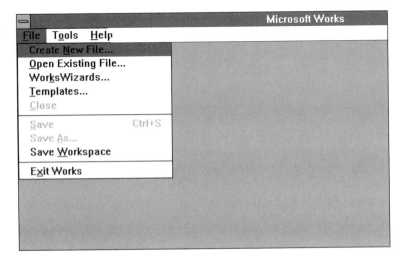

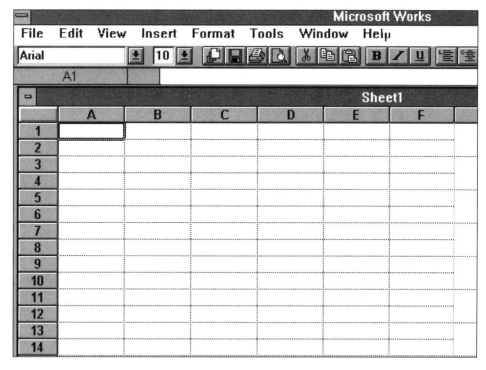

Figure B–2
Blank Microsoft Works Spreadsheet

A1 is B1 and the next is C1. The cell immediately beneath A1 is A2 followed by A3. To enter data, the cell pointer or spreadsheet cursor must be positioned at that cell. The cell pointer always highlights its current position. To develop a spreadsheet, you must have a basic understanding of the cell concept and spreadsheet layout. If familiar with these, continue with this workshop. If not, practice entering data into various cells until you are comfortable with the procedure.

The first object of this exercise is to create a budget spreadsheet as illustrated in Figure B–3 to compare two fiscal years. To begin entering data for this spreadsheet:

Position the cell pointer to B1.
Type NORTH.

Arrow right to C1.
Type CENTRAL.
Arrow right to D1.
Type SCHOOL.

Continue entering the remaining entries for E1 and F1. After each cell entry, either arrow to the right or press the ENTER key to continue. To center nonnumeric data in a cell, use the spacebar.
Next:

Type PROPOSED in C2; BUDGET in D2; and "1997–98 in E2.

Using a quotation marks before a number such as "1997–98 indicates that the entry to follow will be treated as a label and not as a numeric value. From the tutorial, you will recall that cell

	A	B	C	D	E	F	G
1							
2			NORTH CENTRAL SCHOOL DISTRICT NO. 1				
3			Proposed Budget 1997–98				
4							
5							Approved vs
6				1996–97	1996–97	1997–98	Proposed
7	Code	Category		Estimated Expend. ($)	Approved Budget ($)	Proposed Budget ($)	Budget Change ($)
8							
9	1000	General Support		1,993,500	2,111,500	2,063,500	(48,000)
10	2000	Instruction		19,131,000	19,489,000	20,334,500	845,500
11	3000	Transportation		1,757,000	1,733,000	1,985,000	252,000
12	4000	Plant Operations		2,638,000	2,785,500	2,795,000	9,500
13	5000	Employee Benefits		3,650,000	3,720,000	4,356,000	636,000
14	6000	Community Service		1,543,000	1,613,000	1,569,000	(44,000)
15	8000	Interfund Transfer		100,000	100,000	100,000	0
16	9000	Debt Service		3,849,750	3,849,750	3,751,750	(98,000)
17							
18		Totals		34,662,250	35,401,750	36,954,750	1,553,000

Figure B–3
Sample Spreadsheet

entries can be numeric values, labels, or formulas. These are distinguished based on the first character of the cell entry as follows:

Digits 0 through 9 indicate a numeric value.
Letters of the alphabet or quote marks (") indicate labels.
An equal sign (=) indicates a formula.

Numeric values are numbers that can be added, subtracted, multiplied, or have other arithmetic operations performed on them. Labels are simply headings used for descriptive purposes. Formulas are used to derive data from other cell entries such as adding a row of entries to get a

summary total. Continue entering the remaining labels through cell G7.

In designing a spreadsheet, you may need to format the size of columns to accommodate the number of characters that the cell entries will require. Microsoft Works defaults to a column size of 10 characters unless changed. Position the cell pointer anywhere in the A column, pull down the Format menu (ALT T), and select the Column Width (W) option. A dialogue box will appear. Change the column width from 10 to five characters (four characters for the CODE fields and one character as a column separator). The length of column A has been reduced to half (five characters) of its previous size. Following the same procedure, change the lengths of the other columns as follows:

Column B: 16 characters
Column C: 8 characters
Column D: 11 characters
Column E: 11 characters
Column F: 11 characters
Column G: 12 characters

Enter the data for all the remaining label cells (A1 through A15 and B8 through B17).

Begin to enter the actual budget information by entering the digits 1933500 into cell D8 (keep the cell pointer at D8). When entering data for numeric values, you do not have to enter commas or decimal places because the Works program can do this automatically. Pull down the Format menu (ALT T) and select Commas (C). When the dialogue box appears, set decimal places to 0, since the amounts in this exercise are whole dollars with no cents, and respond <OK>. Commas will appear as follows: 1,933,500. Enter the values without commas for cells D9 through D15, E8 : E15, and F8 : F15. In Microsoft Works the colon (:) between two cells means "through" so that E8 : E15 translates into cell E8 through cell E15.

To have Works set the commas and decimal places for these columns, you could follow the same procedure as in cell D8 earlier. To save time, however, the cell pointer may be pointed to the entire group of cells at one time. To do this, position the cell pointer to D8 and holding the SHIFT key, arrow across or drag the mouse across to F8 and then down to F15. All cells from D8 : F15 should be highlighted. Now pull down the Format menu (ALT T) and select Commas (C). As you did earlier, change the decimal places to 0 and respond <OK>, and all the entries in these cells will have commas placed in the proper places.

The only data missing from your spreadsheet should now be cells G8 : G15 and D17 : G17. Although entering the actual numeric values is possible, it would be more appropriate to enter

formulas so that this data can be derived from the other cells. For instance, cell G8 can be derived by subtracting cell E8 from F8. To do so, position the cell pointer to G8, and enter =F8-E8. The entry in cell G8 should now be (48,000). A number in parentheses indicates a negative value. Practice entering formulas in G9 and G10. To save time in entering the remaining formulas, a *copy* of the contents of a cell can be applied to a group of cells as follows:

Position the cell pointer to G8, which becomes the source cell for the COPY command.
Hold the SHIFT key and arrow down to G15, highlighting all the cells in between.
Pull down the Edit menu (ALT E) and select Fill Down (W).

All the cells from G9 : G15 should now have formulas replicated or copied from G8 with their relative cell positions substituted: G9 should be =F9-E9, G10 should be =F10-E10, and so forth.

Try entering the formula for cell D17 and then copying it to E17 : G17. To simplify the addition of the cells, use the arithmetic function "SUM" as follows: =SUM(D8:D15). This is the same as =D8+D9+D10+D11+D12+D13+D14+D15.

Your spreadsheet should now be complete. Check the totals to verify that all the entries you made are correct. At this point, it would be wise to save the spreadsheet by pulling down the File menu (ALT F), selecting the Save As (A) option, and giving the spreadsheet a file name (i.e., BUDGET97.WKS).

If this were an actual application, you would have created a spreadsheet that could be changed at will to answer the popular "what if" questions. Try changing some of the entries to see the impact on the remainder of the spreadsheet. If you wish to save any of these changes, save them under another file name.

Keep practicing until you feel comfortable with this budget spreadsheet. To exit the spreadsheet, pull down the File menu (ALT F) and select Exit Works (X).

Charts

Administrators use charts and diagrams to convey ideas and information, in addition to text and numbers. The use of spreadsheet data for developing bar graphs and pie charts is very popular. Microsoft Works provides an excellent facility for developing charts from spreadsheet data.

To do this, execute the Microsoft Works program as described in the Works Tutorial section. Pull down the File menu (ALT F), and select Open Existing File (O). Works will provide you with a list or directory of available files. Arrow down to the Spreadsheet File named "BUDGET97.WKS," which is the name you gave to the original spreadsheet file, and select it, or type BUDGET97.WKS in the File area at the top of the dialogue box. Either of these two methods will open the spreadsheet file BUDGET97.WKS. The North Central School District No. 1 budget spreadsheet should appear on the screen. Position the cell pointer to E8 and holding the SHIFT key, move it to E15, which should highlight the cells E8 : E15. Pull down the Charts menu (ALT C) and select New Chart (N). A bar graph illustrating the 1996-97 Approved Budget should appear. This chart can be printed, or you can refer to it again as you make refinements to the spreadsheet. To return to the spreadsheet display, open the File menu (Alt F) and Close (C) the Chart 1 file.

The objective of the following exercise is to expand the bar graph to compare the budgets of the two fiscal years 1996–97 and 1997–98. Your final product will look like Figure B–4.

Position the cell pointer to E8 and highlight
E8 : F15.
Pull down the Chart menu (ALT C) and select
Create New Chart (N).

A new barchart, Chart2, will be displayed. Microsoft Works automatically gives each chart a name starting with Chart1, Chart2, Chart3, and so on.

Pull down the Edit menu (ALT E) and select Titles (T) and enter the following into the dialogue box:

Chart Title	Budget Comparison
Subtitle	1996-97/1997-98
X-Axis	Budget Categories
Y-Axis	Dollars $

Respond <OK>. The title, subtitle, X-Axis and Y-Axis descriptions should appear on the chart.

To provide a legend for the two sets of bars:

Pull down the Edit menu (ALT E) and select
Legends (L).
For the 1st Value, type in the Legend area
96–97.
For the 2nd Value, type in 97–98, and
Respond <OK>.

The legends should appear at the bottom of the chart.

To add category headings:

Pull down the Edit menu (ALT E), and select
Data Labels (D).
Enter B8:B15 in the 1st Value Series box.
Respond <OK>.

The category labels should appear at the top of each of the bars. Notice that the labels are too long and are running into each other. The best way to handle this would be to review the existing category labels and abbreviate them, such as

"G.S." for General Support
"Trans" for Transportation
"Plant" for Plant Maintenance
"Benefits" for Employee Benefits
"Community" for Community Service
"I.T." for Interfund Transfers
"Debt" for Debt Service

To do this, return to the spreadsheet and enter the abbreviated labels in cells B8 : B15 as follows:

Figure B–4
Sample Bar Graph

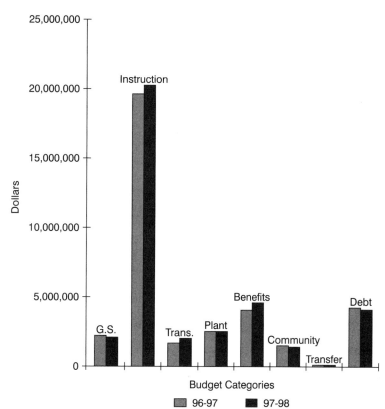

Budget Comparison
1996-97/1997-98

Open the File menu (Alt F) and Close (C) the Chart2 file.

Enter the abbreviated category labels.

Pull down the Chart menu (Alt C) and Open (2) the Chart2 file.

Chart2 should appear with the abbreviated category labels.

To improve the display of the chart, the Format menu provides options for doing things like changing color, adding patterns rather than using solid colors, and changing font styles or sizes. Adjusting fonts and patterns are very important options, particularly if you wish to print the chart with a standard, noncolor printer. The Options menu also provides several style features such as showing a border. It is best to "tinker" or practice with these various features to determine how they might be used in a chart. When the chart looks the way you want it to, open the File menu (Alt F) and select the print option (P). Previewing your work before printing is always recommended. Microsoft Works provides a preview option on all print operations.

Having succeeded with this exercise, good practice would be to create your own spreadsheets with your own data. Suggested applications include budgeting, financial or population projections, student demographics, student performance patterns (grades, standardized test scores, etc.), faculty and staff salaries, and other staff characteristics. Also try different types of charts such as line and pie charts and stacked bar graphs to display the data.

Merging Word Processing and Databases

In the preceding exercise, spreadsheet data were merged with a graphics tool to produce a chart. In the following exercise, we will look at one of the most common of all integrated applications, the merging of text (a letter) with database information (address data). Before beginning this exercise, review the Works Tutorials for word processing and databases.

To merge a letter with the addresses from a database, the following steps must be followed:

Create or access an existing database file that contains the names and addresses of the individuals.

Create or access a Word Processor document containing the text or body of the letter.

Put field inserts or placeholders in the Word Processor document to indicate where you want the names, addresses, and any other database fields to appear.

Print the Word Processor file using the Print Form Letter command.

If you have a database file with names and addresses, you can use it for the following exercise; otherwise, you can create a database file with the data in Figure B–5 by performing the following steps:

Open Works if it is not already open.
Open the File menu (ALT F).
Select New Database (N).

If successful, a blank screen should appear with the database manager menus available above.

Before you enter the actual data in each database record, data fields must be created for each data element (Last Name, First Name, Street, etc.). This is also referred to as developing a database structure. To create a data field, the name of the field is typed followed by a colon (:).

Type "Last Name:" and ENTER. A dialogue box should appear establishing a field width of twenty characters. Respond <OK>. You have just created a data field named "Last Name" that can contain a maximum of twenty characters.

Type "First Name:" and ENTER. Respond <OK> to the field width.

Type "Street:" and ENTER. Respond <OK> to the field width.

Type "City:" and ENTER. Change the field width to 15 characters.

Type "State:" and ENTER. Change the field width to two characters.

Type "Zip Code:" and ENTER. Change the field width to five characters.

Last Name	First Name	Street Address	City	State	ZIP Code
Henson	Sandra	122 Pacific Hwy.	San Diego	CA	92101
Garrison	Linda	34 10th Ave.	San Diego	CA	92101
Brown	Louise	16 Euclid Ave.	San Diego	CA	92102
Gonzalez	George	169 Fairmount Rd.	San Diego	CA	92105
Young	Lenore	67 47th St.	San Diego	CA	92105
Sinclair	Elaine	55 Washington Ave.	San Diego	CA	92103

Figure B–5
Sample Names and Addresses of Staff

You have completed creating all the data fields needed for an address file, and you can now start entering actual data for each record by using the list in Figure B–5 or, better yet, making up your own address list.

Before entering data into the fields, practice moving up and down the fields using the arrow keys and the TAB keys. Arrow keys are used to place the cursor at individual character positions. The TAB key is used to place the cursor at a data field. The regular TAB key moves the cursor forward. Holding down the shift key while pressing the TAB key moves the cursor backward. To enter data for the first record:

Use the arrow keys to position the cursor to the right of the Last Name field just past the colon (:).
Type "Henson" and press the TAB key.
Type "Sandra" and press the TAB key.
Type "122 Pacific Hwy." and press the TAB key.
Type "San Diego" and press the TAB key.
Type "CA" and press the TAB key.
Type "92101" and press the TAB key.

You have completed entering all the data for the first record, and the cursor is positioned to enter the data for the second record.

Type "Garrison" and press the TAB key.
Type "Louise" and press the TAB key.
Type "34 10th Ave." and press the TAB key.
Type "San Diego" and press the TAB key.
Type "CA" and press the TAB key.
Type "92101" and press the TAB key.

You have now completed entering the data for the second record. As practice, enter the data for the remaining four records on the list or use your own list following the exact same procedures.

After entering all the data for the six records, save the database file by opening the File menu (ALT F) and selecting Save As (A). In the dialogue box, give this file the name "STAFF01.WDB."

To create the word-processing document (letter) that will serve as the text to be merged with the database records, open the File menu (ALT F) and select New File (N). Select Word Processing File (W) in the dialogue box that appears. A blank word-processing screen will appear. Enter the text of the letter that appears in Figure B–6. Leave four blank lines between the date and salutation *Dear*.

After completing this letter, you should have two files open on the screen, the WORD1.WPS word-processing file in the foreground and the STAFF01.WDB database file in the background. You are now ready to merge the names and addresses with the letter to the staff. To merge the database fields with the letter:

Position the cursor to the left-most character position (above the *D* in *Dear*) on the line immediately below the date.
Open the Insert menu (ALT I) and select Insert Database Field (F).

In the dialogue box that appears, STAFF01.WDB should be available.

Press ENTER and all the available fields should appear to the right of the STAFF01.WDB.
Arrow over and select First Name.
Respond <OK>.

If successful, the field name "First Name" should appear on the letter as follows:

<<First Name>>

The << . . . >> are placeholders that identify the text positions in the letter where the data from the First Name field will appear.

With the cursor positioned immediately after the placeholder, type a blank space that will be used to separate the First Name field from the Last Name field.

Open the Insert menu (ALT I) and select Insert Database Field (F).

NORTH CENTRAL HIGH SCHOOL

August 5, 1997

Dear

I am happy to report to you that the North Central Board
of Education has approved our request for additional
staff development funds for the new academic year. As
you will recall, North Central High School's Staff
Development Committee had recommended that these funds
be used specifically for training staff in the use of
multimedia technology.

In approximately two weeks, the chairperson of the Staff
Development Committee, Laura Speeks, will be conducting a
survey to determine specific preferences of the staff for
schedules, dates, formats, and so forth. Please consider
these carefully so that we can be assured that the staff
development activities best meet all of our needs.

In closing, I am sure you join me in thanking the board
for approving our request. I look forward to participating with you in our staff development activities.

Sincerely,

Jane Kendall
Principal

Figure B–6
Text of Letter

In the dialogue box that appears, arrow over and select the Last Name field. Insert fields with the Street, City, State, and Zip Code fields. Make sure to put a comma between the City and State fields.

After completing the address, do the following:

Position the cursor two spaces beyond the salutation *Dear.*
Open the Insert menu (ALT I) and select Insert Database Field (F).
Arrow over and select the First Name field.
After the placeholders, type a colon (:).

You are now ready to print your merged letter and database. To print the letters for all the records in the database:

Open the File menu (ALT F) and select Print Form Letters (F).

In the dialogue box that appears, STAFF01.WDB should be available. Respond <Print>.

In the next dialogue box that appears:

Respond Print (P) to the Number of Copies = 1.

Individualized letters (see Figure B–7) should begin printing on the printer.

To save the letter with the placeholders for future use:

Open the File menu (ALT F) and select Save As (A).

In the dialogue box, give the file the name STAFF01.WPS.

To close the files:

Open the File menu (ALT F) and select Close (C).

If successful, the word-processing file (STAFF01.WPS) will close and be removed from the screen.

Open the File menu (ALT F) again, and select Close (C).

The database file (STAFF01.WDB) will close and be removed from the screen.

To exit WORKS:

Open the File menu (ALT F) and select Exit Works (X).

You will be returned to the DOS command prompt or to the Windows Program Manager.

Merging text and database information, especially for form letters, is a very common application. The possibilities existing in a school system are almost endless: correspondence to students, parents, faculty; memoranda to staff; meeting and agenda notices; newsletters; and so forth. A senior administrator might not perform the actual text, database, and merge operations, but someone on the staff should be familiar with these software procedures and be using them routinely.

Summary

The exercises here are but an introduction to some of the facilities available with an integrated software package. Much more can be done, and comprehensive manuals and books are available describing more in-depth activity. Most importantly, remember that learning to use computer software is a skill that develops as one *uses* it. Read whatever written material you feel comfortable with, but to learn to use software, you must work with it.

NORTH CENTRAL HIGH SCHOOL

August 5, 1997

Elaine Sinclair
55 Washington Ave.
San Diego, CA 92013

Dear Elaine:

I am happy to report to you that the North Central Board
of Education has approved our request for additional
staff development funds for the new academic year. As
you will recall, North Central High School's Staff
Development Committee had recommended that these funds
be used specifically for training staff in the use of
multimedia technology.

In approximately two weeks, the chairperson of the Staff
Development Committee, Laura Speeks, will be conducting a
survey to determine specific preferences of the staff for
schedules, dates, formats, and so forth. Please consider
these carefully so that we can be assured that the staff
development activities best meet all of our needs.

In closing, I am sure you join me in thanking the board
for approving our request. I look forward to participating with you in our staff development activities.

Sincerely,

Jane Kendall
Principal

Figure B–7
Sample Merged Letter

References

Beaver, J. F. (1992a). *Microsoft Works for educators on the IBM PC and compatibles*. Pacific Grove, CA: Brooks/Cole.

Beaver, J. F. (1992b). *Microsoft Works for educators on the Macintosh*. Pacific Grove, CA: Brooks/Cole.

Mansfield, R. (1989). *Using Microsoft Works—Macintosh version*. Carmel, IN: Que Corporation.

Microsoft Works reference for IBM personal computers. (1989). Redmond, WA: Microsoft.

Woodcock, J. (1992). *Concise guide to Works for Windows*. Redmond, WA: Microsoft.

Instructional Software Evaluation Factors

General

- Program is useful in a school setting.
- Program avoids controversial teaching methodologies.
- Program allows completion of lesson in one class period.
- Instruction is integrated with previous student experience.
- Program is likely to save time when compared with other means of presentation.
- An on-disk tutorial for the program's command structure is provided.

Content

- Content is appropriate for intended student population.
- Content is accurate.
- Content is current.
- Content breadth is reasonable.
- The processes and information learned are useful in domains other than the subject area of the program.
- Content is free of any bias or stereotyping.
- Content supports the school curriculum.
- Content is relevant to the subject field.
- Definitions are provided when necessary.
- There is continuity between the information presented and prerequisite skills required.
- Content avoids taking a side on controversial moral or social issues.

- There is a need for better than the standard treatment of this topic in the curriculum.

Appropriateness

- Application is well suited to computer use.
- Pedagogic approach is superior to what is available elsewhere.
- Readability level is appropriate for the intended student population.
- Tone of address is appropriate for the intended student population.
- Means of response is appropriate for the intended student population.
- Prerequisite skills required are appropriate for the intended population.
- Time required for use by a typical student does not exceed the attention span of that student.
- Multiple levels of instruction are available.
- Difficulty levels are based on discernible logic.
- Sufficient exposure and practice are provided to master skills.
- Sufficient information is presented for intended learning to occur.

Questioning Techniques

- Questions are appropriate to the content and effectively measure student mastery of the content.
- Questions incorrectly answered can be repeated later in the lesson/exercise.

- Number of trials is reasonable and appropriate.
- Calculation can be accomplished easily on-screen when appropriate.

Approach/Motivation

- Approach is appropriate for the intended student population.
- Format is varied.
- Overall tenor of interaction is helpful.
- Student is an active participant in the learning process.

Evaluator's Field Test Results

- Student understands on-screen presentation and is not confused.
- Student enjoys using the program.
- Student retains a positive attitude about using the program.
- Student maintains the desire to use the program again.
- Student has the desire to pursue the topic in other ways.
- Program involves students in competition in a positive way.
- Program fosters cooperation among students.

Creativity

- Program challenges and stimulates creativity.
- Pedagogy is innovative.
- Program allows the student as many decisions as possible.
- Program provides opportunities to answer open-ended questions and supplies evaluative criteria to assess responses.
- Program demonstrates a creative way of using knowledge.
- Program challenges the student to change an underlying model or design an alternative model.

Learner Control

- Learner can alter program sequence and pace.
- Learner can review instructions and previous frames.

- Learner can end activity any time and return to main menu.
- Learner can enter program at different points.
- Learner can stop in the middle of an activity and at a later session begin at that stopping point with the previous record of progress intact.
- Help is available at likely points of need.

Learning Objectives, Goals, and Outcomes

- Learner objectives are stated, and purpose is well defined.
- Steps taken to make learning generalizable to other situations.
- For programs requiring use over several days, learning outcomes are worth the time invested.

Feedback

- Feedback is positive.
- Feedback is appropriate to the intended student population.
- Feedback does not threaten or reward incorrect responses.
- Feedback is relevant to student responses.
- Feedback is timely.
- Feedback is informative.
- Feedback is corrective when appropriate.
- Feedback remedies and/or explains when appropriate.
- Feedback employs a variety of responses and avoids being boring.
- Feedback remains on the screen for the appropriate amount of time.
- Branching is used effectively to remediate.
- Program uses branching to adjust automatically difficulty levels or sequence according to student performance.

Simulations

- Simulation model is valid and neither too complex nor too simple for intended student population.

- Variables used in the simulation are the most relevant.
- Assumptions are adequately identified.
- Program simulates activities that can be too difficult to demonstrate in reality.
- Time needed to complete both a step and the entire simulation is reasonable and effective.
- Program encourages decision making or calculation rather than guessing.

Teacher Modifiability

- Teacher can easily change or add content.
- Teacher can easily regulate parameters for each class.
- Teacher can easily regulate parameters for each student.
- Parameter setups can be bypassed.

Evaluation and Record Keeping

- Program provides an adequate means of evaluating mastery of the content.
- If tests are included, criteria for success are appropriate for the ability/skills of the intended student population.
- If tests are included, content accurately reflects the material presented.
- Score keeping and performance reports are provided when appropriate.
- Useful information about student performance is stored for future retrieval.
- Useful diagnostic pretest or placement test is provided, where appropriate.
- Useful diagnostic or prescriptive analysis of student performance is available to the teacher, when appropriate.
- Student performance information is easily accessible to the teacher.
- Management system includes adequate security.
- Program allows printout and screen display of student records.
- Program can hold multiple performance records of a single class.

- Program can hold multiple performance records of several classes.

Documentation and Support Material

- Quality of packaging is durable and appropriate for student use.
- Student, parent, or teacher guides and materials are clearly identified.
- Technical and operational explanations for implementation are clear and complete.
- If appropriate, "quick start-up" section is included.
- Useful reproducible student worksheets are provided.
- Other valuable support materials are supplied.
- Sample screen-by-screen printouts of the program are provided.
- Teacher support materials can be separated from student materials.
- Useful suggestions are offered for introductory classroom activities.
- Useful suggestions are provided for classroom activities during the use of the program, where necessary or helpful.
- Useful suggestions are given for classroom logistics in a variety of hardware situations and student groupings.
- Useful suggestions are provided on how to integrate program with the regular curriculum.
- If the program is open-ended, subject-specific suggestions are included.
- Clear explanations of the differences between the various difficulty levels are provided.
- Prerequisite skills are clearly stated.
- Accurate and clear descriptions of content topics are made.
- Accurate and clear descriptions of instructional activities are given.
- Where appropriate, how material correlates to standard textbook series is described.
- Necessary information can be found quickly and easily.

- Quick reference card for program use is included, where appropriate.
- Printed text is clear and readable.
- Printed graphics are clear and readable.
- Printed text is free of errors in spelling, grammar, punctuation, and usage.

Technical Quality

- Audio can be adjusted.
- Audio is clear and used effectively.
- Character sets used in text display are clear, appropriate, and visually interesting.
- Graphics are acceptable on a monochrome monitor.
- Graphics are clear and easily interpreted.
- Program is "crash-proof."
- Program runs without undue delays.
- Program runs consistently under all normal conditions.
- Transitions between screen displays are effective.
- Program guards against multiple key presses advancing the student past the next screen.
- Program avoids unnecessary or inappropriate moving back and forth between screens.
- Special features (i.e., flash, scrolling, split screen) are used effectively.
- Program requires a minimal amount of typing.
- Random generation is used when appropriate.
- Program judges responses accurately and accounts for minor variations in input format.
- Program allows user to correct answer before being accepted by the program.
- Program is capable of accepting partial answers when appropriate.
- Where students must input responses, inappropriate keys are disabled.
- Control keys are used consistently.
- Students require a minimum amount of teacher supervision while using the program.
- Computer operation does not interfere with concentration on activity.
- Program makes effective use of peripheral devices.

- Program considers a previously unexplored potential of the computer.
- Program uses other technologies (i.e., audio, video) to enhance learning.
- Printing is easy to accomplish.
- Procedural and instructional statements are clear.
- On-screen prompts clearly indicate where the user should focus attention.
- Frame formatting is clear, uncluttered, and consistent from screen to screen.
- Presentation of each discrete content topic is logical.
- Sequence of content topics and instruction is logical.
- Sequence of menu items is logical.
- Prompts and cues are clear and consistently and logically applied.
- Hints are clear and not misleading.
- Demonstrations and examples are clear and available when appropriate.
- Interface is simple enough to be used with little or no reading of the documentation.
- Program makes clear where the user is in the program.
- User-computer communication is consistent and logical.
- Prompts to save work are given when appropriate.

Start-up and Implementation

- Software code modifications or unusual manipulations of disks are not required.
- Start-up time for teacher implementation is not excessive.
- Teacher needs a minimum of computer competencies to operate program.
- Start-up time for student implementation is brief enough to permit completion of a lesson.
- Students need a minimum of computer competencies to operate the program.

Graphics and Audio

- Graphics and audio are used to motivate.

- Graphics and audio are appropriate for the intended student population.
- Graphics, audio, and color enhance the instructional process.
- Graphics help focus attention to appropriate content without being distracting.

Probeware and Peripherals Included in the Software Package

- Probes or peripherals are durable.
- Probes or peripherals are sensitive.
- Audio and/or graphic quality are effective.
- Probes or peripherals are easy to install.
- Calibration is accurate and easy.
- Data displays are flexible.
- Data analysis is useful.

Hardware and Marketing Issues

- Potential usefulness of the program justifies its price.
- Peripherals that are difficult to acquire or inappropriately expensive are not required.
- Producer field test data are available.
- Field test data indicate that students learned more or better as a result of using the program.
- Preview copies are available.
- Backup copies are provided.
- Adequate warranty is provided.
- Telephone support is available.
- If allowable, multiple loading is possible.
- Site license is available.
- Network versions are available.
- Multiple-copies discount is available.

Glossary

Access time The time required to fetch data from a source once a request has been made. It is most commonly used to refer to accessing data from a primary or secondary storage device.

Advanced Research Projects Administration Network (ARPANET) A worldwide data communications network established by the U.S. Department of Defense in the 1960s that evolved into the Internet.

ALU See **Arithmetic-logic unit.**

Analog A general term used to refer to any continuous physical property such as voltage, current, fluid pressure, rotation, and so on.

Application software Programs that "apply" the computer to perform specific tasks or solve specific problems. Examples include word-processing, electronic spreadsheets, and graphics programs.

Arithmetic-logic unit (ALU) The part of the central processing unit that performs all arithmetic operations, including comparisons.

ARPANET See **Advanced Research Projects Administration Network.**

ASCII An acronym for American Standard Code for Information Interchange. It is a coding scheme that represents letters of the alphabet, numerals, and special characters as a series of binary digits or numbers.

Audio response unit Any device that produces a spoken word from a computer in response to a question or command.

Authoring language A user-friendly programming language used to develop specific applications such as teaching presentations, computer-assisted instruction, and multimedia. Examples include HyperCard, LinkWay, ToolBook, and Authorware.

Authoring system See **Authoring language.**

Bandwidth In communications, the frequencies within which signals can be transmitted and received. Bandwidth directly relates to data transfer speed. The greater the bandwidth, the faster the data transmission speed.

BASIC An acronym for Beginners All-Purpose Symbolic Instruction Code. It is a high-level computer programming language developed by John Kemeny and Thomas Kurtz at Dartmouth University in the 1960s. Because of its general availability on most microcomputers, BASIC has become the most popular high-level language ever developed.

Benchmark A test used to measure the performance (i.e., speed or accuracy) of computer hardware or software.

Binary digit In the binary number system, the binary digit is either 0 or 1. See also **bit.**

Bit A binary digit. In the binary number system, the bit is either 0 or 1. In electronic storage, it represents the smallest unit of data and is characterized as being either "on" or "off." Groups of eight bits are combined to represent characters of data that are referred to as *bytes.*

Browser software (Web browser) Software that provides facilities for accessing Uniform Resource Locators (URLs) on the World Wide Web. Examples of Web browsers include Netscape and Mosaic.

Bug An error or problem in software or hardware.

Byte The minimum amount of primary storage or memory needed to store a character (letter, numeral, special character, etc.) of information. It usually is eight binary digits or bits.

C A programming language developed at Bell Laboratories in 1972. Designed originally to work with the UNIX operating system, it has become widely popular on many microcomputers.

CAI   See **Computer-assisted instruction.**

CAL   Acronym for computer-assisted learning or computer-augmented learning. See **Computer-assisted instruction.**

Cathode-ray tube (CRT)   The most common type of video display screen. It uses an electron gun to generate a light beam that is scanned across a screen.

CBE   See **Computer-based education.**

CBT   See **Computer-based teaching.**

CD-ROM   An acronym for compact disc–read only memory. It is a form of high-capacity optical storage that uses laser technology.

Central file server   The central or host computer in a network that provides files and programs to other computers.

Central processing unit (CPU)   The part of a computer hardware system that directs all processing activities. It consists of electronic circuitry and includes a control unit, an arithmetic-logic unit, and a primary storage or memory unit. On large computers, the term is used to refer to the entire main computer console. On some microcomputers, it refers only to the control unit and the arithmetic-logic unit.

Character   A letter, numeral, or special character such as a comma or exclamation point that can be represented by one byte.

Client server system   A distributed data communications system in which computers perform two important functions either as "clients" or "servers." The "client" function makes requests for data (i.e., files) from the "server," which locates the data on the data communications system and processes the request for the client.

Clip media   Digital files or libraries containing images, video, sounds, and other media that can readily be incorporated into a multimedia program.

CMI   See **Computer-managed instruction.**

COBOL   An acronym for Common Business-Oriented Language. It is a high-level programming language developed in 1959 that uses English-like commands. It became popular for business applications.

Communications control program   See **Communications controller.**

Communications controller   A data communications device that is used to send and receive messages from multiple sources. A multiplexor is an example of a communications controller. In some networks, communications controlling is performed by computer programs that also are referred to as communications controllers.

Computer   An electronic device that accepts input, processes it according to a set of instructions, and produces the results as output. Computers can be classified as supercomputers, mainframes, minicomputers, microcomputers, laptop computers, and so forth, depending on physical size, speed, and peripheral devices.

Computer-assisted instruction (CAI)   The use of the computer to assist in the instructional process. One of the earliest used terms to refer generically to computer applications in education, it is used now to refer to tutor-type applications such as drill and practice and tutorials.

Computer-assisted learning   See **Computer-assisted instruction.**

Computer-augmented learning   See **Computer-assisted instruction.**

Computer-based education (CBE)   A generic term used to refer to the broad array of instructional computer applications.

Computer-based teaching (CBT)   A generic term used to refer to the use of a computer by teachers as part of an instructional presentation such as an interactive video.

Computer chip   See **Integrated circuit.**

Computer hack   See **Hacker.**

Computer-managed instruction (CMI)   The use of the computer in an instructional process in which student progress is monitored and recorded for subsequent instructions and review. Most CMI applications also are able to adjust material to each individual student's level of understanding.

Computer program   A set of instructions to direct physical devices to perform some task.

Control unit (CU)   The part of the central processing unit that interprets instructions and directs the processing of the other physical devices.

CPU   See **Central processing unit.**

CU   See **Control unit.**

Cyberspace   Descriptive term for the Internet.

Daisy-wheel printer   An impact printer that uses a daisy-wheel-type element to strike a character through an inked ribbon onto a sheet of paper.

DASD   See **Direct access storage device.**

Data communications   The methods and media used to transfer data from one computer device to another. Common data communications media include coaxial cable, telephone, fiber optics, and satellite systems.

Data element   A grouping of characters (letter of the alphabet, numerals, special characters) to represent some specific data characteristic of a person, place, or thing. Examples include a person's name, street address, and gender. Also referred to as a *data field* or *data item*.

Data element dictionary   A table used to identify the content and coding schemes used for all the data elements in a database. The term *data element dictionary* is also used for a document that identifies the content, definitions, and coding schemes used for all data elements in a database.

Data field   See **Data element.**

Data file   A collection of related data records. Examples include a personnel file of all personnel records or a student file of all student records.

Data item   See **Data element.**

Data processing   A general term used for the systematic processing (storing, manipulating, sorting, etc.) of data on computer systems.

Data record   A grouping of related data elements for a single entity such as a person, place, or thing. Examples include a personnel record, inventory record, and financial record.

Data structure   The method by which data is organized in a database.

Database   A collection of data files and records.

Database management system (DBMS)   A package of computer programs that allows users to create, maintain, and access the data on a database.

DBMS   See **Database management system.**

Desktop publishing   The use of computer equipment to develop text and graphics. It usually refers to software that provides enhanced facilities for displaying characters, pictures, and color.

Digital   Related to digits. Computers are considered digital because all data and instructions are represented as binary digits.

Digitizer   Any device used to convert analog (continuous physical property such as voltage or current) signals into binary or digital format.

Direct access storage device (DASD)   Any secondary storage device such as a magnetic disk or optical disc that allows users to access data in a direct or nonsequential manner.

Directory   A grouping or catalog of file names that reside on a secondary storage device such as a disk. On Macintosh microcomputers, a directory is referred to as a *folder*.

Disk operating system   A generic term used to refer to any operating system that resides on a disk device and is loaded as needed into primary storage.

Disk Operating System   See **DOS.**

Distributed system   A form of computer processing that distributes and links hardware over some geographic area as in a network. It assumes that the local hardware can perform some tasks as well as expand its capabilities by connecting to other hardware.

DOS   An acronym for Disk Operating System, the most popular operating system for Intel-based (i.e., IBM PC and PC-compatible microcomputers). It is also referred to as *Microsoft* or *MS-DOS* after the company that developed it.

Dot-matrix printer   An impact printer that forms text and images as a pattern of dots.

Downlink   The transmission of data from a communications satellite to an earth station.

Download   In a computer network, the process of transferring a copy of a file from one computer, generally referred to as a *central file server,* to another, requesting computer.

Drill and practice   A form of tutor software used to reinforce a lesson or material that has already been presented to a student. It is characterized by repetitive questioning or drills.

E-mail   See **Electronic mail.**

EBCDIC   An acronym for Extended Binary Coded Decimal Interchange Code, a coding scheme developed by IBM for use on mainframe and minicomputer systems for representing letters of the alphabet, numerals, and special characters as a series of binary digits or numbers.

Electronic mail (E-mail)   The transmission of messages over a data communications network.

Electronic spreadsheet   Application programming software that provides the user with an electronic grid of rows and columns similar to a ledger worksheet. It is used extensively for budget, forecasting, projections, and other number-based applications. Examples include Lotus 1-2-3, Excel, and SuperCalc.

EPROM   An acronym for erasable read only memory, which is a type of read only memory that can be programmed or written to.

Ergonomics   The study and design of people in work environments. The objective of ergonomics is to develop comfortable and safe conditions so as to improve worker morale and efficiency. Ergonomics is especially important in designing computer hardware such as keyboards and video display devices.

Fiber optics   A term used to describe the method of transmitting and receiving light beams along an optical fiber that is usually made of a thin strand of glass. Fiber optics are destined to change radically the speed and nature of communications throughout the world.

File transfer protocol (FTP)   A popular protocol used for transferring data files on the World Wide Web.

Floppy disk   See **Magnetic disk.**

Folder   A grouping or cataloging of file names that reside on a secondary storage device such as a disk. The term is most commonly used on Macintosh microcomputers. It is similar to a directory on IBM PC and PC-compatible microcomputers.

FORTRAN   An acronym for Formula Translation, a high-level programming language developed in 1954. Although originally developed for scientific and engineering applications, it established several programming concepts such as variables, subroutines, input/output formats, and so forth, that continue to form the basis for many other programming languages.

Frame rate   The number of frames or images per second displayed on a video device. Thirty frames per second is the full-motion video standard.

FTP   See **File transfer trotocol.**

Gigabyte   One billion bytes.

Gopher   A database communications protocol used for locating data files on the World Wide Web.

Graphical user interface (GUI)   The graphic display of software options in the form of icons and pictures that can be selected, usually by a pointing device such as a mouse. It is considered a feature of user-friendly software such as that provided with the Macintosh operating system, Microsoft Windows, and many application software packages.

Graphics tablet   An electronic surface connected to a central processing unit. It comes with a pen, arm, or stylus to draw images that are automatically transferred to the CPU.

GUI   See **Graphical user interface.**

Hacker   A general term used to refer to someone who seems overly involved with computer hardware and software. Also used to refer to people who gain unauthorized access to computer networks and databases.

Hand-held computer   A small portable computer capable of being used (held) in one hand.

Hard disk   See **Magnetic disk.**

Hardware   The physical components of a computer system such as the central processing unit, printer, keyboard, and so on.

High-level language   A programming language that uses common words and symbols that are translated into computer machine language instructions by way of a compiler or interpreter. Examples of high-level languages include FORTRAN, BASIC, COBOL, and Pascal.

HTML   See **Hypertext markup language.**

HTTP   See **Hypertext transfer control protocol.**

HyperCard   An authoring language designed for the Apple Macintosh microcomputer. It established several important new concepts such as fields, buttons, and stacks that have been copied by other authoring languages.

Hypermedia   A computer-based information retrieval system for accessing sound, text, images, graphics, or video in a nonsequential or nonlinear format.

Hypertext   A computer-based text and document retrieval system that can be accessed in a nonsequential or nonlinear format.

Hypertext markup language (HTML)   Software language used to establish data files for access on the World Wide Web.

Hypertext transfer control protocol (HTTP) The most commonly used protocol on the World Wide Web. It runs in conjunction with TCP/IP.

ICAI   See **Intelligent computer-assisted instruction.**

Icon   A graphic image displayed on a video screen representing an object, usually a file or command that can be referenced or executed by a user. Icons are common features of user-friendly software referred to as *graphical user interfaces.*

IIS   An acronym for integrated instructional system. **See Integrated learning system.**

ILS   See **Integrated learning system.**

Information superhighway   Descriptive term for the Internet.

Ink-jet printer   A nonimpact printer that uses droplets of ink sprayed from a tiny nozzle.

Input device   Any device that is used to enter or bring data to a central processing unit.

Input/output device (I/O device)   Any device that can be used to enter data to or receive data from a central processing unit.

Integrated circuit   Combining of two or more electronic circuits (transistors, resistors, etc.) onto a thin wafer of silicon or other type of semiconductor material. A *microprocessor* is an integrated circuit that usually combines a control unit or circuit and an arithmetic-logic unit or circuit. Same as a *computer chip.*

Integrated instructional system (IIS)   See **Integrated learning system.**

Integrated learning system (ILS)   A single computer package for delivering instruction that combines hardware, software, curriculum, and management components. It is usually supplied by a single vendor.

Integrated Services Digital Network (ISDN)   A high-speed (128 kilobits per second) data communications network evolving from existing telephone services.

Integrated software package   A software package that integrates several programs into a single comprehensive program. An example is Microsoft Works, which combines word processing, spreadsheet, database, communications, and graphics.

Intelligent computer-assisted instruction (ICAI) Similar to CAI but also uses a substantial database of information for presenting material and selecting instructional paths.

Interactive   Operating in an interactive or back-and-forth mode. It refers to user and machine dialogue or interaction in which both are active participants in a process.

Interactive video   Combining computer and video technologies to provide for an active video environment in which users can control and select options based on a given application. Interactive video is a major advancement over other video technologies such as film and television, which are considered "passive."

Interface   The point at which two components meet. With computers, it is used for both hardware, when two physical devices connect to one another, and software, when two programs work with one another. It is also used to refer to points at which people connect to computer devices such as with graphical user interfaces.

Internet   The network of networks that provides the basic protocol standard for allowing data communications systems to link themselves together throughout the world.

Intranet   In data communications, the adoption of the standard Internet protocol and software tools for a local network or establishing a mini-Internet within a local system.

ISDN   See **Integrated Services Digital Network.**

Joystick   An input device popular with computer games and used to point to objects on a video screen.

Kilobyte (KB)   One thousand bytes.

Koala pad   A form of graphics tablet or electronic surface connected to a central processing unit. It comes with a pen, arm, or stylus used to draw images on the tablet that are automatically transferred to the CPU.

LAN   See **Local area network.**

Laptop   A type of portable computer that can easily be used by resting it on one's lap.

Laser printer   A nonimpact printer that uses laser technology to produce a high-quality image on a page.

Laserdisc   An optical disc used to store video images and associated audio or sound information in analog format. Same as a *videodisc*.

Light pen   An input device that allows the user to point to objects on a screen with a pen-shaped wand. It can also be used for drawing and designing shapes and figures.

Line printer   An impact printer that prints one line at a time.

Liquid crystal display (LCD)   A flat-panel video display that uses electroluminescent (liquid crystal) material to produce a light image. Very popular in watches and portable and laptop computers.

LISP   An acronym for *list processing*. It is a high-level programming language developed in 1959 and used extensively in artificial intelligence applications.

Local area network (LAN)   Connecting computer equipment using data communications over a limited geographic area such as a room, building, or campus.

Logo   A high-level programming language developed by Seymour Papert in 1968. It is a very popular programming language for teaching young children to use a computer.

Machine cycle   The time required for a central processing unit to perform its fastest operation as determined by its internal clock.

Machine language   Instructions that are represented in binary form (1s and 0s). All computer instructions must be converted or reduced to machine language instructions for the central processing unit to execute them.

Magnetic disk   A form of secondary computer storage that uses electromagnetic technology to store data. A magnetic disk can be made of metallic (hard disk) or plastic (floppy disk) substances. Because the read/write head on a magnetic disk drive can move across the surface of a disk, this technology is used for direct or random processing. A magnetic disk is the actual platter on which data reside. The device that stores and retrieves data on magnetic disk is a *disk drive*.

Magnetic disk drive   See **Magnetic disk.**

Magnetic tape   A form of secondary computer storage that uses Mylar tape to store data. Because the tape passes through a stationary read/write head, this technology is used strictly for sequential processing. Magnetic tape is the actual reel of tape on which data reside. The device that stores and retrieves data on magnetic tape is a *tape drive*.

Magnetic tape drive   See **Magnetic tape.**

Mainframe   Large computer systems capable of processing extensive amounts of data and of controlling many peripheral devices. IBM 3090 and 4300 systems are examples of mainframe computers.

Media distribution system   A computer-based system that integrates several media sources (videotape, videodisc, computer, camera, etc.) and is able to distribute them to selected output devices.

Megabyte (MB)   One million bytes.

Megaflops (MFLOP)   One million arithmetic operations per second.

Megahertz (MHz)   One million machine cycles per second.

Memory   See **Primary storage unit.**

Menu   A presentation of options available that a user can select or request from a program. Menu-driven software anticipates user options and presents them in the form of lists or icons.

Microcomputer   A small computer system that usually uses one central processing unit. Apple II, Macintosh, and IBM PC/PS are among the most popular microcomputers ever manufactured.

Microprocessor   A central processing unit used for most microcomputer systems capable of being integrated on a single chip. See **Integrated circuit.**

Microsecond   One-millionth of a second.

Millisecond   One-thousandth of a second.

Minicomputer   A midrange computer system between a large mainframe and microcomputer. Minicomputers are highly effective in network environments where they are used to control microcomputers and other minicomputers. Hewlett-Packard, Digital Equipment Corporation, and Sun Microsystems are among the leading manufacturers of minicomputers.

MIP   An acronym for million instructions per second. Similar to megaflop.

Modem   See **Modulator-demodulator.**

Modulator-demodulator (modem)   A data communications device used to convert computer digital signals into a telephone frequency or analog signal and vice versa.

Monochrome   A video monitor that displays images in one color.

Morphing   Relating to form or structure. Morphing software is designed to edit and manipulate graphics such as images and video.

Mouse   A hand-held input device that is electronically connected to a video screen. It is used to position a pointer to make software selections by pressing a button.

Multimedia   Combining sound, text, images, animation, and video. With computers, it refers to a variety of applications that utilize CD-ROM, videodisc, and audio equipment.

Multiplexor   A data communications device used to control many or multiple messages by funneling them into a smaller number of communication lines or ports.

Nanosecond   One-billionth of a second.

Network   A group of computer devices connected by a data communications system. Two major types of networks are local area networks (LANs) and wide area networks (WANs).

Notebook   A very lightweight portable computer, usually weighing less than 10 pounds, that can be easily carried under one's arm.

Office automation   The use of computer and data communications equipment to perform office functions electronically rather than manually. Examples of office automation applications include word processing, electronic mail, and desktop publishing.

Operating system   A type of system software that acts as a master control program and directs the processing of all physical devices and application programs. Examples of operating systems include DOS (Disk Operating System) and the Macintosh operating system.

Optical character reader (OCR)   See **Optical scanning device.**

Optical disc   A secondary storage device that utilizes laser technology for storing data. CD-ROM is a form of optical disc.

Optical mark reader (OMR)   See **Optical scanning device.**

Optical scanning device   An input device that uses light sensors to scan paper documents and convert images into digital format. Optical mark readers and optical character readers are types of optical scanning devices.

Output device   Any device that receives data from a central processing unit.

Pascal   A highly structured, procedural programming language developed by Nicholas Wirth in 1967. It is very popular for teaching structured programming techniques to beginning programmers.

PC   An acronym for *personal computer*. See **Personal computer.**

Peripheral   Any hardware device that connects to a central processing unit such as a printer, keyboard, magnetic disk, magnetic tape, and so on.

Personal computer   A generic term used for any microcomputer that is used essentially by one person. It is also the model name (Personal Computer or PC) that IBM adopted for its microcomputers.

Picosecond   One-trillionth of a second.

Pixel   Short for picture element. A point on a grid such as video screen that represents a single dot of light. Text and images are developed by manipulating many pixels.

PL/1   An acronym for Programming Language 1. It is a high-level programming language developed in 1964, designed to combine the best features of FORTRAN and COBOL.

Plasma display   A flat-panel video display that uses neon or argon gas to produce a light image. Also referred to as a *gas-discharge display.*

Platform   The foundation hardware and operating system software technology of a computer system. Examples include Macintosh and DOS/Windows/Intel platforms.

Plotter   An output device used to draw charts, maps, diagrams, and other line-based graphics.

Portable computer   Any computer designed to be carried and moved about. Laptop, notebook, and hand-held computers are examples of portable computers.

Primary storage unit (PSU)   The part of the central processing unit that stores instructions and data. Also referred to as *memory.*

Probeware   Hardware and software used to conduct experiments of physical properties such as temperature, light, and humidity. Probeware is characterized by the use of probes to measure physical surroundings.

PROM   An acronym for programmable read only memory, which is a type of read only memory that can be programmed or written to once.

Protocol   A general term used for a set of rules, procedures, or standards used to exchange information in data communications. Examples of these rules include a code or signal indicating the beginning of a message, a code or signal indicating the end of a message, or a code or signal indicating that a device is busy with another task. Computer manufacturers have established various protocols for exchanging information on their equipment.

PSU   See **Primary storage unit.**

Query language   A user-friendly language that enables users to retrieve and display data from a database.

RAM   An acronym for random access memory. A type of primary storage that can have data and instructions read from and written to it by a central processing unit. It is also referred to as *volatile memory* because it can keep changing.

Read/write head   The read and write or playback and record mechanism on secondary storage devices such as magnetic disk and tape drives.

Relational database   A database structure that uses a table to relate or link one data element with another data element.

Resolution   Clarity of detail available on a video monitor or printer.

Response time   The time required for an operation to be performed once a request has been made. It generally refers to software but can also refer to hardware.

ROM   An acronym for read only memory. A type of primary storage from which data and instructions can be read by a central processing unit. Because ROM is read only, data and instructions on it never can be changed.

Router   An intermediary device on a communications network that accepts and routes messages from one link (i.e., LAN) on the network to other links.

Sampling rate   The rate as measured in KiloHertz (KHz) at which sound can be recorded and played back.

Search engine   Software that provides keyword and other search facilities for locating information on the World Wide Web. Examples include Yahoo!, Lycos, and Alta Vista.

Secondary storage   Input/output devices that are used to store data and instructions other than the primary storage unit. Common examples include magnetic disk, magnetic tape, and optical disc.

Semiconductor   Any substance between a full conductor and a nonconductor of electricity. In computer electronics, silicon and germanium are the most commonly used semiconductor materials used for manufacturing microprocessors.

Simulation   A form of tutor software used to represent a real-life situation on a computer.

Software   Computer programs and instructions that direct the physical components (hardware) of a computer system to perform tasks.

Sound board   A CPU component capable of generating and synthesizing sound.

Sound capture   Term used for converting analog sound into a digital file.

Speech synthesis   Producing spoken words from computer-generated or controlled equipment.

Supercomputer   The largest, fastest, most expensive computers manufactured. They are used to process extensive amounts of data and to make very precise mathematical calculations. Cray XMP systems are examples of supercomputers.

System   A group of interrelated parts assembled to achieve some common goal or end. The three major components of most systems are input, process, and output. Examples of systems include computer systems, ecological systems, economic systems, political systems, and school systems.

System software   Programs that direct, supervise, and support the computer hardware system and all the tasks that are to be performed on it. An operating system is an example of systems software.

TCP/IP See **Transmission control protocol/Internet protocol.**

Terabtye One trillion bytes.

Tool software One of the classifications of instructional software established by Robert Taylor. It assumes that the computer is used to assist in a learning activity. Examples of tool software include word-processing, spreadsheet, database, and graphics software.

Touch-sensitive screen A video screen designed to recognize the location of touch on its surface. It allows users to use a finger to point to options provided on the screen by software. Also referred to as a *touch screen.*

Trackball An input device that functions very similarly to a mouse and is used for pointing to objects on a video screen.

Train the trainer An approach to staff development that relies on developing a cadre of well-trained individuals in an organization who train other staff.

Transfer rate The time it takes to transfer data from one location (device) to another. In computer hardware evaluation, transfer rate would be used to measure the performance of input and output devices.

Transmission control protocol/Internet protocol (TCP/IP) The standard protocol used on the Internet. Originally developed by the U.S. Department of Defense for ARPANET.

Tutee software One of the classifications of instructional software established by Robert Taylor. It assumes that the student possesses the necessary information and controls the learning environment. Examples of tutee applications include programming languages such as Logo, BASIC, and Pascal.

Tutor software One of the classifications of instructional software established by Robert Taylor. It assumes that the computer possesses the necessary information and controls the learning environment. Examples of tutor software include drill-and-practice programs, tutorials, simulations, and educational games.

Tutorial A form of tutor software similar in style and appearance to drill-and-practice software. However, tutorials are designed to teach new material, whereas drill-and-practice programs are designed to reinforce material already learned.

UNIX A powerful multitasking operating system developed at Bell Laboratories in 1969 and written in the C programming language. Variations of UNIX exist that enable it to run on IBM, Apple, and other manufacturers' computers. The UNIX operating system is especially popular for supporting the "server" function in client-server environments such as the Internet.

Uniform resource locator (URL) An electronic address that identifies a unique location of a data file on the World Wide Web.

Uplink The transmission of data from an earth station to a communications satellite.

Upload In a computer network, the process of transmitting a copy of a file from a computer to a central file server.

URL See **Uniform resource locator.**

Video board A CPU component capable of accepting and generating video.

Video capture Term used for converting analog video into a digital video file.

Video display device (VDD) An output device capable of displaying text or images on a video screen.

Videodisc An optical disc used to store video images and associated audio or sound information in analog format. Same as a *laserdisc.*

Virus A computer program designed to reproduce (infect) as it is used in computer networks and copy programs. Some viruses are merely nuisances; others are designed to damage files or programs.

Voice output unit Any device that produces spoken words from a computer. See Speech synthesis and Audio response unit.

Voice recognition device Any device that can be used to recognize and record sounds. It is frequently used with a digitizer to convert sounds into digital format.

WAN See **wide area network.**

Wave format Digital file format used to store sounds as a pattern of oscillatory periodic electronic signals.

Web browser See **Browser.**

Wide area network (WAN) Connecting computer equipment using data communications over a widespread geographic area such as a town, city, or country.

Word processing   The use of computer equipment for entering and editing text. Popular word-processing programs include WordPerfect, WordStar, and Microsoft Word.

World Wide Web   The protocol and file format software incorporating hypertext and multimedia capabilities for use on the Internet.

WORM   An acronym for write once, read many. It is a type of optical disc that allows the recording or writing of data once, which can then be accessed or read many times.

WWW   See **World Wide Web.**

Index